HISTORY'S GREATEST HEIST

THE LOOTING OF RUSSIA

BY THE BOLSHEVIKS

SEAN McMEEKIN

Yale University Press
New Haven and London

Published with assistance from the Louis Stern Memorial Fund.

Copyright © 2009 by Yale University.
All rights reserved.
This book may not be reproduced, in whole or in part, including illustrations, in any form (beyond that copying permitted by Sections 107 and 108 of the U.S. Copyright Law and except by reviewers for the public press), without written permission from the publishers.

Designed by James J. Johnson and set in Sabon type
by The Composing Room of Michigan, Inc.
Printed in the United States of America by Sheridan Books.

Library of Congress Cataloging-in-Publication Data

McMeekin, Sean, 1974–
   History's greatest heist : the looting of Russia by the Bolsheviks / Sean McMeekin.
      p. cm.
   Includes bibliographical references and index.
   ISBN 978-0-300-13558-9 (cloth : alk. paper)   1. Finance, Public—Soviet Union—
History.   2. Pillage—Soviet Union—History.   3. Soviet Union—Politics and
government—1917–1936.   I. Title.
   HJ1208.M36 2008
   336.47′09041—dc22

                                                                                    2008022100

A catalogue record for this book is available from the British Library.

This paper meets the requirements of ANSI/NISO Z39.48-1992 (Permanence of Paper).
It contains 30 percent postconsumer waste (PCW) and is certified by the Forest Stewardship
Council (FSC).

10 9 8 7 6 5 4 3 2 1

FLORIDA GULF COAST
UNIVERSITY LIBRARY

For Nesrin

The knell of private property sounds. The expropriators are expropriated.

— Karl Marx

Contents

II. Cashing In   93

Gallery follows page 92

Abbreviations

AAB	Arbetarrölsens Arkiv och Bibliotek, Stockholm
AN	Archives Nationales, Paris
BB	Bundesarchiv Bern, Bern
DBB	Deutsches Bundesarchiv Berlin, Lichterfelde, Berlin
GARF	Gosudarstvenny Arkhiv Rossiiskoi Federatsii, Moscow
NAA	National Archives Annex, Washington, DC
PAAA	Politisches Archiv des Auswärtigen Amtes, Berlin
PRO	Public Record Office, Kew Gardens, London (now known as the National Archives of the United Kingdom)
QO	Quai d'Orsay Archives, Paris
RSU	Riksarkivet Stockholm Utrikesdepartement, Stockholm
RGAE	Russian Government Archive of Economics, Moscow
RGASPI	Russian Government Archive of Social-Political History, Moscow

A Note on Transliteration, Names, and Translation

For Russian-language words, I have used a simplified Library of Congress transliteration system throughout, with the exception of common spellings of famous or frequently repeated surnames (e.g., Dzerzhinsky, Gorky, Gukovsky, Krestinsky, Novitsky, Obolensky-Osinsky, Trotsky, Tukhachevsky, Yudenich, Yurovsky, Yusupov). I have also rendered Christian names and patronymics in their most commonly used forms (e.g., Georgi not Georgii, Grigory not Grigorii, Natalya not Natalia, Yakov not Iakov, Yuri not Iuri, Alexandrovna not Aleksandrovna). With city names, I have generally followed contemporary, not modern, versions: thus Reval not Tallinn, Tartu not Dorpat. All translations from the French, German, and Russian, unless otherwise noted, are my own.

A Note on the Relative Value of Money Then and Now

Throughout this book I have tried to render the value of gold or other commodities bought or sold by the Bolsheviks in contemporary dollars, with a corresponding equivalent value in today's money. This is, of course, an inherently problematic exercise, as any economist will tell you. Various historical currency converters are available online, but they vary greatly in both methodology and result. At measuringworth.com, the value of a 1917 dollar is rendered into its contemporary equivalent in six different ways, ranging from a low of $12 per 1917 dollar in terms of "consumer price index," to $31 if using a roughly comparable "consumer bundle of goods," to $208 if the measuring stick is "relative share of GDP," or what might be called in layman's terms the size of a particular fish in the economic sea of that fish's time. If we go by a commodity such as gold, the conversion in dollar prices, then-to-now, is about 35 to 1.* One might easily add real estate to the equation: by some measures the value of residential property in many fashionable Western neighbor-

*In a curious coincidence, the market price of an ounce of gold in 2005–6 in dollar terms is almost identical to the price of a kilo of gold, circa 1917–22: both trade(d) in the range of about $650 and $700. At 35.274 ounces to the kilogram, this particular conversion is thus quite easy to perform, although it is not a happy one for anyone concerned about the downward plunge of the U.S. dollar in the last half-century.

hoods has risen by a factor of 500 just since 1950. The price of other essential commodities, however, has actually fallen in past decades, casting all such simple conversion formulas into doubt.

Because of the very nature of Soviet Communism, especially in the early postrevolutionary "maximalist" phase covered in this book, in which all private economic activity (including the use of money) was actively and ruthlessly suppressed, the use of a consumer price index for a dollar conversion would be absurd. Any hard currency the Bolsheviks obtained was used to securitize imports from abroad, not to purchase largely nonexistent "consumer bundles" inside Russia.

The relevant issue in the present narrative, then, is not domestic consumer or per capita GDP indices, but purchasing power in international exchange. It seems therefore more helpful to come up with a conversion formula related to the prices of military-industrial imports. To take an important example from the narrative: state-of-the-art warplanes purchased by the Bolsheviks in Europe from 1920 to 1922 ranged in price from a low of a few thousand dollars apiece for German models (the competitive price of which in hard currency terms was largely due to the collapsing deutschmark) to about $12,000 to $15,000 each for armored Belgian Breguets and Dutch Fokkers priced in hard currencies, to as much as £16,000 (then worth $80,000) for English A. V. and Roe warplanes with Rolls-Royce condor engines mounting the latest Vickers and Lewis guns. The Bolsheviks were thus looking at a price spread of about $2,500 to $80,000 for state-of-the-art imported warplanes.

Although it would perhaps be unfair to compare $2 billion stealth bombers to 1920s warplanes capable of flying only 500 miles or so before refueling, governments today typically pay in the neighborhood of $25 to $120 million apiece for fourth-generation fighters (i.e., those designed and manufactured since about 1980), with Russian MIGs falling at the low end, Eurofighter Typhoons in midrange ($70 to $80 million, depending on the value of the euro), and state-of-the-art United States–made F-22s at the high end. If we do a one-to-one comparison of an A. V. and Roe circa 1922 ($80,000) with an F-22 today ($120 million), the dollar price conversion for state-of-the-art warplanes between today and the early 1920s comes out at 1,500 to 1. If we compare midrange fighter to midrange fighter, such as today's Eurofighter Tycoon ($70 to $80 million) against a 1920s

Belgian Breget mounting double-machine-gun batteries ($12,000 to $15,000), the conversion ratio stands at about 5,000 or 6,000 to 1. If we look at the low end, meanwhile—say, early Weimar-era German warplanes artificially cheap due to postwar inflation (about $2,500), as against prices of 1990s-era Russian MIGs devalued in similar circumstances (about $25 million)—the conversion ratio nears 10,000 to 1.[1]

Now, it may be objected that warplanes today are substantially superior—in range, speed, targeting, and firepower—to anything produced in the early 1920s. This is the military-industrial equivalent of the bundle-of-goods versus quality-of-life comparisons that bedevil economists trying to compare consumer price indices over time. It is certainly true that the warplanes in question are so dramatically different as to render comparison difficult. But this objection misses the point because it ignores *context*. The Bolsheviks of 1920 would indeed have been hard pressed to do much damage with Fokkers and Breguets if they faced White armies that happened to deploy today's latest F-22s (or MIGs), or to beat irregular partisan armies furnished with the latest M16s or AK-47s with their First World War–era Danish Madsen machine guns. But, of course, their enemies did not possess these weapons: in some cases, as in the repression of political opponents by the *Cheka* and the assaults on peasants resisting requisitions, the Bolsheviks' opponents did not possess modern weapons at all. The key question relating to historical currency conversions and the arms trade is *bang for the buck*.

In these terms, the dollars the Bolsheviks used to import weapons in the first half-decade after the revolution must be said to be far more valuable in today's terms than the customary conversion figure of 40 to 1, even if the gold-dollar conversion itself falls at only 35 to 1.[2] The issue at hand is not how much the volume of gold the Bolsheviks sold circa 1917–22 would be worth in dollars today, but rather how much they were able to *buy* with the hard currencies they obtained by selling this gold. To take another relevant comparison: the custom-made "complete outfittings" the Bolsheviks ordered for Red Army officers from Tjernberg and Leth Aktiebol in 1920–21 (consisting of disinfected "English khaki uniforms" with woolen overcoats, black top boots, woolen blankets in custom colors, an American Westinghouse-manufactured three-line repeating Nagan rifle with 1,800 cartridges, etc.) were priced at 269 Swedish crowns per set, or about $65 at then-exchange rates. According to the *Wall Street Journal,* in 2006 it cost the U.S. Army $24,280 to equip a soldier. In terms of the arming and outfitting of infantry in the latest style, then, the rough dollar conversion, now-against-then, is about 375 to 1.[3]

This figure of current military costs may reflect, of course, both the recent fall in the dollar and the onerous new technical requirements of fourth-generation warfare. So, too, might we say that the complexity of modern fighter aircraft, when set against the primitive models manufactured in the early 1920s, renders the conversion figures reached above, of 1,500 to 1 or more, problematic. In contrast, the 35 to 1 figure for gold does not seem nearly right either: today gold is simply one commodity traded among many, a bit more significant than other metals for reasons of symbolism and tradition, but nowhere near as important in facilitating international trade and debt settlements as it was in Lenin's day. Having more than 500 metric tons of gold to dispose of in 1920, as the Bolsheviks did, indicated serious weight in global affairs, far beyond that of a government possessing its converted cash equivalent today ($11 or $12 billion, or roughly the annual GDP of a Botswana or Cameroon). For all these reasons—and for ease of conversion—I have therefore adopted a compromise figure of 100 to 1 for converting dollar figures circa 1917–22 to current suggested values. This figure is a gross approximation, of course, but I hope it will give readers a sense of the scale of the transactions involved.

Prologue: The Patrimony of Imperial Russia

Although Soviet propaganda later succeeded in convincing much of the world that the Communist program of central planning was essential to Russia's rise to world-power status, even a rudimentary glance at the historical evidence shows this claim to be largely hollow. To begin with, of course, Germany did not launch a preemptive war with Russia in 1914 because her leaders saw a weak eastern neighbor ripe for the plucking: the leitmotif of paranoid policy discussions in Berlin that fateful summer was, rather, the unstoppable Russian juggernaut. As Chancellor Bethmann Hollweg famously remarked as the crisis heated up in July, "the future lies with Russia, she grows and grows, and lies on us like a nightmare."[1]

The German chancellor may have been more than usually anxious about Russian power (it is said he told his son not to plant slow-maturing trees on the family estate in East Prussia, as they would eventually enrich only the Russians), but his fears were not entirely ungrounded. Russia's population, after shooting up from 36 to 135 million between 1800 and 1900, had leapt to 175 million by 1914. Nearly every economic indicator showed Russia breaking through the limits of what had recently been believed possible. Her industrial production, measured in output of coal, iron, and steel, was now fourth in the world, behind only Germany, Britain, and America, having shot past even France, Russia's key economic partner. In the last six years before the war, driven in part by heavy French investment in Russia's railways and armaments, the Russian economy grew at an average annual rate of 8.8 percent. By 1914 there were nearly a thousand factories in Petrograd alone, many devoted to producing arms: this targeted expansion of Russia's war industry, along with the expansion of her rail network into Poland, terrified war planners in Berlin.

Considering the frequency of famines during the Communist era, it is even more astonishing to be reminded today that prewar Russia was the world's largest exporter of foodstuffs, shipping 20 million tons of grain abroad in 1913 alone—a surplus never remotely approached under Bolshevik rule. Reflecting both her favorable trade balance and the faith of British and French investors in her corporate and government bonds, Russia had accumulated Europe's largest strategic gold reserves by 1914, nearly 1.7 billion rubles ($850 million) worth, or about 1,200 metric tons. Russian rubles were fully convertible, with the nominal value of all paper notes in circulation backed 98 percent by gold. Even personal savings deposits, in a country where banks were still not entirely trusted by the population, were up dramatically at the time of the war's outbreak, 250 percent since 1910, to over 2 billion rubles. Rather like China at the beginning of the twenty-first century, Russia at the start of the twentieth was turning heads in its seemingly inexorable advance in raw economic power.[2]

Appearances, of course, can be deceiving, and when one probed beneath the frothy surface of the prewar Russian economy, numerous potential trouble areas called out for attention. The trade surplus that underwrote Russia's colossal gold reserve was beginning to erode in the last years before the war, as more and more imported components were needed to modernize Russia's rail network and her booming war industries. From a favorable balance of 430 million rubles in 1910, the surplus had dwindled to less than 200 million by 1913.[3] The trade surplus also masked increasing private and public indebtedness, which would become a major headache for Russia and its bondholders in the cataclysm to follow. Although public revenue nearly doubled between 1900 and 1914, expenses had risen still more, producing an overall debt burden of 9 billion rubles, nearly three times annual public revenue. More than half of this tsarist government debt was now held by foreigners, especially the French, who had also invested heavily in Russian municipal and railway bonds. The prewar Russian boom was thus highly leveraged, dependent on a constant influx of foreign capital, which if it ever dried up, would leave Russia's entire economy vulnerable.[4]

The export of the bulk of Russia's grain surplus each year, moreover, meant that her peasants had less to eat at a time when the peasant population was exploding. Rural overpopulation pushed needed bodies into urban factories, but it was also intensely destabilizing to the agrarian economy. Urban industrial growth was uneven, largely concentrated in Moscow, Petrograd, the Ukraine, and the Urals, to the exclusion of the rest of the country. The fruits of this growth, too, were unevenly divided. In the crowded factories, workers, many of them recently removed from rural life and unaccustomed to factory discipline, were restive. Wages, though rising, were not keeping pace with inflation. Although declining between the revolution of 1905 and 1910, the number of labor walkouts thereafter jumped dramatically. More than a million workers went on strike in 1914, which was hardly encouraging for social cohesion during the war.

Still, the impression Russia left on most foreign visitors in 1914 was not, generally speaking, one of backwardness and poverty. After the October Revolution, an entire literary genre developed to celebrate the vanished wealth of tsarist Russia. These post-facto memoirs must be taken with a grain of salt—the glamour of lost riches nearly always improves in the telling—but this does not mean the riches they celebrate were entirely fictitious. Maurice Paléologue, the French ambassador to Russia, later recalled the scene in the Moscow Kremlin as Tsar Nicholas II performed the necessary rites to sanctify the war in August 1914: "The court choir, in sixteenth-century silver and light blue costume, chanted the beautiful anthems of the Orthodox rite . . . in the aisles on the left was a group of one hundred and ten bishops, archimandrites and abbots. A fabulous, indescribable wealth of diamonds, sapphires, rubies and amethysts sparkled on the brocade of their mitres and chasubles. At the time the Church glowed with a supernatural light."[5]

The Romanovs themselves were almost otherworldly in their opulence. Atop the Imperial Sceptre was the Orlov diamond of 300 carats, "said to have been prised from the eye of a Hindu idol in southern India." The Great Imperial Crown, made for Catherine the Great's coronation in 1762, was "encrusted with 4,936 diamonds weighing 2,858 carats," along with a single ruby weighing 400 carats. The crown jewels comprised "7 chains, 23 stars, crosses and emblems, 12 diadems, 16 necklaces, 6 diamond necklaces (rivières), 56 brooches, 10 clasps, 185 hair-pins, earrings, buttons, rings, lockets, bracelets, buckles, etc., 7 loose stones, 19 gold snuff-boxes and 60 sundry gold trinkets." Altogether the "Russian Crown Treasury," wrote the man later hired by the Bolsheviks to appraise it, contained "25,300 carats of diamonds, 1000 carats of emeralds, 1700 carats of sapphires, 6000 carats of pearls and many rubies, topazes, tourmalines, alexandrites, aquamarines, chrysoprases, beryls, chrysolites, turquoises, amethysts, agates, labradores, almandines." This was not yet to count the famous Fabergé eggs (fifty-four of them), and hundreds of other Fabergé miniatures. Then there were the royal trains (two of them, one a decoy), yachts, and palaces: all in all plenty enough to give the Romanovs a well-deserved reputation as "the richest family in the world," with a fortune, the *New York Times* breathlessly reported after the February Revolution in 1917, of $9 billion (likely an exaggeration—this would be the equivalent of nearly a trillion dollars today).[6]

And the Romanovs may not have been the richest family in Russia. The Benckendorff and Shuvalov properties alone "produced half the annual world output of platinum." The Potockis, Lubomirskis, and Radziwills owned sprawling estates in White Russia and Poland, producing enormous income from grain, sugar beets, alcohol distilling, and mining. Richest of all, perhaps, were the Yusopovs, whose Petrograd palace on the Moika canal was "crowded with valuables: paintings by Old Masters covered the walls, while showcases bulged with miniatures [and] porcelains. . . . Among [the] statuettes . . . were a Buddha made from a ruby matrix and a Venus from a sapphire. . . . Gold and enamelled snuff-boxes and ashtrays made of amethyst, topaz and jade with gem-encrusted gold settings lay scattered on tables or glistened in cabinets."[7]

The dramatic contrast between such extravagance and the lot of Russia's poor was, of course, often highlighted by the Communists and their apologists to justify the revolutionary depredations that followed. According to the Marxist theory of capital accumulation, after all, this national wealth had been accrued through the labor of "proletarians," who had themselves acquired no share in it. At best, this is a half-truth: centuries of often poorly compensated, forced, and unfree serf labor had certainly gone into producing the conspicuous riches of prewar Russia, but this wealth was also drawn from a tremendous bounty of natural resources (grain, timber, furs, platinum and other metals, and more recently Caspian oil) and the financial and intellectual investment, much of it foreign, necessary to exploit them; from quality craftsmanship (Peter Carl Fabergé, hardly a proletarian, certainly "created" value); and from the growing confidence of Russian merchants, aristocrats, and artisans happy to invest their money at home. Peasant smallholders, whose numbers were increasing in the wake of Stolypin's reforms, along with better-paid factory workers, were even beginning to save their earnings in banks. Russia in the last days of the tsars was a substantial net importer of both people and capital, a telling fact that, after 1917, would never be true again.

All this wealth taken together was the national patrimony of centuries, and it would be justly mourned when it was gone. The riveting scenes of the revolution, which saw desperate Russians selling priceless jewels and family heirlooms for food and fuel to survive the winter, would be repeated again after the collapse of Communism in 1991—with one crucial difference. At century's end, in a crude measure of how badly the Bolsheviks had beggared the country, Russia's dispossessed hawked not expensive jewelry, but raggedy mittens and small handfuls of vegetables raised on dacha plots. It was an extraordinary fall: from world-famous opulence to subsistence agriculture in only seventy-five years.

How did it happen? The war unleashed in 1914 may have come, as many tsarist ministers lamented, too early. Stolypin had famously pleaded in 1909 for "twenty years of internal and external peace" to complete Russia's economic modernization: this may have been asking too much, but maybe another five years would have done. Still, historical research on the wartime economy has greatly altered the impression, cultivated deliberately by the Communists for obvious reasons, of a general economic collapse preceding 1917. In his classic study *The Eastern Front,* Norman Stone shows that most of the evidence points instead to a stupendous wartime boom: by 1916 Russia was churning out four times as much artillery shell as Austria-Hungary, for example, and half again as much as Imperial Germany, achieving clear superiority across much of the eastern front. "However astonishing it may appear in retrospect," Stone writes, "the Russian Stock-Exchanges went through something of a boom in the First World War, a process noted elsewhere only in the United States." Over a thousand new corporations were chartered in Russia between 1914 and 1917, issuing more than 2 billion rubles in share capital. Russia's banks invested over 9 billion rubles in the war economy (about $4.5 billion, the equivalent of some $450 billion today).[8]

The economic crisis of 1917 was not, therefore, one of insufficient growth. If anything, the problem lay in distortions caused by economic "overheating" as millions of peasants rushed into the booming war factories. Transport of grain to urban centers was difficult to organize efficiently as the trains not only were clogged with soldiers and war matériel but transplanted rural laborers themselves, going back and forth to the cities. Russia's rail network ultimately proved inadequate to the task, though here, too, the problem was not one of production—the supply of both locomotive engines and rolling stock increased substantially from 1914 to 1917—but the excessive strains brought on by the wartime boom. It was finally inflation, Stone argues, and not stagnation, that produced the bread riots of 1917: there was plenty enough grain to go round (especially now that Russia no longer exported its surplus), but the peasants were reluctant to load much of this surplus onto transport trains in exchange for paper money of uncertain value.[9]

The most important wartime financial developments—the lifting of the gold standard, the Russian bond boom in Paris and London, the explosion in corporate stock issues—bespeak a country not capital-poor, but quite possibly too flush. The mint was working overtime, expanding the number of rubles in circulation from 2 billion in 1914 to 9 billion by early 1917. The growth in the money supply was paralleled by a rise in private bank savings—up from 2.5 billion rubles at the start of the war to over 9 billion rubles by the time of the February Revolution. These deposits were then loaned out to lubricate the booming arms factories, augmented by yet more foreign loans. Nearly 11.5 billion rubles worth of fifty-year Russian war bonds—the principal, $5.75 billion, would be equivalent to almost $600 billion today—were sold between 1914 and 1917, mostly in London and Paris, with an assist from Wall Street buyers beginning in 1916. Foreign capital was also sunk directly into Russian war production, as much as 6 billion rubles ($3 billion) from French investors alone, if we are to credit postwar claims. In some sectors, like mining, more than 90 percent of Russia's share capital was now foreign owned. By 1917, the Russian war economy exhibited symptoms of a dangerous market bubble, with too many speculators chasing lofty wartime returns that could not possibly last forever.[10]

Russia in 1917, then, is best thought of not as an economic backwater but as a kind of gigantic casino of global capitalism on which investors from all over the world had converged to risk their fortunes. The national wealth accumulated slowly over centuries; the hard work and painful reforms of recent decades; and the cascading influx of capital from France, Germany, Britain, and (more recently still) the United States had created a financial and economic colossus but a deeply fragile one. If harnessed properly, Russia's gold and cash reserves, her thriving bond and equity markets, and the whole international network of overlapping obligations tying her to Entente creditors, investors, and military suppliers could help her win the war with the Central Powers and secure a prosperous postwar future for her people. If, however, the country's precariously balanced financial system fell apart, the consequences for Russia, her creditors, and the entire world economy would be devastating.

It was Russia's grave misfortune that a ruthless gang of Marxist ideologues appeared on the scene in 1917, just as the wartime boom had turned her capital cities into vast arsenals of weaponry, backed by a thousand tons of gold bullion in bank vaults and billions more rubles on deposit, with the entire stupendous edifice financed by "capitalist" governments, banks, and corporations the Bolsheviks had expressly targeted for destruction. The casino was loaded and wired to the hilt. All it took was a spark to burn the whole building down.

Introduction to Bolshevik Gold

The Nature of a Forgotten Problem

IN THE MID-1990s, a series of sensational reports appeared on the subject of looted Nazi gold laundered in Switzerland during the Second World War. Helped along by the war's fiftieth anniversary, a Freedom of Information Act lawsuit filed by the World Jewish Congress, and nationally televised hearings on Holocaust survivors' claims against Swiss banks chaired by U.S. Senator Alphonse D'Amato, "Nazi gold" became front-page news. "The greatest theft in history," proclaimed the BBC. The *New York Times* denounced the "Goblins of Zurich." Ambitious journalists turned out books with sensational titles like *Hitler's Secret Bankers: How Switzerland Profited from Nazi Genocide*. Without "the considerable efforts of Swiss bankers," declared Adam Lebor, "the Second World War could have ended several years earlier."[1]

Given the stonewalling of Swiss bank directors when faced with intrusive queries by lawyers and journalists, such heady claims made for good copy. But this was not really a new story. Nazi looting of central banks in occupied countries, the macabre retrieval of gold jewelry and teeth from Holocaust victims, incurious Swiss bankers laundering Nazi gold—all these themes were long familiar to historians. If there was anything novel in the 1990s craze for exposés on Nazi war booty, it lay in the declassification of U.S. intelligence on

Nazi gold movements gathered by Operation Safehaven during the war.[2]

One might expect that this fruitful archival coup would have prompted historians to explore the theme of gold movements further, say, by examining the role of "neutral" bankers in prolonging the First World War or in facilitating the advent and spread of Bolshevism. To take one obvious measure of comparison: of the $398 million in gold shipped by Nazi Germany to Switzerland from 1939 to 1945, Lebor estimates that some $289 million worth was obtained from the looting of central banks in occupied countries, plus an unspecified (though much smaller) amount taken from Holocaust victims. This figure is less than the absolute dollar value of gold sold abroad by the Bolsheviks in *just eighteen months* during the murderous final stretches of the Russian civil war (about $294 million), even without accounting for a quarter-century's dollar inflation.[3] Like the Nazis, the Bolsheviks obtained this gold by looting banks and robbing whole categories of people—and they procured substantially more gold, silver, and other precious stones (especially diamonds) from "class enemies" than did the Nazis from Holocaust victims.[4] Like the Nazis, the Bolsheviks had gold melted down and sold to obtain hard currency, which they used to purchase desperately needed war matériel. Unlike the Nazis, however, the Bolsheviks' audacious looting of an entire continent has attracted little notice from historians, aside from books in the "Anastasia" genre, which examine the legal claims of purported Romanov descendants to the family's lost fortune, and specialist art-historical studies on the provenance of looted paintings, antique books, and icons.[5]

The disparity in attention paid to Nazi and Communist crimes is itself old news: the world still awaits Hollywood's first feature film exposé of the Red Terror or Soviet Gulag, to accompany its first several thousand dramatizing Nazi evil. But in the problem of gold movements, the disparity is not only acute but injurious to historical understanding. To begin with, gold sales, and the imports they financed, were much less important to the Nazi war machine than they were to the Bolsheviks'. The economy of Nazi Germany was almost entirely functional during even the bleakest war years, producing the vast majority of sophisticated manufactures and armaments essential to the Wehrmacht. Famously, the I. G. Farben company even perfected the technology of producing gasoline and fuel oil from coal. Other strategic materials were obtained by the Nazi war machine through conquest, as with iron ore in Norway, or by coercing satellites, like Romania with its petroleum. German gold sales in Switzerland in the early 1940s financed the purchase from neutral states of only a few metals, such as manganese, tungsten, and chrome, admittedly important but hardly dear compared to everything else required by the Wehrmacht. Had the army not been so ravenous, the Nazi government could have simply traded for these metals with surplus German manufactures. Lebor's $289 million in gold meant a lot to the occupied governments being looted, but when set against total expenditures by the German war machine from 1939 to 1945, it is rather small beer.

By contrast, gold was virtually the only moveable asset the Bolsheviks enjoyed for many years after the Russian Revolution. Economic production under the draconian regime of "war Communism" was insufficient to supply food and fuel to Moscow and Petrograd, let alone produce surpluses in traditional Russian export sectors, such as grain, timber, hemp, flax, and furs. A country where emaciated urban dwellers were tearing down entire buildings for wood to heat their apartments was not likely to have export surpluses on hand. In fact, excepting a few leftover stocks of flax and hemp they inherited in 1917, the Bolsheviks had only confiscated gold, silver, platinum, diamonds, and jewelry to "trade" for desperately needed imports.

The flip side of an economy producing nothing worthy of export was that the Bolsheviks, again unlike Nazi Germany, had to import virtually everything their war machine required. War needs money, and the Bolsheviks were fighting many different wars in succession from 1917 to 1920, against Whites, Poles, Finns, at times Germans, and of course Allied expeditionary forces from America, France, Great Britain, and Japan. Thanks to Orlando Figes and others, we now know of the ferocious civil war that erupted in the Russian countryside in 1920–21 as bands of peasant partisans and anarchist "greens," many of whom had cooperated with the Red Army against the Whites and foreign troops, turned their wrath on the Bolsheviks. In 1922, with the peasant rebellion largely broken by the Volga famine, the Bolsheviks fought yet another pitched conflict against the Russian Orthodox Church and the priests and Old Believers who defended it. All along, the struggle against myriad and constantly re-defined "class enemies" required ever-increasing quantities of weapons in the hands of secret police (Cheka) enforcers.[6] Although a few ammunition factories continued functioning for the duration of these conflicts in Bolshevik-controlled territory at Tula, it was at a much-diminished capacity compared to pre-1917 output. As the civil war heated up in 1919, the Red Army and Cheka tore through small arms rounds three to four times faster than they could be replenished. Chronic ammunition shortages would be overcome only in 1920, when the Allied blockade eased up enough for the Bolshe-viks to begin importing war supplies in quantity across the Baltic.[7]

The pent-up demand, by then, was enormous. Like water bursting through a dam, Bolshevik agents rushed through the blockade break-point at Reval (Tallinn) to place import orders as fast as they could. There was no shortage of suppliers. As Lenin famously prophesied, capitalists proved quite willing to sell Communists the rope that they would use to hang them. The Bolsheviks' pariah status was powerful inducement to businessmen eager to exploit their desperation, charging hefty premiums for surplus German automatics and Amer-ican rifles, artillery, and cannon, with shells, rounds, gunpowder, and explosives; poison gas; military aircraft, vehicles, and trains (plus engines and spare parts for all of them); cloth for uniforms and greatcoats; binoculars, goggles, and boots in the millions; foodstuffs, pots, and pans for field kitchens; entrenching equipment, field tele-phones, steel cable, and communications wire; medicines, pain-killers, and cigarettes; and not least, the blank paper, ink, and film stock for the propaganda that was the true mother's milk of Bolshe-vism. Then there was Russia's reeling civilian economy and its own war factories, which after the depredations of War Communism was desperately short of the most basic necessities—rolling stock, fer-rous metals, ball bearings, agricultural machinery and implements, pumps and centrifuges, castor oil and machine lubricants, cotton-spinning machines and thread, dairy processing equipment, even vegetable and legume seeds. In the absence of goods to trade, all this needed to be paid for in hard currency—Swedish, Danish, and Nor-wegian crowns; Dutch guilders; U.S. dollars; German marks; French and Swiss francs; British pounds—which meant selling precious met-als, principally gold.

Considering the greater importance of gold movements for the fortunes of Communism than Nazism, why has the former phenomenon attracted so much less scholarly notice? One clue might lie in archival access. Communist sources relating to precious metals looting and Red Army procurement (mostly located at RGAE in Moscow) have been available to most researchers only since 1991—and this archive remains less well known than the State and Party Archives—whereas captured Nazi files from the war have been combed over since 1945. Still, most of the Allied intelligence reports on the outflow of precious metals from Bolshevik Russia, the post-1917 equivalent of Operation Safehaven, were declassified decades ago. The problem of Bolshevik gold may have disappeared from the history books, but it fairly screams out for attention in the foreign office files of the Entente powers, to anyone who looks at them. Contemporary newspaper accounts of the Russian civil war and its aftermath, too, are full of colorful reporting about Russia's rapidly dwindling precious metals reserves, artfully mixing hard fact, rumor, and the wildest speculation. The ongoing saga of Russian gold movements was, for years, a passing obsession of Entente diplomats and intelligence officers, many of whom left behind copious (though not always accurate) documentation of their findings.[8]

Most striking of all, it turns out that many of the Bolsheviks' principal foreign "financiers of genocide," unlike Switzerland's stubborn "Nazi gold" apologists hiding behind banking secrecy laws, made no attempt to conceal their contributions to the triumph of Bolshevism.[9] If they were ever asked about their role in laundering stolen Bolshevik gold, silver, platinum, jewelry, and diamonds, such men described these activities openly and with pride, even, in one extraordinary case, while under hostile police interrogation.[10] The same can be said of the Bolsheviks' own commercial agents and buyers, the most important of which, like Leonid Krasin, wrote self-glorifying memoirs on the subject.[11] The story of Bolshevik gold movements and their role in assuring the triumph of Bolshevism is, in short, simply waiting to be written.[12]

Lest we forget, the Bolsheviks, unlike the Nazis, *won* their war against the world in the first half-decade after the Russian Revolution, establishing a stranglehold on power that would endure for three-quarters of a century. Whereas many Nazis faced a day of judgment for their crimes, no such fate was in store for Bolshevism after

1922. Although many of Lenin's associates would later feel the wrath of Stalin when he turned on the "Old Bolsheviks," the Russian Communist Party itself has never, to this day, faced its own Nuremberg.

Here, perhaps, we are getting closer to an explanation for the gross disparity in attention paid to Nazi and Bolshevik wartime finances. There is little joy in chronicling an ill-fated Entente blockade of Soviet Russia that failed so miserably to dislodge or contain Bolshevism. Any glory in accounts of the Allied intervention, and the Russian civil war more generally, was on the Soviet side. Little wonder the once-hysterical obsession in Entente statehouses with Bolshevik gold movements, and the menace to Western civilization that they represented, slipped rapidly down the memory hole. In historiography, as in democratic politics, victories will have many proud fathers; a crushing defeat, such as the Allies suffered in trying to quarantine Soviet Russia and its global influence, will remain a political and scholarly orphan.

It is time to rescue the orphan. Now that the Russian archives are open, the last piece in the puzzle of Bolshevik gold movements has fallen into place. This book aims to introduce readers to this long-forgotten subject, which holds the key to the greatest mystery of the Russian Revolution: how the Bolsheviks, despite facing a world of enemies and producing nothing but economic ruin in their path, were able to stay in power. The story is narrated as a historical drama in two acts. In the first, we shall learn how the Bolsheviks came into possession of Europe's largest gold reserve in 1917–18 and how this hoard was then enlarged, as armed detachments fanned out across Russia to fulfill Marx's injunction to "expropriate the expropriators": breaking open safe deposit boxes in "nationalized" banks; withdrawing hundreds of millions of tsarist rubles from other people's savings accounts; looting landed estates, churches, and monasteries; and prying precious stones and other valuables from the bloodied bodies of anyone who dared resist Bolshevik confiscations. To the imperial gold reserve was thus added money, bonds, watches, platinum, diamonds, jewelry, silverware, precious paintings, icons, engraved books: the wealth of a continent, built up over generations.

As we shall see in the second act, once in possession of the colossal patrimony of tsarist Russia, the Bolsheviks proceeded to dump the bulk of it as fast as they could, at well below prevailing world market prices, to anyone who would buy. The reason for haste was simple. Surrounded by enemies both real and imagined, the Bolsheviks needed to arm their supporters to the teeth, first to survive, and then to perpetuate their hold on power. With breathtaking audacity, they transformed the accumulated wealth of centuries into the sinews of class war: armored airplanes, cars, trucks, and trains; colossal factories of agitprop; and most of all, a continent-sized army of enforcers possessed of warm clothing, boots, food, medicine, guns, and ammunition at a time when the economic catastrophe of War Communism meant such things were lacked by nearly everyone else in Russia. Waging a pitiless war on their own people, the Bolsheviks succeeded in monopolizing not only force, but the very means of human subsistence, reducing the once wealthy land they ruled to a bitter penury, which endures to this day. But these ruthless ideologues did not create the grotesquely distorted socioeconomic system of Communism alone. In the final chapters of the drama, readers will be introduced to the bankers and middlemen who, for a price, helped the Bolsheviks launder the loot from the real heist of the century.

I

THE HEIST

The time seemed to drag on terribly. . . . Our nerves were overstrained. Suddenly the door flew open and two dozen armed soldiers entered the room and lined up along the table on which the money lay. The murmurs ceased. The soldiers put the money in bags and dragged them to the car. The money was sent to Smolny.

1 The Banks

*Three times Lenin has sent down to the Bank to fetch ten million Rubles
and three times he has failed to secure them. The last time . . . a battalion
of soldiers with a band at their head marched to the Bank with the necessary vehicles to carry off the spoil . . . all began bawling and shaking their
fists. . . . For a time things looked nasty, but the [Bank] Directors found
their champion in a giant peasant, in soldiers uniform, who roared louder
than any ten and had a larger fist.*

— Francis O. Lindley, "Report on Recent Events in Russia,"
25 November 1917

THE BOLSHEVIK NATIONALIZATION of Russia's banks in
1917 came right out of the playbook of the *Communist Manifesto*.
"The proletariat will use its political supremacy," Marx had instructed, "to wrest, by degrees, all capital from the bourgeoisie."
Such a program "cannot be effected," he emphasized, "except by
means of despotic inroads on the rights of property," including the
"centralization of credit in the hands of the State, by means of a national bank with State capital and an exclusive monopoly."[1] Lenin,
continuing this line of thought, had written earlier in 1917, "The big
banks are that 'state apparatus' which we *need* for the realization of
Socialism and which we *take ready-made* from capitalism. . . . This
'state apparatus' . . . we can 'lay hold of' and 'set in motion' at one
stroke, by one decree, for the actual work of bookkeeping, control,
registration, accounting, and summation is here carried out by *employees*, most of whom are themselves in a proletarian or semi-pro-
letarian position."[2]

This was much easier said than done. Following Marxist theory, Lenin expected bank employees to cooperate in nationalizing bank assets: themselves proletarians, they could hardly object to the transfer of wealth into the hands of the dictatorship of the proletariat. But in practice, as the workers' soviets and Provisional Government had discovered after the February Revolution, the banks could not function without skilled employees trained in Western bookkeeping methods, most of whom had little patience with revolutionary theorizing. Although certain conspicuous assets of the tsarist regime—the imperial palaces, the crown lands and jewels, the royal trains and yachts—had been "nationalized," the Provisional Government stopped well short of sacking the banks. With the German army poised for most of 1917 just a few hundred miles from Petrograd, the workers' soviets and Kerensky's cabinet had resolved that, for the sake of survival, in Norman Stone's words, "the maintenance of the economy must be left to bankers and industrialists who understood these things."[3]

The Bolsheviks made no such compromise with Russia's banking community. In part this was for the obvious reason that Lenin, unlike Kerensky (a Social Revolutionary, and not a particularly ideological one), was an avowed Marxist committed to nationalization on ideological grounds. Lenin's maximalist program, well publicized all year, ensured that bank directors would greet the Bolshevik seizure of power, effected in Petrograd on 7 November 1917 and in Moscow one week later, with hostility.* Most private banks shut their doors immediately. The State Bank and Treasury remained open but refused to honor the Bolsheviks' requests for funds, lodged on behalf of the Council of People's Commissars (*Sovnarkom*), all through November.

Like all governments, Lenin's needed ready cash, if only, at first, to pay the Red Guards—armed sailors, mostly from the Kronstadt garrison—who had staged the Bolshevik coup. And so, beginning on 12 November, Sovnarkom issued a decree threatening bank directors, in particular, I. P. Shipov of the State Bank, with arrest if they contin-

---

*The "October Revolution" is so called because it occurred on 25 October 1917 according to the Julian calendar used in tsarist Russia, which lagged thirteen days behind the Gregorian, to which the Bolsheviks switched beginning in 1918. Because the bulk of the present narrative takes place after 1918, the Gregorian dates will be used throughout.

ued refusing to authorize Bolshevik withdrawals. Led by the stubborn Shipov, the bankers of Petrograd refused to give in. On 17 November, Shipov responded to criticism of his heartlessness by pointing out to the Bolsheviks that the State Bank had paid out, in the preceding week, more than 600 million rubles to the army, representatives of Russia's "real" government, and to public charities, such as soup kitchens for the poor. To the Bolshevik usurpers, he would give nothing, as they did not have the proper paperwork authorizing government withdrawals.[4]

What followed was a tragicomedy of epic proportions, as the Bolsheviks tried, but failed, to steal 10 million rubles from Russia's State Bank. On 20 November 1917, Lenin sent his new commissar of finance, Viacheslav Menzhinskii, along with a battalion of armed sailors to the bank, "with a band at their head," along with "the necessary vehicles to carry off the spoil." The Bolsheviks' armed emissaries, a witness reported, then "began bawling and shaking their fists in the faces of their adversaries who consisted of the [Bank] Directors, some Delegates from the Duma, the Peasants Soviet, and from the workmen employed by the Bank. For a time things looked nasty, but the Directors found their champion in a giant peasant, in soldiers uniform, who roared louder than any ten and had a larger fist."[5]

On 24 November 1917, Menzhinskii returned with a larger force and an ultimatum. Unless Shipov relented and turned over the money requested, Menzhinskii warned, every State Bank employee would be fired, lose his or her pension, and "those of military age would be drafted."[6] By replacing striking bank officials with trusted party comrades, it was hoped, the Bolsheviks could authorize their own withdrawals without filling out official paperwork. But when the Bolsheviks, failing yet again to win compliance, fired Shipov, all but a small handful of State Bank employees walked out in protest, leaving no one in place to advise Menzhinskii's men. The members of the Bolshevik financial team were in over their heads as one of them, Valerian Obolensky-Osinsky, later confessed: "There were people among us who were acquainted with the banking system from books and manuals . . . but there was not a single man among us who knew the technical procedure . . . of the Russian State Bank. We took possession of an enormous machinery, the working of which was practically unknown to us. How the work was carried on, where things were to be found, what were the basic parts of the business machinery—all these were a closed book to us. We entered the enormous corridors of this bank as if we were penetrating a virgin forest."[7]

Inevitably, the Bolsheviks, after bungling the attempted holdup of the State Bank and failing to find any employees willing to facilitate an inside job, began seizing hostages among the staff. To begin with, they needed to figure out how many cashboxes and vaults the bank contained and where the keys were hidden. As Lenin had instructed his bank-storming squad, "as long as we did not get *the keys to the vaults,* we were merely *talking* about the seizure of the bank." By the second day of the State Bank strike (25 November 1917), the Bolsheviks had located and taken into armed custody the Petrograd branch manager, the head cashier, the head bookkeeper, and the guardian of the vaults and demanded, at gunpoint, that the men surrender their keys. This they duly did, whereupon "the keys to the bank's millions were brought to [Bolshevik headquarters at] Smolny and solemnly emptied from a special chamois bag on the table before Lenin." Alas, Lenin, according to Obolensky-Osinsky, "was not satisfied with our first step and demanded from us *money* and not the keys."[8]

Although it took three more days and a great deal of effort, the Bolsheviks finally did succeed in removing money from the Russian State Bank. A degree of legend surrounds this whole episode, but the basic facts are clear. To acquire additional leverage over the striking employees, the Bolsheviks took other Petrograd bank officials into custody, including Epstein of the Azov-Don, Wavelberg of the Commercial Bank, Sologub of the Volga-Kama, Sandberg of the Siberian Bank, and Krilitichevsky of the Bank for Foreign Trade. Lenin reportedly demanded 1 billion rubles for the release of his hostages, before finally settling for "1,000,000 rubles per head, but cash down only."[9] After reaching an agreement to this effect, the Bolsheviks produced a decree from the Soviet of People's Commissars authorizing the withdrawal of 5 million rubles from the State Bank. Still, there were problems, as Obolensky-Osinsky remembered:

> We had to strain our patience to the utmost in order to make the cashier enter this issue of money in the ledger and to make the accountants actually count the money in a steel room and bring it from there on a lit-

tle pushcart to the cash office . . . the time seemed to drag on terribly. There was no guard, and angry murmurs were already heard from the accountants. Piatakov left the room to look for the guard and did not return. Our nerves were overstrained. Suddenly the door flew open and two dozen armed soldiers entered the room and lined up along the table on which the money lay. The murmurs ceased. The soldiers put the money in bags and dragged them to the car. The money was sent to Smolny.[10]

Although grateful to have cash on hand, the Bolsheviks were not home free yet. The employees of the State Bank had made clear they would not cooperate with the Bolsheviks any more than they felt was necessary to save themselves from a massacre. Permitting the withdrawal of 5 million rubles turned out to be a onetime concession: the strike continued on through the winter, ultimately encompassing more than six thousand bank employees in Petrograd alone.[11] Bolshevik "commissars" were stationed at every bank in the capital and those in Moscow as well "in order to supervise that no money was paid out except for wages." Most of these commissars, the Danish manager of the Russian and English Bank lamented, were "ignorant vulgar boys who understood neither accounts or receipts." Not surprisingly, many were disgruntled former employees, fired for incompetence or malfeasance, who now demanded to take over account books they could barely read, let alone understand. Before long, the account books of Russia's leading banks were reduced to "a hopeless condition from which it will take years to recover."[12]

By December 1917, nearly every state employee in Russia was "sabotaging" the Bolshevik government, that is, refusing to recognize Lenin's illegal seizure of power. Not the least irony of the advent of the world's first self-defined "workers' government" was that its first months were largely devoted to strikebreaking. Telegraph and telephone workers walked out as early as mid-November; water transport workers and schoolteachers followed on 20 November; and Moscow municipal staff one week later. Petrograd city employees walked out in mid-December. It was no coincidence that the dreaded Cheka (Chrezvychainaia Komissiia po bor'be s kontr-revoliutsiei, spekulatsiei i sabotazhem, or All-Russian Extraordinary Commission to Combat Counterrevolution, Speculation, and Sabotage) was formed as the state employee strike reached crisis stage. As

Lenin instructed Felix Dzerzhinsky, the man chosen to direct the Cheka, on 20 December 1917: "The bourgeoisie are still persistently committing the most abominable crimes. . . . The accomplices of the bourgeoisie, notably high-ranking functionaries and bank cadres, are also involved in sabotage and organizing strikes to undermine the measures the government is taking with a view to the socialist transformation of society. . . . exceptional measures will have to be taken to combat these saboteurs and counter-revolutionaries."[13]

Among those "exceptional" measures was a rapid escalation of the Bolshevik war on the banks. On 21 December 1917, the new managing director of the State Bank, Grigory Sokol'nikov, decreed that Bolshevik commissars must be appointed to all the banks in Russia. In a telegram sent simultaneously (and optimistically) to 102 different cities, not all of them, by any means, under Bolshevik control, Sokol'nikov ordered that Bolshevik bank commissars in all of them send weekly reports back to him in Petrograd. Most important, said commissars were to transfer to the State Bank for inspection, as quickly as possible, all "gold coin and ingots discovered" in their banks (nemedlenno peredavat' Gos. Banku obnaruzhivaemoe zoloto monetakh' i slitkakh').[14]

Predictably, the Bolsheviks' extension of their bank offensive throughout Russia produced an equal and opposite reaction: the bank strike went national. While withdrawals for "workers" were everywhere permitted, in the form of checks drawn against the State Bank, Petrograd bank employees consistently refused to authorize the release of state funds for the Bolsheviks. Most bank directors preferred, not without reason, to wait for the formation of a legal government by the Constituent Assembly, elected in November and scheduled to convene in Petrograd on 18 January 1918.

Following their own stubborn logic, the Bolsheviks responded to the "sabotage" represented by a nationwide bank strike with ever more imperious decrees subordinating the recalcitrant banks to their authority. Simply appointing commissars, no matter how untrammeled their authority was in theory, had not been enough to bring the "bourgeois" banking community to heel. To show they really meant business, on 27 December 1917 the Bolsheviks proclaimed, in one of the most infamous of their revolutionary decrees, the abolition of all private banks. Further, the Bolsheviks laid claim to all bank deposits in Russia, with the exception of small savings accounts held by workers not belonging to the "rich classes," this crucial condition being defined as possession of 5,000 rubles, or the income of 500 or more per month. So, too, were private joint-stock companies administered by banks nationalized. The Bolsheviks also planned to cancel all loan obligations contracted by the former government (although this would not be publicly announced until February). Private property, whether in the form of cash, gold, commercial capital, or public bonds, was to be "annihilated."[15]

The reaction of Russia's banking community to this frontal assault was marked by a mixture of bemusement and contempt. After summarizing the gist of the nationalization decrees, the manager of the Russian and English Bank of Petrograd wrote to the bank's London headquarters, "I could continue this list of interesting financial experiments for some time yet, but this may be sufficient to show you that we find ourselves in a lunatic asylum, and consequently no use wasting more time."[16] It was indeed hard for most people to believe the Bolsheviks were serious when they further stipulated in the 27 December 1917 nationalization decree, for example, that "all holders of safe deposit boxes are under obligation to appear at the bank upon notice, bringing the keys to their safe deposit boxes," or that "all holders of safe deposit boxes who fail to appear after three days' notice will be considered as having maliciously declined to comply with the law of search."[17] Who in their right mind would obey a "government" that declared illegal any resistance to its attempted robbery of individual bank accounts—a government, moreover, that had not been elected, that could not compel its own essential employees to show up for work, and the days of which (many hoped) were numbered, with a Constituent Assembly (in which the Bolshevik Party, not incidentally, would be a minority faction) slated to meet several weeks later?

The only factor working in the Bolsheviks' favor with the public employee strikers was constant Cheka harassment and a monopoly of armed forces—at least in Moscow and Petrograd. Showing the regime's contempt for the prerogatives of legality and democratic legitimacy, Lenin-loyal Red Guards and a disciplined detachment of Latvian Rifles blanketed "the entire square in front of Taurida Palace" on 18 January 1918 as the Constituent Assembly finally convened.

Armed with "guns, grenades, munition bags, and revolvers," the Lenin-loyal forces intimidated and harassed all non-Bolshevik deputies, which is to say the vast majority of Russia's elected representatives, before dispersing the Assembly outright. Elsewhere in Petrograd, Bolshevik forces actually fired on workers demonstrating in favor of parliamentary authority, killing at least eight and possibly as many as twenty.[18] One might expect this naked display of power would have forced some bank employees to give in and begin dealing with the Bolsheviks as a de facto government. But while most white-collar state employees relented and began serving Lenin's regime, however reluctantly, the bank employees refused to give in. All winter, as the Bolsheviks struggled to pay the Latvian Rifles and to publish party propaganda, the banks persisted in blocking state withdrawals. Both sides were standing on principle, the Bolsheviks unwilling to abandon their bank nationalization program, the bankers unwilling to bow down before Bolshevik tyranny.

An outsider who tried to mediate between the two sides, the Swedish banker Olof Aschberg—the same whose Nya Banken had been implicated by Kerensky for its role in facilitating wire transfers of German funds to the Bolsheviks in summer 1917—left behind an amusing account of the bank standoff. Aschberg, though a successful and well-regarded financier in the banking communities of Stockholm and Petrograd, sympathized with the revolutionaries. While visiting Petrograd in January and February 1918, he made the rounds at various banks, advising his old friends and colleagues "earnestly to try and facilitate the new government's endeavors." Alas, he later recalled with bitterness, "no one would listen to me. They sabotaged everything in the belief that they could thereby overthrow the Bolshevik regime." Still, Aschberg was not happy with the Bolsheviks' revolutionary proclamations either, thinking their proposed cancellation of Russia's government debts, for example, "preposterous." "To announce to the whole world that you have decided to write off your debts," he berated Bolshevik Trade Commissar Mechislav Bronsky, "is quite unheard-of, and will only result in totally ruining your credit with the whole world." Aschberg was right in this, of course, but quite wrong in thinking the Bolsheviks cared about a bourgeois value like creditworthiness: Bronsky laughed in his face.[19]

Aschberg's obtuseness captures, uncannily, the disconnect between the Bolsheviks and the civilized world in the winter of 1917–18. Like so many foreign witnesses to the Russian Revolution, whether sympathetic or unsympathetic, Aschberg was simply unable to believe that Lenin and his comrades meant what they said when they annulled Russia's internal and external debts, abolished the private banking industry, and laid claim to bank assets in cash, gold, and securities.

The Bolsheviks, however, were dead serious. Russia's banking community may not have been cooperating in the maximalist nationalization program, but the Bolsheviks were going to proceed with or without them. On 3 January 1918, notices were placarded around Petrograd announcing that in order "to combat bank speculation and the regime of capitalistic exploitation," the "late private banks have been occupied by armed forces." All of Petrograd's banks, the Bolsheviks promised with a hint of menace, will renew normal operations immediately, "so far as the sabotage of the bank directors and employees permits."[20] On 4 January, the Bolsheviks posted notice that on the morrow "will take place the revision of the safes at the following banks: International, Siberian, Russian Commercial and Industrial, Moscow Merchants', and Moscow Industrial (late Junker's). Owners of safes from Nos. 1 to 100 at the said banks are to appear with their keys at 10 A.M. Safes belonging to those not presenting themselves within 3 days will be opened by the Revision Committee at each bank with a view to the confiscation of the contents."[21]

To maintain a veneer of legality behind their novel policy of mass armed robbery of the citizenry, the Bolsheviks developed a formal protocol to handle the sacking of bank safes. Before each "revision" could take place, it was required that an accredited representative of the workers' soviets was present, along with at least one licensed bank official and the Bolshevik commissar assigned to the bank. After inspection, a report was to be "drawn up in duplicate stating contents of safe: paper money, serial Treasury notes, coupons of State loans and stock, all of which are entered in the lessee's name to his current account at the State Bank"—if, that is, the safe holder's account there had not already been eradicated by Bolshevik commissioners. Next, the written protocol would state "the quantities of:

foreign *valiuta* [currency], gold and silver coin and ingots and bars of gold, silver, and platinum, all of which are confiscated and handed over to the State Treasury."[22] The stated goal of the safe revision initiative was to secure for the Bolshevik government, as soon as possible, 2 to 3 billion rubles, or one to 1.5 billion in 1918 dollars—the equivalent of 100 or 150 billion dollars today.[23]

It was a plan of extraordinary audacity, which, if it succeeded, would yield enough cash and coin for the world revolution to last for years. But the Bolsheviks hit a snag almost immediately. Asking safe holders to appear in numerical order assumed, of course, that they all knew their account number offhand. Although leasers of safe-deposit boxes had likely written their number down for reference, this did not mean said individuals necessarily had the information handy while walking around city streets reading sundry revolutionary proclamations (if indeed most "capitalist" depositors did not fear going out-of-doors). Nor did the Bolsheviks, of course, have any idea which safe at which bank, or which account number, belonged to which person—and the striking bank employees were not about to tell them. And so gradually Sokol'nikov switched to a reference system general enough not to require any assistance from bank staff but specific enough to frighten depositors into immediate compliance. Each day a new letter of the alphabet would be called, marking out all safe holders whose family name began with it as public enemies if they did not show up to open their safe. By late February, the Bolsheviks had moved on to the letter *L* in Petrograd, which prompted, among others, Max Laserson, commercial director of the Shuvalov Mining Company, to visit his bank, bringing, as ordered, the key to his safe-deposit box. Laserson later recalled the scene: "Tables were set up in the vault at which employees were seated. All around stood the safe deposit boxholders whose boxes were to be opened. The plan followed was to remove all valuables (precious metals in bars, objects of platinum, gold, silver, precious stones, pearls, foreign currency, etc.), which were subject to confiscation for the welfare of the state, and to make it impossible for the owner of any particular object later to identify his property. . . . In a case such as mine, where the valuables were wrapped up in packages, the wrappers were torn open and the particular object was tossed on the pile."[24]

In this way many of Russia's "capitalists" began coughing up their accumulated wealth to the Bolsheviks in the interest of self-preservation. In the first six months of 1918, 35,493 safes were "revised" in Moscow alone, yielding the Bolsheviks half a ton of gold, silver, and platinum bullion (mostly gold); some 700,000 rubles in gold, silver, and platinum coin; 65 million tsarist rubles; nearly 600 million rubles worth of public and private bonds; and a substantial quantity of various foreign currencies.[25] This was only a fraction of the total number of safes: most safe owners had either fled or refused to cooperate (see chapter 3). The total take by summer 1918 was far short of the 2–3 billion rubles the Bolsheviks had hoped for. (Sokol'nikov had possibly misinterpreted a statement published by the State Bank in September 1917 listing total savings deposits at 2.54 billion rubles, thinking this amount was available for withdrawal, whereas the greater part was likely lent out or invested.)[26] Still, it was a good start.

Sacking the safes, however, was the easy part. As Obolensky-Osinsky's account of the bungled State Bank holdup in November suggests, most Bolsheviks were clueless about financial paperwork. Grigory Sokol'nikov, for example, was a young Bolshevik activist with no previous experience in the banking industry, which fact one might think would occasion a degree of caution as he took over the State Bank. Sokol'nikov, however, was not a timid man by nature. He refused to be intimidated by established financiers who offered him advice, telling Max Laserson in December, for example, that he "did not know him" and therefore could not accommodate his request for a withdrawal on behalf of his workers. (Laserson was later given an introduction to Sokol'nikov by a Bolshevik friend, Nikolai Krestinsky.)[27] The title Sokol'nikov was given after the 27 December 1917 bank nationalization decree, moreover, was so peculiar to the brave new world of Bolshevism that his lack of banking experience arguably qualified him perfectly for his duties as "managing director of the Commissariat of Formerly Private Banks" (Upravlyaushchy Komissariata byvshimi chastnymi bankami).[28]

As such a job had never existed before, Sokol'nikov could make it up as he went along. The first step, he decided, was to do a quick inventory. And so Sokol'nikov began earnestly assembling data on Russia's thousands of banks, beginning with their addresses and phone numbers.[29] The first reports he received from Bolshevik bank commissioners bristled with talk of sums of "incredible size" (neimovernye razmery) soon to be at the Bolsheviks' disposal. The Volga-Kama Bank, for example, was said to have assets totaling 125 million rubles "under guarantee" (pod obespecheniem).[30]

When Sokol'nikov began looking closer at the account books, however, he began to realize how difficult it would be to turn bank assets into ready cash for the world revolution. Banks, after all, were complicated institutions possessing not only gold and cash reserves but also a bewildering array of obligations to depositors, shareholders, and bondholders. It was one thing to storm the front entrance, as the Bolsheviks had done in November 1917, and demand money. Even forcing safe holders to show up with keys to their safes, as the Bolsheviks began doing in January 1918, was practicable, requiring only terrorizing these unfortunate depositors into compliance.

It was quite another thing, however, to assume control of a bank's affairs, which included not only assets and deposits but also liabilities. The Volga-Kama, for example, turned out to have fiduciary obligations totaling more than 80 million rubles, which made its takeover less appetizing than it first sounded.[31] A quick inventory of the "formerly private banks" of Moscow taken in late December 1917 turned up nearly 200 million rubles worth of private and public bonds, plus a smattering of equities, on the books: assets for the shareholders but an obligation for whatever other bank client— whether a joint-stock corporation or a city or regional government—had issued the shares.[32] Then, too, there were unpaid bills, such as personal or corporate checks recently drawn on a bank's name, regular employee salaries, or dividend and interest payments coming due. These obligations were less imposing than bond or equity principal but hardly trivial: the Russian Commercial-Industrial Bank of Moscow, for example, had 2.7 million rubles in unpaid bills immediately outstanding; the Azov-Don Bank, nearly 400,000; the Russian and English Bank (with its bemused manager), 185,000.[33] All of these unpaid bills represented individuals (or powerful groups of individuals) likely to be very angry when they learned their payments were being held up indefinitely.

Nonetheless, Sokol'nikov pressed on. Not satisfied with having declared war on the banking community and holders of safe-deposit boxes, the Bolsheviks now targeted ever-subtler distinctions of "cap-italist," such as bond and equity shareholders, along with those who had issued the shares. On 11 January 1918, Sovnarkom decreed that "all payments of interest on investments and dividends on shares will be discontinued," that "all transactions in bonds are prohib-ited," and that anyone violating these conditions would be held "criminally liable and their property will be confiscated."[34] Still, without cooperation from bank employees bonds and equities could not be done away with in a physical sense. And so a revised decree, signed by Lenin himself, was posted throughout Petrograd in early February 1918, stipulating, "All bank shares to be immediately de-livered by present owners to local branches State Bank, and if not in owners' hands [the] latter must present lists pointing out exact whereabouts shares. Penalty non-delivery shares of lists within fort-night complete confiscation all property."[35] The annulment of state loans, whether held by foreigners or Russians, was announced on 10 February 1918. In effect, the Bolsheviks had declared illegal the very fact of owing or being owed money, for any reason. There was no limit, it seemed, to the array of ordinary economic (not to say hu-man) activities Lenin's government would criminalize.

The Bolsheviks had opened a Pandora's box with their war on the banks, which in still-developing Russia were hugely important in the running of the economy, especially after 1914, with the leveraging of war production on the international bond market. Employee salaries in all the country's industries needed to be processed through banks headquartered in Moscow and Petrograd, which often themselves owned the companies in question. The effective shutdown of the banking industry in winter 1918 meant that these workers could not be paid. Max Laserson, for example, as commercial director of the Shuvalov platinum mines in Perm, was responsible for paying, and feeding, 29,000 miners and their families, altogether more than 100,000 people. Through assiduously lobbying with Sokol'nikov and other contacts at the Bolshevized State Bank, Laserson was able to transmit some money from Petrograd to Perm during the bank strike—until, that is, he was fired by the company's new Bolshevik commissioners on 16 March 1918. After Laserson's departure, Shou-valov's workers at the Perm mines were on their own.[36]

There was a brutal punitive logic to the Bolsheviks' maximalist program of 1918 which produced a cascading wave of mutual sabotage. The repudiation of Russia's foreign debt obligations caused the Entente powers to retaliate by freezing Russia's foreign assets, thus depriving the Bolsheviks of desperately needed import credits even as they themselves impoverished Russia's millions of foreign bondholders. This impasse between the Bolsheviks and Western creditors would endure for nearly the entire history of the Soviet Union. Closer to home, the nationalization of Russia's banks in 1918 deprived the country's businesses of their ability to pay their employees. Bolshevik factory committees, seeking to blame someone for nonpayment of wages, would then fire managers, engineers, and other senior employees, which made it impossible for a given factory to function. Inevitably, companies thus plunged into chaos were then denounced for insubordination to revolutionary decrees, which served as legal justification for state confiscation of their operations. This would complete the exodus of managerial and skilled personnel, leaving behind only a shell of a company, producing nothing of value.

Sundry nationalization decrees followed one after another all winter with numbing regularity. On 21 December 1917, the Bogosloff Mining Works Company in the Urals was declared Bolshevik property "in view of the refusal to submit to the Workmen's Control decree." Four days later, an identical fate befell the Simsky Mining Works Company, and then four days after that the Russo-Belgian Metallurgical Company. On 30 December, the "1886 Electric Light Company" was confiscated "in view of the Board having brought the undertaking to complete financial ruin." On and on it went: in early January the Bolsheviks confiscated the Putilov Works of Petrograd (which produced artillery shells and locomotive engines), the International Sleeping Car Company's Automobile Workshops, the Kyshtym and Neviansk Mining Companies, the A. A. Anatra Airplane factory at Simferopol, the Rostokino Dye Mills outside Moscow, and the Theodore Kibbell Chromo-Lithographic and Cardboard Mills ("in view of refusal to continue production or to pay [employees]"). In February, an illuminating twist of phrase was added to the genre of confiscation decrees: the Petrograd Fittings and Electric Company, the Karkushevitch Military Equipment Factory, and the Vlokhi Plate-Rolling Works were all seized by the Bolsheviks "owing to the disappearance of the owner and his agents and their thus leaving the Works and men to the mercy of fate."[37] Apparently "capitalist" factory owners and managers were not so superfluous after all.

Singling out companies for compulsory nationalization one by one, however, became tedious rather quickly. And so the Bolsheviks decided to begin appropriating entire sectors of the economy so as to save time. Factories and farms, along with urban real estate, had been nationalized back in December 1917, although this was mostly a rhetorical flourish, in the style of early revolutionary pronouncements. The nationalizations carried out after the dissolution of the Constituent Assembly were meant in earnest, with explicit instructions regarding compliance. On 28 January the Bolsheviks declared a state monopoly over the mining of and trade in gold, silver, and platinum, with specific guidelines regarding pricing and allocation for both coin and industrial use.[38] On 5 February, the Bolsheviks decreed that the production and sale of all Russian pig iron and steel must be "subordinated to the Metallurgical Section of the High Economic Council."[39] On 10 February, the Russian insurance industry was split into three national directorates, for life, fire, and transport.[40] In April, the Bolsheviks abolished the "purchase, sale, or leasing" of commercial and industrial enterprises.[41]

The cumulative economic impact of the nationalization drive was catastrophic. Already disrupted by nearly a year of revolutionary upheaval, the Russian economy began collapsing in upon itself. The sprawling multinational banks had been the lifeblood of the prewar economy, spreading capital liberally across the Eurasian expanse to finance railway construction, colossal timber and mining operations, and urban manufacturing. During the war, their importance only increased, as billions of rubles came into the country through bond sales in Paris and London and via direct foreign investment. The Bolshevik assault on these banks, the "annihilation" of capital in all its forms, unsurprisingly choked off the cash flows lubricating the economy. Ironically, those hardest hit in the "red attack on capital" (as it was deemed in Soviet propaganda) were laborers, thrown out of work by factory closings. In the first three months of 1918, writes Sylvana Malle, "405 undertakings employing 200,000 workers closed down, owing to the stoppage of bank credit."[42] It was only the beginning.

The relentless process of Bolshevik wealth destruction is best illustrated in the fate of multinational bank-industrial combines targeted in the nationalization drive. The Putilov Works in Petrograd, as we have seen, were nationalized in January 1918. Alexei Putilov, the owner, had first acquired notoriety with Russian revolutionaries in 1905, when his firing of four employees belonging to Father Gapon's Assembly had provoked the citywide strike that led to Bloody Sunday.[43] The factory had figured prominently in the upheavals of 1917, as thousands of laid-off or idle Putilov workers took to the streets during both the February Revolution and the July Days. After Putilov refused an 11 January 1918 summons "to appear before the Inquiry Commission of the Petrograd Council of Workmen's and Soldiers' Deputies," Lenin himself signed a decree "confiscating all the real and personal property of Mr. Alexei Putilov."[44]

Expropriating the powerful Putilov must have been richly satisfying for Lenin. To Bolshevik eyes, Putilov was a perfect embodiment of the evils of capitalism: a war profiteer who had received huge commissions from the tsarist government (one such, worth 113 million rubles for artillery shell, had never been fulfilled to the government's satisfaction, causing a major scandal), a man whose payment of wages had failed to keep pace with inflation, and one who fired workers with impunity. Putilov was a notorious villain of the revolutions of 1905 and 1917, and perhaps most important of all, he had suspicious ties to foreign capital (Lenin's confiscation decree noted that Putilov was "president of the Board of the Russo-Asiatic Bank," most of whose shareholders were French).[45]

Precisely because Putilov was so closely connected to foreign investors, however, confiscating his businesses turned out to be a daunting undertaking. The Putilov Works of Petrograd were only the tip of an enormous iceberg of interrelated enterprises fully or partly owned by Putilov's Banque Russo-Asiatique, itself tied to the Banque de l'Union Parisienne.[†] The Banque Russo-Asiatique had been founded in 1910, the product of a merger between two Russo-French banks, the Russo-Chinoise and the Banque du Nord de la Chine. The bank's founding capital was 55 million gold rubles, al-

[†]Because of possible confusion with Leslie Urquhart's Russo-Asiatic Consolidated Corporation, the Putilov conglomerate will be referred to throughout by its most widely used French corporate title, the Banque Russo-Asiatique.

though this greatly understated its real wealth, which included 117 branch offices in Asia, Russia, and Europe, most of them occupying stately buildings in capital cities (international headquarters in Petrograd, for example, were located in a grand fin-de-siècle edifice at 62, Nevsky Prospekt); a large chunk of the Trans-Siberian railway (the stretch running through northern Manchuria had been financed by the bank); timber concessions in Russia and Manchuria; a virtual grain monopoly in northern China; much of China's rail network; and the right to collect customs and issue currency in China (dollars, pounds sterling, taels).[46] Shortly before the war, the bank had acquired a stake in the Putilov plant in Petrograd for 9 million rubles. Putilov himself was named president of Russo-Asiatique in 1914, to underscore the importance of Russian war industry to the bank's future.[47] In its last shareholders statement published before the October Revolution, the Banque Russo-Asiatique listed "active" and "passive" capital totaling 1,679,466,257 rubles, or nearly $840 million: the equivalent of some $84 billion in today's terms.[48] The Banque Russo-Asiatique was a very big fish in the pond of global capitalism, and one that Lenin wanted dearly to reel in.

Putilov and his big bank, however, proved to be an elusive target. Seizing Putilov's headquarters in Petrograd was certainly practicable, but the real wealth of Russo-Asiatique was located elsewhere. What could the Bolsheviks do with such bank assets as Russian war bonds—which Lenin's government had itself repudiated? What use the Trans-Siberian shares or assets in Vladivostok or China, with the Bolsheviks not acquiring control of eastern Siberia until well into 1920, by which time the Petrograd headquarters of Russo-Asiatique had been cut off from them for nearly three years? Even assets closer to hand, like the Putilov shell and locomotive factory in Petrograd, were valuable only so long as the employees produced something there, and for contractors able to pay. But the Bolsheviks proved unable to compensate these workers with anything of value: near-constant strikes continued long after the plant was nationalized. Putilov's (former) workers even introduced a resolution in the Petrograd Soviet in May 1918, demanding the Bolsheviks end their grain monopoly, permit freedom of speech, and allow independent unions and new elections to the soviets.[49]

Private banks like Russo-Asiatique, the Bolsheviks would learn to their chagrin, were valuable only as nodes in a commercial network, connecting the cash accumulated by depositors with capital goods, such as war bonds or the Putilov plant. Cash on hand at any one branch would usually be enough only to cover ordinary withdrawals; the rest of the deposits were out on loan or tied up in investments. As it happened, the Bolsheviks were somewhat fortunate with Russo-Asiatique, in that the lion's share of the bank's available cash reserves at the time of its nationalization—85.4 million rubles— were located in Russian branch offices (about 82 million rubles), whereas most of the loans coming due were slated to be paid out by the Paris and London branches, which themselves each had only about 1.5 million rubles ($750,000) on hand to cover these expenses. Amazingly, the London branch alone continued paying Russo-Asiatique's assorted creditors nearly 200,000 pounds sterling a year, or $1 million, until 1926, despite having been cut off from the bank's Russian capital, having to raise its own bonds in the City of London for the purpose.[50] In effect, the Bolsheviks had taken over the Russo-Asiatique's core cash reserves while leaving foreign shareholders to pay its bills.

Still, what was 82 million rubles, anyway? Compared to the claims held against Russo-Asiatique by bondholders, depositors, and shareholders from Paris to Peking, 82 million rubles were peanuts, and the Bolsheviks did not get even this. They found only 9.8 million rubles listed on current account at the Petrograd headquarters of Russo-Asiatique, for example, of which they appear to have gained access to only 1 million rubles.[51] Most depositors who had entrusted their assets to Russo-Asiatique, meanwhile, refused to cooperate with "nationalization" and "safe revision": as late as September 1920, less than 200 of 960 safes at the bank's Moscow branches had been opened.[52]

The story was repeated again and again in the Bolshevik war on the banks. Colossal multinational enterprises with capital flows in the hundreds of millions or billions of rubles, from the Russo-Asiatique to the Volga-Kama (125 million rubles in passive and active capital on the books) and the Azov-Don (166 million), were nationalized and sacked of whatever moveable assets or credits could be secured without the cooperation of the employees. While the bank strike persisted, the Bolsheviks were lucky, in most cases, to secure a million or two rubles.[53]

In exchange for this meager return, the Bolsheviks destroyed the Russian banking industry, starved Russian businesses of desperately needed funds, threw hundreds of thousands of employees out of work, and antagonized foreign investors. Seeking to get their hands on the 5.8 million rubles listed on current account at the Netherlands Bank of Russian Trade in Petrograd, the Bolsheviks made enemies of institutional shareholders, including five other Amsterdam banks, one Rotterdam-based corporation, and several powerful financiers from the City of London. Asked in April 1918 to explain why he was confiscating the "capital invested in Russia" by "neutral Holland," a country "far from having political goals" in Russia, the new finance commissar, Nikolai Krestinsky, replied blandly that the bank's holdings were being "nationalized, not liquidated."[54]

This was cold comfort to Russia's assorted creditors, who stood to lose more than 60 billion rubles in all ($30 billion) if the Bolshevik nationalization drive continued—or about $3 trillion in today's terms. Only about a quarter of Russia's sovereign debt ($6.5 billion worth) was owed to foreigners, but these creditors, unlike Russia's own expropriated investors, actually had the backing of powerful Entente governments, such as those of Great Britain and the United States, who were prepared to fight for their interests.[55] In France alone, deposed Russian bond and equity holders numbered well over a million, a broad enough constituency to make the restitution of their property a principal object of French governments for decades. On the eve of the debt-settlement conference at Genoa in 1922, the Quai d'Orsay's lawyers levied claims against the Bolsheviks totaling more than 22 billion francs: just under $4 billion at contemporary exchange rates, the equivalent of nearly $400 billion today.[56] This sum, adjusted for interest, represented what French citizens had invested in Russia before 1917 (mostly before the war), helping to build its railroads and industry and to finance its municipal and national governments. In exchange for this colossal investment in Russia's future, France's shareholders would receive from the Bolsheviks little but contempt.[57]

Russia's striking bank employees had good reason, then, to hold out for so long in 1918, hoping the Bolsheviks would be overthrown. The bonds and equities listed on their books represented real value to millions of people, whereas in the upside-down mental universe of the Bolsheviks, such financial instruments only represented evidence of "criminal liability" on the part of the shareholders, to be "annulled" or "annihilated" as soon as possible. Bolshevism was a zero-sum game in the most literal sense, as the value represented by private and public sector investment built up over decades evaporated at a stroke. As Bolshevik Finance Commissar Isidor Gukovsky admitted ruefully at a Central Committee meeting in April 1918, Russia's economy had ground to a halt: "Work has either stopped altogether or only goes on part time." Cash savings confiscated so far "were so negligible that we shall not be able to exist on them for long." "No country," Gukovsky concluded sadly, "can exist without creating new values."[58]

As the economy, and the tax base it supported, disintegrated, Bolsheviks resorted to the same expedient employed by all governments starved of revenue: printing bushels upon bushels of worthless paper money. Although failing to subdue the banks, the Bolsheviks had seized control of the Mint back in November 1917. The paper inflation had already begun during the war (the tsarist government had suspended the ruble's convertibility into gold in 1914), and accelerated under the Provisional Government, with the ruble losing nearly half of its prewar value by 1917 against gold-backed currencies traded in Stockholm and London. This acceleration of inflation in 1917 was due not only to excessive printing of notes by the Provisional Government, but also to the cheapness of the product: unlike the old tsarist rubles, beautiful productions almost impossible to counterfeit, "Kerenskys" (called *kerenki* by Russians, and Kerensky rubles by Swedes and Germans) were smaller and printed on only one side of paper, without either serial number or signature. The Bolsheviks, to save trouble, did not even change the stamps, instead continuing to print (ever-cheaper-looking) kerenki, which were soon referred to contemptuously as "soviet rubles" or *sovznaki*. Ten billion of these rolled off the presses between November 1917 and April 1918.[59]

A dual-track system of economic exchange inevitably evolved, in which the Bolsheviks used billions of (ever-more-worthless) sovznaki to discharge fiduciary obligations for the millions of ordinary Russians thrown onto the payrolls of nationalized enterprises, while reserving "real" tsarist rubles and gold coin to pay security organs on whom the regime depended for survival: Chekists, Red Guards,

Latvian Rifles, and later, Red Army officers. (Intriguingly, Kerensky rubles, though not sovznaki, continued fetching much better value abroad than inside Russia, where most peasants refused to accept them.) "By the action of Gresham's Law," the British consul in Petrograd reported in February 1918, the flood of cheap rubles meant that proper tsarist notes were "rapidly disappearing from circulation."[60] For as long as it endured, the bank strike was therefore a crippling liability for the Bolsheviks' ability to hold onto power. As Lenin complained at a Central Committee meeting on 4 March 1918, "We are suffering from a money famine, we are short of currency notes, the Treasury cannot print all we need. . . . It is a rare week when I do not receive a complaint about money not being paid out."[61]

Fortunately for Lenin, after five months of "sabotage," the banking community finally surrendered, by stages, in the second half of March 1918. The breaking of the bank strike is glossed over quickly in most histories of the Russian Revolution, possibly because the issue seemed moot after the Bolsheviks began laying their hands on bank safe-deposit boxes in January 1918.[62] But in fact it was a development of historic importance. Max Laserson, unemployed and largely broke after surrendering his safe-deposit box in February and being fired from the Shouvalov company in mid-March, offered his services in helping negotiate a settlement. A generous man of remarkable patience and good will, who (likely due to his socialist sympathies) seemed scarcely to resent having his personal possessions confiscated, Laserson would emerge as the prototype of the bourgeois "experts" the Bolsheviks would increasingly have to hire to clean up the economic and financial mess they had created. Lenin's financial advisers, such as Finance Commissar Nikolai Krestinsky (a close friend of Laserson's), knew they needed to keep on at least some former bank employees who knew what they were doing. Still, they wanted to vet the strikers, rehiring only those who were ideologically malleable (or indifferent) enough to ensure they would not "sabotage" confiscations. The Bolshevik negotiators insisted on taking on only 2,000 of the 6,000 strikers in Petrograd. Laserson mediated a compromise, which saw about 4,000 bank employees reinstated to their posts by the end of March 1918, including many whom the Bolsheviks mistrusted.[63]

With trained bank employees now cooperating, even if halfheart-edly, the Bolsheviks could make nearly unlimited withdrawals for the needs of the "state." The cash windfall alone was enormous, if not quite the 2–3 billion (tsarist) rubles the Bolsheviks had hoped for. The Latvian Rifles and Cheka agents could now be paid easily in "real" money, which fact alone bought the Bolsheviks enough confi-dence to expel the last nonparty members, Left Social Revolutionar-ies (the SRs had beaten the Bolsheviks handily in the November elections), from cabinet meetings in early April 1918.[64] Bolshevik couriers were soon being dispatched abroad, carrying hundreds of millions of tsarist ruble notes (and some of the better-looking kerenki) to buy hard currency, foment strikes and sabotage in En-tente countries, and securitize arms purchases.

The most important prize the Bolsheviks gained by breaking the bank strike was access to the imperial Russian gold reserves. By run-ning a substantial trade surplus, and by purchasing bullion in Paris and London with the money secured through sales of government and railway bonds, the tsarist government had assembled Europe's largest strategic gold reserve by 1914: some 1,200 metric tons, worth 1.6 billion rubles, or $823,714,500. This reserve was depleted during the war by shipments of roughly $330 million in gold, mostly to Great Britain, to securitize arms purchases (which gold was now frozen by the British government in retaliation for the Bolsheviks' re-pudiation of Russia's debts). This depletion in Russia's available re-serve, however, was offset by the production of new gold bullion worth $123 million in Siberia between 1913 and November 1917 and the accidental acquisition of the Romanian gold reserves shipped to Moscow for "safekeeping" in 1916, about $62.5 million worth.[‡65] Including the Romanian bullion, most estimates put Rus-sia's gold reserves at the time of the October Revolution at about $680 million, or some 950 metric tons: the largest strategic reserve in Europe, and by a comfortable margin.[66]

‡The Bolsheviks also inherited a cache of Romanian artifacts, jewels, and manuscripts sent to Moscow with the gold reserves. Although little known outside Romania, the saga of this lost treasure is a national obsession there. Lenin decreed that the reserves might be returned if the "Romanian proletariat" ever came to power. As a gesture of goodwill, though rather a cheap one, Brezhnev returned several cracked Thracian gold plates to Communist Romania in the 1960s; these are now pathetically on display in the National History Museum in Bucharest.

This estimate of the gold bullion available in Russia circa 1917–18, however, significantly overstates the amount the Bolsheviks were initially able to dispose of. We must first subtract the reparations the Bolsheviks were forced to pay the German imperial government after the diktat peace of Brest-Litovsk, signed in March 1918. By the terms of a supplementary agreement signed on 27 August, the Bolsheviks began shipping gold to Germany. The first two installments, totaling $80 million or about 110 metric tons of gold bullion, were shipped to Berlin on 10 and 30 September 1918. Coupled with the loss of almost half the imperial gold reserves, which were stored at Kazan—roughly $330 million worth—to anti-Bolshevik forces in June 1918 (first to the Czechoslovak legion of prisoners-of-war who had seized control of long sections of the Trans-Siberian railway, then to the White Army of Admiral Kolchak, which inherited the cache from the Czechs), this meant the Bolsheviks effectively acquired not $680 million in 1918, but more like $270 million in imperial Russian gold bullion, about 380 metric tons (although $205 million worth, about 285 metric tons, would later be recaptured from Kolchak).[67]

This was still an impressive hoard of the world's favorite precious metal. At first, however, it did the Bolsheviks little good. Gold bullion was heavy, difficult to move, and, perhaps most significantly for the outlaw regime created by Lenin, easy to trace. Imperial Russian ingots were clearly marked with a tsarist stamp, familiar to bankers all over the world. Any gold exported from Russia with this stamp after 1918 would excite a great deal of scrutiny. Predictably, following the Bolsheviks' repudiation of Russia's entire public and private debt, the bulk of which was held by Entente creditors, a ban on transactions in looted Russian gold would be enforced in the capital markets of London, New York, and Paris, and (after the Entente powers won the war) in most of the neutral countries as well. This "gold blockade" was not ironclad, as we shall see (chapters 7–8), but it took the Bolsheviks nearly two years to break it, during which time they had to fight a civil war without being able to sell their most valuable commodity.

The nationalization of the banks was thus a good deal less lucrative in the short run than the Bolsheviks had hoped. The tsarist rubles acquired in the breaking of the bank strike did allow the Bolsheviks to outbid their last political rivals in Moscow and Petrograd and to begin financing strategic imports from Scandinavia (see chapters 5–6). Now that most skilled Mint workers who knew how to print such notes had fled, however, tsarist rubles represented a finite resource, one that would be largely exhausted by 1919. In time the gold reserves acquired by the Bolsheviks would allow them to finance the creation of powerful, well-equipped armies strong enough to fight off their domestic and foreign enemies, but this prospect was still a long way off in spring 1918. Disappointed by the failure of the banks to yield the ready cash they needed, the Bolsheviks now moved on to Russia's richest resource: her people.

2   The People

The Old Bolshevik was right when he explained what Bolshevism was about to the Cossack. When the Cossack asked if it was true that Bolsheviks were looters, the old man replied: "Yes, we loot the looters." (Da, my grabim nagrablennoe.)

— LENIN, in *Pravda*, 6 February 1918

THE LOOTING of Russia's rich began long before the Bolshevik seizure of power. The transfer of the nation's patrimony into the hands of "revolutionaries" was effected almost immediately after the February Revolution in Petrograd, when the tsar's many palaces were requisitioned by the Petrograd Soviet. Kerensky famously installed himself in the Winter Palace in July, sleeping in the bedroom once used by Tsar Alexander III, and further helped himself to a Rolls Royce "requisitioned" from a rich foreigner.[1] Peasant-soldiers returning to their villages from the front began dividing up estates owned by absentee landowners long before the Bolshevik land decree of 8 November 1917 offered them a formal legal pretext for doing so (not that most of them needed such justification). Just as the tsar's abdication of power meant that he effectively relinquished title to Romanov family assets, so too did wealthy merchants, foreign businessmen, and aristocrats forfeit enforceable claims on their Russian properties as soon as they fled the country (or were unable to return, in the case of absentees). In all this, Russian revolutionaries could be said to have followed the example of the French Revolution in effecting a swift transfer of wealth from fleeing émigrés into the hands of a new class of rulers.

Nevertheless, the Bolsheviks were radical innovators in the deliberate and declarative manner in which they set about looting areas
that came under their control, beginning with Moscow and Petrograd in November 1917, then spreading east and southeast towards
the Caucasus, the Urals, the trans-Volga region, and central Asia.
Like most Bolshevik policies in the early months after the October
Revolution, the "loot-the-looters" campaign, first announced in
Pravda on 6 February 1918, was a blend of Marxist theory and hasty
improvisation in the face of desperate circumstances. In *Das Kapital*,
Marx had famously thundered that on the day of Communist reckoning, "The knell of private property sounds. The expropriators are
expropriated."[2] As Lenin interpreted Marx while outlining his government's expropriations policy on 6 February 1918: "The bourgeoisie is concealing its plunder in its coffers. . . . The masses must
seize these plunderers and force them to return the loot [i.e., capital
accrued through exploiting proletarian labor]. You must carry this
through in all locations. Do not allow [the bourgeoisie] to escape, or
the whole thing will fail. . . . The Old Bolshevik was right when he
explained what Bolshevism was about to the Cossack. When the
Cossack asked if it was true that Bolsheviks were looters, the old
man replied: 'Yes, we loot the looters.'"[3]

If Marx had provided the ideological impetus for the looting campaign, however, the disappointing intake of the winter bank nationalization drive provided the motivation. Lenin's reference to the
"concealment" of Russia's riches by its exploiting classes was a
thinly veiled complaint at the slow pace of confiscations from bank
safe deposit boxes, which were yielding nowhere near the 2.5 billion
tsarist rubles Sokol'nikov had promised. Lenin lamented the growing deficit in the same *Pravda* article in which he announced the looting campaign, estimating the projected revenue shortfall for 1918 at
20 billion (soviet paper) rubles.[4] With the help of the Red Guards,
armed Cheka agents (many recruited from tsarist prisons), along
with the masses of army deserters now roaming the countryside,
Lenin hoped to procure enough "loot" to plug his gaping budget
deficit and shore up Bolshevik rule.

Anyone familiar with the cruel and bloody depredations visited
upon Russia during the periodic peasant rebellions of tsarist times
(especially the Pugachev revolt of the 1770s) could have predicted

the anarchy that would result from Lenin's invitation to pillage. As Maxim Gorky, himself an early supporter of the revolution, wrote in mid-March of the mobs marauding around the country, "They rob and sell churches and museums, they sell cannons and rifles, they pilfer army warehouses, they rob the palaces of former grand dukes; everything which can be plundered is plundered, everything which can be sold is sold."[5]

By its very nature, a popular mass pogrom such as the one Lenin encouraged was unlikely to leave much of a paper trail. Most of what we know of it has come down to us through memoirs of rich émigrés who escaped with their lives. Baroness Meyendorff, for example, had the jewels stored in her bank safe deposit box confiscated but was lucky enough to sell others for cash to feed herself and her family. The commissars who ransacked her home in Petrograd were thus disappointed when the jewelry boxes in her bedroom were empty. Nevertheless, they made do: "Although the greater part of our silver was at the bank, there was still a certain amount of odd trays, forks, spoons and teapots, all of which they took possession. Anything that was silver they confiscated, from the lids and covers of my toilet set (leaving the crystal bottles and boxes behind), down to the little ikons hanging over the children's beds. It was useless to argue and I no longer cared."[6]

Similar stories were legion, as luxuriously furnished estates were taken over one by one by Bolshevik house committees of the sort made famous to the world in *Doctor Zhivago*. The richest families, like the Yusupovs and Stroganovs, fled almost immediately after their palaces and most (though not all) of their contents were confiscated by the Petrograd Soviet. Prince Felix Yusupov was fortunate to escape southwards with two Rembrandts in his luggage, along with many family jewels. Grand Duke Peter Nikolaevich was able to save some of his butler's silver, though not the far more imposing collection owned by his own family. Grand Duke Nicholas, through assiduous planning and a bit of luck, "had managed to save all of his family plate, gold as well as silver, along with his Sword of Honour with a gold hilt studded with diamonds."[7]

Others were not so lucky. The émigré dancer Igor Shvetsov, who grew up in a twelve-room house in Petrograd, later lamented the loss of all of his family's "furniture, pictures, pianos, bronzes, carpets, porcelain, books—everything that goes to furnish a comfortable home."[8] From dressing chambers and drawing rooms, Russia's colossal collections of jewelry and precious stones now spilled out onto the streets. As Orlando Figes writes, "the flea markets of Petrograd and Moscow were filled with the former belongings of fallen plutocrats: icons, paintings, carpets, pianos, gramophones, samovars, morning coats and ball dresses." Family heirlooms passed down from generation to generation over centuries now passed through the hands of opportunistic strangers, heedless of their emotional value.[9]

In Baku, the millionaires born of the fin-de-siècle oil boom watched in horror as their estates were ransacked by Bolshevik mobs in April 1918. Lev Nussimbaum later recalled what had become of his father Abraham's fine neighborhood, where a "block of elegant mansions [now] lay in ruins: broken coaches, collapsed lampposts, scattered clothes, and dead camels." The Nussimbaums were lucky, however: by bribing the right Bolshevik commissars, Abraham was able to arrange an exit visa, fleeing on an outbound steamer across the Caspian to Krasnovodsk (today's city of Turkmenbashi), "with only his sheltered son in tow and his cash, jewels, and oil deeds sewn into the pant legs of his fashionable European suit."[10]

The most famous story of loss, of course, was that of the Romanovs. Russia's ruling family had accumulated an enormous fortune over the three centuries they had ruled the empire, which had increased in nominal cash value even as the tsar's old patrimonial claim to own *all* the property in his domain had been eroded by the ending of the nobility's service obligation in 1762, and then with the freeing of the serfs in 1861. Estimates as to the family's net worth in 1917 vary widely, the *New York Times*'s breathless early claim of $9 billion (or $900 billion in today's terms) being as famous as it is likely erroneous. For the purposes of the present narrative, what is important is not so much what the theoretical value of the imperial patrimony may have been before it all went poof, or the relative merits of descendants' claims to pieces of this wealth; rather, the key question is, how much Romanov property that was "liquid" or otherwise saleable came into possession of the Bolsheviks after the revolution?

In the short term the answer to this question was, not very much.

Despite all the mountains of ink spilled on the "lost fortune of the Romanovs," the fact remains that the expropriation and murder of Tsar Nicholas II in 1918 was of far greater political than financial importance for the Bolshevik regime. Most of the cash savings of the tsar, Empress Alexandra, the tsarevitch, and the four grand duchesses (Olga, Tatiana, Marie, and Anastasia)—altogether not more than about 12 million tsarist rubles, or some $6 million, of which less than half was held in Russian banks—had already been exhausted by the Provisional Government paying for the upkeep of the Romanovs after the tsar's abdication in March 1917. The crown lands nationalized first by Kerensky, then by the Bolsheviks, had a book value of some 100 million rubles ($50 million), producing "appanage" income of 2.5 million rubles annually.[11] But with the tsar's abdication of title to this land came also the end of the political system that had made it valuable. It was a typical problem produced by the breakdown of law, public order, and tradition in the Russian Revolution. Just as the nationalization of the banks had choked off their capital flows until they were effectively bankrupt (see chapter 1), the confiscation of the Romanov crown lands eroded their value immediately. With no one paying these rents, there was no income to collect.

Lenin did help himself to three imported luxury cars from the imperial garage at the Alexander Palace at Tsarskoe Selo, of which two were Rolls-Royce. At first the Bolshevik leader was driven around in the tsar's old Delauney-Belville limousine, until, in an amusing turnabout of the loot-the-looters campaign, it was stolen from him at gunpoint in March 1918. Thereafter, Lenin used the 1915 model Rolls formally belonging to Mikhail Romanov for hunting trips to Gorki (where it may be found today in the local museum). Still, however satisfying it must have been for Lenin to drive the Romanovs' Rolls-Royce, expropriating it did nothing to raise funds for his regime (in fact the car proved quite a financial burden, demanding costly maintenance).[12]

There were still the Romanov crown jewels, of course, the illustrious provenance of which has excited the attention of claimants and storytellers ever since the revolution. Most of the famous items, like the Imperial Sceptre, the Orlov diamond, the crown regalia, along with thousands of other jewels and paintings, had been transferred to Moscow for safekeeping at the outbreak of war in 1914. In July 1917, the crown jewels were moved into the Kremlin Armory, where they remained, undisturbed by the Bolsheviks (who did not know where they were) until March 1922.[13] Not the least of ironies in the Bolsheviks' looting of tsarist Russia is that the most glittering prize of all remained out of their reach for years. Even after being located, the crown jewels proved nearly impossible for the Bolsheviks to sell, though they did try (see chapter 8).

The robbery-murder of the Romanovs in July 1918 was still a crucial episode in the Bolsheviks' loot-the-looters campaign, not so much for the overall "take," which was mediocre, as for what it showed about the logistical problems in controlling an officially encouraged looting pogrom. The basic outline of the story is now well known. After his abdication, Nicholas Romanov, the former tsarina Alexandra, their children, and most of their immediate retinue, were maintained by the Provisional Government at the Alexander Palace at Tsarskoe Selo. On 31 July 1917, due in part to the danger posed by the Bolsheviks' attempted putsch earlier that month, Kerensky ordered them moved eastward to Tobolsk, east of Ekaterinburg in the Ural mountain region, where they remained until being transferred by the Bolsheviks to Ekaterinburg itself in April 1918. Other Romanovs, including Grand Duke Sergei Mikhailovich, Grand Duke Constantine, and his three sons, were also put under house arrest in the Perm region nearby. In April and May, when these transfers took place, the Perm-Ekaterinburg area in the Urals seemed safe for the Bolsheviks, far from both the German occupying forces in Ukraine and the anti-Bolshevik, White "Volunteer Army" being formed in the northern Caucasus under General Anton Denikin. But the revolt of a Czechoslovak legion of former prisoners-of-war on the Trans-Siberian railway in June 1918 opened the path for a White advance from Siberia, threatening Bolshevik rule in Ekaterinburg. The prospect that the Romanovs might be rescued from captivity, and be able to make a renewed claim to the imperial throne, seems to have served the Bolsheviks as a pretext for eliminating them. Lenin's government, at its weakest point that summer, may also have simply needed a dramatic public relations coup to rally the faithful. Whatever the reason for the decision to execute the Romanov captives, there is now little doubt that Lenin approved the order himself.

Yakov Yurovsky, the head of the Ekaterinburg Cheka tasked with the executions, was possessed of a peculiar rectitude typical of the Bolshevik mentality. Ironically, in view of his mandate from Moscow to expropriate the Romanovs, Yurovsky was initially welcomed by the family as a protector against popular predations on their remaining property. There were many would-be royal looters running about in Ekaterinburg, trying to claw their way into the house, owned by an engineer named Ipatev, where Nicholas and his family were being held. The guards assigned to the family, too, were not above helping themselves to valuables, sometimes by enlisting bribes in exchange for helping members of the tsar's family deliver messages. After taking over responsibility for the captives on 4 July 1918, Yurovsky put an end to such practices. He also took an inventory of the Romanovs' property, placed an enormous amount of jewelry in a sealed box, and put a lock on the storage room where the royal luggage was stowed away.[14]

As would become clear in the course of events, however, Yurovsky was not doing all this out of solicitude for the sanctity of the Romanovs' property (or their lives) but preparatory to "expropriating" them in the proper Bolshevik manner. Just as he "protected" the family from would-be robbers before the executions, so afterwards Yurovsky would jealously guard their corpses against the vulture-like attention of rival looters (though with mixed success). The Romanov executions themselves were carried out on the night of 16–17 July 1918, without any semblance of a trial, but only a pro forma sentence of guilt (for "continued aggression against Soviet Russia"). In the basement of Ipatev's house, Yurovsky's execution squad fired a ferocious hail of bullets into the bodies of Nicholas Romanov, his doctor Botkin, the tsarina, their daughters, and their ladies-in-waiting. Only Nicholas was killed on the spot. (The gun that fired this fatal bullet was later put on display at the Museum of the Revolution in Moscow.) The other victims, writhing around in pools of blood after the initial volleys, were finished off with shots to the head or bayoneted repeatedly. The gunshots, despite Yurovsky's having taken the precaution of running a loud truck engine outside, were heard on the street, which caused a crowd to gather. Word quickly spread to would-be looters that one of the Romanov daughters had been protected by diamonds sewn into her dress (in so thick a layer that the dress could scarcely be pierced by bayonets).[15]

What transpired next was a gruesome spectacle, which revealed

volumes about the difficulty the Bolsheviks were having in controlling the furies of ressentiment they had unleashed. Yurovsky, proud
of his role in supervising the executions and the disposal of the
corpses (for which services he would be promoted and congratulated
personally by Lenin), left behind an extraordinary description of the
scenes following the Ekaterinburg executions, which deserves to be
quoted at length:

> Then they started carrying out the corpses and putting them into the car,
> which had been covered with heavy blankets so the blood wouldn't seep
> out. At this point, the stealing began: three reliable comrades had to be
> assigned to guard the corpses while the procedure continued (the
> corpses were brought out one by one). All of the stolen goods were re-
> turned under the threat of execution (a gold watch, a cigarette case with
> diamonds, and so on). . . .
>
> After driving a little more than 3 miles past the Upper Isetsk factory,
> we bumped into a whole encampment—about 25 people—on horse-
> back, in light, horse-drawn carts. . . . The first thing they exclaimed
> was: "Why didn't you bring them to us alive!?" They thought the Ro-
> manovs' execution would be entrusted to them. . . . They immediately
> began to clean out [the corpses'] pockets—it was necessary to threaten
> them with being shot and to post sentries here as well. . . .
>
> Then it was discovered that Tatiana, Olga, and Anastasia were
> dressed in some kind of special corsets. It was decided to strip the
> corpses bare, but not here, only at the place of burial. But it turned out
> that no one knew where the mine was that had been selected for the pur-
> pose. . . . When one of the girls was being undressed, it was noticed that
> the bullets torn the corset in places, and diamonds could be seen in the
> holes. The eyes of those all around began burning brightly. . . .
>
> The detachment began to undress and burn the corpses. A. F. was
> wearing a whole pearl belt made of several strands and sewn into cloth.
> Around each girl's neck, it turned out, was a portrait of Rasputin with
> the text of his prayer sewn into the amulets. The diamonds were in-
> stantly removed. They [things made of diamonds, that is] amounted to
> about eighteen pounds. . . . After we put everything valuable into bags,
> the rest of what was found on the corpses was burnt and the corpses
> themselves were lowered into the mine. While this was going on, a few
> of the valuables (someone's brooch, Botkin's dentures) were dropped . . .
> it was evident that the corpses were damaged and that certain parts were
> torn off some of them.[16]

The Four Brothers mine where the bodies were dumped, unfortunately for the Bolshevik disposal team, turned out to be not quite as

deep as Yurovsky had been told. Thus the bodies were lifted up again. Because of heavy rain, the roads were too muddy to continue on to the deeper mine where Yurovsky planned to rebury the Romanovs. And so, after some debate, the disposal team simply stopped along the Yekaterinburg-Moscow road and poured sulfuric acid onto the bodies. Yurovsky then covered the decomposing corpses with dirt and brushwood and drove over them with a truck to mangle the corpses beyond recognition in case the bodies were discovered by the Whites. Buried in a shallow grave, the remains lay undisturbed until 1989. For good measure, the very next day the Romanov blood relatives held at nearby Alapaevsk—including two more grand dukes, a grand duchess, and their children—were strip searched, robbed of all of their valuables, shot, and dumped in a mineshaft, while at least several of the victims were still alive.[17]

What was the total Bolshevik take from the various Romanov murder-robberies? Yurovsky personally secured for the regime, by his own boast, some eighteen pounds of diamonds and other jewelry, sewn into the corsets of the tsar's daughters, along with a pearl strand belonging to the tsarina later appraised at some 600,000 gold rubles, or $300,000. (Because of the rapid advance of the Czech legion and the embryonic Volunteer Army of Siberia, which reached Ekaterinburg on 25 July 1918, all these items had to be hidden temporarily underground, being transferred to Moscow only after the Whites were expelled in 1919.) From the quarters in which the grand dukes had been housed in Alapaevsk, Yurovsky's men also discovered "a number of valuables—more than a wagonload," most of it "hidden in things down to their underwear."[18]

No matter how hard Yurovsky tried to micromanage the expropriations, however, the fabulous Romanov riches were too alluring to keep prying hands away. Andrei Strekotin, one of the guards, later recalled that his "comrades began removing various items from the bodies, like watches, rings, bracelets, cigarette cases." Yurovsky, after learning of this, "suggested that we voluntarily give back the various items we had taken . . . some gave it all back, some just part, and some nothing at all."[19] To induce them to leave Ekaterinburg, Yurovsky finally had to buy the guards off with 8,000 rubles apiece, presumably to prevent them from stealing more.[20] Stories of buried treasure percolated around Ekaterinburg and Tobolsk for years, rumors thought to be fictitious until Soviet archives were opened in

1991. These reveal that as late as the 1930s, locals were being searched systematically by Cheka agents, who on one occasion turned up "154 valuable objects," including several brooches mounting 100-carat diamonds, altogether worth 3.2 million gold rubles, or $1.6 million.[21]

Yurovsky himself was so preoccupied on the fateful night of 16–17 July, keeping the mob at bay and figuring out how to dispose of the bodies, that he let many valuable items slip right through his fingers. The rain and mud did not make it any easier. At the Four Brothers mine where the Romanov bodies were first buried before being hastily removed, White investigators later discovered a ten-carat platinum-gold brilliant, a jeweled cross with emeralds and diamonds, porcelain miniatures, silver portrait frames, imperial belt buckles, coins, thirteen intact pearls, a broken ornament, and all manner of splintered and damaged jewelry (emeralds, earrings, almandines, adamants, topazes). Scattered in amidst body parts (including a human finger), ripped corsets, "the corpse of a female dog," melted lead and loose bullets, here was macabre evidence of the brutality of the Bolsheviks' loot-the-looters campaign and also its ineffectuality. Having committed one of the most audacious crimes of modern times, theoretically in order to wrest back the "plunder" the Romanovs had amassed by exploiting the Russian people, the Bolsheviks were too careless to count up all the plunder.[22]

Although the story of the Romanov murders continues to shock and titillate readers, it does not seem to have prompted many tears from Russians at the time, at least in the major cities where we have reliable reports on popular reaction to the news.* Far more shocking to pious Orthodox Russians, at least, was the Bolsheviks' assault on church property. On 19 January 1918, the Petrograd Soviet attempted to commandeer the Alexander Nevsky Monastery to be used to house war veterans. After the monks rang the monastery bells for help, "soon a large and hostile crowd gathered to heckle the armed Soviet emissaries. . . . The sailors grew increasingly nervous and angry under the taunting of the crowd; monks circulated among

*Foreign consuls still resident in Moscow, Petrograd, and other cities were unanimous in reporting "amazing indifference" to the news of the Romanov murders. Pipes, *Russian Revolution*, 784–785.

the bystanders, stirring them up to shout at the troops. Finally the armed men fired on the unarmed. The confrontation ended with one priest dead and the monastery unoccupied.[23]

The following day (20 January 1918), the Bolsheviks announced the nationalization of all church property. In theory, this included 827,540 desiatines (approximately 2.3 million acres) of church-owned land, on which stood "31,000 parishes, more than 75,000 churches and chapels, over 1,100 monasteries, some 37,000 primary schools, 57 seminaries and four university-level academies." The monastic latifundia also comprised orphanages, factories, farms, hostels, hospitals, nursing homes, and asylums. More to the point for the Bolsheviks, Russia's churches were filled with millions of church vessels made out of precious metals (especially silver), icons, and other valuable artwork.

What was once sacred was now open game for the mob. In many cities where the Bolsheviks were ascendant, revolutionary activists "took away from the churches church vestments, Episcopal mantles, altar cloths—all these were sewn up into revolutionary flags as if intentionally to outrage the feelings of the believers." Other looters helped themselves to church silver and raided the monasteries' wine cellars, which had the effect of turning raiding detachments into a drunken rabble.[24]

Little wonder the Bolshevik assault on the Church rapidly turned murderous. According to Soviet sources, which likely downplay casualty figures, 687 clergymen and parishioners were killed between February and May 1918 "while participating in religious processions or attempting to protect church properties." Of some 1,025 monasteries in Russia, 673 had been sacked by the Bolsheviks by 1920, with all of their assets turned over to the state. According to Soviet statistics published that year, monastic property confiscated to date included "84 factories, 436 dairies, 620 cattle barns, 1112 rented dwellings, 708 hostels, 311 apiaries, and 277 hospitals and asylums." In Moscow alone, the Bolsheviks took possession of church property including "551 dwellings, 100 commercial buildings, 71 almshouses, 6 orphan asylums, and 31 hospitals." Monks and other clergymen living on these properties were, one later complained, discarded "like cockroaches swept out from under the stove by the hand of a tidy housewife." They were replaced by regime supporters, mostly workers and soldiers, some 1.7 million of whom were installed on church lands between 1918 and 1920.[25]

Nevertheless, church supporters in Russia, as the story of the Alexander Nevsky Monastery suggests, still sometimes outnumbered revolutionary looters. As Lenin himself warned his followers in November 1918, "We must be extremely careful in fighting religious prejudice. . . . By giving too sharp an edge to the struggle we may only arouse popular resentment."[26] In cash terms, the pace of confiscations remained relatively slow. Not until October 1919 were the first accounts prepared on proceeds from the church robberies, which listed income of only 30 million rubles from the Moscow region. The following year, the regime boasted it had secured 4.2 billion rubles nationwide from the Church, but this was merely a crude estimate of monastic capital holdings listed on paper. Like the crown lands, the monastic latifundia were valuable only so long as rents were paid and the properties were put to productive use. In practice, the forcible nationalization of these properties rendered their capital value nugatory. Had the campaign against the Church really yielded 4 billion rubles in ready cash by 1920, the campaign to loot church wealth launched in 1922 would have been unnecessary (see chapter 4).[27]

Foreign owners of Russian property, without a popular constituency to protect them, fared worse than the Orthodox Church. British consulates in Russia were besieged as early as December 1917 by businessmen of many nationalities, afraid their offices and homes would be ransacked. "Hardly a day passes," wrote British Ambassador George Buchanan to Foreign Secretary Arthur Balfour, "without the Embassy receiving from some firm a request for protection, which I am powerless to afford."[28] Some came in from businessmen still trying to make a go of it in Russia, like H. H. Charnock, whose textile factory in Vladimir employed 17,000 workers and provided housing and medical care for another 13,000 dependents. Charnock's position became precarious once the looting campaign was underway. When his workers demonstrated to protest ongoing Bolshevik depredations against their factory and its benevolent manager, Red Guards opened fire, "killing and wounding . . . over 100 people." Charnock was able to escape, though not before his house, "with all contents, horses, carriages, clothing etc. were confiscated or 'requisitioned' by the local soviet. In addition all my holdings in the firm, including shares and loan money were taken over by the Central Government, and jewelry, Plate and papers placed in the safe of the library at the Anglican Church and furs stored in cold storage in Moscow were confiscated by the Moscow tribunal."[29]

After the news of the sacking of safe deposit boxes filtered out of Russia in January 1918, British consulates around the world were deluged with desperate pleas from property-owning subjects. Frank Reddaway, founder of a Manchester-based rubber firm, which manufactured hoses, rollers, and conveyer belts, had opened an office in Moscow before the war. Reddaway had also deposited, in a safe at the Bank of Foreign Trade,

> the deeds of his landed property near Moscow
> The scrip of One Million Roubles Russian War Loan
> Some few Bills of Exchange falling due during the current year
> Various Work books and papers having reference to the business of
>   F. Reddaway & Co. which he has directed for the last 30 years.[30]

Reddaway himself sent the key to this safe in January 1918 to the Foreign Office in London, which forwarded it on to the British consulate in Moscow. But the key arrived only in March, by which time Reddaway's safe had been emptied of its contents.[31]

It was not only foreign businessmen who lost their shirts. Margherita Johnson and her recently widowed mother, as she wrote the British ambassador in Switzerland on 4 February 1918, had left Petrograd at the outbreak of the war in 1914, after "locking up all our papers, bonds, Government loans, etc., our jewellry [sic], and various gold and silver articles of value, in our safe at the Azov-Don Bank." There were other family heirlooms, and a good deal of silver kitchenwares, in their Petrograd apartment. Although the Johnsons did not know it yet, all these family treasures would be lost forever.[32]

Less well-heeled foreigners unlucky enough to leave property behind in Russia often lost their entire life savings. There was Ethel Jane Small, who fled Russia after the October Revolution without being able to retrieve cash and securities deposited at the Volga-Kama Bank, about 22,000 rubles worth, "which represent to myself and my brother our total fortune." Likewise, Miss E. M. Nicolson, who had spent most of her life teaching English in Russia, had saved up some 15,000 rubles in cash and another 8,000 worth of bonds in Credit Lyonnais's Petrograd branch but was now unable to return to Russia to make a claim.[33] Mrs. Tatiana Walton owned a quarter-share in a house in Moscow on Bolshaia Nikitskaia, for which she had paid 5,000 British pounds.[34] Frank and Ethel Taylor had deposited some 80,000 rubles at the Azov-Don Bank in Petrograd, a sum that represented, Taylor lamented in a letter from Southampton to the Foreign Office in London, "the whole of our life savings."[35]

By the time the Anglo-Soviet trade accord was signed in March 1921, 38,000 British subjects had already filed claims for restitution against the Bolsheviks for stolen property, and fresh claims were coming in "at the rate of about 50 to 60 per week."[36] In France, the number of private claimants would run into the millions. Despite assiduous lobbying by the French government (which had itself lost billions of tsarist rubles), few would ever receive a kopek for their trouble.[37] Even the Germans, granted immunity from property nationalization in the Brest-Litovsk Treaty of March 1918, succumbed as soon as the Western armistice rendered the Brest accords moot. The German consulate in Petrograd was sacked in mid-November 1918, with everything from secret papers to personal luggage (Privatgepäck) snapped up by euphoric Bolshevik looters.[38] By spring 1919, Bolshevik looters had already helped themselves to no less than 250 million rubles from the German consulate in Petrograd alone, most of which they found stuffed inside thirty extremely heavy diplomatic mailbags.[39]

Of course, we should never lose sight of the ordinary, mostly nameless Russians who lost most. Most émigrés made little effort to find out what happened to their property in Russia, giving it up as lost unless the Bolsheviks were ever overthrown. Still, a few *burzhui* who remained in Russia did apply later for restitution of lost property. Anna Ivanovna Nozhina of Riga, for example, had taken her family heirlooms to Saratov in 1915, to keep them from falling into German hands. In October 1917, she "registered" them voluntarily with the Saratov workers' collective (Saratovskaia trudovaia artel'), which happily took into possession some forty items of her personal jewelry, including "one gold brooch mounted with stones, one gold woman's watch, one pair of diamond brooches, silver and gold, in cases, one gold bracelet with a strongly radiant white diamond . . . a gold pendant with chrysolites, silver medallions with French stones, a woman's gold ring with diamonds, a woman's gold ring with chrysolites, a woman's gold ring with two pearls . . . a silver cigarette-holder inscribed 22/IX/1782 . . . 12 silver tea spoons, 12 silver table spoons made in 1884."[40] Although she held receipts (kvitantsii) for all her items, Anna Nozhina's repeated queries with the Saratov Soviet were unavailing: she was told, again and again, to wait. Finally, in 1920, it emerged that the Nozhin family heirlooms had been requisitioned and confiscated, before being transferred to Moscow.[41]

The Nozhins were not alone. Red Guards, Cheka committees, and armed bandits pledging vague allegiance to the revolution were extremely inventive in coming up with new ways to expropriate those with material assets of any kind. In different towns, the Bolsheviks tried various approaches. In Ekaterinoslav, armed looting detachments were instructed to "wrest from the bourgeoisie those millions taken from the masses and cunningly turned into silken undergarments, furs, carpets, gold, furniture, paintings, china. . . . We have to take it and give it to the proletariat and then force the bourgeoisie to work for their rations for the Soviet regime."[42] In Nizhny Novgorod, a revolutionary levy of 22 million rubles was imposed on local notables, "while the Cheka arrested 105 bourgeois citizens and held them hostage until the levy was paid." Rich burghers in Moscow and Petrograd were ordered in October 1918 to cough up a onetime "contribution" of several billion rubles in each city (although, predictably, nowhere near this amount could be collected).[43] Everywhere merchants, landowners, and educated professionals were subject to special confiscations or onerous taxes, irregardless of their ability to pay. As Orlando Figes writes, "many of those persecuted as 'the rich' were no more than petty traders or half-impoverished teachers, doctors, and clerks."[44]

Another Bolshevik innovation in wealth appropriation was the exit visa bribe, a fund-raising method commonly practiced by Communist regimes in the twentieth century, most famously in Ceausescu's Romania. Like the Nussinbaums, many émigrés were willing to cough up serious money to buy their freedom from Bolshevik terror. Another oil baron from Baku offered Soviet Finance Minister Isidor Gukovsky no less than 1 million rubles in exchange for a travel visa to Stockholm in August 1918. Gukovsky accepted the offer on behalf of the Commissariat of Finance, adding the magnate's bribe to the suspiciously huge hoard of tsarist rubles (50 million, all told) he was amassing for a trip to Sweden. Gukovsky and the oil baron departed Petrograd for Stockholm in early September, accompanied by Max Laserson: the trio carried fifteen suitcases bulging with cash.[45]

In Moscow and Petrograd alone, thousands of lives were ruined by the Bolsheviks' sacking of the bank safes. Anyone who had put his or her money into war bonds or corporate equities; real estate; foreign currency; gold or silver coin; jewelry, platinum, or precious stones lost the entire investment, whether or not they showed up with their safe deposit key to turn it over "voluntarily." Most, in fact, did not show up, whether because they had already fled or did not wish to give obnoxious commissars the satisfaction of pawing through their valuables. It would take several years of safecracking, but eventually the Bolsheviks would have their way (see chapter 3).

As for less well-off Russians who had deposited their earnings in savings accounts, these small savers were, it is true, exempted from the laws of confiscation in 1918. Prominent among this category were Russia's peasant smallholders, the kind who had prospered under Stolypin's reforms and from rising grain prices during the war. By some estimates, peasant savers had accumulated 3 or 4 billion rubles in state banks by 1917. But as Richard Pipes has pointed out, the paper inflation deliberately fanned by the Bolsheviks—who printed 40 billion ever-cheaper-looking ruble notes in 1918—"rendered these deposits as worthless as if they had been confiscated overnight."[46]

It is likely that Russia's peasants, still not entirely trusting banks, had stored billions more rubles "under the mattress," many of them tsarist notes. These did retain a nominal value higher than the "Kerenskys" printed in 1917 and the soviet notes printed by the Bolsheviks. But money is valuable only so long as there is something to buy with it. This is why the Bolsheviks took nearly every tsarist and Kerensky note they could get their hands on in 1918 to Stockholm, where Swedes were willing to exchange them for Swedish crowns or import credits (see chapter 5). Russia's peasants, of course, did not have this option.

Here was a lose-lose situation typical of Bolshevik economic policy. By deliberately inflating the money supply, the Bolsheviks wiped out the wealth held by successful peasant smallholders, those miniature rural "capitalists" denounced in party propaganda. This inflation, in turn, had the effect of choking off the flow of grain to the cities. As Isidor Gukovsky, the Bolshevik finance commissar, complained as early as April 1918, "All our efforts to induce the peasant to give us his foodstuffs have been rather fruitless, because in exchange for his produce we offer him paper money which cannot buy anything."[47] Soon Lenin was denouncing the "bloodsucker kulaks" who were "ready to suffocate, to carve up hundreds of thousands of workers" by refusing to supply food. And so he proclaimed a "Merciless war against the kulaks!" in August 1918, before an audience of workers tasked with bringing the loot-the-looters campaign to the countryside.[48] As Lenin described the objectives of these new "urban food detachments" in a directive to the Penza Soviet on 10 August 1918, "The kulak uprising in your five districts must be crushed without pity. . . . (1) Hang (I mean hang publicly, so that people see it) at least 100 kulaks, rich bastards, and known bloodsuckers. (2) Publish their names. (3) Seize all their grain. (4) Single out the hostages per my instructions. . . . Do all this so that for miles around people see it all, understand it, tremble, and tell themselves that we are killing the bloodthirsty kulaks and that we will continue to do so." As in the assault on the Church, however, the Bolsheviks proved too weak to win a war with the peasants that fall. Resistance to confiscations predictably led the Bolsheviks to take ever-crueler measures against resisters, which begat yet more resistance. When executions and hangings proved unavailing to induce compliance with confiscation decrees, Lenin suggested hostage-taking: "In all grain-producing areas, twenty-five designated hostages drawn from the best-off of the local inhabitants will answer with their lives for any failure in the requisitioning plan." What was important, he explained, was that "the rich, just as they are responsible for their own contribution, will also have to answer with their lives for the immediate realization of the requisition plan." When this threat, too, failed to improve grain yields, Lenin ordered that all uncooperative kulaks, along with "priests, White Guards, and other doubtful elements" be interned "in a concentration camp."[49] But nothing seemed to work. As Richard Pipes writes, despite "all that effort and all that brutality—troops firing machine guns, pitched battles, hostages with death sentences hanging over their heads," the anti-kulak pogrom "brought in only one hundredth of the harvest" in 1918, or about 570,000 tons of grain. In January 1919, the Bolsheviks abandoned forced confiscations in favor of a policy of collective grain contributions from peasant districts, the *prodrazverstka*.[50]

Class war, in short, was nowhere near as profitable as the Bolsheviks had hoped. The confiscations policy had actually backfired in the agricultural sector, producing what was likely a negative yield in grain supplies to the cities. Much of the jewelry procured through ad hoc popular confiscations, meanwhile, was secreted away in the pockets of those doing the looting, who had little incentive to turn it over to the Soviet government. Even with a heavily armed Cheka execution squad on an official Bolshevik mission in Ekaterinburg, as we have seen, Yurovsky had not been able to beat off rival looters. Ideologically satisfying as the loot-the-looters campaign must have been, ultimately it did even less for Moscow's bottom line than did bank nationalization, which at least produced a significant hoard of tsarist rubles and gold bullion that Bolshevik procurement agents could use to securitize imports.

An important reason for the disappointing cash yield from the looting campaign was the flooding of the black market in jewelry. Fleeing émigrés, lucky looters, and Bolshevik officials were all selling in 1918, but who was buying? Almost no one—no one interested in jewels for their intrinsic value, anyway. With property rights under siege, there was no guarantee traders would even get to hold these items for more than a day or two. In such circumstances, desperate pawners would receive only what the market would bear, which was not very much. As Baroness Meyendorff recalled, "Small pieces of jewellery, such as my favourite emerald and diamond rings . . . would fetch nothing." After failing to obtain anything of value for her expendable jewels, the baroness was finally forced to part with a brooch covered with "six large diamonds the size of peas, the middle ones slightly smaller than the ones on either side, graduating from two to three carats each." In exchange for this priceless family heirloom, she received enough money to buy . . . a single bag of white flour.[51]

Frustrated by the poor cash flow from jewelry sales, the Bolsheviks gradually hit on the idea of forced levies on traders akin to the peasant prodrazverstka, which might produce cash directly. A decree issued in May 1918, the first of many similar to follow, targeted "pawn shops, loan offices, banks and any type of establishment taking possession of, for storage or under any conditions, precious stones and metals or watches made from them." Instead of paying commissions when they sold their loot, the Bolsheviks would now *charge* traders on all items traded worth more than 5,000 rubles, beginning at 40 percent of value and ramping up thereafter.[52] This might yield tax revenue, or it might simply shut down illicit jewelry trading. Either result would be welcome.

Slowly, reluctantly, the Bolsheviks were beginning to relearn the laws of economics that Lenin had so desperately wished to repeal. There was a reason the value of precious stones plummeted when street bazaars were flooded with them, just as the price of bread shot through the roof when it became scarce in the cities. As the Soviet government was now itself the single largest owner in Russia (and likely, the world) of jewelry and other precious metals, it was imperative to shut down the thriving black market trade that was driving down their value. Although continuing to denounce, in party propaganda, those despised "hoarders" of scarce goods who were profiting from the people's distress, the Bolsheviks would soon become the biggest hoarders of them all.

3   The Gokhran

Confiscated silver, gold, precious stones and pearls . . . had been accu-
mulated in such enormous quantities as could hardly be conceived. . . .
I passed through . . . vast halls crammed on both sides up to the ceiling
with all sorts of luggage-cases (trunks, baskets, boxes, satchels, and
so on).

— MAX LASERSON

THE REGIME LENIN began erecting on the ruins of the tsarist empire was, as he himself never tired of repeating, no ordinary government. If the principal function of most governments is to cultivate law and public order, that of Lenin's was precisely the opposite: to eradicate all existing law and institutions and to encourage class war. As no government of this kind had existed before, it is not surprising the Bolsheviks struggled to define the roles of various governing bureaucracies. Having dissolved the elected parliament (Duma) and defanged the worker soviets (where the Social Revolutionaries remained strong) by spring 1918, the Bolsheviks legislated mostly through the Council of People's Commissars (Sovnarkom), theoretically a kind of executive branch answerable to the Soviet, although most of these commissars were simply appointed by the Bolshevik Central Committee. The execution of laws (if instructions on the order of "hang the bloodsucker kulaks" may indeed be called "laws") was then theoretically entrusted to local workers' soviets. On the ground, however, as we have seen, property nationalizations decreed from Moscow were carried out by whoever wished to loot and rob their neighbors: house committees, Red Guards, Cheka agents, execution squads like Yurovsky's, random mobs of greedy onlookers, armed food detachments, and so on. If this was a government at all, it was a most peculiar one and, judging by its inability to control the looting campaign or feed its urban population, not a very effective one.

Governing a nation on Marxist-Leninist principles was evidently not an easy task. The class war encouraged and enflamed all year by revolutionary decrees had upended the Bolsheviks themselves on numerous occasions, from the holdup of Lenin's limousine in March to the famous 30 August 1918 assassination attempts on Lenin and Petrograd Cheka chief Moisei Uritsky, which furnished the pretext for the Red Terror. By encouraging people to rob and murder their "oppressors," Lenin had evidently given at least some of them the notion to attack the Bolsheviks themselves. A war between the haves and have-nots could spiral onward without end, as looting have-nots turned into haves, thus becoming targets for new looters. At some point distinctions would need to be drawn between those allowed to possess property and those not.

Where to draw the line? Part of the answer lay in the ever-expanding list of Bolshevik Party members and Cheka agents, both of whose ranks had expanded into the tens of thousands by fall 1918, and would continue to grow so long as Bolshevik rule in Russia seemed assured: the Cheka alone would employ 280,000 by early 1921. By proclaiming their allegiance to the new government, registered Communists and Chekists acquired de facto, if not quite de jure, protection of their own property from regime confiscations and, of course, the predations of other looters. By contrast, property rights were forfeited by anyone targeted as an "enemy of the people" in the Red Terror: kulaks; "the rich"; White officers; "doubtful elements"; "Menshevik counterrevolutionaries"; "bandits"; "members of the families of bandits taken as hostages"; those guilty of "parasitism, prostitution, or procuring"; "hostages from the *haute bourgeoisie*"; "functionaries from the ancien régime"; and so forth.[1]

Still, there was a nebulous category of people in between the extreme status of loyal class warriors and outright class enemies. So long as they paid the new jewelry tax and helped suppress illegal trading, pawnshop owners and loan sharks would now receive protection (see chapter 2). Then there were "capitalists" like Max Laserson, who, despite much of his personal property having been confiscated, was willing to be of service to the regime. Because such men voluntarily relinquished their possessions and even helped catalogue them properly, "Lasersons" were much more valuable to the regime than either uncooperative "class enemies" or those who robbed them and pocketed the proceeds. If other well-off Russians could be encouraged to follow Laserson's example and voluntarily turn over their precious valuables, the Bolsheviks could be spared the logistical headaches produced by the popular pogroms of 1918.

Just as the new prodrazverstka sought to improve the yield of grain shipments to the cities by enlisting collective district compliance with requisitions, a series of Bolshevik decrees passed in fall 1918 sought to streamline looting by abandoning the popular pogrom in favor of "voluntary" registration of valuable property by the rich—those who had not yet fled the country in terror, that is. On 10 November 1918, the Commissariat of Finance decreed that anyone whose bank safe still contained gold watches or other personal jewelry would get to keep them (for now), so long as they paid a levy beginning at 15 percent of value (for items worth 1,500 to 3,000 rubles) and topping out at 75 percent for jewels worth 80,000 rubles or more.[2] In part, this was an admission of defeat: the Bolsheviks had not yet figured out how to crack open safes and had reached an impasse now that most remaining safe owners had fled or gone into hiding.

Somewhat more promising were the prospects of "registering," that is, confiscating, valuable antiques and artwork from apartments and estates. In October 1918, a Sovnarkom decree ordered owners of artistic and antiquarian artifacts, whether individuals or institutions, to register them with the Soviet government. Overseeing this project would be a new subagency of the Commissariat of Education (Narkompros), the "Commission for the Storage and Registration of Artistic and Historical Monuments" (Komissiia po okhrane i registratsii pamiatnikov iskusstva i stariny).[3]

The new Bolshevik arts registration venture of winter 1918–1919, though (understandably) receiving much less attention from historians than the concurrent onset of the Russian civil war, was given high priority by the government. Top-ranking Bolshevik Party members of the caliber of Trotsky and Stalin predictably took on military commands that winter. Still, the new Narkompros arts commission was hardly shortchanged. Its leading lights would be three ostensible party outsiders with credibility in the worlds of culture and business, but who had been quietly involved in Bolshevik finances since the turn of the century: the famous novelist Maxim Gorky; Gorky's common-law wife, the actress and reputed thief Maria Fyodorovna Andreeva; and Leonid Krasin.[4] Gorky and Andreeva offered a patina of glamour to the new commission, which could be promoted as a campaign to make amends with Russia's beleaguered intelligentsia and preserve what was left of her culture after the worst revolutionary excesses. But the presence of Krasin, an engineer, fund-raising maestro, and accomplished terrorist, should have given the game away.

Although far less well known to historians and the educated public than most Bolshevik leaders (or Gorky), Krasin was the true éminence grise of the Russian Revolution, without whose skills and contacts Bolshevism could never have triumphed. Born in 1870, the same year as Lenin, Krasin was first exposed to revolutionary ideas while studying chemical engineering at the Technological Institute in St. Petersburg. The timing was apt for a socialist awakening: the years of Krasin's enrollment (1887–91) coincided with the spread of the German-style Marxism of the Russian Social Democratic Party (RSDRP) through Russian student circles, where it began to rival homegrown populism as the fashionable revolutionary orientation. With his engineer's mentality (and his budding knowledge of German), Krasin was primed for the "scientific" pitch of Marxism, though he seems to have been less interested in Marxist theory (he was bored by *Das Kapital*) than in the more practical aspects of revolutionary politics, like bomb making. Like his exact contemporary Lenin, Krasin was placed under surveillance by the tsarist secret police (Okhrana) at an early age and was banished from St. Petersburg in April 1891, while only twenty. Still, Krasin's engineering talent and his elegant manners won him a degree of sympathy from tsarist officials. Despite periodic imprisonments for his involvement with revolutionary organizations, on other occasions Krasin was entrusted with prestigious government engineering commissions, such as the section of the Trans-Siberian railway abutting Lake Baikal.[5]

Krasin's appearance of respectability would prove exceedingly useful to the Bolsheviks both before and after the Russian Revolution. After taking a full-time job at an electrical power company in

Baku (Elektrosila) in 1900, Krasin was finally taken off the Okhrana's full-time surveillance list. This compliment from the tsarist regime, however, did not prevent Krasin from offering his services to Lenin's radical "Bolshevik" faction of the RSDRP (which had split from the "Mensheviks" at a party congress in London in 1903). Krasin's social graces allowed him to organize Bolshevik charity balls and music recitals, selling tickets to Baku's oil magnates and unsuspecting tsarist officials. It was in this capacity that Krasin became acquainted with Maxim Gorky and Maria Andreeva, who raised money for the Bolsheviks in a similar manner in Moscow and St. Petersburg (the pair also raised 50,000 rubles for Lenin on a celebrated literary tour of the United States in 1906). Together, Gorky, Andreeva, and Krasin helped Lenin publish the first legal Bolshevik publication in Russia, *Novaia zhizn'*.[6]

What Gorky and Andreeva may not have known about their cultivated colleague, however, was that Krasin was also raising funds for the Bolsheviks in other, less savory ways. After taking a job at a Belgian electrical firm in St. Petersburg in 1905, Krasin developed a network for smuggling dynamite and weapons into Russia from Finland. Using chemical firms and camera shops as cover, Krasin helped design bombs, grenades, and other hand projectiles personally. After the fizzling out of the 1905 revolution, which had provided their ostensible purpose, Krasin's underground weapons factories would supply the explosives and arms used by Bolshevik bank robbers in Moscow, St. Petersburg, and most famously, in the Caucasian holdups in which the young Stalin first made his name. Krasin was also involved in ruble counterfeiting operations.[7]

Krasin, like Gorky, later had a falling-out with Lenin, but this would not prevent either man from offering his services to the Bolsheviks again after the revolution. The arts registration agency formed in November 1918 was an ideal commission for both men, combining their genuine concern with Russia's cultural heritage (though this motive was likely stronger in Gorky's case) with a hidden fund-raising angle perfectly suited to Krasin's talents. It is conceivable, at least, that Gorky remained unsuspecting as to the ultimate goal of their new enterprise; but there is little chance Krasin was so naïve.

With Gorky as the main public face of the operation, the three old comrades set to work with energy and enthusiasm. The arts and antiques registration commission was, in fact, only one of a series of ventures Gorky undertook that winter with the aim of "saving Russian culture," which also included a kind of writers' colony he installed in an expropriated merchant's house in Petrograd at the corner of Nevsky Prospekt and Bolshaia Morskaia, and a publishing house devoted to mass-producing novels by Russian writers, many of whom had become destitute during the revolution.[8] Still, Gorky was by no means simply a figurehead in the antiquarian commission, the initial Petrograd headquarters for which, at 3 Chalturin ulitsa (later Piatnitskaia), he himself selected. The priority assigned to the venture was manifested in the size of the staff, which rapidly grew to eighty full-time employees. Together, the members of Gorky's team scoured the apartments, houses, pawnshops, and bookshops of Petrograd for artwork, old books, jewelry, and other antiques and artifacts, confiscating the most promising items while theoretically "registering" them to their owners (if these were still alive and in Russia).[9]

Gorky and Andreeva likely told their charges that the confiscated valuables were destined to go on display in "proletarian museums" being organized under the auspices of Narkompros, but this was at best a half-truth. As early as February 1919, Gorky's operation was subordinated to the Commissariat of Trade, particularly its Foreign Trade Commission (Narkomvneshtorg), in order to prepare the most saleable artwork and antiques for possible export. This is where Krasin came in. During the war, Krasin had developed a formidable array of contacts abroad, especially during stints with the German firm Siemens-Schuckert in both Stockholm and Berlin. He moved easily in business circles in both cities and for this reason was empowered by Lenin to negotiate with Swedish and German firms in 1918 (see chapter 5). Krasin, intimately familiar with the difficulty the Bolsheviks were having capitalizing trade deals because of their repudiation of foreign debts, was on the lookout for financial alternatives to loans that might serve as security for imports—like valuable art, antiques, jewelry, and precious metals. Gorky's arts and antiques commission seemed like a perfect vehicle for streamlining collection of Russia's most saleable artifacts, and so it is not surprising Krasin began supervising the project in 1919.

Unlike the informal loot-the-looters campaign of 1918, the antique "registration" drive of 1919 produced written accounts, which allow us to get an idea of the operation. The files are not systematic, but those that do exist recall the "maniacal accuracy" of the tsarist bureaucracy, listing "antiques" acquired in numbing detail.[10] Thus in one Petrograd house search, carried out by a team led by Andreeva on 5 October 1919 at 30 Koresa ulitsa, the Bolsheviks registered the following items: "a silver chain, a silver frame, watches with watch-cases—bronze. Gloves. A bottle of wine. Bronze watches. A silver pin. A decorated chain [Tsepochka s ordenami]. Four bronze medals and one silver one. A fine gold ring with a red stone and five diamond pieces [oskolkov ot brillianta]. Red fabric [krasnaia materiia] and a collection of coins."[11] Unsatisfied with the paltry total of items from this first visit, the Andreeva team returned to the same apartment nine days later, and further registered:

> One salt-shaker, five silver spoons, ten silver forks, eight knives . . . a silver cigarette lighter, a silver glass, two little tumblers, a magnifying glass, gold watches, a perfume bottle, three chamberlain keys [kamer-gerskikh kliucha], three tea spoons . . . a woman's silver cigarette holder [portsigar], a fan, a knife, a silver ashtray, women's gold watches with [precious] stones, men's watches with chains and trinkets [s tsepochkoi i brelkami], a writing-pad case, a women's cigarette-holder and jewelry box, lace, twelve monogrammed silver knives, forks, and spoons with silver handles, twenty-four spoons and twenty-four forks.[12]

By the end of the year, Gorky, Andreeva, and Krasin had registered and appraised "antiques" worth 36 million gold rubles (about $18 million) in Petrograd alone, divided up into seventeen categories, including paintings by European Old Masters, Orthodox icons, furniture, silverware, porcelain and crystal objects, silver and bronze artifacts, along with "archaeological curiosities" native to Russia and antique weapons.[13]

Progress assembling valuables in Petrograd, then, was relatively rapid. In the provinces, with civil war engulfing the country, collection proceeded much more slowly, or at least was more slowly reported. Judging from the volumes of artwork, jewelry, and precious metals sent to Moscow in the early 1920s, there must have been a great deal of effective provincial hoarding by Red Army officers and Chekists even in 1919. For example, Tambov province, located some

350 kilometers southeast of Moscow, was systematically looted in winter 1918–19. Although not as wealthy as Petrograd's aristocrats and merchants, Tambov's peasants were well blessed with a variety of items made from silver, including tablewares (forks, knives, spoons, tea sets), goblets (charki), and trays (podnosy). Tambov's peasants had also collected flower vases in great numbers. After the Red Army pacified the province in early 1919 (temporarily: Tambov would rise repeatedly in 1920–21), eighteen large trunks filled with these sorts of modest silver antiques were catalogued and sent in to Moscow.[14]

Tambov, however, was the exception that proved the rule. Its population of peasants was prosperous enough to offer possibilities for plunder and hostile enough to the regime to justify their expropriation. Most important, its assorted loot was near enough to Moscow for transport to be arranged fairly inexpensively. Few other provinces met these criteria so perfectly. In general, with the British blockade shutting off Bolshevik access to Baltic ports throughout 1919, there was little justification to load looted treasures onto scarce railcars needed by the Red Army to move men and munitions, as there was no chance they could be exported even if they made it to Moscow or Petrograd. Precious valuables, moreover, could easily be stolen by Whites, peasant partisans, or roving bandits if the trains carrying them were sabotaged.

The effective collapse of the White armies in November–December 1919, along with Lloyd George's unilateral lifting of the British Baltic blockade, altered this equation dramatically. Suddenly it seemed possible not only to ship looted treasures across Russia by rail or road routes safe from White (if not partisan and anarchist) harassment, but also to export them. The logistical problems posed by such an operation were immense, of course. The port of Petrograd had been severely damaged during the revolution and civil war, and so most of the treasures the Bolsheviks wished to ship abroad would need to go through a nearby Baltic port like Reval (Tallinn), Estonia. Krasin himself wrote most of the terms of the Tartu peace treaty with Estonia, ratified on 2 February 1920, which guaranteed nearly unlimited Bolshevik use of Estonian rail lines and seaports (see chapter 6). Two weeks later, Krasin ordered the Gorky-Andreeva commission (now controlled by the Foreign Trade Commissariat) to begin assembling all "valuable antiques in the vicinity of the northern district" for possible export, with emphasis on "articles made of gold, silver, and platinum, as well as precious stones and pearls."[15] Krasin himself, however, would now be spending most of his time abroad, placing Soviet import orders for desperately needed locomotive engines, weapons, cars, and airplanes. In Krasin's absence, the task of running the suddenly urgent arts and antiques registration operation fell to the finance commissar, Nikolai Krestinsky.

Krestinsky was not, at first glance, a promising candidate for such an important and politically sensitive commission, though he was certainly a step up from Sokol'nikov, whose lack of experience had been painfully evident during the bank nationalization drive. (Sokol'nikov's inexperience extended to politics: only a greenhorn would have agreed to be the sacrificial lamb who signed the humiliating terms of the Brest-Litovsk Treaty in March 1918, which act of political self-immolation predictably led to his losing the Finance Commissariat.) Krestinsky had at least had some work experience before the war and revolution, as a trial lawyer. Like Alexander Kerensky, Krestinsky had represented primarily poor clients out of socialist conviction, though unlike Kerensky, he lacked the courtroom charisma that might lead one to think he had a future in politics. Krestinsky was not the sort of man who turned heads very easily. Max Laserson, who had known Krestinsky intimately since 1908, reflected that his friend "was no orator and in no respect rose above the circle of his colleagues."[16]

Krestinsky, however, had other qualities that augured well for the task at hand. Laserson remembered him as having always been "extraordinarily ambitious," the kind of careerist who "took the pains to make up for his lack of any surpassing talent through hard work, persistence and research." Krestinsky's diligence was not matched by great curiosity, which might have made him ask uncomfortable questions about the origins of the treasures he was processing. So blind was Krestinsky to the social horrors engulfing Russia during the Red Terror and civil war that he remained unaware as late as spring 1919, according to Laserson, that the Cheka was killing, or even torturing, suspected class enemies. Krestinsky was, in the illuminating description of one of his employees, "a great man in small matters" (ein großer Mann in kleinen Dingen).[17]

Such a man was perfect for the simultaneously grandiose and petty job of hoarder-in-chief of the looted treasures of a continent. Krestinsky's new mandate was announced on 3 February 1920, the day after Krasin's Tartu Treaty was signed with Estonia. In a Sovnarkom decree signed by Lenin himself, Krestinsky was appointed director of a new "State Treasury for the Storage of Valuables" (Gosudarstvennoe khranilishche tsennostei), or Gokhran, with responsibility for the "centralization and accounting of all valuables on the territory of [Soviet Russia], consisting of ingots of gold, platinum, and silver or articles [made from] them, diamonds, precious stones, and pearls." From Siberia to the Polish border, the Black Sea to the Baltic, Russia's tremendous patrimony of riches was now to be collected, preparatory to export, in a single building complex abutting Strastnaia Square at 3 Nastas'inskii pereulok, which formerly housed the Moscow Loan Office. The only exceptions to Gokhran's claim on Russia's immense stores of precious metals, jewelry, antiques, and artistic treasures were a limited allowance of gold and platinum for industrial purposes and an exemption for valuables set aside for use by "religious communities, like objects of worship."[18] Although the language was left deliberately ambiguous, this last exception likely reflected Lenin's enduring fear of the wrath of peasants, which had caused him to pull back from the assault on the Church in 1918.

The Gokhran mandate was broad yet vague enough to offer almost limitless potential for the connoisseur of administrative minutiae. Like Sokol'nikov in the bank nationalization campaign, Krestinsky attacked his appointed task with great plodding energy, if little imagination. There were responsibilities to be delegated— analysis of artifacts' cultural and historical provenance to Lunacharskii's Commissariat of Enlightenment; budgeting and accounting to Krestinsky's own Finance Ministry; security matters to the new "Workers and Peasants' Inspectorate," or Rabkrin; sorting for export to Krasin's Commissariat of Foreign Trade.[19] There were committees to be created, like the "Commission for the Depersonalization, Sorting, and Appraisal of Valuables" (Komissiia po obezlicheniiu, sortirovke i otsenke tsennostei pri Gokhrane), on which would sit delegates from all relevant commissariats.[20] There were jobs to be created, salaries apportioned—30,000 rubles a month for

Gokhran branch managers, 25,000 for top managerial staff, 22,000 for the chief accountant and chief inspector, slightly less for their assistants, 15,000 for the main cashier, the same for gold and precious stones sorters, 12,000 rubles for those handling the silver, and so forth.[21]

In a reflection of the priority Krestinsky gave to staffing the Gokhran, the salaries he offered were far superior to those of his employees at the Finance Commissariat (which ranged from 400 to 1,200 rubles).[22] All the remuneration in the world, however, could not help Krestinsky conjure up competent workmen. In fact Krestinsky had not a single jewelry or art expert on staff equal to the immense problem before him, and he would not have one until 1923. The only problem Krestinsky was really competent to tackle on his own was *sortirovka*, the crude sorting of valuables into categories. On 16 March 1920, he instructed his workers to begin separating precious metal objects into piles of platinum, iridium, gold, and silver; then jewels, into pearls and colored stones, and these according to size; and of course diamonds, which, after being removed from objects onto which they were mounted, would be sorted by carat. Jewelry or antique items not containing diamonds were simply weighed as is and labeled according to whichever metal (gold, silver, platinum) seemed to predominate.[23]

The first Gokhran accounts date from 6 April 1920, although they were not actually prepared until later. They are peculiar documents, reflecting the unprecedented nature of the job being done by Krestinsky's men. Most businesses produce records of revenue and expenditure. The Gokhran, by contrast, was more like a giant abacus rigged to move in only one direction: its sorters and accountants counted up the intake of various items on the credit side of the ledger, with no debits. By mid-July, the Gokhran abacus reported a "yield" of 21,563 carats of diamonds; 20,305 of pearls; along with some 3,000 gold, silver, and platinum watches; 11 poods (about 400 pounds) worth of gold jewelry items "of an artistic character"; 5 poods (190 pounds) of gold ingots and nuggets; some 8,000 gold-plated artifacts made of gold (izdeliia iz zolota); 27 poods (half a ton) of gold scrap (lom zolota); 1,614 poods (about 30 tons) of silver; plus 41,845 as yet unweighed artifacts made of silver—kitchenwares, antiques, and so on. In crude approximation of world market prices, these wares would be worth some 225 million rubles, or about $112.5 million, with over 80 percent of value coming from the pearls (optimistically appraised at 2,500 rubles per carat) and diamonds (at 6,000 per carat) alone.[24] There were also bronze artifacts and antiques (23 poods, or 800 pounds) and copper and silver coins (about three or four tons of both). By the end of November 1920, the total intake at Gokhran had surpassed 490 million rubles by theoretical valuation—$245 million, the equivalent of almost $25 billion today, including 51,479 carats of diamonds, 39,840 carats of pearls, a hundred tons of silver, and 35,000 items of gold jewelry.[25] Throughout 1921, diamonds and pearls continued arriving in thousands of carats per month, augmented by rubies, sapphires, and precious stones the overmatched Bolshevik sorters were unable to categorize.[26] By December 1921, the size of the Gokhran hoard had roughly doubled again, to an estimated value of 900 million gold rubles ($450 million, or about $45 billion today).[27]

Where did all of these Gokhran treasures come from? Although Krestinsky's mandate implied that he would be assembling loot from across the Eurasian continental expanse, in its first six months the Gokhran drew primarily on the bank safes of Moscow and Petrograd, just as Sokol'nikov had done during the bank nationalization drive. Evidently, neither the threats of winter 1918 nor the decree in November of that year legalizing possession of valuables in safes (if the owner would pay an onerous tax) had succeeded in convincing most Russian safe depositors to collaborate with the Bolsheviks in robbing themselves. Lasersons remained the exception, not the rule. Some 35,000 safes had been opened by summer 1918, but thereafter progress was halting. Of 50,901 bank safes confiscated by the Bolsheviks due to their owners' not having appeared with their keys, by September 1920 only 12,727 had been emptied of their contents (osvobozhdeno). Another 14,900 had been broken open by force (vzlomano), while 23,274 safes had resisted all efforts at safecracking.[28]

Not surprisingly, the slow progress of safe opening convinced Krestinsky to establish yet another Bolshevik bureaucracy, the Safes Commission (Seifovaia Komissiia), which began operations in late August 1920. In ministerial terms, the Safes Commission was subordinate to the Finance Commissariat, but its operations would be overseen by the Cheka, and the materials it collected (minus a commission of 300 rubles per safe for the safecracking teams) would be sent to the Gokhran. Although not as large as the Gokhran bureaucracy, the Safes Commission employed more than a hundred full-time employees, roughly fifty each for safecracking (po vskrytiiu seifov) and for the "depersonalization" of the safes (po ikh obezlicheniiu), which is to say, the removal and transport of their contents to Gokhran.[29] Missing no trivial detail, the Safes Commission instructed the depersonalization teams to make at least two car trips to Gokhran for each bundle of treasure they obtained, so as not to risk losing everything in a single holdup.[30]

Just as Krestinsky's sorters had little idea how to classify and appraise the materials they received at the Gokhran, the safecracking teams of the Seifovaia Komissiia were often struck dumb by the magnitude of their task. If we count simply by numbers, their progress was not insubstantial: the fifty-man operation cracked open 17,166 safes between 10 September 1920 and 1 January 1921, or about 1,000 per week, and did this in "unbelievably difficult and unhealthy conditions." Most of the banks in Moscow were now damp, unheated, and poorly lit, and the men worked with their bare hands. And yet, due partly to these trying conditions, progress was uneven: rapid at the Unified Bank (Soedinenny Bank) on Kuznetskii Most, which contained 2,229 safes, but virtually nonexistent at the Siberian Bank branches on Sukharevskii, where the vaults remained inaccessible because of flooding, or at Preobrazhenskaia Square, where 1,159 of the bank's 1,184 safes were located in impenetrable vaults. Asked to explain why they had not been able to access these vaults, the safecrackers complained that the metallic doors had rusted so badly they could not be opened. Only in May 1921, after the spring thaw, were they able to open these vault doors, by oxidizing the air enough to break through the rust (or perhaps simply to be able to breathe in the damp reaches of the inner bank corridors).[31]

What the depersonalization teams found inside opened safes seems to have varied greatly from bank to bank. At the former Moscow Private Bank of Commerce on Il'inka, the main item stowed away in the vaults was gold, platinum, and silver watches, of which more than 7,500 had been removed and sent to Gokhran by March 1921.[32] From most other Moscow banks, the safes seem to have yielded mostly diamonds, judging from the dramatic upswing in the

Gokhran abacus beginning after the Safes Commission went to work—nearly 8,000 carats of diamonds were processed in September 1920, the highest monthly total yet.[33] Intake was fairly steady all winter, before a new record was set in April 1921, when in just the first fifteen days the Gokhran took in 13,000 carats of diamonds, valued at over 50 million rubles ($25 million, or some $2.5 billion today).[34]

Some of the acceleration of diamond intake at the Gokhran in winter 1920–21 may have followed the sack of Bokhara by the Red Army in September. Sitting on the throne of a fabled city astride the old Silk Road trade routes and, more recently, at the heart of Great Game territory between the Russians and the British, the emir of Bokhara was rumored to dispose of fabulous wealth, the fruit of centuries' worth of trade and customs taxes, not to mention gifts and tribute offered by rulers seeking his favors. The bazaars of central Asia, from Khiva and Kokand to Bokhara and Tashkent, were inviting prey for Red Army officers, many of whom amassed impressive personal collections of carpets, jewelry, and antiques in the course of the campaigns there in 1920–21. The Bokharan operation of August–September 1920 was commanded by Mikhail Frunze of the Fourth Army, who may have had occasion to regret taking the command after being engulfed in acrimony surrounding the fate of the city's wealth after the emir fled to Afghanistan. Yakov Peters, Dzerzhinsky's powerful deputy in charge of Cheka counterintelligence, accused Frunze of secreting away "gold looted from Bokhara" and other priceless valuables belonging to the emir. Frunze, for his part, expressed indignation at Peters's foul "personal insult" (moral'ny udar).[35]

The "Bokharan loot" rapidly became a political football in Moscow, with Grigory Sokol'nikov, the former banks commissar, sent to Tashkent to investigate on behalf of Gokhran. Sokol'nikov unearthed plentiful evidence of corruption in the Bolsheviks' Turkestani commission there. Even before the conquest of Bokhara, the *Turkkomisii*'s executive jewelry collection was imposing, consisting of ornate cigarette cases, platinum bracelets, diamond brooches, gold and silver watches, gold and diamond rings, antique weapons and daggers, and Persian currency.[36] It would soon be reinforced by (some) of the loot stolen from the emir of Bokhara, which Sokol'nikov ordered transferred to Tashkent "for safekeeping" on 11 October 1920, prior to its delivery to the Gokhran.[37]

The Bokharan controversy was typical of the difficulties the Gokhran and Safes Commission were having in enforcing their writ in the provinces. The original founding decree of 3 February 1920 had been updated in April to make official the Gokhran's claim to all personally owned jewelry, coin, and precious metals in Russia (thus overturning the earlier exemption in case owners paid a punitive tax) and to delineate the subordination of regional soviet financial committees (Gubfinotdela) confiscating them to the Gokhran. Not all regions, however, played along. The financial committee of the Smolensk Soviet, for example, had opened 130 safes in 1920, but as of April 1922 had still not sent any of the valuables obtained to Moscow.[38] The Gubfinotdel in the Urals industrial center of Ekaterinburg, where both Volga-Kama and Russo-Asiatique had huge bank branches filled with safes, was similarly recalcitrant, turning over nothing to Moscow in either 1920 or 1921.[39] The story was much the same in the Penza Soviet, whose accountants were reprimanded in March 1922 for delinquency and ordered to expedite "as quickly as possible the packing and dispatch of safe valuables to [Moscow]."[40] Saratov was particularly notorious for the "disorder" prevailing in its Gubfinotdel's "storage of valuables and safes," along with what were deemed euphemistically "misunderstandings arising in their dispatch to [Moscow]" (voznikaiushchikh nedorazumeniiakh po vysylke ikh v Tsentr).[41] Novgorod's financial team, too, was asked to clean up the "chaotic condition" of its safe confiscation operation, which had as yet produced neither proper accounts nor turned over any valuables to Moscow.[42] Astrakhan's Gubfinotdel, at least, had produced thorough reports outlining the volumes of "gold and silver in coin and bullion," valuable precious stones, along with Romanov and Kerensky rubles, which had been acquired in raids on local bank safes. None of these treasures, however, had yet been forwarded on to Moscow.[43] Only Irkutsk, the Siberian city where Admiral Kolchak had been captured in February with the remainder of the old Kazan gold reserves ($210 million worth, or about 270 tons), proved reliable in sending boxes of loot regularly to the Moscow Gokhran, doing so at monthly intervals between July 1920 and November 1921.[44]

The relatively anodyne language of such reports conceals great drama in the Gokhran's struggle to streamline the looting of a continent. As ever, the logistical problems—recalcitrant local hoarders, trouble securing safe transport—inspired the creation of yet another Bolshevik bureaucracy. This was Fininspektsiia, the "Financial Inspectorate," which answered to Krestinsky's Commissariat of Finance but was actually run out of Stalin's Workers' and Peasants' Inspectorate (Rabkrin, or RKI). Rabkrin had been created in February 1920, alongside the Gokhran, specifically to root out corruption in the collection of loot. Eventually, its tentacles would ensnare nearly every corner of the Bolshevik government, famously allowing Stalin to spy on anyone he liked. Fininspektsiia was a typically open-ended Rabkrin operation, spinning off new divisions almost immediately, such as the one for train security (Raboche-Krest'ianskoi Inspektsii bankovskikh vagonov), which would guard each railcar carrying Gokhran loot into Moscow from the provinces. Fininspektsiia officers would also be responsible for applying official stamps and seals to the containers in which the Gokhran loot would be stored en route to Moscow and for numbering them.[45]

No matter how elaborate the supporting bureaucracies became, however, Krestinsky's Gokhran could not shake off a strong whiff of ad hoc amateurism. The imposing, officious tone of the decree laying out the rules of the road for Gokhran train convoys was belied by the description of the vessels in which looted jewelry, precious stones, and antiques would actually be stored en route: "trunks, suitcases, bags" (bauly, chemodany, sumki), and "hand luggage."[46] Lacking any sort of expertise in the transport of fragile and valuable cargo, the Bolsheviks simply used whatever random containers they could find. That they did this is amply confirmed by Max Laserson, who returned to Russia in 1923 to appraise the Gokhran treasures accumulated to date in Moscow. "I passed through the vast halls," he later recalled, "crammed on both sides up to the ceiling with all sorts of luggage-cases (trunks, baskets, boxes, satchels and so on). To all the parcels and packages labels bearing numbers were attached. The greater portion of all these parcels had not yet been opened or sorted, while a certain number had been superficially, so to say roughly, sorted, pending the so-called 'detailed' sorting."[47] By 1923, some 20,000 of these "parcels," stuffed full with "confiscated silver, gold, precious stones and pearls . . . in such enormous quantities as could hardly be conceived" had been piled up in the halls, of which over 17,000 had not yet had their seals broken. Meanwhile, 400 new parcels were arriving every week, accompanied by the Rabkrin Fininspektsiia train-security teams.[48]

The amateurism carried over to sorting and appraisal at the Gokhran, which was a mess from the start. Predictably, the temptations posed by such a vast quantity of treasure proved too strong for many of the sorters, who stole anything they could get their hands on. Employee pilfering was more or less a constant irritation at Gokhran, but from time to time it got to be so bad that the Bolsheviks ordered high-profile crackdowns. On 3 November 1921, for example, seven Gokhran workers "found guilty of stealing precious stones and other valuables" were sentenced to death by a revolutionary tribunal. The accused, it was reported in Moscow newspapers, "pleaded poverty and hunger," but Lenin personally insisted they be executed *pour encourager les autres*.[49] Apparently others were not so encouraged, as the very next month sixteen Gokhran guards "were shot for stealing 3,000 carats of diamonds."[50]

Aside from being easy to steal, Gokhran diamonds were difficult to sell abroad at a good price, in part due to scrutiny from Entente spies, but more fundamentally because the Bolsheviks simply did not know what they were doing. Prices offered by diamond dealers in Stockholm, Copenhagen, and London were better than those on the black market in Soviet Russia, but it was still a buyer's market. One particularly promising collection of diamonds, rubies, turquoises, and emeralds was appraised by Gokhran in early 1921 at a value of a million pounds sterling and shipped to Copenhagen. The Bolsheviks finally settled for one-third of the asking price.[51]

In the Bolsheviks' defense, we might note that the diamond business has always been a rigged buyer's market, at least since the discovery of the huge South African mines in 1870 led to the creation of the De Beers Cartel. Through shrewd marketing ("diamonds are forever"), De Beers gradually was able to convince most diamond owners never to sell their stones, ostensibly because of their emotional value as romantic symbols or family heirlooms, but actually to keep prices artificially high. The Bolsheviks were, in one sense, De Beers's worst nightmare, threatening to destroy the artificial price ceiling by dumping their diamonds in Reval, Stockholm, Copenhagen, and even London (where Krasin himself sold 40,000 pounds sterling worth of stones in 1920). But the Bolsheviks had also fallen into De Beers's trap, taking diamonds away from owners for whom they had emotional value—owners who had, in effect, already overpaid for them.[52] Stripped of any intrinsic or personal significance, many literally torn off from brooches and jewels on which they had been mounted, Gokhran diamonds would not fetch anywhere near their theoretical value by carat from shrewd dealers, who knew they had Bolshevik sellers over a barrel. Far from suspecting the real reason they were unable to get good prices for stolen diamonds, however, the Bolsheviks in fact expressly courted the De Beers consortium in the hope they could sell off the Gokhran hoard in bulk.[53]

Still, the Bolsheviks' poor performance in the European diamond market was part of a general pattern. The flooding of the Russian jewelry market in 1918 cut the legs out from under the loot-the-looters campaign, which had to be abandoned. The Gokhran had at least succeeded in streamlining collection of jewels and antiques and in keeping precious metals and stones off the market. But as soon as Bolshevik sellers tried to sell them abroad, the value of such metals would invariably plummet. Platinum, for example, sold for forty-two pounds sterling an ounce in Copenhagen in early 1920. After the Gokhran reserves began to be dumped there in quantity later that year, the price dropped to fifteen. Litvinov, mystified by the plunging prices, oddly blamed a collapse in world demand for platinum and advised Moscow to abandon hopes of financing strategic imports with Gokhran stocks of diamonds, jewels, and platinum. When it came to obtaining hard currency and import credits, Litvinov concluded sadly in a letter to Lenin, only one Russian commodity truly sufficed: gold.[54]

The problem was that little gold remained in Russia to be exploited. The imperial reserves, once the largest in the world, had been run down almost to zero by the end of 1921 (see chapters 7–8). The general economic breakdown had spread even to the high-priority gold mines of Siberia, where starving miners were now roaming the countryside, looking for food.[55] After three years of looting and safecracking, Russia's banks were dry of everything but now-worthless paper assets, like bonds, equities, and property deeds, most of which "were still lying in boxes and baskets waiting to be sifted" as late as 1923.[56] The great landed estates had been ripped apart from end to end, long since denuded of any saleable jewelry, antiques, or gold and silver wares.

There was one major precious metals repository left in all Russia which had been spared by Bolshevik looters and the mandate of the Gokhran: the Church. It had been spared, of course, not out of moral scruple but due to Lenin's fear of the wrath of pious peasants who might have objected to the wholesale robbery of Orthodox Churches and monasteries. By 1921, however, Russian peasant power was slipping at last. The colossal famine that began spreading across the Volga region that summer was an embarrassment for the Bolsheviks, who were forced to hire Herbert Hoover's "capitalist" American Relief Administration (ARA) to feed their starving subjects. But the famine was also an opportunity. Weakened, demoralized, their ranks decimated by starvation, Russia's beleaguered peasants would no longer offer much resistance to the regime. If the Bolsheviks were not to be bankrupted by their own precious metals famine, it was time to go on the offensive again.

4   The Church

It has become imperative for us to carry out the confiscation of church valuables in the most decisive and swift manner, so as to secure for ourselves a fund of several hundred million gold rubles (we must recall the gigantic wealth of some of the monasteries and abbeys).

— LENIN, "top secret" telephone message to the Politburo, 19 March 1922

EVER SINCE THE Emperor Constantine established the legal position of the church in the Roman Empire, churches, convents, abbeys, and monasteries have served as storehouses for the vast spiritual and material wealth of the Christian community. Whether nationalized or simply carted off en masse by ravenous armies, the rich silver, gold, and artistic wares of the church have often enticed looters in times of revolutionary upheaval, from the Vandal sack of Rome in the fifth century to the Crusader sack of Constantinople in the thirteenth, to the appropriation of the English monasteries in the 1530s by Henry VIII, to the nationalization of church lands by the French revolutionaries in 1790.

If there is anything surprising about the wholesale Bolshevik assault on church property, then, it is simply that it was delayed for so long. The nationalization of church assets was proclaimed, at least, as early as January 1918. But confiscating church property in practice proved to be difficult because of the enduring piety of Russia's peasant parishioners and even some urban workmen and soldiers (themselves recently removed from the peasantry), who objected to church nationalization on principle and physically defended many churches from Bolshevik attack. Because there were so many other rich institutions to rob and loot in 1918, it is easy to see why Lenin pulled back from the confiscations of church valuables late that year, which, at the time, had proved to be more trouble than they were worth.

Lenin's surrender to necessity on this front, however, was little more than a truce, a Brest-Litovsk with the Church, which enabled the Bolsheviks to bide their time prior to a renewed offensive. Confiscations of monastic property were never abandoned entirely, but they were not carried out with great rigor during the civil war. Most of the paper assets held by the Orthodox Church, including war bonds, property deeds and accompanying rents, corporate equities, and so forth, had been confiscated during the bank battles of 1918, but as we saw in chapter 1, this did not mean the Bolsheviks acquired more than a fraction of this wealth; most of it simply evaporated, benefiting no one. As for the 2.3 million acres of church land, the problem was the same as with the crown estates: once no one paid rents on them, or raised saleable crops, there was no income for Bolshevik nationalizers to collect.

For most of the civil war, the Bolshevik assault on the clergy remained on low boil, fought out in local skirmishes, a priest murdered here, a church or monastery defiled there. The Orthodox community did not escape the Red Terror, but the best estimates of clergical casualties between 1917 and 1921 come out at around 1,500 victims, out of some 140,000 clergymen: hardly negligible but not quite genocide either.[1]

The Church fought back, for the most part, with words. Patriarch Tikhon, elected Orthodox Patriarch by church elders shortly after the Bolshevik coup in October 1917 (the first since Peter the Great had abolished this office in the eighteenth century), did not wish to provoke greater repression by openly opposing the new regime. Still, Tikhon signed a circular on 1 February 1918, shortly after the Bolshevik assault on the Alexander Nevsky Monastery in Petrograd, calling down anathema on "the monsters of the human race . . . who have begun to persecute the [Orthodox Church] and are striving to destroy Christ's cause by sowing everywhere, in place of Christian love, the seeds of malice, hatred, and fratricidal strife." In October of that year, the patriarch went further still, admonishing Lenin to "celebrate the anniversary of taking power by releasing the imprisoned, by ceasing bloodshed, violence, ruin, constraints on the faith." If they did not do so, Tikhon warned the Bolsheviks, "all the righteous blood you shed will cry out against you (Luke 11:51) and with the sword will perish you who have taken up the sword (Matthew 26:52)."[2] In response, the Soviet government charged Tikhon with complicity in the plot to kill Lenin in August 1918 and accused him of collaborating with Entente spy rings in Moscow. Not wishing to create a martyr around which pious Russians could rally against the regime, however, the Bolsheviks did not carry through with the prosecution, although they did place Tikhon under house arrest.[3]

As the survival of Patriarch Tikhon suggests, the war against the Church remained something of a strategic stalemate, with the Bolsheviks possessing a monopoly of armed force but the Orthodox clergy a stronger hold on public opinion. Both parties were still at the mercy of the peasant masses, few of whom had much sympathy for the drumbeat of atheistic propaganda emanating from Moscow. While many peasants were happy to take over church lands for themselves, they were less pleased with Bolshevik seizures of sacred Orthodox objects—crosses, icons, and embellished Bibles. The exception in the Gokhran mandate granted for such "objects of worship" reflected Lenin's grudging acceptance that certain boundaries could not be crossed without turning the whole nation against the Bolsheviks. As late as April 1921, Lenin warned his Politburo colleagues that they must give "absolutely no offense to religion."[4]

In light of what we know of the renewed assault on the Church that began in early 1922, such a statement seems astonishing. But like every one of Lenin's political utterances, the timid warning he had issued the previous April reflected a cold grasp of power relationships. Spring 1921 was a trying time for the Bolsheviks, who were barely able to weather the famous Kronstadt rebellion of February–March, let alone hundreds of concurrent peasant uprisings stretching from White Russia to the Urals. April, in particular, was a brutal month, when the crisis posed by Alexander Antonov's partisan army in Tambov province reached crisis stage. The repression of this single peasant *bunt* alone required the organization of a special army organized "for the Internal Defense of the Republic," which numbered more than 100,000 regulars, backed by armed Cheka execution squads. It was not until summer 1921 that the peasant wars began to simmer down—not because the Bolsheviks had won them decisively but rather due to the onset of a nationwide famine which rendered most peasants unable to fight.[5]

The Volga famine of 1921 was both crisis and opportunity for the Bolshevik regime. It was a grotesque political embarrassment, to be sure: otherwise the Soviet government would not have denied for months that it was happening, before admitting publicly, in late June, that 25 million Russians were on the brink of starvation. It was a serious blow to Communist pride that the only organization capable of feeding the hungry masses was Hoover's ARA.[6] Still, in strategic terms, the famine provided a desperately needed respite for the regime, which had been at war with a world of enemies ever since 1917. The Anglo-Soviet accord, signed in March 1921, had opened the floodgates for strategic military imports, which were now pouring into Russia in vast quantities even as the Bolsheviks' last remaining enemy—Russia's peasant masses—were being weakened by hunger and starvation. The problem was that these imports were expensive, eating up the imperial gold reserves at a furious rate. Because the Bolsheviks, presiding over a ruined economy producing nothing worthy of export, could securitize imports only by exporting bullion, by the end of 1921 dozens of long-term military import deals would have to be put on hold by suppliers due to the regime's declining reserves (see chapters 7–8). If the famine were broken—as it would be by summer 1922, thanks largely to Hoover and the ARA— the peasant wars might resume with a vengeance. If they did not want to lose the next round, the Bolsheviks would have to be ready.

The confluence of temporary peasant weakness and desperate financial straits produced a perfect political storm in winter 1921–22, which finally overrode Lenin's last hesitations about wholesale robberies of church valuables. All that was needed was a political pretext for resuming the assault. The famine was an obvious possibility, although with the Russian Orthodox Church itself contributing generously to relief efforts, it was unclear on what pretext the expropriation of church valuables could be justified. In a series of resolutions passed in November and December 1921, the Politburo gave Trotsky a new high-priority commission to oversee the "sale of Gokhran treasures" abroad, ostensibly for the purpose of famine relief.[7]

With Lenin himself ill for much of the winter, Trotsky began articulating a political line to justify the coming assault. At first, he dropped hints that Orthodox clergymen and parishioners were not "doing enough" for relief. In an article widely circulated in the Soviet press in January 1922, the Bolsheviks suggested that Russian "religious societies" could use their "gold and silver valuables" to buy "several million *puds* of grain and could save several million of the hungry from starvation." Soon similar suggestions were being made by "the people," in the form of thousands of (highly suspicious) "citizen letters" sent nearly simultaneously to Soviet newspapers like *Izvestiia* and *Pravda,* supporting confiscations of church valuables. Many of these were dispatched from the pens of "progressive" clergymen of middle rank—those regime collaborators in the clergy who would become known as "renovationists"—who hinted darkly that Patriarch Tikhon was threatening generous famine donors inside the Church with excommunication. The public slogan of Trotsky's agitprop campaign, "Turn Gold into Bread!" was an ingenious concoction, combining the invitation for popular mobs to rob churches with the motivating insinuation that reactionary ("Black Hundred") clergymen were responsible for sabotaging relief efforts.[8]

It was a lie from start to finish. To begin with, revenue raised by Bolshevik sales of gold and other precious metals abroad in 1921 (some $200 million, or the equivalent of $20 billion today) had been devoted not to famine relief, but to pay for strategic imports, especially high-end military aircraft, and even—perhaps more significantly, in the context of a nationwide famine—luxury food items, including tens of thousands of tons of Swedish herring, Finnish salted fish, German bacon, and French pig fat.[9] Concern about starving peasants played little role in the decision taken by the Politburo in October 1921, for example, to ship a special 12 million gold ruble fund to London to pay for weapons, boots, and Red Army uniforms.[10] Nor were humanitarian considerations for famine victims evident when Krasin spent 16,400 gold rubles in London that January on spare parts for the fleet of Rolls-Royces driven by Lenin, Trotsky, and other Bolshevik bigwigs.[11] Certainly few in the Politburo batted an eye later that winter when millions of marks were dispatched to finance Communist propaganda in central Europe, along with 10 million gold rubles for emergency purchases of refined gasoline for the Red Army.[12]

As for the suggestion of recalcitrance on the part of the Church hierarchy, which became more and more insistent as the "Turn Gold into Bread" campaign heated up in winter 1922, this was a grotesque slander. Patriarch Tikhon had been active for months in famine relief, organizing a church committee for the purpose as early as June 1921. The patriarch issued a passionate appeal for help to his flock, admonishing them to "take the suffering into your arms with all haste . . . with hearts full of love and the desire to save your starving brothers." No less than 200,000 copies of this appeal were printed at church expense for nationwide distribution. The patriarch's famine relief committee began work with great fanfare on 1 August 1921 in the Church of Christ the Savior on the banks of the Moscow River. The problem with the patriarch's approach to famine relief, from the Soviet perspective, was hardly that he was not doing enough, but quite the opposite: his energetic efforts put the Bolsheviks' own paltry response to shame. Patriarch Tikhon even wrote the Soviet authorities on 22 August 1921, asking permission for the Orthodox Church to buy food supplies directly and organize relief kitchens in famine areas. Apparently this was a step too far: the patriarch's request was denied. In September 1921, the Bolsheviks dissolved the church committee for famine relief, arrested its leaders without trial, and exiled them to Russia's far north.[13]

Still, Patriarch Tikhon did not give in entirely. Although the persecution of his relief committee dampened the enthusiasm which had greeted his first appeal, church collections for famine victims continued, with some 9 million rubles donated by parishioners in the second half of 1921. The Church was not allowed, however, to distribute this money or purchase food itself, being forced instead to turn over every kopek it raised to the Soviet government's own famine relief committee, Pomgol.* When the All-Russian Central Executive Committee (VTsIK) ordered the expropriation of Orthodox Church valuables on 23 February 1922, the patriarch did declare this Bol-

---

*Pomgol was a contraction of the Russian for "hunger relief," *pomoshchi golodaiushchim.* Ostensibly a private agency independent of the Bolsheviks, headed by nonparty luminaries like Gorky, Pomgol was in fact legally subordinate to the All-Russian Central Executive Committee (VTsIK).

shevik decree a "sacrilege" (Sviatotatstva) and threatened to excommunicate anyone who removed "sacred vessels" from the Orthodox Church, "even if for voluntary donation." But in the same statement, issued on 28 February, Tikhon reaffirmed his earlier suggestions that parishioners donate saleable church valuables to help feed the hungry, as long as these objects "had not been consecrated for use in religious ceremonies" (neosviashchennykh, ne imeiushchikh bogosluzhebnogo upotrebleniia). A week later, the Orthodox metropolitan of Petrograd, Veniamin, spelled out in greater detail the Orthodox position on the use of church valuables for the benefit of the hungry: they could be surrendered to the government only if the Bolsheviks could provide assurance that all government resources were truly exhausted, that the "proceeds would truly benefit the hungry," and that Orthodox clergymen would be allowed to "bless the sacrifice." For thus calling the Bolsheviks' bluff about the real purpose of the church confiscations, Veniamin and Tikhon were both arrested and labeled "enemies of the people."[14] It would soon become clear to disinterested observers just how little the Church confiscation campaign had to do with famine relief.

To understand what this systematic assault on the last pillar of Russia's traditional civilization was really about, it is necessary to look closely at the timing. February 1922, when the renewed Bolshevik attack on the Church began, was certainly a dire time for the Volga peasants enduring both hunger and bitter winter cold. It was not, however, a time of particular importance as regards the financial requirements of famine relief. In fact, according to Herbert Hoover himself, the Soviet government requested, at precisely this time, that the ARA slow down shipments of food aid coming into Russian ports, "owing to their inability to handle such large quantities." By summer 1922, the ARA, helped along by a number of other American and European charities, had largely broken the famine and provided enough seed to ensure Russia a fall harvest expected to be "three to four times" as large as the previous year's.[15]

If it was of no particular significance in terms of the finances of famine relief, however, February 1922 just happened to be the very month in which the imperial Russian gold reserves the Bolsheviks had inherited in 1918 finally ran out. The last major shipment of Russian imperial gold (40 metric tons worth) left the port of Reval on 6 February 1922, aboard the Estonian steamer *Gladiator*. The very next day, Trotsky, just then putting the finishing touches on the agitprop line for the Bolshevik campaign against the Church, temporarily revoked authorization for Soviet purchasing agents abroad. In terms of gold bullion—which they needed not for famine relief, but to pay for military and luxury imports—the Bolsheviks were broke.[16]

If we understand this, then the ferocity of the church robberies of spring 1922 begins to make sense. So too does it become apparent why an operation ostensibly devoted to relieving the hungry was entrusted primarily to the Cheka, now renamed the State Political Directorate or GPU, and directed by Trotsky, the commissar of war.[17] With Trotsky in overall command, the offensive against the Church was meticulously planned at a series of closed sessions held in December and January 1921–22 of the Sovnarkom, the Politburo, and the Central Committee of the Russian Communist Party. Although the famous church confiscation decree was not made public until late February, the policy was in fact hashed out much earlier, with a secret VTsIK policy resolution "on the liquidation of church property" (o likvidatsii tserkovnogo imushchestva) passed on 2 January 1922. We can thus dispense with the claim that the campaign was launched in retaliation to the patriarch's resistance to aiding the hungry, as his protest against the Church expropriation decree was not lodged until two months later. We may also put to rest any lingering claims that the confiscations were devoted to famine relief, as the 2 January VTsIK resolution explicitly stated that saleable valuables obtained from the Church would go not to famine victims but to the Gokhran. Two subsequent decrees, passed on 14 and 23 January 1922, expressly mandated that each regional Gubfinotdel dispatch church valuables to the Gokhran "without delay." All trains on which church plunder was transported would be accompanied by Red Army officers, who were required to inform the Gokhran by telegram before their trains left each provincial station of "the number of the train, the number of the wagon, and the time of departure." All communications, before and after the arrival of church loot trains in Moscow, were to be conducted only with senior Gokhran officials.[18]

Propaganda was central to Trotsky's conception of the confiscations: they must appear to have come from a groundswell of popular outrage against the Church (thus the letter-writing campaign). Trotsky's plan was also premised on widespread popular resistance to GPU church-looting teams, which could then be blamed on "inhuman and greedy" clergymen who would be hauled in for sensational show trials. The expected defense of many churches and monasteries by crowds of faithful parishioners would also, of course, serve as justification for bringing in the Red Army to crush the resistance.

Russia's parishioners did not disappoint Trotsky's expectations. By mid-April 1922, no less than 1,414 "bloody excesses" had already been reported in confrontations between the GPU and church defenders, according to *Izvestiia*.[19] Resistance was particularly fierce in the countryside, but there were also major incidents of violence in Rostov-on-the-Don, Smolensk, Novgorod, and even Moscow and Petrograd. The most notorious clash in the early days of the campaign occurred at Shuia, a textile factory town northeast of Moscow. There, as if to intentionally enrage the faithful, the GPU looting team raided the church on a Sunday, the twelfth of March. The crowd of worshippers was strong enough to repel them, which may have been the idea. On Wednesday, the GPU returned "in the company of troops equipped with machine guns" and opened fire on the parishioners defending the church. Although the figures were later disputed, it appears at least four or five were killed and another eleven injured.[20]

The Shuia incident was important not so much for the casualty count, which was relatively insignificant in the course of the Bolshevik war on the Church in 1922, as for the reaction it occasioned in Moscow. The Politburo convened a series of crisis meetings following the clash at Shuia. Trotsky, in particular, was incensed by the scale of the resistance. He would now lay down a tougher line on church confiscation protocol, which included the issuance of threats to leading clergymen that they would be held personally responsible for resistance to confiscations in their churches.[21]

The news from Shuia seems also to have awakened Lenin from his winter slumber, at least long enough for him to dictate instructions for stepping up the assault on the Church to the Politburo on 19 March 1922, over the phone from his current country retreat at Korzinkino. Although Lenin expressly insisted that no copies be made of this top secret dictation, the original was well preserved in the party archives in Moscow. Published in full for the first time in 1990, Lenin's stunning instruction has acquired great notoriety since the collapse of Communism, and for good reason. In it Lenin reveals, in his inimitably vituperative style, the true political and financial motivation for the Bolshevik assault on the Church in 1922, and the reason it was launched during a crushing famine (despite all the agitprop, it had absolutely nothing to do with famine relief). It is a statement of such breathtaking cynicism, such utter callousness and cruelty, that it deserves to be quoted at length:

> Concerning the events at Shuia . . . I believe that the enemy here commits a major strategic blunder, trying to engage us in a decisive struggle when it is for him especially hopeless and unfavorable. For us, on the contrary, the present moment . . . offers us a 99 percent chance of overwhelming success in shattering the enemy and assuring our position for decades. It is now and only now, when in the famine regions there is cannibalism [ediat liudei], and the roads are littered with hundreds if not thousands of corpses, that we can (and therefore must) carry through the confiscation of church valuables with the most rabid and merciless energy, stopping at nothing in suppressing all resistance. . . .
>
> It has become imperative for us to carry out the confiscation of church valuables in the most decisive and swift manner, so as to secure for ourselves a fund of several hundred million gold rubles (we must recall the gigantic wealth of some of the monasteries and abbeys). Without such capital no government work is possible, no economic reconstruction, and especially no defense of our position at [the upcoming inter-Allied debt settlement conference in] Genoa. We absolutely must take into our hands this capital of several hundred million (or perhaps several billion) rubles . . . no other moment except that of desperate hunger [krome otchaiannogo goloda] will give us such a mood among the broad peasant masses such as will assure us [their] neutrality, that victory in the battle to remove the [church] valuables will remain unconditionally and completely on our side.[22]

Lenin's reaction was wholly in character, combining both his life-long detestation of the Russian peasantry (note there is no mention of famine relief!) with a cold calculation of the possible gains from destroying them. But in political terms, Shuia fit Trotsky's plan perfectly. Each successively bloody clash lent credence to his claim that the Church was impeding famine relief. As *Izvestiia* intoned darkly on 28 March 1922, "What should the workers and peasants do, if they do not wish the deaths of millions of dying peasants? Give a re-buff to this band of rabid 'dignified' priests. Burn out the 'most holy counterrevolution' with a hot iron. Take the gold out of the churches. Exchange the gold for bread."[23]

And so the hot iron of repression descended on Russia's belea-guered Orthodox community. On 13 April 1922, some thirty-two clergymen were arrested in Moscow for, in effect, failing to cooper-ate in sacking their churches. By the time the anticlerical show trial opened on 26 April in the theater of the Moscow Polytechnic Mu-seum, another twenty-two defendants had been hauled in. Trotsky himself took charge of the press campaign, smearing them as "black hundreds" and "counterrevolutionaries." Eleven were sentenced to death, the first of hundreds to follow, as the show trials moved on to Petrograd (86 defendants, 4 executed), Shuia (3 death sentences), and many other cities. Lenin, according to a document unearthed by Dmitri Volkogonov, demanded to be informed "on a daily basis" how many priests had been shot. He was not likely disappointed, al-though at least 2 bishops, in Perm and Tobolsk, were drowned to death instead of being shot, perhaps to save the expense on bullets. Estimates vary as to the total number of victims of the church terror of 1922, but we can confirm that at least 28 bishops and 1,215 priests were killed, according to the regime's own estimates. Another 20,000 or so parishioners perished, many of them elderly Old Be-lievers who defended their beloved churches with pitchforks and were mowed down with machine guns.[24]

If the assault on the Church did not produce the worst violence of the revolution, it was the most shocking in spiritual terms. The Bol-sheviks scaled new heights in sacrilege all spring, with perhaps their most audacious crime yet committed in late May 1922, when a spe-cial looting team, working on behalf of the old Gorky-Andreeva an-tiques registration commission, invaded the Petropavlovsk Cathe-dral in Petrograd. According to a rumor that spread quickly through the city, the cathedral had been targeted by the Bolsheviks expressly with the intention of raiding the tsars' tombs. At first, the looting team proceeded calmly, removing the silver coffin of one tsarina con-sidered to be saleable (and placing her body in another, less valuable receptacle) and noting that "the body of Alexander I was not in his coffin." Next, "a pearl necklace was removed from the body of

Catherine the Great." When the grave robbers reached the tomb of Peter the Great, however, even these ruthless Bolsheviks, we are led to believe, were taken aback by the magnitude of the crime they were committing: "The body of the Emperor, very carefully embalmed, is practically intact. The appearance of the Tsar who has been lying in a coffin for 200 years and who looked as if he had just been placed there gave a violent shock to the workmen, who insisted that the coffin should be closed immediately, and would not allow anything to be taken off his body."[25]

Another legend of the time concerns the Troitsky-Sergievskaia Monastery, located in what is now the town of Zagorsk, some seventy kilometers north of Moscow, which Lenin had specially ordered to be converted into a "museum of atheism."[26] When the Bolsheviks seized this monastery, the story begins, they put in a team of Red Army soldiers as guards for the night. When an apparently pious Orthodox "intruder" rang the church bells overhead, one Bolshevik immediately ran up to the belfry threatening to kill the "scoundrel." A few minutes later, however, the unfortunate Bolshevik "came down headfirst and dead." Three more guards mounted the belfry mouthing vile threats, and each was cut down. At last one of the Bolshevik soldiers, it was said,

> [promised] that he would go up without any arms or threats. Crossing himself he climbed up. When he came to where the bells were, he saw an old man with a white beard who asked him why he came and whether he too had murder in his heart. The soldier said he did not. Then the old man took him by the hand and led him to where he could look out and there he saw conflagration of cities and villages, from this scene he was led to another where war was going on, where one Russian massacred his brother, the third scene showed parched fields, hunger, pestilence, and the fourth scene human beings reverting to savagery and idolatry. After showing him all this the old man told the soldier that what he saw was the fate of Russia under the Bolsheviki and asked him to go and tell them to desist.[27]

Hopeful parables aside, the Bolsheviks did not, of course, desist from their war on the Church. The material temptation was simply too great. In Moscow alone there were 764 Orthodox churches and another 74 chapels, each and every one of them housing, in the words of Natalya Krivova, "one of a kind works of art, the priceless treasures of a thousand years of Russian history": illuminated bibles and rare church manuscripts mounted on silver bindings, icons embroidered lovingly with pearls, gold vessels, chalices encrusted with precious gems. Targeting these assets were Bolshevik looting commissions for each of the seven main districts in Moscow housing significant church property, each staffed by around twenty-five men, of whom usually about ten were heavily armed enforcers from the security organs (either GPU or the Red Army). By 5 April 1922, these "commissions" had stolen 367 poods (about 6.5 tons) of treasures from 43 Orthodox cathedrals and monasteries. In an extraordinary acceleration, in just three days, from 5 to 8 April, no less than 106 different Moscow churches were raided, yielding some 700 poods of valuables (nearly 13 tons). After pausing to catch their breaths, the Bolshevik looting squads pulled off an even more stupendous feat between 24 and 26 April, attacking over 130 churches and 3 chapels and carting off another 13 tons of silver, and about 50 pounds of gold, plus untold quantities of sacred church vessels.

The acceleration of the Moscow looting campaign after 5 April 1922 was touched off by an explosive incident that day at the Church of the Epiphany in the Khamovnicheskii district, which likely inspired the parable of the Troitsky-Sergievskaia monastery recited above. This legendary cathedral, constructed in 1625, was second only to the Church of Christ the Savior in the Russian hierarchy, frequently hosting Orthodox religious councils (sobory). When a detachment of Red Army soldiers raided the church, a crowd of nearly 3,000 angry parishioners assembled to beat them off. Suddenly the church bells sounded plaintively, as if in protest against the unholy intrusion. It emerged that a small boy was the culprit, having squirmed his way past the guards. When the soldiers tried to shoo him away from the belfry, the boy slipped and crash to the ground, badly injured. In real life under the Bolsheviks, unlike in parables, there were no happy endings. Undeterred by the omen, the looting team carried off more than 14 poods (in all about 500 pounds) of priceless Orthodox treasures. The Church of the Epiphany, after being stripped of its most sacred relics, would be dynamited on Stalin's orders in 1931.[28]

Crowning the April campaign was the looting of the very Church of Christ the Savior on the Moscow river embankment where Patriarch Tikhon had read out his appeal to aid Russia's famine victims the previous summer. Constructed to commemorate the victory over Napoleon and finally consecrated in 1883, this stunning cathedral was far too richly endowed to escape the attention of the Bolshevik church-looting battalions: it contained "five gold domes, the highest of which was as high as a seventeen-story building." Fourteen enormous silver church bells had been carefully lifted into four cavernous belfries, which bells together weighed some 65 tons. The cathedral walls were adorned with 177 marble panels, each depicting "heroic battles with the French" and commissioned from Russia's leading nineteenth-century artists. Still, the very size and immense weight of the endowments of the Church of Christ the Savior made their removal a logistical nightmare. In April 1922, only 34 poods, or about 1,000 pounds, of church vessels were carted off, mostly silverwares.[29] Not until 1931 were the church's towering gold domes and the massive church bells finally torn down wholesale by an enormous team of "secret police operatives and young Komsomol workers." Like the Church of the Epiphany, the Church of Christ the Savior was blown to smithereens that year by Bolshevik demolition experts: Stalin wanted to build a towering statue of Lenin in its place. Groundwater soon seeped through the foundation of Stalin's would-be statue, however, leaving only "an enormous, stagnant pool" of dank, muddy water where once had stood Russia's most beautiful Orthodox Church.[30]

Although the Russian Orthodox community suffered most, the Bolsheviks were ecumenical in selecting targets in the church-rich environment of Moscow. In April 1922, for example, churches targeted by looting squads included several Armenian and Greek Orthodox facilities, one Protestant-Evangelical church, and Jewish synagogues. The most lucrative acquisition was Armenia's national church treasure, which—like the Romanian patrimony—had ironically been brought to Moscow for safekeeping back in 1915 from Etchmiadzin, near Batumi.[31]

The Anglican Church of Moscow had been singled out in summer 1920, a calmer period in Bolshevik-church relations, which had allowed a team of unhurried Gokhran appraisers enough time to produce the kind of detailed inventory lacking in the superheated 1922 looting campaign. They catalogued items in numbing detail, including: "37 antique watches of faded metals. 2 men's gold watches. 3 women's gold watches. 2 silver medals. 1 bronze medal. A crystal vase embellished with garnit. One porcelain figurine. . . . Theater monocles. 3 cigarette holders. 15 gold bracelets. . . . 7 gold chains. . . . 42 charms, brooches, and medallions [brelokov, medal'onov broshek]. 112 fine metal objects and other flashy trinkets in a box [v korobke neustan. metalla melk. predmetov roskoshi]. 182 trinkets in a box."

The Gokhran inventory of the Anglican church of Moscow continues in this vein for four more pages, moving on from tsarist government and war bonds (millions of rubles worth, in about twelve different denominations) to furniture, armoires, clothing, mirrors, and table lamps, before concluding with kitchen silver (231 dinner knives, 315 dinner forks, 98 dinner spoons, 179 tea spoons, 62 dessert forks and knives, 14 ashtrays, 32 candleholders, and, not to be forgotten, 12 silver sugar holders and 10 pepper shakers).[32]

Petrograd did not have as many churches as Moscow, and those it did have were of course much newer, with fewer ancient church vessels and icons. But what they lacked in liturgical history, they made up in material wealth, especially in diamonds, which were scarcer in the older Moscow cathedrals, built in a poorer time. By 29 April 1922, Petrograd looting committees had collected 30 tons of silver from local churches, 4 poods (about 145 pounds) of gold, 3,690 diamonds, and another 367 precious stones. Most of the gold and silver was forwarded to the Moscow Gokhran, but about two-thirds of the diamonds (2,672) remained in the vaults of the Petrograd Gubfinotdel, in part to lessen the risks of losses to sabotage or theft en route.[33]

In the provinces, Orthodox churches and monasteries were not quite as well endowed as those in Russia's capital cities, but there were so many of them that mere volume sufficed to produce a cornucopia of riches. The Kaluzhskaia and Viatskaia Gubernii alone yielded more than 1,000 poods of church loot (about 20 tons). Nizhny Novgorod yielded 51 poods of silver (nearly a ton), although only 3 pounds of gold. The story was similar in Astrakhan, Kazan, Cheliabinsk, the Penza region, and the Ukraine. Still, by mid-May 1922, church treasures confiscated by the Bolsheviks included not only gold (about 14 poods) and silver (9,236 poods), but also "12,124 diamonds and brilliants (weighing 1,145 carats), one pood, twenty-two pounds of pearls, and 26,708 precious stones of various kinds (weighing one pood, fourteen pounds)."[34]

The pace of Bolshevik church confiscations remained brisk through the summer and fall of 1922, although, as in the earlier looting campaigns, not everything collected by regional looting committees made its way to the Moscow Gokhran. In part this was by design: the Politburo expressly ordered that provincial Gubfinotdel committees be allowed to keep some of the church treasures to keep party bosses happy: many used confiscated ecclesiastical furniture, paintings, and silverware to furnish their apartments.[35] Silver, despite its bulk, was actually the material regional soviets most easily parted with, perhaps because it offered the least temptation for pilfering and did local Bolshevik Party bosses little good. All but about 5,000 of the 24,000 poods (about 450 tons) of silver collected by November 1922 had been shipped on to the Moscow Gokhran. By early 1923, so much church silver—about 30,000 poods, or 550 tons— had accumulated at Gokhran that a nearby building on Borovaia ulitsa had to be emptied to house it. By contrast, only about half of the 33 poods of gold (about 1,250 pounds) confiscated from provincial churches was forwarded to Moscow, barely one-seventh of the 35,000 diamonds, and only a tenth of the 14 poods of pearls. Another 52 poods, or nearly 1 ton, of various jewels were hoarded by provincial Bolshevik finance committees, along with 72,000 precious stones other than diamonds.[36]

Orthodox icons, too, were confiscated in enormous quantities during the looting campaign of 1922, although no accurate count seems to have been kept. Thousands of these unique Russian artistic treasures spilled out onto street bazaars, where many were snapped up by foreigners at bargain prices. Olof Aschberg bought no less than 277 unique icons personally, dating from the fifteenth to the nineteenth centuries. In his inimitable tone of cheerful incuriosity, Aschberg fondly recalled his experiences browsing through a Moscow market on Smolenskaia with his Swedish friends in 1923 and 1924: "One thing that amused us was to go to what was the Russian equivalent of the Caledonian market, where everything imaginable could be bought. . . . It was there that I bought my first icons. They came partly from private families and partly from churches and convents, from which presumably they had been stolen during the Revolution. . . . When the icons reached Stockholm I hung them in my villa." Some 250 items from Aschberg's collection of looted Russian icons were later donated to the Rijksmuseum in Stockholm.[37]

In Aschberg's defense, it must be said that he did a much better job preserving Russia's religious and artistic patrimony than the Bolsheviks did. Most of the icons and other church loot sent in to the Gokhran in 1922 were systematically dismantled for scrap. Icons embroidered with pearls, for example, were collected in several rooms where "women tore out these pearls one by one, washed them and sorted them out on strings according to size." Other icons had been "doubled up or even bent fourfold" long before their embroideries were picked apart, simply to fit the boxes they were stored in. In this manner, Max Laserson reported after being hired by Gokhran in 1923, "hundreds of icons were hopelessly and irretrievably destroyed," "many dating from the eighteenth century, and a number of them even from the seventeenth." The story was much the same with antiquarian manuscripts and religious service books, which were being ripped from their bindings to procure silver. So, too, would "vestments and chasubles, crosier and mitre, crosses and cups" be melted down for silver, which was then sold by volume.[38]

How much revenue did the Bolsheviks secure from the church robberies in 1922? A report published in September boasted that the Soviet government had already sold 6.6 billion (soviet) rubles worth of church loot. But as the British commercial attaché in Moscow noted, on the black market this was equivalent to only about 350,000 pounds sterling, or $1.75 million.[39] The best estimates of the amount of silver and gold obtained from the Church as of April 1923 come out at around 26 poods of gold (about half a ton) and about 30,000 poods of silver (some 550 tons). At even the most favorable prices, this hoard could not have netted the Bolsheviks more than about $10 million, barely enough to pay for a month's worth of strategic imports. The income side of the Gokhran abacus actually *declined* in 1922 from the furious pace of 1920–21, with only 40 million gold rubles ($20 million) worth of valuables sorted and appraised from January to October.[40]

Never was the process of wealth destruction under Bolshevism more apparent than in the destruction of icons and service books for scrap metal. When Laserson asked his party minder why sacred objects were being defaced, the Bolshevik coldly replied, "This is being done with a view to destroying Church property."[41] And so a campaign launched in order to secure, in Lenin's words, a "fund of several hundred million gold rubles" ended up yielding forty or fifty times less. The Orthodox Church, it turned out, was not wealthy because it exploited "the people," but rather because it inspired them to work hard, donate their earnings, and create beautiful objects. Now that these objects had been stolen from their owners and physically pried apart, they had almost no value at all.

Almost forgotten in the hot blaze of publicity surrounding the church campaign of 1922 was the Bolsheviks' attempt to appraise and sell off the Romanov crown jewels, which they finally found hidden away in the Kremlin Armory, after a frantic search, in March. But even this famous collection of priceless jewels and stones was valuable only if it could be sold for hard currency. The appraisal of the "Romanov treasure" solicited by Grigory Sokol'nikov in early 1922 came out at 900 million gold rubles ($450 million), which colossal sum would have exceeded even Lenin's wildest expectations for the church robberies. But this presumed, of course, a buyer willing to risk international opprobrium for purchasing the world's most famous stolen treasure. Without finding such a buyer, the crown jewels were just as worthless as expoliated church property.[42]

At every point in the progressive looting of Russia's national patrimony from 1917 to 1922, the Bolsheviks ran up against the same problem. The nationalization of the banks in 1917 had choked off capital flows and rendered bonds and equities worthless. The "looting of the looters" in 1918 had flooded the market with jewelry and family heirlooms, once priceless to their owners and now scarcely worth a bag of flour. Although the Gokhran drive of 1920–21 had helped shut down the thriving black market in precious stones, the dumping of its hoard of platinum and diamonds abroad would eventually drive down their value as well. In the church campaign, sacred items of inestimable value were turned into heaping piles of low-quality silver. In every one of these expropriations, the Bolsheviks had killed the goose which laid the golden eggs.

Still, not all the news was bad for the Bolsheviks. No matter how much they had impoverished Russia as a whole by tearing down its patrimony root and branch, the sale of this patrimony abroad brought their regime significant, if not overwhelming, revenue. The sacking of the bank safes in 1918 had not yielded the 4 billion tsarist rubles Sokol'nikov had hoped for, but it brought in more than 500 million ($250 million) just the same. The 380 hundred metric tons of gold bullion removed by the Bolsheviks from bank vaults later that year (and another 285 metric tons taken off Kolchak in 1920) might, ideally, yield another $400 or $500 million. Gokhran treasures collected in 1920–21, according to rough estimates, might have netted another $400 to $500 million (800 to 900 million gold rubles), if dealers could be found willing to systematize sales abroad without flooding the market or to accept them in lieu of bullion for bank credits. Although the church campaign proved disappointing, netting barely $10 million at best, the Romanov crown jewels discovered in the Kremlin in 1922 might—just conceivably—net another $450 or $500 million or be used as collateral for loans close to that amount.[43] All told, then, the Russian national patrimony offered the Bolsheviks potential foreign trade reserves, in bullion, cash, and Gokhran collateral, equivalent to about $1.6 billion, or some $160 billion in today's terms. This would have been more than enough to jump-start the world revolution Lenin and Trotsky dreamed of, if the loot had been used for this purpose. So unpopular were they with the people they claimed to rule, however, the Bolsheviks needed to dump most of Russia's patrimony abroad in great haste simply to pay for the weapons they needed to stay in power. It is to this story that we now turn.

1. Albert Engström's portrait of Olof Aschberg from their trip to Moscow, November 1923. Swedish National Portrait Gallery, Gripsholms Castle, inv. nr 3198.

2. Leonid Krasin at work in London, circa 1920–21. From Lubov Krassin, *Leonid Krasin: His Life and Work* (London: Skeffington and Son, 1929).

3. Members of the Soviet Railway Mission in Berlin, March 1921. Professor Georgi Lomonosov, who led the mission, is the bearded gentleman in the center, front row. Photo courtesy M. J. Larsons, envelope A, Hoover Institution Archives, Stanford University.

4. The Commission for Classification of Antique Silver at the Gokhran, June 1923. From left to right, seated, are Gokhran director Gromadsky; Dr. Ernst Cohn-Wiener, a German expert on antique silver; Serge Troinitsky, director of the Hermitage Museum in Petrograd; Max Laserson (in the center, wearing glasses); D. D. Ivanov, director of the Armory Museum; Vishnevsky, an expert on antique Russian silver; and Dubrovitsky, a member of the Commission for the Realization (i.e., sale) of State Valuables. Standing are three Gokhran classification officials. Photo courtesy M. J. Larsons, envelope A, Hoover Institution Archives, Stanford University.

5. The Gokhran. Seated, from left to right: Serge Troinitsky (holding a rare Scythian antique silver platter dating to the third century A.D.), Dr. Ernst Cohn-Wiener, Max Laserson, Vishnevsky, and Gromadsky. Photo courtesy M. J. Larsons, envelope A, Hoover Institution Archives, Stanford University.

6. The Great Imperial Crown made by Posier in 1762, among the Romanov jewels appraised as collateral for Western loans in the early 1920s but ultimately not sold abroad. Photo courtesy M. J. Larsons collection photo envelope, Hoover Institution Archives, Stanford University.

7. Small Imperial Crown made in the reign of Emperor Paul I (1796–1801). Photo courtesy M. J. Larsons collection photo envelope, Hoover Institution Archives, Stanford University.

8. The Imperial Sceptre made in 1784 containing the famous Orlov diamond. Photo courtesy M. J. Larsons collection photo envelope, Hoover Institution Archives, Stanford University.

9. The Imperial Globe made in 1784.
Photo courtesy M. J. Larsons collection
photo envelope, Hoover Institution
Archives, Stanford University.

10. The Diamond Chain of
the Order of St. Andrew made
in 1795. Photo courtesy M. J.
Larsons collection photo
envelope, Hoover Institution
Archives, Stanford University.

11. Pearl Necklace made
in 1860. Photo courtesy
M. J. Larsons collection
photo envelope, Hoover
Institution Archives,
Stanford University.

II

CASHING IN

They bought up Russian gold, set another stamp on the ingots and melted down the coins. The Royal Mint worked at top pressure. Afterwards the gold with the Swedish stamp could be sold at a fantastic profit.

5 Brest-Litovsk and the Diplomatic Bag

In summer 1918 several hundred million rubles in all were transported from Russia to Stockholm. . . . Cautious observers estimate, that the amount sent was not less than 200 million; others believe that a total as high as a half billion would not be an exaggeration . . . the largest consignments were taken to Stockholm by couriers of the Soviet government.

THE PROPER FINANCIAL HISTORY of Bolshevism begins in the last week of March 1918, with the breaking of the winter-long bank strike (see chapter 1). Absent reliable income, the sovereignty Soviet Russia had achieved by signing the Brest-Litovsk Treaty with Germany earlier that month was nominal at best. While the bank strike persisted, the Bolsheviks subsisted by printing rubles backed by nothing but the paper they were printed on, which lost value by the hour. There were simple party dues, augmented since early February by small quantities of gold and silver coin stolen from private citizens as part of Lenin's loot-the-looters policy. But the mass robberies of winter 1918, though officially encouraged, at first yielded the central government little more than petty cash as looters preferred to line their own pockets. One measure of the regime's financial desperation was the circulation of *Pravda,* which, after peaking at 220,000 in November, was down to 85,000 by March 1918. As Yakov Sverdlov reported on 6 March 1918 to the Bolsheviks' first postrevolutionary party congress in Petrograd, "As yet the Soviet government has given nothing to the party. It is true that the Soviet of People's Commissars had approved the appropriation of 250,000 rubles, but there was no money in the [state] treasury and the appropriation could not be realized."[1] Without access to the hard currency and coin in Russia's bank vaults, the Bolsheviks were running on fumes.

This is why the breaking of the bank strike was of historic importance: it brought the Bolsheviks their first real financial independence, ultimately sealing their triumph over remaining rivals in the Congress of Soviets (several Left Social Revolutionaries allowed to attend Bolshevik cabinet meetings, beginning in December 1917, were expelled in early April 1918).[2] As Lenin explained obliquely in his famous 4 April 1918 speech celebrating the "breathing spell" afforded by Brest-Litovsk, "Up till now measures connected with the expropriation of expropriators occupied the foremost place, but now the organization of accounting and control must take precedence."[3] Now that the expropriators had finally been expropriated, that is, the Bolsheviks could begin spending their money.

But on what? It would take months to build a serious army, and the terms of Brest-Litovsk expressly forbade the Bolsheviks from doing so. At the least, Lenin could now afford to pay the Latvian Rifles who had dispersed the Constituent Assembly in January and who guarded the Moscow Kremlin after the Bolsheviks transferred their headquarters there in March. Throughout spring and summer, the three Latvian brigades commanded by the former tsarist officer Colonel I. I. Vatsesis, 35,000 strong, were the only crack troops the Bolsheviks could rely on, a kind of praetorian guard of the revolution. Vatsesis himself was far from loyal to Lenin—he expressed willingness, at one point, to desert the Bolsheviks if the Germans desired him to—but so long as his men were paid, Vatsesis defended the Communist regime with vigor, helping suppress a rebellion by Social Revolutionaries in July and recapturing Kazan and Simbirsk for the Bolsheviks in September.[4]

Were the Bolsheviks concerned with more than immediate regime survival in 1918, they might have invested some of the ruble-denominated portions of the bank loot—gold and silver coin, tsarist ruble notes—in the domestic economy, which had come to a virtual standstill. But if they flooded the market too quickly with "real" rubles, even these would start quickly to lose value. Peasants were already suspicious of "paper money which cannot buy anything," as Isidor Gukovsky, the beleaguered Bolshevik finance commissar, reported to the Central Committee on 15 April 1918. There were no urban manufactures to trade for food. Taxes, in the ordinary sense, had ceased to exist as there was little organized economic activity to provide the necessary revenue stream. Even the seeming windfall acquired by breaking the bank strike would not amount to much, Gukovsky feared, were the economy not to recover: "We have nationalized the banks, but we have not as yet created anything new to take the place of the old credit machinery. . . . The more [money] we issue the more we seem to need. . . . We adopted the line of least resistance and began to expropriate the expropriators. However our savings are so negligible that we shall not be able to exist on them so very long. . . . No country can exist without creating new values."[5]

Swallowing their pride, the Bolsheviks began inviting deposed factory owners back to restore productivity, even tempting foreign "capitalists" to invest in Soviet Russia. The premise for the latter was the nationalization of foreign trade, announced by Sovnarkom on 22 April 1918. Before long, the Bolsheviks had opened negotiations with both Germany and the Entente powers over the possibility of commercial concessions in Russia. Some of the concessions—for example, the mining rights and rail construction contracts Lenin dangled before an American representative in May—may have been conceived, as George Kennan wrote, "in coldest cynicism and contempt," to play Entente powers off against one another in their greed to dominate the postwar Russian market.[6] Richard Pipes also sees clever "guile" at work in the Bolsheviks' efforts to thaw relations with the capitalist world in spring 1918, as they sought to "compensate for their appalling weakness, [by] luring foreign powers with prospects of industrial imports in exchange for food and raw materials which they did not have."[7] Cynical or not, the concessions game was serious: without some investment in Russia's economy, the Bolsheviks would soon find themselves ruling over a barren wasteland. And evidently, the Bolsheviks did not want to use their hard-stolen capital to make the needed investment themselves.

The foreign concessions stratagem was also a clever way to manipulate the German government, which, Lenin knew, had ambitious plans in store for Russia's economy. The Brest-Litovsk accords spelled out in raw form what was expected of the Bolshevik government—the only possible Russian government, the Germans knew, that would sign them. Aside from exempting the property of German nationals from Bolshevik nationalization decrees, the Brest peace deprived Russia of territories from the Baltic to the Black Sea, altogether some 750,000 square kilometers. Through satellites, the Germans would now rule over 55 million previously Russian subjects, control more than half of Russia's factories, and could exploit three-quarters of her coal and iron deposits. The German draftsmen of the Brest accords, in great haste to wrap things up in the east so the generals could proceed with Ludendorff's spring offensive in the west (launched, as planned, on 21 March 1918), had left many of the economic details of the peace diktat, from expected parameters of trade to the amount the Bolsheviks were to pay in reparations, to be hashed out later.[8] This gave Lenin the opening he needed: with one hand he could exploit the greed of German industrialists by offering them unheard-of concessions in the Russian economy, which they wholly expected to be able to recoup in the near future. This would keep the Bolsheviks in good graces with the German government while, with the other hand, Lenin could use Berlin as a springboard to world revolution.

Thus was born the Janus-faced diplomacy of the first-ever Bolshevik ambassadorial mission, which arrived in Berlin on 19 April 1918. At its head was Adolf Abramovich Joffe, a polished intellectual of "striking Jewish appearance," sporting a smart beard and a pince-nez, who had impressed the German diplomats at Brest with his civilized manners. Although deeply distrusted by Ludendorff and the generals, Joffe was indulged by the German Foreign Office, which had put great stock in the Bolsheviks and did not wish unduly to offend them. Setting up shop in the grand former Russian Embassy on Unter den Linden, Joffe wasted no time before unfurling the Red Flag, complete with Bolshevik hammer and sickle. In true revolutionary style, Joffe ostentatiously refused to present his credentials to the kaiser, preferring an audience with Karl Liebknecht and Rosa Luxemburg, the most radical socialists of the Spartacist faction that would soon form the nucleus of the German Communist Party.[9]

Joffe went about his business in Berlin with an insouciant confidence belying the position of dependence on Germany the Bolsheviks actually found themselves in. Together with Leonid Krasin, the old Siemens-Schukert hand seconded to Berlin because of his German contacts, Joffe established a working rapport with Berlin business circles, offering favored access to Russian raw materials in the postwar period. Joffe and Krasin were courted by officials from Deutsche Bank and the House of Mendelssohn, and even Gustav Stresemann, the nationalist politician and future German chancellor. Stresemann, impressed, recommended that Germany "establish a far-reaching economic and political understanding with the present [Russian] government." An internal German Foreign Office memorandum, prepared in May 1918, went so far as to describe the Bolshevik leaders as "Jewish businessmen," perhaps mistaking the Jewish Joffe for a businessman, which he definitely was not. The concessions stratagem was paying off: despite continued complaints lodged by the general staff about Joffe's covert revolutionary activities, Wilhelmstrasse placed no obstacles in Joffe's path.[10]

The most important privilege the German Foreign Office granted Joffe was use of the diplomatic bag, immune from hostile searches and seizures. So great was the traffic of self-styled Soviet "diplomats" through the Berlin embassy offices, "accompanied by a vast amount of luggage, boxes, and bags," that it became a kind of spies' game to keep count of them: first a hundred men, then two, now three hundred.[11] Few Entente observers doubted these couriers were carrying Bolshevik propaganda, along with funds to foment antiwar demonstrations and destabilize Western governments. The key question was where they were headed: elsewhere in Germany or to Entente capitals by way of neutral states like Denmark or Switzerland?

Berlin was not, understandably, the Bolsheviks' first choice for a foreign staging post, sensitive as they were to the widespread impression that they were German agents. The impression was not entirely false: from Foreign Office files captured in 1945 we now know that the Germans in fact seeded Bolshevik operations both before and after the October Revolution, spending in all some 50 million gold marks, the equivalent of nine or ten tons of gold.[12] The responsible Germans certainly believed themselves to have been instrumental in financing the Russian Revolution. Germany's State Secretary for Foreign Affairs Richard von Kühlmann, who appears to have been the mastermind of the whole operation, wrote in a confidential report on 3 December 1917, "It was not until the Bolsheviks had received from us a steady flow of funds through various channels and under different labels that they were able to build up their main organ, *Pravda,* to conduct energetic propaganda and appreciably to extend the originally narrow basis of their party."[13] If true, this would explain the contained euphoria of a 26 November 1917 telegram from Kühlmann's right-hand man Kurt Riezler, the Wilhelmstrasse's liaison to the Bolshevik Foreign Mission in Stockholm, in which he cautioned his Foreign Office colleagues not to be overwhelmed by "joy" (Freude) at the decisiveness with which the Bolsheviks were sabotaging Russian war efforts.[14] According to Kurt von Lersner, the Foreign Office liaison to German military headquarters on the eastern front, Lenin contacted the German generals shortly after the October Revolution with a personal request for a cease-fire, transmitting this German-language telegram en clair. In the same telegram in which he informed Berlin about Lenin's cease-fire request, Lersner further noted that the bank strike in Petrograd (about which he was suspiciously well informed) meant the Bolsheviks were starved of funds. Lersner added that the members of the German general staff "considered it very desirable, if it could be arranged, to send money to the Lenin regime."[15] Even without knowledge of these secrets revealed from German archives after 1945, the belief that the Bolsheviks were beholden to the Germans was widely held by contemporaries party to the events in question, and not only by the deposed Kerensky and Entente officials. Social Revolutionaries in the Congress of Soviets greeted Lenin with shouts of "Down with the Traitor!" after he signed the Brest-Litovsk Treaty in March 1918.[16]

Knowing full well what people would suspect following his controversial voyage across Germany under military escort in April 1917, Lenin had taken considerable pains to set up a foreign headquarters in Sweden that would remain (ostensibly) untainted by the German connection. Stockholm had, in fact, been the capital of the "northern underground" used by Russian revolutionaries ever since the 1860s.[17] So it was not surprising that Lenin's trusted associates Karl Radek, Jakob Fürstenberg (alias "Hanecki"), and Vatslav Vorovsky established a "Bolshevik Foreign Mission" there on Kaptensgatan, right behind the Imperial Russian Legation on Strandvägen. Although Sweden did not formally recognize the Soviet government, the Bolshevik Mission in Stockholm was given the use of a diplomatic cipher for its communications with Moscow as early as November 1917, in part because it was favored by the powerful German Legation.[18] Swedish public opinion was "about 90 percent pro-German" in the world war, according to Stockholm banker Olof Aschberg, which meant the Bolsheviks found a much warmer welcome in Sweden than they would have in a country more sympathetic to the Entente (like Switzerland, of which more below). The Swedish government allowed Vorovsky to publish *Korrespondenz Prawda,* a thinly disguised Bolshevik propaganda organ, and all but encouraged Swedish businessmen to visit the Soviet Mission on Kaptensgatan.

Swedish neutrality in the First World War was misleading. Sweden had virtually cornered the market on illicit wartime trade between the belligerent powers, profiting hugely from the war (as it would from the Second World War as well). Encouraging a separate peace between Germany and Russia—the goal of both Lenin and his German sponsors—was even an unofficial policy of the Swedish government, if we are to judge by a well-orchestrated press campaign launched in Stockholm after the October Revolution. As *Aftonbladet* intoned on 4 December 1917, in an editorial picked up by most leading Swedish newspapers, "If a separate peace is not followed by a general peace, and the Entente becomes hostile to [Soviet] Russia, then the Russian market will remain open only to the Central Powers and neutral states. In this case Sweden will be in an especially favorable position, because of its proximity, its rail contact with Russia, and the interruption of normal trade relations by the war. Every day must be exploited to strengthen trade ties [with Russia], so that in the postwar period Sweden will be able to compete with great powers like Germany, England, America and Japan."[19]

Olof Aschberg himself was the perfect embodiment of Swedish neutrality. Aschberg's Nya Banken, or "New Bank," was already suspected by the Entente due to suspicious wire transfers in 1917 to Petrograd, including (famously) 750,000 rubles sent to the Siberian Bank account of Evgeniia Sumenson, a relative of Fürstenberg-Hanecki. Kerensky's Ministry of Justice also obtained a copy of

"German Imperial Bank Order No. 7,433 dated 2 March 1917 authorizing payment of money . . . for peace propaganda in Russia," which was transferred to "the New Bank of Stockholm [e.g., Nya Banken] . . . opened on order No. 2,754 of the German Imperial Bank." (This file was later confiscated by the Bolsheviks and destroyed on Trotsky's orders, but not before Kerensky had reported its contents to Entente intelligence.)[20] Because of ongoing transactions with Bolshevik agents like Vorovsky in Stockholm, Nya Banken was put on an Entente blacklist in 1918, with its American and British assets frozen.[21] Undeterred, Aschberg sold his shares, formed a new bank out of his personal capital in a back neighborhood on Stockholm's Fredsgatan, called Svenska Ekonomie Aktiebolaget or "the Swedish Finance Company, Limited," and continued right on buying rubles from Vorovsky's men.[22] Was Aschberg, then, a Bolshevik? Hardly: in 1916 he had secured an American loan of $50 million for tsarist Russia through J. P. Morgan's Guaranty Trust Company in New York. Aschberg also lent two million rubles to Kerensky's beleaguered Provisional Government in 1917 to help launch its "Liberty Loan" campaign.[23] Aschberg's financial support for the Bolsheviks grew not out of ideological conviction, but out of an incurious lack thereof. He would have offered Kerensky equal support had the Bolsheviks not triumphed in October.

Likewise, Sweden's avid interest in commercial relations with the Bolsheviks was a logical outgrowth of its profitable relationship with the tsarist government until February 1917, and then with the Provisional Government, which had, in fact, deposited $2.5 million in Russian gold in Stockholm in October 1917 to finance future Russian imports—Kerensky's final gift to Bolshevism.[24] So it was not surprising that Swedish businessmen courted Vorovsky, the Bolsheviks' man in Stockholm, so assiduously after Lenin had seized power in Petrograd.

There was a problem, however. Now that the "northern underground" had helped the Bolsheviks seize power in Russia, the Germans were no longer so enthusiastic about facilitating Bolshevik communications with Stockholm. Although German State Secretary Kühlmann was leaning heavily on the Swedish government to recognize the Bolsheviks, his hope was that the Swedes would remain subordinate to the Wilhelmstrasse in their relations with Moscow.[25]

Kurt Riezler, Kühlmann's liaison to the Bolshevik Foreign Mission in Sweden, reported optimistically to Berlin in December 1917 that "Stockholm will soon cease to be of any importance as regards Russia because of the poor communications with Petrograd."[26] When a delegation of Swedish trade negotiators requested passage, via Germany, to Petrograd, in March 1918, the German government refused. There was no reason for Germany, the director of the Reich Export-Import Commission declared, "to make easier in any way the unmediated trade traffic between Sweden and Russia."[27] Although a smaller Swedish trade delegation was allowed to visit Moscow in June, its activities were closely watched.[28] Count Mirbach, the German ambassador in Moscow, ordered the German navy to subject all seagoing traffic between Scandinavia and Petrograd to "surveillance in the English style" (nach englischem Muster).[29]

Easy or not, Swedish business interests would not be denied. Although transport between Stockholm and Petrograd remained at the mercy of the German Baltic fleet, this did not stop Soviet commercial agents in Stockholm and their Swedish counterparts in Russia from negotiating ambitious deals—to be realized whenever the Baltic *would* open. (A typical deal specified that shipment would begin within four months "of the opening of seagoing traffic between Petrograd and Stockholm.")[30] While the Swedish trade delegation was still being held up en route to Russia, K. N. Widerström, the Swedish consul in Petrograd, signed a general trade agreement on 29 April 1918 with Gukovsky, the Soviet finance commissar, under which the Bolsheviks would buy Swedish agricultural implements and machinery in exchange for gold, flax, and hemp.[31] Most of the details were worked out in Stockholm, where Vorovsky's Bolshevik Mission was being courted by Swedish firms eager to resume business with Russia. Joining Vorovsky in spring 1918, by way of Berlin under diplomatic cover, were Krasin, Isaak "the engineer" Steinberg,* and Aaron Sheinman, the Bolsheviks' chief expert on the gold and platinum markets, who was entrusted as far as Stockholm with no less than 17 million tsarist rubles to finance imports.[32] The working orders from Moscow were clear: do nothing that might antagonize the Swedish government and focus on desperately needed imports—pa-

---

*"The engineer Steinberg" had acquired notoriety the previous year in allegations surrounding Lenin's receipt of German Foreign Office money through Aschberg's Nya Banken.

per (already running out with the furious pace of Bolshevik decrees), agricultural implements, locomotive engines, and foodstuffs.[33]

Unlike Joffe, that is, who was teasing Berlin industrialists with mostly phantom concessions in order to throw the German Foreign Office off the scent of his revolutionary activities, Vorovsky's men really were trying to do business in Stockholm. And they were fairly successful, at least at placing orders. Between April and June 1918, deals were struck with such Swedish firms as A. Johnson and Company (axes, sickles, scythes, grindstones, and saws); Nyman and Schultz (for copper wire and telephone switching equipment); and Baltik (for separators, ploughs, mowers [kosilki], and reapers).[34] The Bolshevik Mission also tried, on 31 June 1918, to place a 16 million ruble order for 6,000 tons of Norwegian codfish.[35] Military orders were off, for the time being, as they would have raised the hackles of the powerful German Legation in Stockholm (even locomotives, unfortunately for Moscow, fell into this category).[36]

Without German connivance, though, it was difficult for even nonmilitary items to reach Petrograd. The two ships permitted regular passage between Stockholm and Petrograd, the *Runeberg* and the *Elias Sehstedz*, had a carrying capacity of only 400 and 500 tons, respectively. They were invariably held up en route by German destroyers, which would stop the vessels to search for Entente correspondence on board.[37] There was often trouble even for shipments passing through German screen. The first Johnson and Company shipment of agricultural implements was seized by the newly declared independent government of Estonia, in Reval (Tallinn). The Nyman and Schultz telephone equipment, meanwhile, was held up by the Entente Commission in Stockholm, then seized by Finnish authorities while being transported overland to Petrograd. Even the fish order was a bust: the Bolshevik buyer was arrested in Oslo. By the end of 1918, some 3.5 million Swedish crowns worth of goods had been fully paid for in Stockholm but not yet delivered.[38] Still, the willingness of Swedish businessmen and export officials to disregard both German and Entente objections to trading with Soviet Russia was obvious. Swedish supply had happily met Bolshevik demand: all that was needed was an unmolested route for shipment.

With the Bolsheviks, due to German surveillance, unable to fully exploit their base in Stockholm, many of the couriers passing through Joffe's Berlin headquarters in 1918 set off instead for the great neutral to the south, Switzerland. What they hoped to accomplish there is not immediately evident. The Swiss government, backed by the wholehearted support of Switzerland's Socialist Party, was united behind its popular policy of "armed neutrality" in the European war, with the Swiss militia on full alert against penetration by agents of any of the belligerent powers. Under heavy German pressure, Switzerland did allow a "Soviet Foreign Mission," similar to Joffe's and headed by Jan Berzin, to set up shop in Bern on 18 May 1918, but kept its activities under close watch. The Swiss government, naturally enough, saw itself as the prime target of Bolshevik subversion, but this is unlikely. It is fortunate for historians, in any case, that Swiss paranoia prompted a full investigation into Berzin's operations later in 1918, which produced an extraordinary snapshot of international Bolshevism in its infancy.[39]

Compared to Joffe, who later boasted about his generous expenditures aimed at "preparing the German revolution," Berzin was fairly tight-lipped about his own motivations.[40] The aim of Berzin's mission seems to have been neither openly revolutionary like Joffe's, nor primarily commercial, like Vorovsky's. From the materials later confiscated by the Swiss government, it appears that Berzin's working orders from Moscow were mostly to sell off tsarist and Kerensky paper rubles the Bolsheviks had acquired in the bank windfall. Some of the proceeds from these sales were to be used for propaganda sheets like Berzin's *Russische Nachrichten,* which, like *Korrespondenz Prawda* in Stockholm, regurgitated slanted news reports from Soviet Russia for the Bolsheviks' Western sympathizers. But clearly not all of the enormous sums of prerevolutionary rubles arriving in Bern were destined to pay journalistic drones editing Bolshevik wire copy. By opening numbered accounts in Swiss banks, Berzin and his bagmen could spread the wealth around as widely as possible. Ideally, keys to numbered deposit boxes could then be transferred repeatedly to different Bolshevik agents, which would frustrate Swiss or Entente investigators trying to trace or sequester Moscow funds.

It was an ambitious operation, although not quite as ambitious as Swiss authorities initially suspected. Bolshevik bagmen arrived in Bern all summer overland from Joffe's embassy in Berlin, laden down with piles of luggage. One courier, Karl Brand, a former em-

ployee of the city bank of Petrograd given a Soviet diplomatic pass-
port signed by Karl Radek, was entrusted with no less than eleven
suitcases as far as Bern—though many of these probably contained
merely propaganda.[41] It is unlikely that these lower-ranking agents
carried sums as imposing as Sheinman's 17 million. A courier named
Alexander Schreider later claimed, under interrogation, to have been
given 400,000 rubles in June 1918, direct from the Bolshevik Central Committee, but he may have been exaggerating.[42]

The handoffs to Berzin's trusted associates would usually proceed
in the alleyways behind the Genfergasse, near Bern's train station.[43]
Most of the cash carried in by couriers was turned over to the chief
legal counsel (Legationsrat) and de facto treasurer of Berzin's Soviet
Mission, Dr. Grigory Shklovsky, a Russian socialist exiled to Switzerland after the revolution of 1905 and an intimate with Lenin, who
had gone to Russia on one of the "exile" trains to participate in the
Russian Revolution in 1917 before returning to Bern with Berzin in
May 1918. (Brand, for example, said his orders were to turn his
diplomatic bags over to no one but Shklovsky.)[44] Shklovsky's chief
currency conduit, in turn, appears to have been the Bern lawyer and
future chairman of the Swiss Communist Party, Dr. Boris Lifschitz,
with whom he was witnessed to be in constant contact during the
summer of 1918. Both men did a booming business with Wilhelm
Tschudy, a currency dealer in Bern, Shklovsky selling him 400,000
Romanov rubles in three August installments, Lifschitz unloading
600,000, at variable rates averaging around 80 Swiss francs per 100
rubles. Lifschitz sold Tschudy a further 1 million Kerensky rubles, at
60 francs per hundred.[45] Lifschitz also sold Zurich dealer Adolf
Dätwyler 750,000 tsarist rubles. Dätwyler was disappointed when
Lifschitz cut off this business, as he "had the impression that Lifschitz had only sent me a small amount of the rubles that he had to
sell."[46]

Sure enough, Lifschitz was selling to other banks as well. The
Swiss government estimated that in the course of 1918, in addition
to the cheaper Kerensky notes, Lifschitz laundered some 2.5 million
proper tsarist ruble notes, scattering the transactions across a half-
dozen banks and buying up primarily Swiss francs, at a rate of between 75 and 85 francs per 100 rubles.[47] Added to the Kerensky
notes Lifschitz sold, and the tsarist rubles laundered by Shklovsky,

these transactions alone would have netted the Bolsheviks some 3 million Swiss francs, or over 1 million U.S. dollars. This was serious money in 1918, plenty to finance strikes and industrial subversion in several West European countries at once, as Allied officials feared.

Swiss authorities later received a tip that Lifschitz had squirreled away another "16 to 18 million" Swiss francs for Berzin's Soviet Mission "in diverse banks in Bern, Lucerne, and Geneva"—about $5 or $6 million worth, or the equivalent of more than $500 million today.[48] But they were unable to find these funds. The closest the Swiss government came to tracing monies laundered by Lifschitz was an account held in his name at the Cantonal Bank of Bern, which saw frequent traffic in sums of "hundreds of thousands of francs." This account carried a balance of 350,000 francs when Swiss officials queried the bank: significant but much less than investigators had hoped to find. Three other banks in Bern did report holding accounts in Lifschitz's name, some of which had seen significant traffic in 1918, but they were mostly cleaned out by November. Lifschitz had covered his tracks well. By 1919, he had disappeared from sight of the Swiss investigators: a Geneva bank produced a forwarding address in Paris for one "Bernard Lifschitz, jewelry merchant," but French police suspected it was fictitious.[49]

Nor did the Swiss authorities have better luck with Lifschitz's less prolific colleagues. Despite aggressive pursuit and a circular sent to every bank in Switzerland, the government was unable to turn up more than a few accounts held in the names of suspected Bolshevik money launderers like Shklovsky, Alexander Schreider, and Isaak Steinberg (fresh in from Stockholm). These findings were disappointing: accounts at the Bern Federal Bank of 1,000 Swiss francs for Shklovsky and 50,000 francs each for Schreider and Steinberg.[50] By the time the ponderous Swiss bureaucracy finally got around to expelling the Soviet Mission on 12 November 1918, Berzin and his men had found plenty of time to burn account books at the Schwanengasse headquarters in Bern, leaving behind little but a smattering of propaganda.[51]

So what happened to the 3 million Swiss francs (or likely five or six times this amount) Shklovsky and Lifschitz had purchased? Doubtless a portion of this money did indeed support the publication of

Russische Nachrichten until it was banned in November, as Berzin later claimed. But this could hardly have been a great sum. The copy was mostly recycled Soviet agitprop, and its editor, James Reich, received a monthly salary of only 500 Swiss francs (though he was given 5,000 francs by Shklovsky to "liquidate" its operations when the authorities closed in, which included severance payments to Swiss employees he fired).[52]

Some of the Berzin mission's cash was also deposited in transferable numbered accounts, intended for future use by the international Bolshevik movement. It is unclear how much, however, as heavy-handed Swiss investigators had given the Bolsheviks several months' notice to clean out these accounts. One suspected Bolshevik account with a transferable key, opened by Schreider and Steinberg at the Federal Bank of Lausanne, contained 40,000 Swiss francs, and 104,500 tsarist rubles when it was sequestered by the government late in 1918.[53] Berzin, Shklovsky, and another Soviet "diplomat" named Stephan Bratmann, who was witnessed traveling frequently between Berlin and Bern, opened a total of five numbered accounts at Bern banks, but these were nearly empty when opened by government investigators in November 1918.[54] A Geneva bank did later agree to freeze a suspicious numbered account holding 500,000 tsarist rubles ($250,000, roughly equal to $25 million today), deposited by the elusive Comintern agent Mikhail Borodin under the name of Michel Gruzenberg, when a reputed Bolshevik agent named Julius Fox turned up with the key, demanding access. Borodin was not one of Berzin's men, though: after spending most of 1918 in Scandinavia he had arrived in Geneva only in April 1919, long after the Soviet Mission had been expelled, using not the Soviet but the Mexican diplomatic bag.[55]

The most likely explanation of what happened to the hoard of Romanov and Kerensky rubles Bolshevik couriers smuggled into Switzerland is also the simplest: after exchanging it for Swiss francs and other Western currencies, they smuggled it right back out. Remarkably, when Berzin and his men were expelled from Switzerland on 12 November 1918, the policemen escorting them, following the letter of the law (or possibly, Entente officials suspected, obeying orders from Swiss parliamentarians who feared having evidence of bribes exposed), *did not search their luggage*.[56] We can only guess, therefore, how much hard currency the Bolsheviks purchased in Switzerland. At the least, the Swiss sting operation nipped such laundering before it grew really serious, sending the "Berzin band" (as Allied intelligence officers referred to the Soviet Mission) across the German border, where many would rejoin Joffe in Berlin.

Joffe's operation, meanwhile, had branched out in a number of fruitful directions. With the cash carried in by Moscow couriers, he later boasted, the Soviet Embassy in Berlin "subsidized more than ten left-socialist newspapers," along with the printing of "hundreds of thousands of revolutionary pamphlets" and the placement of "agents in various German ministries." With his other, accomodationist hand, Joffe negotiated supplementary provisions to the Brest Treaty in August 1918 which provided a German guarantee of Soviet port access at Reval and Riga—presumably to capitalize on Vorovsky's commercial negotiations in Stockholm. Joffe also secured Moscow the right to import German arms and ammunition: he immediately requested 200,000 rifles, 500 million bullets, and 20,000 machine guns.[57]

Despite generous expenditures, Joffe's savings account at the German Bank of Mendelssohn nearly doubled in size during his tenure in Berlin, from an initial deposit of 12 million marks in April to a total of 22 million in December. It is likely a sizable portion of this increase was made up by Berzin's couriers returning overland from Switzerland after their expulsion in November: 3 million Swiss francs would have netted some 5 million marks at summer 1918 rates, and much more after the German collapse sent the mark tumbling. At any rate, Joffe was not short for cash. In October he even purchased, directly on the German market, some 200 handguns for Soviet Embassy personnel, possibly hoping to capitalize directly on the chaos sure to engulf Berlin following a military defeat.[58]

The German Foreign Office (again, winning out over the objections of the General Staff) continued approving Joffe's sometimes brazen requests—excepting only the machine guns—because of the belief that Berlin was benefiting from Bolshevik rule in Russia. The truth of this perception is difficult to evaluate. On the positive side of the ledger, the Bolsheviks did agree to pay enormous war reparations to Berlin, 6 billion marks in all (about $2 billion at pre-armistice

1918 rates, roughly equivalent to some $200 billion today): a significant payoff on the money the Germans had invested in Lenin. One-quarter of the reparations principal was to be paid promptly in cash and gold. The Bolsheviks duly shipped the first two of five planned installments, totaling 662.5 million marks, half in tsarist rubles and half in fine gold (about 93,500 kilograms, or 100 tons), to Germany on 10 and 30 September 1918.[59] The tsarist rubles in the reparations package were intended to cover German occupation expenses in the Ukraine.[60] As for the weapons Joffe requested for Moscow, the German Foreign Office wanted them to be used in a campaign to eject Allied forces from Murmansk, under German command, as one of the secret clauses to the Supplementary Treaty to Brest-Litovsk spelled out in depth. The weapons were not, in fact, dispatched before the armistice rendered the agreement moot, suggesting the Germans still had considerable reservations about the Bolsheviks.[61] Still, so long as the army of occupation remained in the east, one million strong, it seemed to Berlin that the Bolsheviks could do German interests no harm.

Still, Joffe's lavish outlays on revolutionary propaganda, much of which was destined for the German armies on both fronts, may have contributed to the overall breakdown of morale, which Ludendorff later blamed for Germany's defeat.[62] Gold aside, by the time the Germans sued for an armistice in October, Moscow had delivered very little of the 1 billion marks worth of raw materials (lumber, oil, flax, nickel, and hemp) it had promised to Germany as part of the reparations settlement, sending, possibly in contempt, only one ship containing some brass shavings and metal scrap. From the German side, meanwhile, a shipment of 40 thousand tons of coal and coke had arrived in Petrograd by the time of the November armistice, of 100 thousand tons promised, for which the Soviet trade officials claimed to have prepaid an additional 722,000 gold marks (as if to excuse the nondelivery of raw materials to Germany—clearly the Bolsheviks had little to offer besides gold).[63] Added to the gold bullion already shipped as reparations, we might say this was a heavy price for Moscow to pay for a relatively small shipment of coal. But the gold shipped to Germany in fall 1918 bought the Bolsheviks the most precious commodity of all: immediate regime survival for the coming winter in Moscow and Petrograd.

It remains somewhat curious, nonetheless, that the Bolsheviks shipped more than 100 tons of gold to Germany in September 1918, at a time when the imminent defeat of the Central Powers in the world war was expected by nearly everyone in the West, the German generals included.[64] Richard Pipes, for example, has suggested that "the Bolsheviks believed in the victory of their German friends as late as the end of September 1918."[65] This is possible. It is also possible that Moscow expected the German government to fall to a Soviet-style revolution, which would effectively put the gold right back in Bolshevik hands, to be used as security against desperately needed weapons imports from Germany (including those Joffe had already ordered), along with coal, locomotives, and rolling stock. Joffe himself is said to have told the Spartacist leader Karl Liebknecht on 2 November 1918, on receipt of the news of the recent naval mutiny at Kiel, "Within a week the Red Flag will be flying over the Berliner Schloss." So it did, albeit briefly, as the German Republic was proclaimed by Liebknecht himself on the steps of the imperial palace in Berlin exactly seven days later. Had Liebknecht and the Spartacists then seized power, Joffe's revolutionary gambit might well have succeeded, bailing the Bolsheviks out of bankruptcy by placing the wealth of Germany at their disposal.

Joffe, though, overplayed his hand. The Soviet Embassy's increasingly public support for German revolutionaries and mutineers finally provoked the seemingly imperturbable German Foreign Office enough to approve Joffe's expulsion, along with that of his entire staff, on 5 November 1918.[66] The provisional German government of Friedrich Ebert then sequestered Joffe's accounts at Mendelssohn, and under Allied pressure forwarded the Russian gold the Bolsheviks had shipped to Berlin on to Paris.[67] The last blow to Bolshevik ambitions in Germany came when the national congress of Germany's own workers' soviets voted in December to abdicate power to an elected "bourgeois" parliament, which turned out to be quite hostile to Bolshevism.

Still, the failure of Germany to "bolshevize" did little to dispel the euphoria in the Kremlin following the German collapse. A German diplomat reported to Berlin in early October that the Bolsheviks were already treating Brest-Litovsk as an empty letter (wie einen verbrecherischen Akt). "Our influence with the Bolsheviks," he continued, "is completely exhausted. They do with us now what they wish." In an ironic twist, the Bolsheviks were confiscating the diplomatic bags used by German embassy staff in Moscow.[68] After the November armistice, the Bolsheviks began looting the German consulate in Petrograd, in delirious violation of the exception-to-nationalization status accorded the Germans by Brest-Litovsk.[69] There they eventually found 250 million rubles stashed away in thirty diplomatic mailbags. Accounts held by German nationals in Russian banks, also exempt from confiscation according to Brest-Litovsk, were turned over to the so-called German Revolutionary Worker and Soldier Council of Moscow, assembled from freed German prisoners-of-war who had chosen to remain in Soviet Russia rather than be repatriated.[70] In this way Lenin and the Bolsheviks avenged their German occupiers, turning the diktat peace of Brest-Litovsk squarely on its head. Whether this was wise is another matter: the Bolsheviks' gleeful anti-German retribution won Moscow no friends in Berlin, which accomplished the difficult trick of winning Lenin the simultaneous enmity of both the defeated Central Powers and the victorious Entente.

The Bolsheviks' triumphant reaction to the German defeat was not entirely irrational, of course. The German military jackboot was lifted from Moscow's neck, opening up the prospect of the Bolsheviks winning back the prosperous regions of the Baltic, White Russia, and the Ukraine. More immediately, Vorovsky and his team in Stockholm could now order imports of what Moscow really needed—war matériel—across the Baltic without German interference.

Without missing a beat, Sweden's industrialists, who had profited handsomely by supplying the armies of both tsarist Russia and Imperial Germany during the war, began filling huge military orders for the Bolsheviks once the war was over. On 23 November 1918, just twelve days after the armistice rendered Imperial Germany impotent and unable to enforce the Baltic blockade, the Bolshevik Mission in Stockholm signed a contract with the Swedish firm Axel Christiernsson for delivery of 255 aero-engines (10.9 million Swedish crowns), leather pilots' jackets—a favorite fashion plate of leading Bolsheviks—and drivers' and pilots' goggles (862,000 crowns), along with 2 million crowns worth of steel cable (stal'nykh trossa) and string wire (strunnoi provoloki). In all, the Bolsheviks appropriated 19 million crowns (about $4.5 million, or some $450 million in today's terms) from the new Extraordinary Commission for Red Army Procurement (Chrezvychainaia komissia snabzheniiu krasnoi armii) for Swedish purchases via Axel Christiernsson. The firm required an advance payment of half this sum (9.5 million crowns).[71] The Red Army also authorized the deposit of 672,000 Swedish crowns in Stockholm to securitize an order for twenty locomotive engines to be manufactured by Munktell-Eskilstuna (this is the base firm that would eventually evolve into the Volvo conglomerate). Another 73,000 crowns was spent on an initial order of 50,000 gun barrels (oruzheinykh stvolov) manufactured in the Husqvarna factory in Stockholm, to be delivered overland via Haparanda on the Swedish-Finnish border (where the order seems to have been held up in customs).[72]

There were new civilian deals as well. Soviet trade officials in Stockholm signed another contract in November for 3 million Swedish crowns worth of milk separators, to be deposited in advance in Swedish banks before shipment to Petrograd.[73] A particularly ambitious deal would bring Russia 15 million crowns worth of mechanical Swedish manufactures (mostly agricultural machinery) by 31 January 1919, in exchange for leftover stocks of flax, hemp, and linseed oil that had been sitting in warehouses in Petrograd since 1917. Bolshevik commercial vessels, according to this agreement, would also be guaranteed access to Swedish coaling stations and all necessary port facilities.[74] As security, the Bolsheviks were to deposit cash directly in the Swedish national bank.[75]

The flurry of commercial activity in Stockholm following the armistice naturally attracted a great deal of scrutiny from the Entente missions there. But Allied officials seem to have mistaken heavy traffic in Russian rubles in Sweden for a laundering operation similar to the one rooted out in Switzerland, aimed at financing propaganda in the West. Marcus Wallenberg, a Swedish financier sympathetic to the Allies, reported to the American Legation in November 1918 that Vorovsky's Soviet Mission had deposited 3 million crowns at his bank alone, which he estimated to be about one-fifth of Bolshevik assets in Sweden. Fearing this money would go to fund agitation in Entente countries—not an unreasonable suspicion, as it was rumored that Vorovsky had acquired 250,000 pounds sterling, along with comparable sums in dollars and French francs—the Allied Legations asked the Swedish government for a full accounting of Bolshevik deposits in Swedish banks.[76] Neither Washington nor London suspected that Bolshevik deposits in Sweden were made, instead, to securitize strategic imports.

From Soviet files opened in 1991, it is now clear that Wallenberg's estimate of Soviet cash reserves in Sweden was far too low. An internal memorandum prepared in January 1919 by the Bolshevik Commissariat of Finance estimated that Russians had sent "not less than 200 million rubles" and possibly as much as "half a billion" to Stockholm in 1918, "the greatest consignments [of which] were taken to Stockholm by couriers of the Soviet government." Sheinman's 17 million rubles was not the largest single sum dispatched to Stockholm: Gukovsky himself, the first Bolshevik finance commissar, was entrusted with 50 million, along with 500 kilograms of platinum. In addition to frequenting Aschberg's Nya Banken and (after it was blacklisted) Svenska Ekonomie Aktiebolaget, Vorovsky's men also sold millions of rubles to Affärsbank, Köppmanebank, and the Stockholm branches of the German Reichsbank and the House of Mendelssohn. Perhaps because Aschberg was under Allied surveillance, he was not the most prolific buyer of the Bolsheviks' money in 1918: this honor belonged instead to a lesser-known dealer named Dardel von Hagling, whose ruble turnover "totaled more than a million every day" (oboroty koego ezhednevno sostavliaiut' ne menee milliona rublei).[77]

Allied pressure on Stockholm to suppress Bolshevik currency transactions was ratcheted up in the weeks after the armistice, but the Swedish government responded only with piecemeal gestures. Vorovsky, a Swedish official assured the British Legation, was told "that cable and courier facilities would no longer be given him," and Swedish police were given a list of twenty-five Bolsheviks "with instructions to let none of them leave Sweden without special authority." This fell far short of sequestering Bolshevik funds, much less the expulsion of Vorovsky's mission demanded by the Allies. Either action would likely have met the loud objections of Swedish business interests that, as we have seen, had lucrative contracts pending with the Bolsheviks. The formal excuse the Swedish government offered London for not freezing Bolshevik accounts was to protect "an estimated 300,000,000 crowns worth of property owned by Swedes in Russia." This did not impress the British, who knew that Swiss firms held substantially more Russian assets at risk than this—which fact had not prevented Switzerland from summarily expelling Berzin's Soviet Mission in November.[78]

Finally, in early January 1919, the Swedish government acceded to at least one of the key Allied demands, forbidding the buying and selling of paper rubles on Swedish territory.[79] But the ban did not extend, as the Entente powers had requested, to sales of Russian gold. This crucial exception, we shall see below, would in time allow the Bolsheviks to establish a crucial lifeline to Western capital markets. In the meantime, the Swedish ban on paper ruble transactions was applied somewhat cynically. Heavy traffic throughout fall 1918, in anticipation of a Swedish-Russian trade boom following the armistice, had driven up the ruble's value in Sweden, with tsarist notes selling as high as 68 per 100 rubles on October 31 (from 50 in September). Even ostensibly worthless "Kerenskys" were still fetching 56 crowns per 100.[80] In Helsingfors and Stockholm, ruble trading had become something of a popular sport. That thousands of individual Swedish speculators, along with bankers like Aschberg and Hagling, now held Russian paper was another reason the government had hesitated before banning it. So what were Swedish ruble holders to do now that Stockholm had banned their sale?

The Swedish government's answer to this problem was typically mischievous: send them to Germany. By the time of the armistice, the German Reichsbank was heavily invested in the Russian ruble. The Reichsbank president had even stipulated earlier in 1918 that German occupation officials in Ukraine not be allowed to purchase grain with German marks, preferring they use Russian currency instead. After the influx of rubles following the reparations settlement of August, the Reichsbank's ruble hoard had grown to more than 200 million.[81] With the Reichsbank, Deutsche Bank, and Mendelssohn all deeply leveraged in Russian currency, it was only natural that ruble holders, blocked in Sweden, would come to Berlin to sell. Before long, the German Legation in Stockholm was besieged with visa requests from Swedes seeking to unload their rubles. The Reichsbank, doubling down on a bad hand, agreed to buy.[82] Lenin would have appreciated the irony: by basing their plans to colonize

Russia on an alliance with Bolshevism, the Germans had become harnessed to shaky Bolshevik finances and would suffer the consequences as the ruble inflated. The chickens of Brest-Litovsk, we might say, had come home to roost in the German Reichsbank.[83]

The last laugh of 1918, though, would be had by the Allies. With the collapse of German power on land and in the Baltic, the Bolsheviks had caught a heady whiff of independence, freed by the force of Entente arms from the clutches of Brest-Litovsk. German oversight and surveillance, it seemed for a brief shimmering moment, would give way to a mutually profitable relationship of equals between Russian Bolsheviks and Swedish bankers and tradesmen. But it was not to be. By the onset of winter, the British had moved in to replace the German Baltic fleet, imposing a blockade that made the German screen look like child's play.

6 Blockade

To allow the Bolshevik government to grant [commercial] concessions would be to gravely jeopardize the rights of Russia's real creditors.

— LETTER FROM FRENCH LEGATION IN STOCKHOLM TO SWEDISH FOREIGN MINISTRY, 5 April 1919

ALTHOUGH THE BOLSHEVIKS later placed the Allied intervention in Soviet Russia from 1918 to 1920 at the heart of their civil war mythology, the truth is that none of the Entente powers that deployed troops ever sought seriously to overthrow the Communist government, with the possible exception of Great Britain for a few months in summer 1919. The earliest Allied deployments, involving small contingents of American, French, and British soldiers sent ashore at Murmansk, Archangel, and Vladivostok in spring 1918, were actually made at the behest of Trotsky, the Soviet war commissar, to protect war stores in these port cities from German capture. A more substantial British-led expeditionary force under General F. C. Poole did occupy Archangel in early August 1918, but Poole's orders emphasized "resisting German influence and penetration," with no mention of combating Bolshevism.[1] A joint American-Japanese landing at Vladivostok later that month was likewise conceived in order to aid the Czechoslovak legion in Siberia, whose services the Allies still hoped to employ on the western front, and was in no way aimed at engaging the Bolsheviks directly. True, the Japanese, who sent the most soldiers (about 70,000) into Russia, did so with the sort of "imperialist" ambitions denounced in Communist propaganda, but these ambitions were confined to eastern Siberia, where

117

Bolshevik rule had not yet penetrated. There is no evidence any of the Entente governments planned to overthrow the Bolsheviks at a single point in 1918. The aim all along, rather, was to bring Russia back into the fold of the world war against Germany.[2]

After the armistice rendered the German threat in the east largely moot, the Allied intervention in Russia took on a new complexion. But the collapse of the Central Powers also removed the unifying factor in Russia policy among the Entente powers. Without the German bogeyman to concentrate the mind, Allied statesmen and diplomats rapidly fell to bickering over what to do about Bolshevism. France, whose banks and private bondholders together owned the greatest portion of prewar tsarist government debt, was most adamant about overthrowing the Communist regime, which had repudiated these obligations, but also the most exhausted materially and emotionally by the world war and thus least able to support a sustained intervention. By contrast, the United States had easily enough men and money to intervene but little desire to meddle in Russia's internal politics, especially if this meant supporting White troops who might, President Woodrow Wilson feared (largely incorrectly), try to restore tsarism. As one recent historian of the American intervention summed up the atmosphere in Washington in winter 1918–19, policymakers were "totally confused about what to do about Russia on the eve of the peace negotiations in Paris." Japan, meanwhile, eyeing Siberia, had no great concern about what sort of government held sway west of the Urals and thus no cause for confronting Communism.[3]

Of the victorious powers, only Britain had both the means and possible motivation to intervene seriously in Russia, but its government was far from united about doing so. Winston Churchill, minister of munitions and (from January 1919) minister of war, was the only consistent advocate of a large-scale campaign to overthrow Bolshevism. But the closer he came to pursuing such a strategy, the more roundly he was rebuked by his colleagues. When Churchill met with French officials in February 1919 to discuss ways of strengthening White forces in Russia, Lloyd George expressed "alarm" and told his war minister not to trust French "incitement." He begged the bellicose Churchill "not to commit this country to what would be a purely mad enterprise out of hatred of Bolshevik principles." Not that Britain would abandon the anti-Communist cause entirely:

Lloyd George had no objections to "supplying Armies in non-Bolshevik areas."[4] Expressing the traditional British distaste for ideological crusades, Foreign Secretary Arthur Balfour justified Lloyd George's policy of halfway intervention on the grounds that Britain not suffer "a serious loss of prestige" by "letting down her friends," while recommending that all cabinet officials declare publicly that they had "no desire to intervene" in Russia's internal affairs. The idea was not to destroy Bolshevism but, as Lord Milner put it, "to confine it to the area it had already ravaged."[5]

In this way the Allies settled on a limited containment policy regarding Bolshevism. It was the path of least resistance, offering conservatives in each country the promise that *something* was being done about the Communist threat while reassuring critics—mostly Labour politicians in Britain, socialists in France, and isolationists in the United States—that no one was starting a new conflict with Russia with the crippling world war finally over. The cliché of the hour was a cordon sanitaire against Soviet Russia, a kind of quarantine against the disease of Bolshevism, which, it was hoped, deprived of outside support, might soon exhaust itself. As illustrated by the equivocating of Lloyd George, the Bolsheviks were not entirely wrong to complain about the fecklessness and hypocrisy of Entente statesmen who denied they were at war with Soviet Russia, even while openly aiding the Bolsheviks' enemies. Here was an anti-Communist crusade lacking the courage of its convictions.

Still, no matter how little resolution or principle lay behind it, the Allied cordon sanitaire was more than enough to give the Bolsheviks fits as the civil war heated up. With both Denikin's Volunteer Army in the south and Admiral Kolchak's Siberian People's Army in the east poised for spring offensives, Moscow was desperate to equip the Red Army—expanding in line with Lenin's 1 October 1918 decree to three million men—with the stores it needed to sustain long battles. As we have seen, Moscow had a number of important military procurement deals pending with Swedish suppliers, which would be held up indefinitely by the British-led Baltic blockade. In addition to the November 1918 deal with Axel Christiernsson for steel cable, string wire, leather jackets, pilots' and drivers' goggles, and aero-engines (see chapter 5), Vorovsky's Bolshevik Mission in Stockholm placed orders in February 1919, totaling more than 100 million rubles, for Danish-made pots, pans, and plates for field kitchens; American-made leather boots and Swedish boot-making equipment; and Bosch spark plugs for military vehicles.[6] Further nonmilitary orders were placed in Stockholm that winter for Danish electrical equipment, plus Swedish and German agricultural machinery, chemical dyes and paper products, and pharmaceuticals.[7] The idea, apparently, was to camouflage dual-use military purchases with simultaneous orders of civilian items so that shipments would be less likely to be held up by British vessels patrolling the Baltic. Although he had done some preliminary negotiation in Stockholm on gun barrels and locomotives, for example, Vorovsky dared not place such obviously military orders just yet.

But the Entente screen was much tighter than the Germans' had been. Three Swedish ships, carrying grindstones, seed, saws, scythes, and excavation machines, did make it through in early December 1918, but this was only because lax British patrols had not expected them to brave the ice floes. As a German agent reported from Petrograd on the incredible arrival of the Swedish vessels at a time when the "Neva was nearly frozen," Stockholm's public "breaking off of relations" with the Bolsheviks after the armistice had only been a "dirty trick" (Schikane): "Sweden will allow nothing to interfere with trade with Russia" (Schweden unterliess nichts, die Warenaustausche mit Russland zu fordern).[8]

Once the British resumed aggressively patrolling the Gulf of Finland in February, the backlog of Swedish orders began to pile up, with bare dribs and drabs of desperately needed imports arriving in Petrograd. By March, only a small consignment of axes (about 18,000) and saws (15,400) had arrived in Petrograd.[9] Part of the problem was that the Bolsheviks had only now-illegal paper rubles to offer Swedish firms in compensation for imports. Only one hundred tons of flax had been sent to Stockholm by the end of 1918, with the rest rotting in warehouses in Petrograd.[10] After learning in February that the Baltik Company was holding up shipments to Russia due to nondelivery of promised goods, the Soviet Trade Commission offered yet more phantom exports, this time of precious furs (tsennykh mekhov). Baltik, skeptical that such furs would ever arrive in Stockholm, did not even reply to this offer.[11]

The Bolsheviks, belying their reputation for boldness, were afraid of shipping almost anything across the Baltic lest it be seized by British destroyers en route. Enlisting the services of Vorovsky's Stockholm lawyer, Wilhelm Hellberg, who was visiting Moscow in May 1919, the Bolsheviks offered to send to Stockholm, at long last, the promised flax and hemp on three Russian ships (the *Karl Marx,* the *Red Petrograd,* and the *Freedom*), but only if their safe passage was legally guaranteed by the Swedish government.[12] Hellberg, a Swedish citizen, was given power of attorney to sign commercial contracts in Sweden and Denmark on behalf of Moscow, which provided the Soviet government a useful end-around for commercial negotiations in Stockholm now that Vorovsky himself was on the Allied watch list.[13] Hellberg bought the Bolsheviks time that summer, reassuring the Swedish Foreign Office that the trade potential with Moscow remained quite real, with contracts for Swedish manufactures possibly totaling as much as 500 million crowns (over $100 million)—everything from agricultural machinery to locomotive engines and gun barrels—just over the horizon.[14] But such deals remained largely fantasy so long as neither Sweden nor Russia could assure safe passage of vessels across the Baltic.

Another problem was port capacity in Petrograd. Because the Gulf of Finland usually iced over in December, Russia had traditionally relied on its warm water ports for the long winter months. But the British, who now controlled Constantinople, were blockading the Black Sea as well. Even after the ice melted, Petrograd's capacity was severely limited. Port infrastructure had been severely damaged during the upheavals of 1917, and dockworkers, apparently not convinced that the Bolsheviks were truly a workers' government, continued to strike frequently. Unable to count on the laborers in whose name they had staged their revolution, in early 1919 the Bolsheviks hired a private Swedish shipping firm, Transbalta, to renovate the port of Petrograd and provide tugboats and barge service, appropriating 2 million rubles for the purpose from the Red Army budget.[15]

Port capacity remained relatively undisturbed at both Reval and Riga, which were both also somewhat less vulnerable to ice than Petrograd. But because of the spirited defense organized by newly independent Estonia—whose embryonic army was reinforced by Finnish and White Russian troops and generously supplied with munitions from Great Britain—Reval would remain off-limits to the Bolsheviks throughout 1919.[16] As for Riga, it had been captured by the Red Army in late December 1918, but supply lines from Petrograd were vulnerable. The North-Western Army of Nikolai Yudenich was menacing the Red Army in northern Latvia from a secure base in Estonia. A Yudenich offensive on Pskov in early May disrupted Red supply lines from Petrograd to Riga from the northern direction, while from southern Latvia they were threatened by a German army under the command of General von der Goltz, which had been left in place by the Allies after the armistice to help stem Bolshevik penetration there. The Baltic region, in short, was in chaos. Even had the British allowed Swedish imports through at Riga, they would likely have been seized in transit by Yudenich or von der Goltz long before they reached Petrograd, much less the eastern or southern fronts where the Red Army most desperately needed them.

It is little wonder, then, that seaborne imports to Soviet Russia dropped to virtually zero in 1919, with exports, likewise, so negligible as barely to register in international trade statistics. The prewar volume of annual Russian exports had sometimes surpassed 50 million tons (mostly grain, foodstuffs, furs, and raw materials like flax, hemp, and timber), which ensured a positive trade balance in most years against smaller volumes of imported manufactures.[17] Exports dropped severely during the world war and even more so after the revolution, to an anemic total of 60,000 tons in 1918, against 300,000 tons of imports, with nearly all of this traffic coming from Germany and Scandinavia, especially Sweden. The trade balance under Bolshevik rule had thus flatly reversed, with the growing deficit, as we have seen, made up by cash deposits of tsarist rubles and promises of future shipments of gold, flax, and hemp, which had not yet materialized. In 1919, due mostly to the British blockade of imports destined for Petrograd but also to the Bolsheviks' inability to pay, Russian imports dropped to only 16,000 tons, mostly the agricultural tools and implements Vorovsky had ordered the previous year in Stockholm. Many of these came in aboard the Swedish ship *Eskilstuna,* whose adventurous Captain Erikson braved the blockade, reaching Petrograd in late August. Total Soviet Russian exports for 1919, meanwhile, consisted of a mere 1,500 tons, mostly flax and hemp.[18] It was as if an entire continent, once central to the functioning of the world economy, had dropped off the map.

The Bolsheviks had only themselves to blame for their economic isolation, of course. By repudiating Russia's debts and seizing the property of foreign nationals, Lenin had ensured the enmity of Western governments, even Germany's, after he repudiated Brest-Litovsk in November 1918. Only the wartime neutrals—Sweden, Norway, and Denmark—remained relatively unperturbed by the ongoing Communist depredations against property, in part because the Bolsheviks actively courted them, offering to exempt their nationals from Soviet taxes and nationalization decrees if they would trade with Moscow.[19] Heavy Allied pressure following Germany's collapse had forced all three countries to ban transactions in paper rubles, but the bans did not extend to Russian gold or raw materials.[20] Entente officials knew that the Bolsheviks were negotiating deals on the sly with the northern neutrals in 1919 and lodged protests accordingly. As the French Legation in Stockholm declared, "to allow the Bolshevik government to grant [commercial] concessions would be to gravely jeopardize the rights of Russia's real creditors."[21] Evidently the Swedish government did not see things the same way, but the British blockade ensured there was little such concessions could yet amount to anyway.

With Scandinavian trade neutralized for now by Allied surveillance, the Bolsheviks naturally sought to find suppliers elsewhere. One possible source was directly south, where Mustafa Kemal, the victorious Turkish commander at Gallipoli, was busy setting up a nationalist regime just as hostile to the Western Allies as was Lenin's Russia. Kemal's new landlocked capital, Ankara, was secure from harassment by the Allied fleet patrolling the Bosphorus and Black Sea. An illicit traffic inevitably developed in summer 1919 between the two pariah regimes, with several ambitious Turkish gunrunners braving the British Black Sea blockade. But this was not really a trading relationship. Turkey's economy was even more devastated than Russia's, and Kemal had little to offer the Bolsheviks in compensation for small-scale deliveries of arms and gold besides cooperation in ejecting the British from the Caucasus. This he provided, by sending military officers to aid the Bolsheviks in Dagestan and by urging Azeri Turks to cooperate with Bolsheviks in Baku, from which city the British withdrew their last troops in March 1919.[22]

Azerbaijan would remain independent until April 1920, but the departure of the British from the area in 1919 made it possible for Moscow to begin importing goods overland from neutral Persia, where the economy had mostly escaped the ravages of the world war. In early July 1919, the Bolsheviks placed an open-ended order with a consortium of Muslim merchants for 63 million rubles worth of Persian tobacco, dried fruit, oranges, and opium, although as sporadic fighting continued in the northern Caucasus, it would take months for these goods to reach Russia.[23] In Moscow, several tons of opium, brought in by a Persian trader the previous year, were requisitioned in March 1919 by the Red Army to produce morphine (the Persian was later compensated at a rate of 500 tsarist rubles per kilo).[24]

Still, imports from the Orient could only go so far. Manufactured goods, machinery, metals, medicines, and painkillers other than morphine could only be procured in Europe. Simply to function on a daily basis, the Red Army needed not only small arms ammunition and artillery shell (at least these were still being produced, though at much lower volume than before 1917, mainly at factories in Tula, south of Moscow, where workers were given highest priority as regarded rations and pay), but also boots and clothing (of which virtually none was now being produced in Russia), plus eyeglasses and modern medicines (not yet produced in Russia), and typewriters, ink, and paper on which to issue orders.

Unable to realize most of the seaborne orders placed in Stockholm, the Bolsheviks resorted to ever-more-desperate measures to secure such supplies overland. Without the advantage of diplomatic couriers the Germans had granted at Brest-Litovsk, Moscow now had to rely on shady middlemen, the kind of smugglers and petty profiteers the Bolsheviks denounced in their own propaganda. With the possession of money inside Soviet Russia now illegal under the draconian system of War Communism, this was a dangerous game for would-be agents to play. Even before they reached the military demarcation lines, Bolshevik buyers carrying large sums of cash, such as the unfortunate Sergei Levshin, were sometimes arrested and tortured by suspicious Cheka agents.[25]

Here was a central paradox of Communism. By declaring buying and selling illegal—except when it was done by the government—the Bolsheviks in effect made their own contractors into suspected criminals. For this reason, the Foreign Trade Commissariat compiled special lists for the Cheka of authorized Bolshevik purchasing agents who, unlike everyone else in Russia, were allowed to carry cash and pursue normal business activities.[26] The irony was well captured in the facetious title Trade Commissar Leonid Krasin bestowed on Georgi Solomon, his former Siemens-Schukert colleague, now chief foreign trade deputy: "minister of state contraband." Because so many of the goods smuggled in by Bolshevik agents were later resold at a premium on the black market, Solomon himself described his role as that of overseeing "plunder and theft" (Ich arbeitete also für Plünderer und Diebe).[27]

Despite the risks involved, the desperate economic circumstances ensured that there would be no shortage of volunteers for commercial missions offering the possibility of profit. Commissions were generous, usually between 3 and 5 percent of gross, with some agents receiving as high as 15. Agricultural implements and other civilian items would fall at the low end of the scale, whereas those goods most desperately needed by the army, like pharmaceuticals, would come with the highest fees.[28] A former agronomist named Leontii Lukhianov received one such high-end commission to buy German optical equipment and medicines.[29] Another volunteer receiving a generous commission—including 150,000 rubles just to cover expenses—was Nikolai Terletskii, a Serbian tasked in May 1919 with importing typing machines and ink cartridges for the use of government officials and Red Army commissars.[30] To similar end, an engineer was sent to Finland with 20,000 British pounds sterling to cover the purchase of "technical material and accessories" for Russia's languishing paper mills (although he was rebuffed there and placed the order instead in Stockholm).[31] Paper was of the highest priority, as an import plan prepared by the Soviet Commissariat of Foreign Trade in March 1919 emphatically confirmed, along with the chemicals needed to treat it.[32] One of the more unusual commissions was that given a German national named Henrich Zaks in June 1919, for tooth powder and dental equipment, a luxury presumably destined for high-ranking Bolsheviks and Red Army commanders.[33]

Inevitably, many of the purchasing agents dispatched from Moscow were German or German speaking. The Bolsheviks still had high hopes for Germany, despite the souring of relations following Joffe's expulsion the preceding November. Karl Radek, one of

Lenin's closest associates from wartime Switzerland, had been dispatched to Berlin in December, where he helped to organize and finance the German Communist Party (KPD). The KPD had played a significant role in the so-called Spartacist rebellion, which erupted in Berlin in January 1919, and in defending the short-lived Bavarian Soviet Republic in Munich that April, although neither movement was ever fully in control of either German Communists or Moscow agents. Like Bela Kun and his short-lived Soviet Republic in Hungary, the German Spartacists had only irregular access to Moscow funds, which were still being distributed in the Brest-Litovsk–era style of cash handouts and jewelry smuggling.[34] In all, the Communist International or Comintern, founded in March 1919, had distributed some 5.2 million rubles to foreign Communists by August, along with "diamonds, sapphires, pearls, rings, bracelets, brooches, earrings and other Tsarist treasures worth hundreds of thousands of rubles."[35] One agent alone, Borodin (Gruzenberg/Berg), was sent to Berlin in April 1919 with 500,000 Romanov rubles and another half million dollars worth of diamonds "sewn into the lining of two bulky leather suitcases," though he continued on through Germany to Switzerland (where the rubles were confiscated) and the United States.[36]

Without an official Soviet ambassador, or even a semi-official trade mission like Vorovsky's in Stockholm, the chain of command in Berlin was murky. While Radek handled liaison with would-be revolutionaries, and old Berzin associates like James Reich and Karl Moor sold off rubles and jewels to finance the underground KPD,[37] a charismatic operator named Franz Rauch emerged as the leading Bolshevik commercial agent in Berlin, although it was unclear what his mandate from Moscow really entailed. Rauch, who hailed from the German-speaking communes of the lower Volga, had been captured by the Czechoslovak legion at Orenburg in spring 1918. Freed when the Czechs withdrew in October, Rauch immediately offered his services to the Russian Communist government, in particular his fluency in German and what he claimed to be long experience in business. He impressed the Swedish consul general in Moscow with a scheme for German investment in Russia's languishing factories, to be financed through Swedish banks.[38] The idea, Rauch explained, was to throw the Allies off the scent of German involvement and, if necessary, place the whole "undertaking under Swedish direction if the Entente will make trouble" (falls die Entente Schwierigkeiten machen sollte, das Unternehmen unter schwedische Führung zu stellen).[39]

Rauch was only too happy to promote such a scheme, so long, of course, as he was at the center of it. In the first half of 1919, Rauch poured all his energy into resuscitating the lost dreams of Brest-Litovsk in German business circles, trying to break the Allied blockade almost single-handedly across the treacherous territory connecting East Prussia to Red Russia. The zigzag path Rauch traveled between Berlin and Moscow was also the route he offered for exporting German manufactures (chemicals and dyes for paper factories, equipment for textile spinning mills, glass and kitchen wares, optical equipment, and pharmaceuticals): across Prussia to the heavily fortified German frontier post at Kovno, in what is now Lithuania, via Eydtkuhnen; then veering southeast to Vilna via Koschedary; then nearly straight south to Minsk, before at last turning east for a comparatively uncomplicated rail journey to Moscow.[40] The contested territory between Lithuania and Red Latvia, noted one German businessman, was animated by a "lively smuggling trade, especially in saccharin, cocaine, and morphine."[41] Why not, Rauch proposed, use the smuggling route for legitimate trade?

Not surprisingly, Rauch reported, after returning to Berlin in early April 1919, that the Soviet government—specifically Leonid Krasin, appointed special Soviet commissar of transportation in March—was prepared to pay up to 800 million rubles for legitimate German imports, if train cars, locomotive engines, and spare parts were included in the deal.[42] As if to underscore the seriousness of Krasin's colossal offer of cash (though not, perhaps, producing quite the effect he desired), Rauch informed the German Foreign Office that the Bolsheviks had recently acquired 250 million rubles by sacking the German consulate in St. Petersburg.[43]

Rauch's overtures were initially welcomed in Germany, particularly in the stricken industrial heartland of Saxony, where the state government gave him a special pass to negotiate in Russia on behalf of local business concerns.[44] But just as the German generals had mistrusted Joffe in 1918, so too did they hesitate before allowing Rauch, a self-described Bolshevik commercial agent, to cross into

Red Russian territory with nine truckloads worth of German goods when he reached Kovno on 26 April 1919. It would be "crazy" (sinnlos), argued the German commander in a dispatch sent to Berlin regarding Rauch, "to spend millions on the struggle against Bolshevism [in Germany] and at the same time to support it at its source."[45] In a sharp turnabout from its attitude in the Brest-Litovsk era, the German Foreign Office agreed, replying that Rauch's convoy should "not be allowed to proceed in any circumstances."[46] Feeling betrayed based on what was probably a misreading of German policy towards Russia in 1919, Rauch later sued the Foreign Office for restitution and lost.[47]

Rauch was not the only ambitious middleman to be disappointed by Germany's apparent discovery in 1919 of anti-Bolshevik principles. Ludwig Baehr had concocted a similarly ambitious deal with Moscow, specifically tailored to Soviet propaganda needs. He envisioned supplying the Bolsheviks with "25 to 50 million rubles" worth of Russian-language school textbooks, printed in Germany to Soviet specifications, along with German-made printing presses and film stock. The materials were to be shipped in successive installments via the Russian-German demarcation line in Lithuania, against Bolshevik deposits in a consortium of Danish banks.[48] After months of work putting the deal together, Baehr was informed by the German Foreign Office in early July 1919 that he would not be allowed to proceed until the resumption of normal trading relations with Russia.[49] A similar fate awaited Isaak "the engineer" Steinberg, who surfaced again in Berlin in April 1919, seeking to reactivate Joffe's sequestered funds from the Mendelssohn account to finance a Soviet order for one million German-made scythes, at 30 marks each. Although Steinberg was allowed to make the rounds, visiting bankers at Mendelssohn, Disconto-Gesellschaft, and Deutsche Bank, the German Foreign Office refused to authorize his deal.[50]

So long as the Allies deliberated Germany's fate at Versailles, Berlin remained wary of antagonizing the Entente by permitting German firms to trade openly with the Bolsheviks. A Foreign Office position paper drafted in April 1919 spelled out the dangers inherent in trusting Bolshevik agents and negotiators and warned German diplomats and businessmen that Moscow might be using them cynically, as a means of manipulating the Entente powers into removing the blockade, for fear Western capital would be cut out of Russia entirely.[51]

Quietly, however, negotiations with Bolshevik buyers were allowed to proceed inside Germany, so long as they took place out of view of the Allies. A Dresden firm finalized a deal in March 1919 to supply the Bolsheviks with 30,000 kilograms of cigarettes, a quantity small enough, it was hoped, to stay under Entente radar.[52] Another deal, concluded soon after Brest-Litovsk with the pharmaceutical firm of Finkel and Oksner for eyeglasses, film stock, and various medicines, to be paid in tsarist and Kerensky rubles, had been languishing since the collapse of the German armies in the east had rendered transport unworkable, although the German government was still trying to make it work.[53] It was renewed, in theory, by a new declaration of legal intent signed by the main Moscow trade agencies in May 1919, though it was still unclear how the goods would ever reach Moscow.[54]

After 9 July 1919, when the Versailles Treaty, with its notoriously punitive measures against Germany, was ratified by the Reichstag, it must have seemed to Berlin that little was left to lose by opening up trade with Soviet Russia. In the last week of July, Dr. Julius Brendel, an engineer who had represented Krupp in German-occupied Ukraine between spring 1918 and January 1919, requested permission to lead a new trade mission to Moscow on behalf of Krupp, along with Mannesmann, a consortium of steel firms from Dusseldorf, and the Huckauf and Bulle machine works of Altona.[55] His request was granted.[56] In August, two representatives of the agricultural machinery firm Ackerbau-Gesellschaft m.b.H were authorized to make a sales pitch to the Bolsheviks in Petrograd, by way of Stockholm, where they would arrange financing (though in mid-September they gave up the quest after reaching Helsingfors, possibly fearing to brave the Allied Baltic screen).[57]

Of much greater lasting importance was the arrival in Berlin, on 13 August 1919, of the Russian professor and railway engineer Georgi Lomonosov.[58] As the Germans knew better than the Allies, Russia's rail network was in pitiful shape in 1919, with nowhere near enough functioning locomotives and rolling stock to handle the Red Army's deployment needs, let alone commercial and civilian transport. The cities were literally starving, as fuel and foodstuffs could not be delivered in bulk: the population of St. Petersburg actually dropped from 2.5 million to 500,000 by the end of 1919. Krasin, as Rauch's report to the German Foreign Office indicated, was willing to pay almost any price to rescue Russia's ailing railway sector. A German intelligence officer reporting from Moscow in June 1919 claimed that Krasin was now "more powerful than Lenin," regarded by many Bolsheviks as the only man who could rescue Red Russia by restoring its transportation infrastructure.[59] Lomonosov, an intimate of Krasin, had been Kerensky's rail consultant before joining the Bolsheviks in 1918. He was considered one of the leading experts on the technical requirements of Russia's train lines (which employed, then as now, a much wider grade than those in Europe). Lomonosov had spent much of the preceding winter visiting bankers and lawyers on Wall Street, seeking (but failing) to arrange credit for Soviet rail purchases in America.[60] In June and July 1919, Lomonosov was in Stockholm, where, unmolested by the Swedish government, he kept up a busy wireless communication with Krasin in Moscow as outlines of a major rail deal began taking shape. The German government was more suspicious but allowed Lomonosov to move freely around Berlin.[61]

Although the fine print, especially the legal complications involving trade with a Bolshevik regime still not recognized by international law, would be sketched in only later, the broad outlines of the budding Krasin-Lomonosov locomotive deal were already in place in 1919. Rail engines, train cars, and spare parts would be manufactured in both Germany and Sweden, with Swedish banks arranging the financing, that is to say, processing Russian gold. The ultimate objective was to procure "one thousand new locomotive engines and all the railway material appertaining to them," altogether "an order to the amount of twenty to twenty-five million pounds sterling, such as had not been placed on the market for years." Such an order alone would amount to $125 million in gold, or nearly half of the Bolshevik-captured portions of the imperial Russian gold reserve (although Bolshevik reserves would soon be augmented by the $210 million worth of gold ingots captured after Kolchak's surrender at Irkutsk in February 1920). With the British Baltic blockade still active, making both the export of the Russian gold and the import of the locomotives impossible, it was too soon to sign contracts. But Lomonosov left no one involved in the rail industry in either Stockholm or Berlin in doubt that the Bolsheviks wanted their business.[62]

Just as the boom in ruble transactions in October 1918 had alerted the Entente powers that something was afoot in Stockholm, so the preliminary German-Swedish-Soviet railway negotiations of summer 1919 set alarm bells ringing in London, Paris, and Washington. The Allies had been on high alert for suspicious shipments of Russian currency since April, when Lenin's old Zurich associate Fritz Platten had been arrested at the Finnish border, en route to Stockholm, carrying no less than 100 million rubles in his personal luggage.[63] Naturally, the Allies assumed this huge pile of cash was intended to finance "Bolshevik revolutions" in Western countries.[64] So, too, did they assume that cascading rumors of cash-laden Soviet couriers heading for Sweden and Germany in summer 1919, carrying not only rubles but large sums of French francs, German marks, and British pounds presumed to be counterfeit, heralded another revolutionary offensive in the West, cooked up by the old Germano-Bolshevik nexus. Lists of suspected German and Bolshevik agents in Stockholm were duly prepared; wire traffic from Berlin to Petrograd was daily monitored; and report after report was filed warning of "enormous sums of money" leaving Petrograd for points unknown. Most ominously, the name of Olof Aschberg began surfacing again as the mastermind of illicit Bolshevik money trafficking. With Aschberg's help in laundering rubles, a French agent reported, the Bolsheviks could now send checks directly to Western countries, using the accounts of individuals who might "not even be aware of the consequences of their cooperation."[65]

As they had in 1918, most Allied (and Swiss) officials assumed Bolshevik money smuggled across the Russian frontier in summer 1919 was destined to fund subversion in their own countries. Once more they were barking up the wrong tree. The weight of the available evidence suggests that most rubles sent to Stockholm were meant to stay there as security against imports. As we saw above, cash and jewels distributed to Comintern member parties totaled, at most, some 6 million rubles in 1919; this was dwarfed by ruble deposits and sales made by Vorovsky's agents in Stockholm for commercial purposes, which were already in the hundreds of millions by the end of 1918. Fritz Platten's suspicious 100 million was almost certainly dispatched with commercial intent: the next time Platten was entrusted to cross the Russian frontier with a comparable sum (20 million in gold ruble coin), he brought with him a carefully prepared license, signed by Lenin himself, which authorized him to use the money to open savings and checking accounts abroad to finance the purchase, for Soviet Russia, of "all manner of goods, materials, and moveable property."[66]

What is remarkable about such episodes is that the Bolsheviks employed couriers of such widely varying ranks to smuggle money. Unaccredited volunteer middlemen might be entrusted with as little as a few tens of thousands, whereas Old Bolsheviks might carry thick suitcases stuffed full with 500-ruble and 250-ruble tsarist notes: Sheinman with 17 million worth, Gukovsky with 50, and Platten 100 million. It was this sort of volume, naturally, that attracted Allied attention.[67] The Bolsheviks may even have courted this attention, for example, by leaking the summer 1919 report that Aschberg's banking expertise now enabled them to send money wherever they wished. Aside from terrifying Entente intelligence officials, spreading such rumors could also enhance Moscow's reputation for liquidity with European business interests. Shrewd Soviet negotiators such as Krasin, as we saw in the Rauch affair, repeatedly talked up Bolshevik cash reserves to impress possible suppliers.

For the moment, though, it was still mostly talk. At times in 1919 the Bolsheviks themselves turned down eager suppliers, knowing that there was no way to transport goods from central Europe across the German lines at Kovno. One complex deal, negotiated in spring and summer 1919 by the agronomist Lukhianov in Breslau, would have seen the German firm Zaudig supply drills, mowers, and threshing machines, paid for in Stockholm and dispatched from a German Baltic port on "American, or neutral ships to Petrograd." Telegrams were sent from Budapest and Breslau to Frederick Ström in Stockholm (like Hellberg, Ström was a Swedish sympathizer hired by the Bolsheviks to deflect scrutiny from Vorovsky) and to Krasin in Moscow. Krasin expressed lively interest in the deal but warned Lukhianov and the Zaudig negotiators in July that he would not send money through Stockholm "unless your side can give a real guarantee" as to "where the goods are and what route is envisioned for sending them to us." By autumn, it had become clear that no such guarantee was in the offing. In November 1919, Krasin killed the deal definitively.[68]

The Bolsheviks' strategic position was still precarious. Although Kolchak's spring offensive across the Urals had been emphatically repulsed by the forces of future Red field marshal Mikhail Tukhachevsky, Denikin's Volunteer Army, reinforced by the Don Cossacks and Wrangel's Caucasian Army, was methodically advancing from the south, taking Tsaritsyn in July and then advancing on a broad front through the Ukraine. On 12 September, Denikin ordered all his armies, "from the Volga to the Romanian border," on the offensive, with Moscow the objective. The "Southern Army," writes Richard Pipes, "went from victory to victory, piercing the defense perimeter set up by the enemy." Denikin's forces rapidly took Kiev, Kursk, and Voronezh; on 13–14 October they conquered Orel, only 250 miles from Moscow and less than half that distance from Tula and its munitions factories. Almost simultaneously, on 11 October, Yudenich's North-Western Army began its second push for Petrograd, reaching the old tsarist Summer Palace at Tsarskoe Selo on the sixteenth and the outer suburbs of the city four days later. In support of Yudenich, the British navy shelled Kronstadt and sank two Soviet battleships. With both Petrograd, the birthplace of the revolution, and Moscow, Lenin's capital, under threat, it was a bleak moment for the Bolsheviks.

The Whites, however, had stretched out their offensives too thin. Hoping to conquer Russia's capitals with a single, powerful thrust which might induce panic among the Bolsheviks' supporters, neither Denikin nor Yudenich had brought up adequate reserves. Trotsky himself famously rallied the Red defenders of Petrograd while mounted on horseback, pushing Yudenich back toward Estonia. In the south, the Second and Third Latvian Brigades performed their last great service to Bolshevism, leading an assault on Denikin's left (western) flank, which pitched White forces into retreat, the Latvians losing in the battle more than half their officers. While retreating, Denikin's Volunteer Army was further menaced by the Red Cavalry Corps commanded by Semen Budenny. By November, the Red advance had reached Kursk, with Denikin in headlong retreat.

It was at this stage, on 8 November 1919, that Lloyd George gave one of his most famous speeches at the Lord Mayor's banquet at

London Guildhall. Taking Churchill, the other cabinet members, the other Entente powers, and Soviet officials entirely by surprise—he had given no prior indication of an imminent change in Britain's Russia policy—Lloyd George announced that Britain was giving up the game. "Russia is a quicksand," he intoned darkly, which had swallowed up foreign armies before. The time had come to admit that Britain could not "afford to continue so costly an intervention in an interminable civil war." The coming winter months, Lloyd George hoped, would give time "for all sections [in Russia] to reflect and to reconsider the situation." The effect of this speech on White morale, a British journalist accompanying Denikin's army later wrote, "was electrical." White volunteers who had believed they were fighting the last battles of the world war, with all-powerful Great Britain as an ally, "suddenly realized with horror that England considered the War as over and the conflict in Russia as merely a civil conflict." Within days, "the whole atmosphere in South Russia was changed. . . . Mr George's opinion that the Volunteer cause was doomed helped to make this doom almost certain."[69]

In December 1919, Entente journalists recorded tearful scenes at Novorossiisk on the Black Sea, as huge crowds of White Russian soldiers and civilian émigrés tried to evacuate on the last British and French ships leaving the port, fearing the worst if they were captured by the vengeful Red Army. Hundreds were killed, with tens of thousands more dispatched all winter to Bolshevik concentration camps, which now dotted southern Russia and Ukraine. Many had foreseen just such a catastrophe in the event of an Allied withdrawal. One U.S. officer had written presciently, back in June, that a pullout would amount to "deserting good friends to the danger of starvation and a hideous orgy of rape and massacre by the Bolsheviks."[70] The White armies were not yet broken: the rump forces of the Volunteer Army would regroup under a new command in spring 1920 farther west, in the Crimea. But without a renewed commitment by the British, it was clear that Denikin's day was done.

Farther north, the retreat of Yudenich's forces from the gates of Petrograd toward Estonia, though attracting much less media attention than the collapse of Denikin's army in the south, may have been the real death blow for White hopes. Estonia's own army, commanded by General Johan Laidoner, had broken with Yudenich in

June 1919, refusing to supply him during his fall offensive. So long as Yudenich had seemed poised to take Petrograd, British pressure had assured that the Estonian government hesitated before making a separate peace with the Bolsheviks, despite repeated overtures from Moscow in August and September. With Yudenich's army now in disarray, and Lloyd George's public abdication of the anti-Bolshevik cause, Reval was ready to sue for peace.[71]

On 31 December 1919, Estonia accepted an armistice with Soviet Russia. Peace talks begin immediately in Tartu (Dorpat), a university town Estonians fondly referred to as the "Baltic Heidelberg," with Krasin heading up the Bolshevik delegation. The Tartu Treaty, signed on 2 February 1920, though not generally well known outside Estonia, was of great historic significance for Communism: it represented the first official recognition of Soviet Russia by a sovereign European state since Brest-Litovsk. The diplomatic bag would soon be back in force. As if to highlight the importance of the Estonian relationship, Moscow's first ambassador posted to Reval was Maxim Litvinov, the deputy commissar for foreign affairs and future Soviet foreign minister. Perhaps most significantly, Tartu secured for the Bolsheviks port access to the Baltic which they would never surrender.[72]

It was no accident that Krasin, the Soviet transportation commissar and leading trade negotiator, was the man Moscow sent to Estonia in December 1919. Nor was it a coincidence that Krasin was accompanied by his leading goods-smuggling expert, Georgi Solomon, and the commissar of finance, Isidor Gukovsky.[73] The provisions of the Tartu Treaty negotiated by Krasin, Gukovsky, and Solomon went well beyond mutual recognition, exchange of ambassadors, and use of the diplomatic bag. At Krasin's insistence, Estonia guaranteed unlimited Russian use of its rail network for commercial freight and even created "special zones" in Estonia ports, use of which would be set aside exclusively for the Bolsheviks.[74]

The British were already loosening the Baltic blockade. By October 1919, only ships carrying obvious military stores were still being denied access to Russian ports, and on 20 November the British cabinet decided not to renew the blockade in even that form after the winter ice melted. As Lloyd George himself laid out the historic new policy in typically equivocal language to the House of Commons, "It is not proposed that the British Fleet should undertake the patrol of the Baltic in the spring."[75] Wired to the world, this declaration was music to Moscow's ears—and to interested parties in Stockholm.*[76]

Although legal obstacles remained, especially regarding the sale of looted Russian imperial gold in the financial markets of London, Paris, Amsterdam, and New York, a small window to the Baltic Sea was just what the Bolsheviks needed to clear the backlog of Swedish orders going back to April 1918. The Krasin-Lomonosov locomotive deal was now a realistic possibility. For the first time in its short history, Soviet Russia could import war matériel without harassment by either Germany or the Entente. But with an economy producing nothing worthy of export, how would Moscow pay?

It was to answer this question that the Bolsheviks established the Russian State Treasury for the Preservation of Valuables, or Gokhran, on 3 February 1920, under Nikolai Krestinsky. The Gokhran's expressly stated purpose was to centralize storage and valuation of loot coming into Moscow from regions conquered (and reconquered) by the Red Army.[77] The sense of urgency was palpable. Shortly before departing abroad to place import orders, Krasin ordered Petrograd employees of the Foreign Trade Commissariat to "take immediate measures toward the registration and valuation" of "all reserves of materials, wares, goods, and valuable antiques in the vicinity of the northern district," particularly "articles made of gold, silver, and platinum, as well as precious stones and pearls." All valuations were to be made in accordance with the "resolution of Gokhran."[78] With the colossal wealth of Imperial Russia piling up in the Gokhran vaults, two years of pent-up demand for war matériel seeking release, and the Baltic finally open for trade, Stockholm was about to see a gold-laundering boom the likes of which the world had never witnessed. The Bolsheviks were in business.

---

*Ironically, Lloyd George's abandonment of the Baltic blockade was announced just one month after the Entente powers had issued an angry communiqué demanding that it be enforced by the Scandinavian neutrals. In Stockholm, a major protest demonstration had been organized on 15 October 1919 *against* enforcement of the very blockade Lloyd George was about to jettison. Little did the protesters know their fondest wishes were about to be granted by the maverick British prime minister.

7   Stockholm

They bought up Russian gold, set another stamp on the ingots and melted down the coins. The Royal Mint worked at top pressure. Afterwards the gold with the Swedish stamp could be sold at a fantastic profit.

— OLOF ASCHBERG

AS SPRING DAWNED in 1920, the Bolsheviks' overall strategic position seemed more secure than at any point since the October Revolution. The armies of Denikin and Yudenich had disintegrated, removing the White threat to Moscow and Petrograd. Kolchak, along with more than $200 million worth of imperial gold ingots from the Kazan reserve, had been turned over to Bolshevik custody by the departing Czechoslovak legion in Irkutsk.[1] Kolchak was shot the night of 6–7 February 1920, his body pushed under the ice of a river. With the British giving up the fight and the Tartu peace with Estonia quieting the crucial Baltic region and opening up its ports, the Bolsheviks now reigned supreme in Russia, with no White or foreign armies directly threatening to depose them.

The human and material price the Bolsheviks had paid for these gains was enormous. Red Army casualties were rapidly approaching one million, with millions more having deserted due to the Bolsheviks' inability to adequately feed and clothe their soldiers. The rural economy was in disarray, with armed "food detachments" sowing chaos as they tried, and often failed, to requisition foodstuffs. Pogroms had devastated the Jewish population in the old Pale of Settlement. As Richard Pipes described the "vicious circle": "Jews were persecuted for being pro-Communist, which had the effect of turning them pro-Communist for the sake of survival; this shift of allegiance served to justify further persecution."[2]

In the cities, civilized life was a memory. By early 1920, the prewar population of Petrograd had been reduced by four-fifths, with the emaciated survivors stumbling around in a perpetual half-stupor, with barely the energy to stand in line at government rationing centers for bread, which sold on the black market at the astronomical price of 1,000 rubles per kilo. Moscow was little better off. Both cities had nearly run out of fuel, with entire buildings being torn down for wood. Water pipes had cracked in the cold. The streets were dark and menacing at night in the absence of functioning streetlamps. Trams and trolleys had long ago stopped running. Colonel Edward Ryan, the American Red Cross commissioner for North Russia and the Baltic states, crossed Bolshevik lines from Estonia without official authorization in March 1920 to investigate the humanitarian situation. He left behind a vivid description of the horror which had overtaken Russia's once-great capital cities: "Both Moscow and Petrograd are indescribably filthy in outward appearance. . . . [I] was told the streets had not been cleaned for more than three years. . . . The dirt and rubbish is in all places at least ankle deep and in most places it is up to one's knees, and there are many places where it is as high as one's head. In Moscow a few women from time to time endeavor to clear up a little space by throwing and sweeping the dirt to the sides of the street so as to permit traffice [sic] to move in a narrow channel. There has obviously been no attempt to haul anything away."[3]

Unable to bathe or dispose of trash properly, city dwellers were set upon by rats, cockroaches, mosquitoes, and other vermin. In such conditions, epidemic disease was rampant. Those suffering from the outbreak of the flu, cholera, typhus, or dysentery found little solace in the hospitals because the doctors and nurses were dying, too. Colonel Ryan, on an impromptu visit to a facility in one of the wealthier neighborhoods of central Moscow, learned that "during the preceding three months seventy-five percent of the personnel of this hospital had died." The hospital did have sheets and mattresses, but surgeries were rarely performed because there were "very few surgical instruments and few anesthetics." Ryan was not allowed to visit hospitals in poorer districts, which presumably were even worse off. So many people were dying in Petrograd that "morgues and cemeteries could not cope, and corpses lay around for months waiting to be buried."[4]

As long as foreign-supplied armies had been perched on Russian soil, the Bolsheviks had a ready scapegoat for such privations. The departure of Denikin, Kolchak, Yudenich and the British navy was, therefore, a moment of reckoning for Bolshevism. If social and economic conditions did not soon improve, it would become clear that it was not the blockade and White armies but the policies of War Communism that had reduced the Russian people to nearly prehistoric conditions of scavenging and widespread starvation. One way the Bolsheviks might have alleviated the urban food crisis, if not the fuel shortages, was by freeing grain prices and re-legalizing the use of gold coin, to convince peasants they had more to gain from supplying the urban population than yet more worthless paper rubles. But in his moment of triumph over the White armies, Lenin was not about to abandon his dream of a world in which gold "would only be used for building toilets" or to cede control of agriculture.[5]

It was not hard for the Bolsheviks to find a catchall explanation for the sorry state of the economy: the railroads. As Krasin wrote to his wife Lubov (herself comfortably settled in Stockholm) in 1919: "Distribution is very difficult with the railways in such a state of disorder. . . . Everything has to be taken for the Army, metals, leather, cloth, etc. Any number of factories are idle; the Volga fleet is paralysed for lack of fuel."[6] An internal memorandum prepared by the Commissariat of Economics in early 1920 estimated that the production of locomotives by Russian factories had dropped to 40 in 1919, against 800 to 1,000 annually prior to 1917. The production of new engines was expected to cease entirely by August 1920. Nor could more than 15 percent of defunct engines be repaired.[7] Functioning train cars, Georgi Solomon later recalled, "had become an archaeological curiosity" (Droschken waren eine archäologische Seltenheit geworden).[8]

It was a comforting illusion to believe that the breakdown of the railways explained away the economic catastrophe of War Communism, but one made more convincing by the circumstantial evidence.

Russia's economy was entirely dependent on its rail infrastructure, which itself relied on a steady stream of imports to function, ergo the blockade was at the root of the problem. It was not as if Krasin and his colleagues had not been *trying* to replenish Russia's rolling stock. As we have seen, Soviet Russia's leading rail consultant, Georgi Lomonosov, had made the rounds in New York, Stockholm, and Berlin, and Krasin had himself proposed an 800-million ruble deal to Franz Rauch in summer 1919.

By 1920, it was an open secret in European business circles that a major Soviet rail deal was brewing. Krasin and Deputy Foreign Secretary Maxim Litvinov did everything possible to publicize Bolshevik trade negotiations. Before he was accredited to Estonia as Soviet ambassador, Litvinov was sent to Copenhagen in late January to handle negotiations with Entente representatives over the exchange of prisoners of war and the lifting of the blockade of Soviet Russia, which had not yet been made official. To demonstrate that Soviet commercial ambitions were serious, Litvinov met with the Allies' banker bête noire Olof Aschberg and a Swedish parliamentary deputy and businessman named Sten Stendahl, signing a tentative trade agreement on 4 February 1920. Although it never came into legal force, Litvinov's would-be Swedish-Soviet trade accord, signed just two days after the Tartu Treaty with Estonia, put the Allies on notice that Moscow's isolation was rapidly eroding.[9]

Krasin, unlike Litvinov a man with real business experience, was able to ratchet up the pressure on the Allies even more. Splitting time between the capitals of neutral Sweden and Denmark in March and April 1920, Krasin took on competing bids on a possible railway blockbuster, carrying out his business in as public a manner as possible. In Stockholm, Krasin invited representatives from fourteen Scandinavian firms to rail negotiations he conducted in April with A. B. Nydquist and Holm Company.[10] In Copenhagen, Krasin, on behalf of the Central Board of Russian Cooperative Organizations (Tsentrosoiuz), which he was using as a front for diplomatic negotiations under the pretense it was independent of the Soviet government, negotiated two very public deals. The first, a statement of intent Krasin signed on 23 April 1920 with a Danish consortium, would create a clearinghouse "to facilitate import-export operations" between Copenhagen and Moscow. The financial details were to be worked out later, but it was fairly clear to Entente observers of these negotiations that Krasin's first rail import deals would be financed by Soviet gold deposits in Copenhagen.[11]

Krasin's timing was fortuitous. At the very moment he was tempting Allied consuls by publicly dallying with locomotive firms in Copenhagen, Lloyd George was at the Supreme Allied Council at the Italian resort of San Remo (18–26 April 1920), trying to cajole the other Entente powers into opening trade discussions with Soviet Russia. Lloyd George himself was already convinced of the crucial importance of opening up the Russian market, believing that "trade . . . will bring an end to the ferocity, the rapine, and the crudities of Bolshevism surer than any other method."[12] With a characteristic mixture of tactical shrewdness and strategic blindness, Lloyd George laid out his case at San Remo by contrasting Litvinov, an unwholesome "political agitator" who "knew nothing of trade" and should thus be shunned in all Allied capitals, with the supposedly trustworthy Krasin, who was "a good businessman and might be useful." Won over by Lloyd George's persistent arguments, the French and Italian delegates agreed to wire Krasin an invitation to bring his "Russian Trade Delegation" to London "with a view to the immediate restarting of trade relations between Russia and other countries," so long as Litvinov would not be included.[13]

The dissembling inherent in Lloyd George's new Russia policy played right into Krasin's hands. Lloyd George knew perfectly well that Krasin and the Tsentrosoiuz delegation accompanying him abroad were just fronts for the Soviet government: he admitted as much when asked by his friend Lord Riddell on 6 March 1920. But publicly and in the House of Commons, Lloyd George maintained the fiction that Krasin's trade team was independent of the Bolshevik regime.* Because Lloyd George was still being coy about announcing an official end to the Baltic blockade, Krasin could present the Allies' 26 April 1920 telegram inviting him to London to corporate negotiators in Stockholm as evidence that London would not interfere in their business with the Bolsheviks.[14]

*Asked by Lord Riddell whether the members of Krasin's Tsentrosoiuz delegation were "representatives of the co-operative societies or the Bolshevist Government," Lloyd George replied, "The Soviet, undoubtedly." Nine days later, Lloyd George, asked the same thing while addressing the House of Commons, gave the opposite answer.

Lloyd George's pro-Soviet démarche came just in time for the fortunes of Communism. The very day his telegram was dispatched to Krasin, ten Polish divisions, led by Marshal Józef Pilsudski, launched an offensive across Soviet lines into the Ukraine. The Poles reached Kiev on 7 May. Armed with the San Remo invitation from Lloyd George, which seemed to ensure that Soviet gold would not be sequestered by Allied creditors, Krasin signed a historic deal in Stockholm on 15 May 1920 with Gunnar Anderson of the Nydquist and Holm consortium. The Bolsheviks would send 25 million crowns worth of gold bullion (about 8,000 kilos) to Stockholm, as security—guaranteed by the Swedish government—against 100 million in strategic imports, mostly of rail engines and rolling stock. Just two days later, Krasin's Tsentrosoiuz advance team arrived at London's First Avenue Hotel, where the British government provided them with access to wireless and telegraph for their communications with Copenhagen and Stockholm, "in cipher if necessary."[15]

The reversal in British policy was nearly complete. On the same day Krasin was exploiting his invitation to London to conclude his historic gold-for-locomotives deal in Stockholm, English stevedores at the East India docks refused to load a consignment of field guns and ammunition onto the *Jolly George* before it debarked for Danzig. At a union meeting three days later in Plymouth, Ernest Bevin called on the entire Labour movement in Great Britain to boycott any manufacture or transport of "munitions for purposes which outrage our sense of justice"—such as to the Polish army fighting Soviet Russia. Bevin was pushing against an empty door: the *Jolly George* arms consignment was in fact nearly the last in a series of shipments Britain had promised to the Poles back in October 1919. Under heavy pressure from the Labour opposition and believing the public to be weary of the failed intervention in Soviet Russia, Lloyd George's cabinet had no plans to send more. "No assistance," Conservative Party leader and cabinet spokesman Andrew Bonar Law assured the Commons on 17 May 1920, "has been or is being given to the Polish Government."[16]

Had he wanted to, Lloyd George could have compensated for his abandonment of the Poles by shunting Krasin aside and ordering the British navy to block Soviet gold and Swedish arms shipments across the Baltic. Throughout 1920, a British naval squadron remained poised offshore at Helsingfors. But, despite a constant barrage of complaints from conservative cabinet colleagues and the French, Lloyd George did no such thing.

By the time Krasin arrived in London for his audience with Lloyd George, the Nydquist and Holm deal had set off a gold-trading boom across the Baltic. By early June 1920, the Bolsheviks had transported 80 million Swedish crowns worth of captured imperial Russian gold ingots via the Estonian railways to Reval, or nearly 30 metric tons. So colossal was the initial influx that the vaults (coffre-forts) of the Estonian national bank, formerly the fairly insubstantial Reval branch of the Russian Imperial State Bank, "were no longer sufficient to house such a quantity of metal."[17] Fortunately for the structural integrity of Estonia's bank vaults, most Bolshevik gold was not long for Reval, destined to be shipped as soon as possible to Copenhagen and Stockholm.

The first Nydquist and Holm installment, representing 17 million crowns of gold ingots, arrived in Stockholm on 1 June 1920. The French ambassador in Stockholm, Louis Delavaud, launched a vigorous protest, warning Swedish Foreign Minister Baron Erik de Palmstierna that France regarded Russia's gold reserves as the "guarantee of the external creditors of this country" and that "this gold would be legally subject to seizure" in Western countries if reexported from Sweden.[18] Without British backing, however—and with Krasin, the author of the Nydquist and Holm deal, being received with honor just then on Downing Street—the French protest predictably fell on deaf ears. Palmstierna, in an interview with the *Times of London,* justified Swedish purchases of Bolshevik gold by citing Lloyd George's lifting of the Baltic blockade the previous winter and his San Remo resolution of 26 April, in which, in Palmstierna's somewhat exaggerated interpretation, the Entente powers had "authorized and recommended the resumption of commercial relations with Russia" (où les puissances ont autorisé et conseillé la reprise des relations commerciales avec la RUSSIE). With Lloyd George having himself opened trade relations with Soviet representatives like Krasin, Palmstierna concluded, the Swedish government could hardly "prevent the import of gold by Tsentrosoiuz into Sweden in payment for its purchases in this country."[19] Sweden's socialist prime minister, Hjalmar Branting, even chided the French for "refusing to participate" in the London negotiations.[20] Krasin had driven a wedge through the heart of the Entente.

The triumphant Nydquist and Holm deal also sealed Krasin's position back in Moscow. Before the Stockholm contract was finalized and he was received by Lloyd George in London, Krasin had received an urgent telegram from the Kremlin warning him that he must "economize gold with all [his] power" and sign trade agreements only if they had "already been approved by the Politburo" (predvaritel'no shli na utverzhdenie Politburo).[21] (We can thus dispense with Lloyd George's disingenuous claim that Krasin was operating independently of the Bolsheviks.) By mid-June, with gold-securitized imports entering Soviet Russia through Reval, Krasin received a very different sort of message from Lenin, Trotsky, and Gokhran director Nikolai Krestinsky, which authorized him to negotiate purchases up to the amount of 300 million gold rubles ($150 million worth, or the equivalent of some $15 billion today) "without arranging advance approval from Moscow" (T. Krasin imeet pravo ne zaprashivaia predvaritel'nogo soglasiia Moskvy).[22] Moscow's miracle man now had virtual carte blanche to sell off Bolshevik gold.

There was no shortage of buyers. Years of speculation about the fate of Russia's reserves ensured that bankers from throughout the Western world would line up to stake their claim. Shrewd buyers went directly to Reval to snatch up "illegal" looted imperial Russian gold ingots at bargain prices before Sweden's mints had recast them. Overseeing such sales from the Bolshevik end were the former Finance Minister Isidor Gukovsky and Georgi Solomon, who together headed a standing "Soviet Trade Mission" in Reval. Gukovsky, the money man, set up shop in the Hotel Petersburg, whose rooms—all of them—were rented at cut-rates to the Bolsheviks by the Estonian government, which itself had commandeered the facility during the war with Soviet Russia in 1919. Solomon, the procurement expert, was installed in the Hotel Goldener Löwe to meet with suppliers. The man accredited as "financial representative" of the Soviet Mission was, unsurprisingly, Olof Aschberg—an old friend of Solomon from the latter's Stockholm days at Siemens-Schuckert.[23] The principal legal counsel, in charge of drafting contracts between bankers, suppliers, and middlemen, was Wilhelm Hellberg, Vorovsky's old lawyer from the blockade days in Stockholm, who was now viewed by the Quai d'Orsay, like Aschberg, as one of the most formidable opponents in preventing the French from being able to sequester Soviet gold.[24]

Reval rapidly took on a Wild West atmosphere, becoming a kind of Bolshevik boomtown on the Baltic. The Hotel Petersburg had been entirely Bolshevized. Because Gukovsky's team did most of its business right in their hotel rooms, leaving top secret papers lying around, the hotel's cleaning staff was not allowed to keep house. The rooms were therefore a mess, with "dirty laundry, articles of clothing thrown all over the place, files and invoices." Solomon, courted by would-be arms suppliers at the Goldener Löwe, felt himself besieged by "petty international con men" (kleine internationale Schieber).[25] Boomtime Reval, Olof Aschberg recalled with a certain fondness, was "chock-full of people from the whole world who wanted to do business with the Russians. They were mostly jobbers and adventurers, but there were also representatives of reputable old firms"—like J. P. Morgan's Guaranty Trust Company of Wall Street, and Comptoir Lyon Allemand, a French house. Max May bought gold directly from Aschberg for Guaranty Trust; a Monsieur Rivière bought gold, precious stones, and diamonds for Lyon Allemand. Remarkably, Bolshevik precious metals trading was conducted with the connivance of General Johan Laidoner, the hero of Estonia's war of independence against Soviet Russia, who was now chairman of Harju Bank.

The transactions worked like this. Prospective buyers would place orders for Soviet gold through Aschberg's bank, or another Bolshevik-friendly house like G. Scheel and Company. Gukovsky would then turn over Soviet gold (or other precious metals) to Aschberg or another middleman, who, for a fee, would transport the metals across the Baltic, often accompanying the shipments in person. Aschberg usually took to sea on the Estonian steamer *Kalewipoeg*, carrying, on one typical voyage, "a consignment of gold representing many millions of kroner." In Stockholm, the gold was then melted down, with the old tsarist Russian insignia replaced by a Swedish one. "The Royal Mint," Aschberg recalled, "worked at top pressure." "Afterwards," he explained, "the gold with the Swedish stamp could be sold at a large profit, especially to USA." Everyone involved in these transactions was happy—not least Solomon and the procurement end of the Soviet Mission, which used the credits obtained through Aschberg's bank to pay for strategic import orders. [26]

Once the gold-laundering boom was underway, it seemed there was no limit to what the Bolsheviks could buy abroad. The railway deal grew bigger and bigger in 1920, as more Swedish, and then German, firms signed on. Krasin ultimately ordered more than $200 million worth of engines, rolling stock, and spare parts for renovating Russia's rail infrastructure, all securitized by gold deposits in Stockholm: a similar deal today would be worth some $20 billion. By 1921, sixty-nine factories in Sweden alone were working to fulfill the railway order, which had grown in size to 1,700 locomotives and all accessories pertaining to them.[27]

Locomotives, however, took a long time to manufacture and even longer to deliver. By the end of 1921, only 135 had reached Petrograd.[28] What the Red Army needed most in summer 1920, as the Poles pressed east and peasant rebellions began erupting in the Bolsheviks' rear, were basic supplies for infantry, especially clothing, guns, artillery, shell, small-arms rounds, and medicines. Of these, medicine was easiest to procure in bulk, due to the small volumes involved and because such imports were least likely to raise the hackles of the Western powers. Krasin ordered a good deal of what the Red Army needed right in London in July 1920, through the English pharmaceutical firm Ralph L. Fuller and Company: aspirin, camphor quinine, iodine, menthol, potassium bromide and iodide, zinc oxide, castor oil, cocoa butter, olive oil, and petroleum jelly. The initial order, worth some 30,000 pounds sterling, was to be paid "in gold ingots against documents in Reval."[29]

Later in July, the Soviet Trade Mission in Stockholm signed an even bigger drug deal with Roche. The Basel-based Swiss pharmaceutical firm would supply the Bolsheviks with aspirin, santonin, codeine, cocaine, opium, and other high-end pharmaceuticals in exchange for (what else?) gold. Upon signing the contract (as they did on 26 July 1920), the Bolsheviks were to "instruct their representatives in Reval to immediately hand ROCHE's bankers, G. Scheel & Co., Reval, a quantity of fine gold ingots, WITH EXPORT LICENSE, of the value approximately equaling the amount of the order (about 715 kilos on the basis of 1000/1000 purity)." G. Scheel and Company was a favorite of Western firms doing business with Moscow via Reval: by the end of 1920, it had processed more than $50 million worth of Soviet gold.[30] Scheel's precious metals team would then transport the gold to the Royal Assay Office in Stockholm. The Roche drugs and medicines would be turned over to Solomon and the Soviet Mission. The commission on sale was a rather steep 8 percent. As if to underline the precarious nature of a contract signed with the Bolshevik regime, Roche's lawyers affixed an explicitly worded condition that would soon become standard issue for trade deals with Moscow: "Revolution, explosions, civil war, war, fire and all risks included under *force majeure* are reasons for ROCHE demanding an extension of time for the execution of this contract, and in the event of any of these calamities arising ROCHE cannot be held responsible for not keeping within the stipulated delivery of six to eight months."[31]

Food was also now easy for the Bolsheviks to buy in bulk for gold, so long as it was not in perishable form (such as the ill-fated multi-million ruble Norwegian codfish deal from 1918). With an urban famine raging and a low-scale war being fought to alleviate it by specially organized "food armies" in the countryside, Russia's agricultural production and distribution networks were in crisis state. Not trusting the peasants either to supply the cities or to grow what was needed, the Bolsheviks boldly decided to overhaul Russia's agriculture, as if from scratch. With the 1920 harvest a disaster, Krasin's new trade mission in London, ARCOS (an English-derived acronym for the Bolsheviks' All-Russian Cooperative Society) negotiated ambitious deals with Danish agribusiness companies to import massive quantities of seed for the new forcibly collectivized farms (the Statute on Socialist Land Organization passed in February 1919 had officially declared peasant farming "obsolescent").[32] It was an order that would have perplexed Russia's peasants, had they known of it. Evidently tiring of bland bread and thin potato soup, the Bolsheviks optimistically planned to raise red and white cabbage; five varieties of carrot; several each of parsley and beetroot, spinach, celery, leek, chicory, cauliflower, field turnips, onions, radishes, tomatoes, squash, beans, and peas.[33]

This was, of course, no ordinary trade deal. There was no pretense ARCOS was able to offer commodities in exchange for hundreds of thousands of tons of vegetable and legume seeds—to pay in any other way than by shipping looted gold to Reval. The contract signed in November 1920 with Theodore Jensen and Company, of Copenhagen, was just as explicit as the Roche deal regarding means of payment. ARCOS (i.e., the Soviet government) was required to make an initial deposit of some 300,000 Danish kroner worth of gold in the Jensen account at the National Bank of Estonia "within ten days," to "procure and to deliver to the Seller the Export Licenses of the Esthonian [sic] Government in respect of all gold which will be paid to the seller under this Contract" and to cover all "freight and insurance" costs. "If and when payment is made," Jensen's lawyers further stipulated, "the gold bars available are not of the exact weight required to make up the amount of the respective invoice the deficiency may be made up in Russian gold coins."[34] When it came to supplying the Bolsheviks, it was a sellers' market: companies willing to brave the opprobrium of Entente critics for accepting looted gold for payment could evidently set whatever conditions they wished.

Clothing and boots were also fairly easy for the Bolsheviks to procure, although the volumes involved were naturally larger than with agricultural seed or pharmaceuticals. One of the highest priorities for Red Army procurement in 1920, Krasin later recalled, was wool for greatcoats, outer uniforms (mundiry), and undershirts.[35] Krasin placed many of the orders himself in London, from September to November 1920, totaling roughly 2 million arshins (an arshin is about 71 centimeters) of smooth woolen cloth. Another 5 million arshins were purchased by Soviet agents from Western textile firms through branch offices in Estonia. Only about half of the wool ordered had been delivered to Moscow via Reval by November, but this was still enough to produce uniforms and greatcoats for several hundred thousand Red Army soldiers. Another 2.35 million arshins of precut "greatcoat" wool was ordered by Red Army procurement in October, and 5.25 million arshins of uniform wool. Better still was clothing of the ready-to-wear variety. Premade tunics, trousers, and greatcoats were all ordered in bulk in Reval in fall 1920: 200,000 of each. Another 400,000 finished woolen greatcoats were purchased in Berlin in early November. [36]

The most ambitious textile orders were placed by the Soviet Foreign Mission in Stockholm, with a consortium called the Eastern Trading Company. Traditionally, Eastern Trading had bought its wool and fabric in Great Britain and sold it to Russia via the Baltic provinces, but during the period of the Allied Baltic blockade, the firm had begun using Swedish suppliers to circumvent possible political obstacles being erected in London. Just as with railway supply firms, the Swedish textile industry, too, saw a huge boom after Bolshevik gold started arriving in Stockholm. As security against wool imports for Red Army uniforms, in early August 1920 the Bolsheviks deposited 15 metric tons of gold in the name of Eastern Trading at Stockholm's Enskilda Bank.[37] By fall, Eastern Trading was reported in the Swedish press to be sending 2 million yards of cloth per month to Soviet Russia, fulfilling a long-term order worth 150 million Swedish crowns in gold (about $35 million, or the equivalent of some 3.5 billion dollars today).[38]

Boots, too, were desperately needed on the front lines in Russia. The Bolsheviks bought all kinds of foreign-made footwear for gold in 1920, from leather riding boots to American-made waterproof designs and simple rubber galoshes. Leather was also ordered in vast bulk, especially precut leather boot soles (kozha podoshvennaia), at 2,889 gold rubles a ton. The Red Army's procurement agency, SPOTEKZAK, employed no less than four Bolshevik boot buyers, tasked with obtaining 5 million pairs by the end of 1920: Solomon in Reval, Litvinov in Copenhagen, Fürstenberg-Hanecki in Riga, and Viktor Kopp in Berlin. The first consignments of mostly American-made boots and leather boot soles began arriving in Reval in early September. If boot purchases are added to the foreign buys of greatcoat and uniform wool, along with winter underwear (teploe bel'e) and infantry helmets, the Red Army laid out about $30 or $40 million worth of gold in 1920 on imported clothing alone, or some $3 or 4 billion in today's terms. This was far more, for example, than the Bolsheviks were spending on Comintern propaganda and agitation.[†39]

Boot buyer Viktor Kopp, a relatively obscure Soviet agent previously unknown to Allied intelligence analysts, emerged in 1920 as one of the Bolsheviks' most important commercial agents. Kopp's

---

[†]The subsidy for the British Communist Party in 1920, for example, was 55,000 pounds sterling—a significant sum, the equivalent of some $27.5 million today, but small beer compared to outlays on Red Army procurement.

first major commission had come in May 1919, when he was named the representative of the Soviet Central Bank in Belorussia and Red Latvia. Kopp was personally entrusted then with 2.5 million rubles worth of precious metals and other valuables, plus 100,000 tsarist ruble notes to cover expenses.[40] Later that year, Kopp surfaced in Berlin under cover as director of the Russian Red Cross, meeting with German Communists and beginning to negotiate illicit trade deals. In addition to boots and greatcoats, Kopp procured for the Red Army in 1920 American-made linen blankets, field telephones and telephone wire, binoculars, Bosch spark plugs, automobile tires, and tire covers. So valuable was Kopp's business to German firms that the Weimar government elevated him to the rank of plenipotentiary in July 1920, granting him diplomatic immunity.[41]

Kopp's real talent, however, was for under-the-radar arms deals. The German army demobilization mandated by Versailles meant that huge quantities of surplus weapons were available in central Europe on the black market. Inevitably, German arms dealers sought out Soviet agents in 1920, hoping to cash in on the Bolshevik gold boom. Kopp forwarded such offers on to Moscow by way of Soviet agents in Reval or Copenhagen. One such deal, originating in mid-May 1920, would have seen 1.5 million Mauser rifles, at a cost of 650 marks each (including 200 rounds per rifle), shipped to Murmansk and Archangel. Details of this billion-mark order were sent from Berlin to Litvinov in Copenhagen before being forwarded on to Lenin, Trotsky, and Soviet Foreign Minister Chicherin in the Kremlin. According to the dealer, the German government itself had approved the sale.[42] The Bolsheviks balked, however, feeling that the risk of such an enormous shipment being lost en route was "not acceptable" (ne priemlemo). Besides, Chicherin informed Litvinov and Kopp, a "colossal quantity" of used rifles less expensive than these Mausers were available on the market.[43] In early September, Kopp found a cheaper supplier, willing to sell him 1 million prewar 1898 model Mausers, with 200 rounds per, for 430 marks each. This time, Moscow agreed to buy, but only 100,000 rifles, for 43 million marks in gold.[44] Kopp was nothing if not persistent: he sold Moscow on another 200,000 Mauser rifles in November 1920 (plus 2,000 rounds for each), along with 1,000 machine guns (pulemety), each with 150,000 clips.[45] Kopp racked up enormous debts in Germany placing these orders before G. Scheel and Company deposited 10 million reichsmarks into his account at Deutsche Bank, calculated against Soviet gold deposits in Reval.[46]

German Mausers, although easy to obtain on the Weimar black market, were not necessarily the Bolsheviks' weapon of choice. Trotsky, the commander of the Red Army, had been quite taken by American-style capitalism while living in New York City during the war: he was enamored of U.S. goods and wanted only the best. When he heard in August 1920 that a German dealer in Minsk was looking to move 15,000 U.S.-made Browning rifles and 250 Browning pistols, Trotsky approved the purchase immediately.[47] Authentic Westinghouse rifles were harder to come by, but the Bolsheviks did find a supplier in Stockholm, Tjernberg and Leth Aktiebol, willing to give them the next best thing: Russian-style Nagan "three line" repeating rifles that had been made, at least, in the Westinghouse foundry in America, in accordance with a now-defunct commission given Westinghouse by the tsarist government back in 1915. In November 1920, Tjernberg and Leth made an offer to Krasin of 1.2 million Nagans, with 1,800 rounds each, for roughly $37.5 million in gold, plus another $2 million for insurance. Trotsky was enthusiastic but could not get authorization from the Commissariat of Finance to spend this much on one single order. The Bolsheviks ultimately agreed to pay $9 million in gold, for 300,000 Nagans and 5 million rounds.[48]

Not everything needed to be imported by the Red Army, which could still draw on at least the arms factories at Tula, which turned out rifles and a few machine guns. But capacity was limited, nowhere near enough to handle the Red Army's crude wastage of rounds, shell, and poorly maintained weapons. The Treaty of Riga, signed in mid-October 1920, which formalized Poland's gains in Belorussia and Ukraine—nearly 200 kilometers past the "Curzon lines" proposed by the British—brought respite for the Red Army and with it the opportunity to think seriously about large-scale imports.[49] An inventory prepared by the Red Army's artillery command (Glavnoe Artilleriiskoe Upravlenie) in October 1920 estimated that Russia's factories, even under best case scenario, could produce only one-third of the 2 million rifles desperately needed to replenish Red Army stocks (1.8 million had been either lost, captured, or had broken down since 1918, leaving only 437,377 functioning rifles), less than half the 13,000 machine guns needed to replace those lost during the civil war, out of 18,036 inherited from the tsarist army depots, and a quarter of the 3 billion clips these would require. Revolvers and pistols used by officers were nearly wiped out during the war with the Whites: only 15,012 of 167,264 acquired from tsarist stores remained in Red hands, and Tula could turn out, at best, only about 50,000 of the 430,000 officers' guns the artillery command had ordered. Hand grenades, too, were nearly gone, with only some 91,000 left of a stock of 1.56 million inherited in 1918. Howitzers (gaubitsy) were also disappearing: only about 200 remained of the old tsarist stores of over 500 English-made Vickers heavy (artillery) guns, and it was not yet clear if Krasin would be able to order new ones. Many other crucial stores falling under the artillery command's purview—binoculars, gun sights (stereotruby), flares and signaling equipment, incendiary rounds (patrony zazhigatel'nye), and explosive cartridges (patron. razryvn)—could not be manufactured in Soviet Russia at all. They, too, would need to be imported.[50]

Besides, with Russia's mines nearly empty of able-bodied workers and no trains running on which mined metals could be transported across the Urals anyway, Tula's factories needed imports of ferrous metals simply to keep operating at bare minimum capacity. Enormous orders for lead, tin, zinc, steel, and pure tungsten (wolfram) were placed by Red Army procurement agents in summer 1920, although it was not until September that the metals began arriving in Reval, and then only the lead. The tin, zinc, and steel would not start arriving in bulk until December 1920, and the wolfram even later.[51]

Soviet agents had to be extremely careful in placing orders with such obvious military application: large volumes would inevitably raise suspicions in London and Paris and possibly force Lloyd George to have second thoughts about lifting the blockade. The Entente powers were aware as early of August 1920, for example, that "small arms and ammunition [were] being shipped into Russia from Germany . . . in violation of the treaty of Versailles."[52] More shocking still was the report published in *Echo de Paris* that Grigory Zinoviev had used the United German Communist Party founding congress at Halle in November 1920 as cover while placing an order for German poison gas.[53]

It was only in November–December 1920, with the Polish threat neutralized and the Red Army preparing for a final push into the Crimea, that war matériel finally began pouring into Soviet Russia in bulk. Many of the orders had been placed earlier in 1920 or even before but were held up as suppliers awaited the outcome of the Polish war, fearing seizure of arms by British ships in the Baltic or of Bolshevik gold by Allied creditors. In addition to clothing and medicines, SPOTEKZAK was now able to restock the Red Army with serious volumes of imported rifle ammunition, machine guns, horse saddles (sedla), tires and spare parts for military vehicles (Dunlop, Fiat, Goodrich, and Michelin), Bosch spark plugs, binoculars (binokli), micrometers (mikrometry), nails, sewing machines and needles, steel tape, and field telephones. By December 1920, all of these wares, along with the lead, tin, zinc, and steel needed by Russia's own war factories, were arriving in quantities measured in thousands of tons via Riga and Reval.[54]

Military airplanes were also now fair game for the Bolsheviks to import. Viktor Kopp took the lead here, as with rifles and automatics, ordering fifty "LVG" planes outfitted with 200-horsepower Mercedes-Benz engines in Berlin in September. The first 12 military airplanes the Bolsheviks ordered began arriving in Russia in November 1920, with another 78 on the way, and 560 slated to arrive by the end of 1921.[55] Aaron Sheinman, the man sent to Stockholm with 17 million rubles in 1918, was dispatched in November 1920 to Tiflis, Georgia, with several million French francs to buy 50 airplanes with Fiat engines.[56] In December, Bosch airplane spark plugs (aviatsionnye svechi) were purchased in Germany.[57]

The arms import surge of fall and winter 1920, like the huge locomotive deal negotiated in Stockholm, was securitized by gold deposits. In just eight short weeks, from 4 November 1920 to 1 January 1921, 70 metric tons of Bolshevik gold were shipped from Reval to Stockholm and several other European ports, worth nearly $50 million.[58] Added to military procurement orders made prior to November, we can estimate that the Red Army laid down at least $200 million on imports of war matériel in 1920, the equivalent of some $20 billion today. These orders, of course, were all securitized with gold deposits in Reval, Stockholm, and Copenhagen, in all more than 130 metric tons by the end of 1920.[59]

Did these imports have an impact on the major Soviet military engagements of 1920? Once they learned the Bolsheviks were importing weapons from Germany, Allied officials and journalists certainly thought so. In a bitter October 1920 dispatch from Stockholm, Delavaud denounced the "nefarious traffic" in gold that allowed the Soviet government to purchase "arms, clothing, anything which might benefit its spring offensive."[60] Wrangel's defeat in November seemed only to confirm the worst. "Before being defeated in the Crimea," wrote the Stockholm correspondent of *Echo de Paris* mournfully, "Wrangel was defeated economically by a conspiracy of freebooters [flibustiers] blanketing the Baltic."[61]

Was this true? Since the campaign to oust Wrangel from the Crimea did not heat up until 7–11 November 1920, by which time reinforcements transferred from the Polish front allowed the Red Army to break through heavily fortified White positions at the entrance to the Isthmus of Perekop, it is possible that the Brownings and Mausers Kopp ordered in summer 1920 may have had an impact on Wrangel's defeat. Likewise, the woolen shirts, boots, helmets, and greatcoats (which began arriving in September) might have improved Red morale during the Perekop offensive, along with the imported medicines and painkillers ordered in July. The colossal volumes of locomotives and rolling stock ordered through Nydquist and Holm, although not beginning to arrive until fall 1920, certainly contributed to Red Army mobility. The imminent influx of ammunition, grenades, flares, gunsights, Nagan rifles, auto and aviation spare parts, along with ferrous metals for the arms factories slated for delivery in winter 1920, may also have reassured Red commanders that they would soon be able to replenish stores exhausted in the offensive. Certainly ammunition was used liberally by the Red Army in the Crimea, not least in the summary executions of 50,000 civilians carried out during the months of November and December.[62] Still, although the French complaints were not without justification, it would be hard to argue conclusively that gold-securitized imports made the difference in the Crimean offensive. Wrangel's forces were probably doomed without large-scale British aid, which Lloyd George—again, over French objections—had declared in June 1920 would not be forthcoming under any circumstances.[63]

Why, then, the major uptick in gold shipments to finance military imports in November 1920, by which time, with the Polish treaty and the departure of the last White armies from Russian soil, we might suppose that the Bolsheviks no longer faced serious opposition? The short answer is that they did, in fact, face such opposition: from their own people, or at least from the 80 percent or so of the Russian population that comprised the peasantry. Periodic rural uprisings behind the front lines had been a constant leitmotif during the civil war and would emerge with a vengeance after Wrangel's departure. Historians are still reconstructing the outlines of the Russian peasant wars, but it is now abundantly clear they were a greater test of strength for the Bolshevik regime than the more publicized conflicts with the Whites, Entente expeditionary forces, and Poles.[64] Cheka files opened since 1991, for example, record the numbers of peasant *bunts* behind (or alongside) military lines during the civil war on a month-by-month basis. There were surges in October–November 1918, which saw 44 separate uprisings; in spring 1919, when the mid-Volga and Ukraine were engulfed in rebellion; and in February–March 1920, when from the Volga to the Urals the so-called Pitchfork Rebellion, encompassing an irregular peasant army of 50,000, faced Red Army regulars "armed with cannons and heavy machine guns." In the Cossack regions of eastern Ukraine, Nicolas Werth estimates, "between 300,000 and 500,000 people were killed or deported in 1919 and 1920, out of a population of no more than 3 million."[65]

In fall and winter 1920, as if in lockstep with the departure of the last foreign-supplied armies from Russian soil, the most ferocious peasant rebellions yet erupted against the Bolshevik dictatorship in the eastern Ukraine, western Siberia, the northern Caucasus, central Asia, the Volga region, and Tambov province, only a few hundred miles from Moscow itself. As Richard Pipes writes, "The 'masses,' who during the Civil War had been told by the regime that the Whites and their foreign backers bore responsibility for all their hardships, refused to accept such explanations once the war had ended." Nestor Makhno's anti-Bolshevik bandits in the Ukraine numbered 15,000. The partisan armies in the Caucasus counted twice as many, and in Siberia more than 60,000. In Tambov, the rebel army led by Alexander Antonov, able to draw on no less than 110,000 Red Army deserters hiding out in the surrounding countryside, at its height put as many as 50,000 men under arms, divided up into 18 or 20 "regiments."[66]

This was a class war of the most brutal kind, fought not only against rich, city-dwelling commercial and aristocratic "expropriators," like those targeted in 1918–19, but against the entire class of independent peasant farmers. The zero-sum nature of the conflict was perfectly captured in the 23 October 1920 order of Sergo Ordzhonikidze, president of the Revolutionary Committee of the Northern Caucasus, for "the inhabitants of Ermolovskaia, Romanovskaia, Samachinskaia, and Mikhailovskaia to be driven out of their homes, and the houses and land redistributed among the poor peasants." Further, "all males aged eighteen to fifty from the above-mentioned towns" were to be "deported under armed escort to the north, where they will be forced into heavy labor." Last, Cheka officers were to seize "all the cattle and goods of the above-mentioned towns." The Cheka obliged: by mid-November 1920, two entire towns had been "emptied of all inhabitants," one razed to the ground, and over 10,000 class enemies cleansed from the Caucasus, with another 5,500 "awaiting deportation." Such brutal treatment of Russia's rural poor was justified by Lenin on the grounds that the peasants were "far more dangerous than all the Denikins, Yudeniches, and Kolchaks put together, since we are dealing with a country where the proletariat represents a minority." Little wonder the Bolsheviks suffered such appalling losses in the rural wars of 1920–22, with one recent casualty count coming to 237,908, and this in a war against desperately poor, badly fed peasants who, lacking firearms, fought mostly with pitchforks and farm implements.[67]

There was an intriguing reverse symmetry involved in the evolution of Bolshevik relations with the peasantry from 1918 to 1921, which neatly parallels the history of their import policies. In the first year or so following the October Revolution—the time of German supremacy and the Brest-Litovsk settlement, while the world war still raged—the Bolsheviks had been so weak that they needed to appease the rural population of Russia: thus Lenin's famous promise of "peace, land, and bread." In this period, as we saw in chapter 5, the little foreign exchange Moscow enjoyed, in the form of diplomatic suitcases bulging with cash, went mostly to purchase peasant-friendly agricultural implements in Stockholm, nonmilitary orders that, it was hoped, would be able to pass German inspection (although military orders, predictably, were placed soon after the German collapse). In 1919, while the Bolsheviks still needed the acquiescence of the peasantry as they fought the foreign-supplied Whites, the anemic foreign exchange they could procure for paper rubles and empty promises of gold, flax, and hemp exports went to dual-use civilian and military items ordered in Sweden, Denmark, and Germany, many of them agricultural. The Allied Baltic blockade, like the German screen, thus had the unintended effect of winning the Bolsheviks grudging sympathy among their rural subjects, as both faced the same enemies and suffered the same material deprivations. Lack of access to imported war matériel in 1918–19 also forced the Bolsheviks into a kind of marriage of convenience with peasant conscripts, whose endless manpower allowed them to field armies poorly equipped but large enough to overcome the assorted armies of Kolchak, Denikin, and Yudenich by sheer weight of numbers.

The effective end of the Allied blockade in 1920 produced precisely the opposite situation. With foreign-supplied White armies and the Poles at bay, the Bolsheviks faced only internal opposition while enjoying, at long last, the freedom to import weapons and other war matériel without German or Allied interference. That the Polish war ended, and Wrangel was defeated, before the greater portion of these arms started arriving was a kind of crowning symmetry: it was only in fall and winter 1920, by which time there were no foreign enemies left in Soviet Russia, that the *real* war began, the one between the Bolsheviks and the vast majority of their own people.

At root, the peasant wars were fought over who would control the food supply. The "food levy" or prodrazverstka, in force from 1919 to 1921, saw the requisition level of all foodstuffs set by planning officials in Moscow, without any regard for "the actual size and location of the food surpluses." The peasants' inevitable resistance to forcible requisitions by Soviet "food armies" (prodarmii) and "military food brigades" (voenprodotriady) set a vicious cycle in motion, as peasants either hid their grain or deliberately stopped growing it, leading the frustrated Bolsheviks to denounce the "devious methods" of "kulak grain hoarders" and demand yet more brutality in dealing with them. Absurdly, the Bolsheviks' attempts to nationalize food distribution meant they were now directly responsible for feeding some 30 million people—and they were doing it very badly. "By the end of 1920," Orlando Figes writes, "there was so little food left in the state depots—and so many people on the rations system—that even those on the first-class ration were receiving only just enough to slow down the rate of their starvation." As for the food growers themselves, the plague of the urban food armies meant that "by 1921 much of peasant Russia had been brought to the brink of a terrible famine." Even Red Army commander Vladimir Antonov-Ovseenko admitted that, by January 1921, "half the peasantry was starving."[68]

In such conditions, one might have expected the gold being sold abroad to be used to finance the import of something, anything, that might have helped peasants grow more grain and entice them to sell it to the cities—agricultural machinery, consumer goods, durables, fuel, tools. But with the Russian people rising against them, the Bolsheviks were no longer as interested in importing such civilian-friendly wares as they had been during the German and Allied blockades. As the rural rebellion deepened in winter 1920–21, precious metal sales in Reval and Stockholm went more and more exclusively to military purchases. The Swedish supply house of Tjernberg and Leth Aktiebol signed a lucrative contract on 11 January 1921 worth nearly 40 million crowns, or about $9 million in gold, to supply the Red Army with "150,000 sets complete Outfittings, consisting of":

> One Nagan (Russian 3 Line-Rifles, new American make) each with 1,800 cartridges for same (Crowns 200.—)
> One complete English uniform, khaki, without tears and patches cleaned and disinfected, consisting of coat, trousers and over coat . . . (Crowns 25.—)
> One pair black topboots, new [Crowns] 30.—
> One woolen blanket, new 80 percent wool, 58 mal 90′, weight abt 4. 1/2 lb, grey or brown colour . (crowns 14.—)
> The price per set being : Swedish crowns 269.—cif Reval.[69]

That January SPOTEKZAK was busy, placing yet more orders for American boots (300,000 pairs); leather boot soles (230 tons); some ten thousand sets of American, German, and English tires and tire covers; 2,650 American-made carburetors; another 46,500 Bosch spark plugs, along with thousands of tons of wool and linens for army uniforms.[70] At a single Red Army procurement meeting in late

January 1921, Maxim Litvinov signed off on an "emergency request" (ekstrennuiu zaiavku) for 200,000 imported rifles and 500 million rounds, at a cost of more than 96 million rubles ($48 million) in gold, along with several million dollars worth of difficult-to-obtain materials like wolfram (500 poods, or about 9 tons), centrifuges, sterilized tubes, and steam pumps (parovye nasosy).[71] In February 1921, as the peasant rebellion was compounded by a wave of workers' strikes in the northern cities, the Bolsheviks were fortunate to receive the 400,000 woolen greatcoats Kopp had ordered in Berlin, along with some 2.5 million arshins of English wool and 150,000 pairs of boots.[72] Later that spring, the Bolsheviks ordered 1,000 Danish-made light Madsen machine guns, half for Red Army infantry units and half for cavalry, through a middleman in Copenhagen.[73]

Lenin's fear of the wrath of the peasants and workers was reflected in the dramatic upsurge in precious metals outflow from Soviet Russia in winter 1920–21. If, as Niall Ferguson has suggested, the bond market is the best way to track the political fortunes of modern capitalist governments, in the case of Bolshevik finances the key index is the twists and turns of the gold-laundering market.[74] And the Bolsheviks' reserves were now disappearing rapidly. Between December 1920 and February 1921, no less than 400 million rubles ($200 million) worth of gold was transferred from Moscow to the Uritsky Palace (formerly Taurida) in Petrograd, in preparation for immediate dispatch abroad via Reval.[75] The gold was pouring out so quickly that Krasin was given a new commission by the Politburo in February 1921 to research the potential of diamond and jewelry sales to fund foreign arms purchases.[76]

This is not to say the Bolsheviks required the confidence of their people, much less foreign investors, to rule. The price of Bolshevik gold did not really reflect foreign estimation of Bolshevik strength: Western bankers, like everyone else, remained ignorant of the scale of the peasant wars in Russia. Looted Russian imperial gold ingots sold in Reval at well below London market value throughout 1920–21, with the amount depending only on the wiles of the buyer: from as high as 105 shillings per ounce (vs. 118 in London) to as low as 95 shillings.[77] In Stockholm, Soviet gold sold for much of 1920 at around 2,600 crowns per kilo (about $650), as against a price of 3,000 crowns for "clean" gold ($750).[78] The Bolshevik regime's perception of its security vis-à-vis its own population, rather, was reflected in the *speed* with which it dumped precious metals abroad. The greater the sense of panic (or of strategic opportunity), the more frantic the military orders and the faster the gold poured out.

Western intelligence was largely flying blind on the matter of Bolshevik currency and gold laundering, but not so blind as to fail to notice the upswings. Thus in fall 1918, the Swedish ruble-trading boom induced fears that the Allied victory would be undermined by Bolshevik-funded strikes and industrial sabotage (whereas in fact the rubles were mostly being deposited as security against imports). In summer 1919, the boom in Bolshevik money smuggling pushed panic buttons in Paris and London that another copycat Soviet-style revolution was being prepared in Allied countries, although it more likely heralded preparation for the coming Krasin-Lomonosov railway blockbuster.

The Stockholm gold boom of 1920–21 was no different, although, as we have seen, the French took note of it long before the other Entente powers. "For many months," British commercial attaché H. Kershaw wrote London, somewhat belatedly, on 2 November 1920, "the Swedish Press has bristled with paragraphs reporting the arrival in this country of Russian gold." Summarizing the state of British knowledge to date, Kershaw informed the Foreign Office, "Russian gold amounting in the aggregate to about Kr. 225,000,000 has arrived in Sweden presumably since the opening-up of negotiations with the Soviet Authorities, but that only about 10 percent of this amount has remained in Sweden. It appears that licences for the re-export of about Kr. 190,000,000 have been issued, of which 42,500 Kgs. consisted of bar gold, and 35,350,000 Russian gold rubles." As to what happened to Bolshevik gold after it left Sweden, Kershaw warned London, "Imported fine gold which finds its way to the London market, and which bears the stamp of an officially recognized foreign Government, may have been replaced in the country of origin by Russian gold." The Swedish Mint, by melting down looted Russian gold ingots, made it possible for Bolshevik gold to reach the City of London, right under the nose of Whitehall.[79]

A similar fear was now haunting Treasury officials in Washington. The U.S. government had been somewhat late in getting on the anti-Bolshevik bandwagon, due to both the resurgence of isolationist sentiment following the 1918 armistice and the hostility of President Wilson to the White generals, which ensured that America's contribution to the cause was confined to cash and ineffective rearguard support (U.S. troops did not engage in combat once during their nine-month deployment in Russia in 1918–19).[80] By fall 1920, with lame-duck President Wilson largely incapacitated by a series of strokes and America undergoing its first "Red scare," Washington was on high alert against Bolshevism. It helped that gold movements, unlike a complicated multifront Russian civil war being fought thousands of miles away, was something U.S. government officials were reasonably confident they could do something about, if only by cutting off suspicious shipments of Soviet origin before they polluted American financial markets.

This was the premise of a U.S. government crackdown on Soviet gold movements launched in November 1920. Anyone selling gold to the Federal Reserve was now expected to fill out a "Certificate of Ownership," prepared by Treasury officials, confirming, "The undersigned owner of a lot of gold . . . delivered to the United States Assay Office at New York on the _____ day of _____, 1920, does hereby represent and warrant that said gold is not of Bolshevik origin and has never been in the possession of the so-called Bolshevik Government of Russia, and further that it is not involved in any credit or exchange transaction with the so-called Bolshevik Government."[81] The policy was meant to apply to private Wall Street banks as well. "From the fact that there has recently been a number of [gold] shipments from certain countries contiguous to Russia of Bolshevik origin," the U.S. Treasury superintendent explained to James Hecksher of Irving National Bank in New York on 17 November 1920, "suspicion has attached to all shipments proffered from these countries. For this reason all the inquiries as to gold known or suspected to be of Russian or Bolshevik origin must be referred by me direct to the Treasury for instructions before tenders are accepted or payments made."[82] Any hopes such bankers might have had about having Bolshevik gold re-minted, Swedish-style, in Washington, were dismissed in no uncertain terms. "All gold known to be of Soviet origin," S. P. Gilbert, the assistant secretary of the Treasury, ruled on 26 November 1920, "will be rejected by United States Mint and Assay Offices, no matter by whom tendered."[83]

The difficulty in enforcing this Bolshevik gold quarantine lay in the phrase "known to be of Soviet origin." If such gold had already been re-minted in Stockholm, then either the buyers did not know it was of Soviet origin or else had purchased it intentionally at a discounted price precisely because it was of Soviet origin. In the former case, Washington was relying on self-policing by bankers who shared its concerns about Bolshevik laundering of the improperly looted wealth of Imperial Russia. In the latter case, it was unlikely that knowing Bolshevik gold buyers would voluntarily submit gold for inspection at the Federal Assay Office, which might reduce its resale value by calling its provenance into question. Such gold profiteers would likely submit to the U.S. Mint only gold already clearly marked with a Swedish or other non-Russian stamp, which would pass the inspection anyway.

In practice, all the U.S. government could do was monitor the outflow of precious metals through Reval and the influx of precious metals into New York from Europe and try to ferret out possible connections. Without voluntary compliance, it was like putting together a puzzle with pieces that never quite fit. In Reval, the Customs House reported the volume of Russian gold shipped across the Baltic, the names of the ships, and their reported destinations. In New York, customs authorities required "gold invoices," which also included the name of the shipper and the consignee. But such invoices told nothing about the origin of the gold, aside from what currency designation the ingots and coins were marked with. In between Reval and New York, of course, were the mints of Stockholm, where buyers made sure their discounted Soviet gold was cleansed of its suspicious origins.[84]

French and American officials knew something was amiss in Reval and Stockholm but were not sure quite what to do about it. Charles Westcott, commercial attaché of the U.S. Embassy in Paris, was aghast that huge volumes of precious metals "looted from palaces, churches, monasteries and private owners" were being "shipped through devious channels." "Doubtless millions of dollars in Russian gold thus exported," Westcott wrote Washington in spring 1921, "are being applied to ceaseless anarchical-bolshevik propaganda to subvert the existing political, economic and social order of civilization."[85] Just as in 1918 and 1919, Entente officials feared the impact of Bolshevik money laundering on their own governments, failing to suspect that foreign gold deposits were mostly devoted to financing arms purchases by a Soviet regime fighting desperately for its own survival. But without shutting down the Swedish Mint, there was nothing the Entente powers could do about such gold sales anyway.

By 1921, the chance the Swedish government would listen sympathetically to Allied complaints about Bolshevik gold laundering in Stockholm was zero. Swedish textile and railway factories were churning along at full capacity, fulfilling hundreds of millions of crowns worth of long-term Soviet orders. Swedish banks had all but cornered the market on lucrative gold commissions and were flush with cheaply acquired Gokhran loot—jewelry, diamonds, platinum—as well.[86] The Swedish government was itself heavily implicated. The Royal Mint alone melted down 70 metric tons of looted Russian imperial gold ingots, 100 million rubles or $50 million worth, between May 1920 and March 1921.[87]

The Bolsheviks knew all this, of course, and were not above periodically reminding the Swedish government how invested it had become in the continuance of their dictatorial rule in Russia. As Lenin's regime faced its most serious internal crisis yet, the famous Kronstadt uprising of February–March 1921 launched by angry sailors' soviets from the very Petrograd garrison that had given the Bolsheviks their most reliable support back in 1917, rumors reached Moscow that foodstuffs were being transported to the Kronstadt rebels through Sweden. Taking the imperious tone of one who enjoys superior leverage, Platon Kerzhentsev, Vorovsky's successor as president of the Soviet Trade Delegation in Stockholm, wrote to Count Herman Wrangel, the new Swedish foreign minister: "I have no doubt that the Swedish Government, which have commercial relations with the Russian Soviet Government, will neither help to such transportation for rebels against the Russian Soviet Government nor allow such transport to take place. I think you will find it necessary to deny above-mentioned statements and that you will not allow the fantastic writing of the newspapers to damage in any way the good relations between Sweden and Soviet Russia." Count Wrangel replied the following day with an emphatic denial.[88]

Kronstadt, then, was not only a test of military strength for the

Bolsheviks but a milestone in their efforts to break out of political and economic isolation. Stockholm had not yet offered Moscow formal diplomatic recognition, but this hardly mattered if the Swedish government was acting as a de facto ally of the Soviet regime, and this at a time when the Bolsheviks' internal enemies, unlike the Whites before them, were cut off from outside support. Whether or not Swedish Foreign Ministry officials knew or cared, the Bolsheviks were barely holding onto power in early 1921. Only 2 percent of industrial laborers still belonged to the Bolshevik Party by winter 1920–21. The urban bread ration was cut by one-third in late January, costing Lenin's regime the support of its most diehard former factory supporters. On 23 and 25 February, with thousands of workers marching in the streets to protest the Bolshevik dictatorship, Moscow and Petrograd were placed under martial law. The Kronstadt rebellion was just the final straw of a cascading wave of worker unrest that nearly broke the back of the Soviet regime.

Gorged on nearly five months' worth of continuously imported war matériel, the Bolsheviks were ready. The counterattack against the Kronstadt island garrison was organized by Trotsky himself, who famously ordered women and children of the mutineers taken hostage and vowed the rebels would be "shot like partridges." With some 50,000 Red Army soldiers, now well-clothed and well-armed, supplied with enough ammunition to bombard the rebels from the mainland for days before the final assault, Trotsky was able to make good on his promise. After Kronstadt was taken, at a cost of 10,000 Red Army deaths, some 2,500 rebels were shot without trial and another 6,500 deported to the Soviet far north, where three-quarters would die within a year. Crowning Trotsky's assault on Kronstadt were bombs dropped by recently imported military airplanes. Battle deaths were so heavy that the Finnish government famously requested the removal of corpses from the ice, "lest they should be washed up on the Finnish coast and create a health hazard following the thaw."[89]

In similar fashion, the Bolsheviks' newfound access to imported war matériel allowed them to fight off dozens of peasant rebellions. The greatest battles were fought in Tambov province, where Red Field Marshal Tukhachevsky was sent in early May 1921 at the head of a special army organized "for the Internal Defense of the Republic," numbering more than 100,000 and backed by Cheka execution squads. Tukhachevsky's army enjoyed superior mobility compared to those he had commanded against the Whites: his cavalry now rode on imported horse saddles, his lorries were well supplied with tires, spark plugs, and spare parts, and he could deploy state-of-the-art foreign warplanes for surveillance and area bombing. The incendiary rounds imported over the winter came in handy as Bolshevik terror detachments burned down villages "suspected of assisting or collaborating" with Antonov. Tukhachevsky was also authorized to use "asphyxiating gas" to "smoke out" rebels hiding in forests (this was likely the poison gas Zinoviev had purchased in Germany at the time of the Halle Congress). Tukhachevsky's orders were to "shoot on sight any citizens who refuse to give their names," along with the "eldest son" of "any family that has harbored a bandit" or given refuge to "other families who have harbored bandits." Houses of "bandit families" were "to be burned or demolished," with their property redistributed "among peasants who are loyal to the Soviet regime." In all, Orlando Figes estimates, "100,000 people were imprisoned or deported and 15,000 people shot during the suppression of the revolt."[90]

The price the Bolsheviks paid for such victories was measured not only in the number of corpses but in the rapid exhaustion of the Bolsheviks' precious metals reserves. Between the beginning of the arms import surge in November 1920 and the temporary petering out of the most serious peasant rebellions (due largely to the onset of a nationwide famine) in July 1921, nearly $120 million worth of gold ingots and coin were shipped abroad through Reval (about 170 metric tons), and an untold volume of diamonds and jewels from the Gokhran. Added to the $100 million worth of gold exported before November 1920 (about 140 metric tons), the original imperial reserve inherited in 1917–18, though reinforced by the expropriation of gold bullion from Kolchak back in February 1920, was now depleting fast.[91]

Exactly how fast no one really quite knew, including the Soviet government itself. It is indicative of the Bolsheviks' ignorance about the gold reserves they had inherited that they hired as a consultant in 1921 none other than V. I. Novitsky, who had been Kolchak's finance minister before consulting for the Entente powers.[92] Novitsky himself had little idea: his report on the Russian gold reserve, published in the *New York Times* in July 1920, had been prepared earlier that spring, *before* the gold-laundering boom in Stockholm had begun. In Novitsky's absence, Charles Westcott, commercial liaison at the U.S. Embassy in Paris, emerged as the leading Allied expert. Westcott, building on Novitsky's 1920 report and the latest intelligence from Reval, estimated in April 1921 that Bolshevik gold reserves stood at some $228 million, a number barely larger than the $214 million exported since the gold boom began in May 1920. The latter figure, of Bolshevik gold exports to date, was fairly accurate, as it was based on the published reports of the Reval Customs House. Westcott's estimation of remaining reserves, however, was little more than an educated guess.[93]

If Westcott was right and Red Army expenditures continued on at the same pace, the Bolsheviks' gold reserves would barely last another year. In Moscow, too, a sense of panic was building over the rapid depletion of the gold reserves. A major battle was brewing between Krasin and Litvinov about the high risk premium the Bolsheviks were paying for gold-securitized imports.[94] Litvinov, who had spent most of 1920 in Copenhagen and Reval, in part because the Entente powers refused to host him, was convinced Krasin was wasting his time in London. Krasin's procurement front, ARCOS, was paying through the nose for imports, such as the Danish agribusiness deal, which could have been done much more cheaply in Copenhagen. Why negotiate deals in London, computed in Danish, Swedish, or Norwegian crowns, when the gold to pay for them was being sold in Reval and melted down in Stockholm? Some of Krasin's deals, Litvinov complained, had cost the Bolsheviks as much as 40 percent on the head, when one factored in not only gold processing and middlemen fees but also the complications of currency arbitrage.[95]

There was also the sheer inexperience of Soviet negotiators. Gukovsky, according to Solomon, sometimes sold Bolshevik gold for as much as 30 percent below world market price, especially to G. Scheel and Company. By contrast, Olof Aschberg, whose perceived persecution by the Entente had turned him into a Soviet sympathizer, was willing to charge lower premiums. At one point Aschberg even promised Litvinov that he could ship Bolshevik gold directly to the

U.S. Mint and avoid the high premiums of Stockholm entirely.‡[96] Solomon himself was hardly blameless—some of his shadier Reval deals, he later confessed, were lubricated by a booze and entertainment budget (Trinkgelder), which alone amounted to a 40 percent surcharge. But Solomon blamed most of the financial waste in Reval on Gukovsky's corrupt habits. At one point, Gukovsky even confessed—proudly—to pilfering a diadem that had belonged to the Tsarina Alexandra.[97]

Krasin himself later admitted that the risk premium involved in circumventing the unofficial Allied gold blockade was costing the Bolsheviks more than 15 percent on every major transaction, and sometimes as much as 25 percent.[98] But Krasin insisted it was best to sign import contracts quickly, no matter the cost, so as to keep suppliers happy and entice other Western businessmen eager to profit from the Bolsheviks' desperation. Each successive Scandinavian trade deal, Krasin wrote Moscow in July 1920, would drive the message home to British industrialists that he and other Soviet trade officials "prefer to use our free time giving dozens of additional orders in Sweden, which otherwise could be placed in England."[99]

London, Krasin knew, may not have been the best place to negotiate Scandinavian trade deals with low commissions. It was, however, the perfect place to lobby Whitehall into removing the last remaining legal obstacles to the export of gold, precious metals, and revolutionary loot of all kinds from Soviet Russia. If Bolshevik gold did not have to be sold on the sly in Reval and then melted down in Stockholm—if, that is, it could be legally sold anywhere, at full market value—the risk premium paid on Soviet arms import deals might soon drop dramatically. David Lloyd George had not yet given his last gift to Bolshevism.

‡Aschberg made this offer in October 1920, shortly before the U.S. government crackdown on Soviet gold was announced. It is likely the idea was quickly dropped.

8   London

Curzon! Be a gentleman!

— LLOYD GEORGE scolding Lord Curzon for refusing to shake hands
with Bolshevik Trade Commissar Leonid Krasin

DAVID LLOYD GEORGE and Leonid Borisovich Krasin made for a
very odd couple, but in some respects the two men complemented
each other perfectly. Lloyd George was both resented and admired
for his skill in balancing seemingly irreconcilable positions held by
his cabinet members, as in his halfway intervention in Soviet Russia,
followed by his sudden abandonment of the intervention, with no
prior notice of a change in policy. As Richard Ullman writes of Lloyd
George, "The master of compromise and temporizing, . . . he did not
commit himself until he sensed the direction and strength of the political winds, but in allowing his ministers a fairly free hand he always
made certain never to close off options which in the future he might
wish to pursue himself." Likewise, Krasin was viewed suspiciously
by his Kremlin rivals due to his ability to mouth Communist rhetoric
with apparent sincerity inside Soviet Russia while consorting easily
with Western businessmen and diplomats when abroad. Krasin's
Politburo colleagues referred to him, half-affectionately, as the "red
merchant." Perhaps sensing a similar maverick temperament, Lloyd
George pronounced himself "much impressed" after his first meeting
with Krasin on 31 May 1920. The prime minister even insisted that
all members of his cabinet present shake Krasin's hand. (Fortunately

for Lloyd George, the bellicosely anti-Bolshevik war minister, Winston Churchill, was absent.) Foreign Secretary Lord Curzon, who initially refused even to face Krasin, reluctantly obliged.[1]

Considering the serious doubts about Krasin's character and motives expressed by Curzon, Churchill, and the French, it was remarkable that Lloyd George was receiving him at all. The invitation dispatched to Krasin from San Remo in April 1920 had envisioned bringing together all the Entente powers for general discussions of debt and trade with Soviet Russia. Before Krasin's arrival in London, the French had repeatedly expressed the hope that any Allied negotiations with Tsentrosoiuz be conducted by trade specialists of low rank, so as not to confer implicit recognition of the Soviet regime. Krasin himself was, in the French view, "an extreme Bolshevist, imbued with their worst and most dangerous theories."[2] This was hardly an exaggeration in light of Krasin's long history of involvement in the Bolshevik movement, including his supervision of fundraising expropriations, that is, armed robberies, carried out in 1906–7 by Bolshevik bandits, such as Stalin in the Caucasus. Makeshift bombs used in bank heists were manufactured in a laboratory Krasin, an accomplished engineer, had designed personally. The most notorious operation masterminded by Krasin, which saw three bank guards murdered in broad daylight in Tbilisi, netted 340,000 rubles.[3] This was the man Lloyd George wished to assure the French was "a good businessman."

Even without knowing the sordid details of Krasin's past, the French had good reason to be concerned about his surprisingly welcome reception on Downing Street, concerns shared by Japan and the United States.[4] Whereas Britain's share of tsarist Russian debt was larger than France's—more than 600 million pounds sterling in all—this sum was owed mostly to the British government (which had underwritten the vast majority of the Russian war bonds issued from 1914 to 1917), whereas in France, deposed Russian bondholders included more than a million private citizens. French claims were spread across a wide spectrum of the Russian economy, including railway loans, bank and industrial equities, and municipal bonds. French Banque Russo-Asiatique shareholders alone had seen Russian holdings worth $750 million go up in smoke (see chapter 1).[5] Any recognition of a Soviet government that had repudiated these obligations threatened to render all such claims obsolete, by making legitimate the authority that had annulled them. As the French premier, Alexandre Millerand, complained to Lloyd George at an inter-Allied summit held in Boulogne on 21–22 June 1920, the negotiations he was conducting with Krasin conferred on the Bolsheviks "prestige and authority," which they did not deserve.[6]

Lloyd George was therefore skirting a very fine line in the series of almost weekly meetings he held with Krasin in May–June 1920. Earlier that spring, the prime minister had repeatedly assured the British parliament and public that Krasin and his Tsentrosoiuz team were independent of the Bolshevik regime (see chapter 7), an assertion Lloyd George knew to be patently false. He made a similarly tortured justification to Millerand at Boulogne, explaining that he was negotiating with representatives of the Soviet regime "not as a regular Government, but as being in de facto control."[7] The French saw right through this ruse: on 16 June, even before the Boulogne summit, the Quai d'Orsay had sent a circular to French embassies abroad warning that "lawyers of the British crown have put forth the position that Soviet power constituted a de facto government," implying that Soviet gold shipments abroad would not be molested by the British navy.[8] To assuage French concerns, Lloyd George did demand Krasin's assurance that Moscow "accepted in principle the obligations contracted by the Russian Government towards private Allied subjects." Lloyd George even suggested postponing consideration of the issue of "debt owing to the British or other foreign Governments"—the kind most important to Great Britain—until after the resumption of normal trade between Britain and Soviet Russia.[9]

This remarkable concession played right into Krasin's hands. Krasin's instructions, wired via Litvinov in late June, were "to agree on a platonic promise of recognition of *private* claims but that should be done in the most careful manner, and, if possible, for the present only as regards the English so as to excite French jealousy." "We can give a promise," Litvinov continued, "only against a guarantee that all obstacles in the way of beginning trade and the free sale of gold be immediately removed, and that no new conditions be laid upon us."[10] It might take time for Lloyd George to be able to justify such a guarantee to his cabinet, especially while the Polish war still raged. Meanwhile, Krasin could remind British negotiators what they were missing. In late June, Krasin informed Lloyd George personally that he was already receiving "numerous appeals from English traders about their desire to start commercial dealings."[11]

This was no bluff. Krasin had been approached on his very first day in London, 27 May 1920, by Standard Oil officials who wanted petroleum concessions in the Caspian (Baku had been reconquered by the Bolsheviks that April). These negotiations were "of serious importance," Krasin wrote to his Politburo colleagues, "in view of the clear desire of Standard Oil to embarrass England in this matter" (vvidu iavnogo zhelaniia 'Standard Oil' podlozhit' svin'iu Anglii v etom dele).[12] If a company as prominent as Standard Oil was willing to disregard the British ban on Soviet gold, the blockade seemed ripe to fall. Although Krasin did sound the usual pro forma denunciations of British imperialism in a formal June memorandum to Lloyd George, he also included the revealing suggestion that, even if Britain was unable to pursue "official negotiations on the restoration of peaceful relations," the "quick resumption" of commercial relations was "nonetheless possible." All that was necessary was a "temporary suspension of property claims" until they were "regularized" at a final peace conference.[13]

Had Lloyd George read Krasin's memorandum carefully, he would have realized that talk of a final peace conference was a red herring. Krasin's real goal, as Litvinov's telegram (decrypted by British intelligence) made clear, was to cajole Lloyd George into removing legal obstacles to the export of looted Russian gold while making only "platonic," that is, empty promises regarding repayment of Russia's colossal debt obligations. Lloyd George's Tory critics, like the French—who themselves rejected Krasin's cynical overtures toward a debt settlement out of hand*—understood Krasin's true aims much better than the prime minister.[14] As Richard Ullman describes the 7 June 1920 Commons debate following Lloyd George's opening of trade negotiations with Soviet Russia, "One after another half a dozen Conservatives on the Government back benches rose to attack Bolshevism as abhorrent and to assert that there were, in fact, no goods in Russia to be traded, and that there-

---

*The basic idea had been for the French to front Moscow 1 billion rubles—that is, to float a major new loan to a regime that had just repudiated all previous loan obligations—in exchange for a long-term bond worth 10 billion rubles, payable over fifty years.

fore the Bolsheviks would have to use confiscated gold which, in France at least, would be regarded as 'stolen goods.'" All of this was, of course, quite true. But in Lloyd George's mind, moral objections to trading in illegally looted gold were irrelevant. "It would be very pleasant," he lectured the Tory backbenchers in a tone of benevolent condescension (the Labor delegation, predictably, was wholly in favor of opening trade with Soviet Russia), "if there were no trading relations except with people just like ourselves—those who had a sane government, and who show the same wisdom and judgment. But we cannot indulge in these things; they are a luxury. . . . We must take such governments as we find them."[15] This was a remarkable apologia for the Bolshevik government: it may not have been "sane," but to refuse to trade with it was a "luxury" Britain could no longer afford.

Here, yet again, was the silver lining of Communist economics, which Krasin grasped and exploited brilliantly. No matter how wretched the condition of the Russian economy due to the depredations of War Communism, no matter how many domestic and foreign property holders had been brutally "expropriated" without any hint of compensation, there would always be new "capitalists" who wished to profit by taking their place. It was actually easier to do business with the Bolsheviks than it had been with legitimate Russian firms before the revolution: the nationalization of industry and foreign trade in 1918 meant that Western firms could now deal with monopoly trade offices, like those in Stockholm and Reval, without even needing to travel to Russia. Formal diplomatic recognition, as we have seen, proved entirely unnecessary in Sweden, where the Vorovsky Trade Mission had rendered the opening of a formal embassy moot.

Krasin hoped to turn a similar trick in London with ARCOS, incorporated on 9 June 1920. Chartered as a joint-stock corporation in accordance with British commercial law, ARCOS was in reality a subsidiary of the Soviet Commissariat for Foreign Trade, its one and only shareholder.[16] Nominally independent of even Krasin's Tsentrosoiuz delegation (which itself claimed to be independent of the Soviet government), ARCOS was buttressed by several institutional layers of plausible deniability as it negotiated contracts with Western firms on behalf of the Bolsheviks. Would-be suppliers needed only visit Arcos House at 68 Lincoln's Inn Fields and sign contracts with the innocuous-sounding "All-Russian Co-Operative Society, Limited."

For ARCOS, there was no shortage of eager suitors. Long before the formal Anglo-Soviet trade accord was signed in March 1921, ARCOS was doing a booming business in London, courted not only by Standard Oil but by dozens of lesser-known firms willing to supply Soviet Russia with everything under the sun. Military orders, naturally, took precedence. In August 1920, Siemens Brothers and Company signed a contract to supply the Red Army with four deluxe sets of telegraph equipment and accessories. Each "Terminal Station Telegraph Apparatus" would include "Complete Wheatstone Duplex Terminal Station Sets for Transmitting and Receiving," "cast iron Punching Sticks," along with tape wheels and winding machines. Accessories would include "air-tight tin canisters," receiver paper, "Special Ink for Receivers," and clock oil, all "of the highest quality as regards workmanship and material." The cost was 380 pounds sterling per set.[17]

Most of the ARCOS deals signed in London before the trade accord were similarly small-scale but high-value, designed to give English firms a taste of the profits possible in doing business with the Bolsheviks while whetting their appetite for more. The general idea was for ARCOS to pay in cash, while making clear that much larger orders would be forthcoming once the invidious "gold blockade" was lifted. Krasin himself signed off on a contract in September for 169,000 Swedish crowns worth of table and wall telephones, which included silk-insulated wire, along with coils, fuse tubes, and dry cells of the highest Western standards.[18] Still more lucrative was the deal signed by Aronstein and Company, Ltd. of Dunster House, to supply the Bolsheviks with 600 tons of cocoa powder ("containing about 22 percent fat") and 50 tons of "CHOCOLATE, sweet eatable manufactured with sugar (not saccharine)," for 30,540,000 tsarist rubles.[19]

Any gold-securitized deals ARCOS signed in London had to be of particularly small volume, so as to fly under the radar of the British Trade Office, which, Lloyd George's pro-Soviet lobbying efforts aside, still forbade the import of looted imperial Russian gold ingots. This was true of the pharmaceutical order Krasin placed in July, which totaled only about 30,000 sterling worth of gold (see chapter 7). In a similar vein, the gold contracts ARCOS signed in September 1920 with the textile firms J. Ross and Company and S. Barling measured greatcoat wool in the thousands, not millions, of yards, while emphasizing expensive cuts ("lightweight overcoatings assorted 6 ways"; "fancy suitings," etc.). All such gold contracts were handled by numerous middlemen in Reval, raising the premium paid by the Bolsheviks.[20]

The ARCOS deals paid in currency, by contrast, were publicized intentionally by Krasin and his team. A contract signed with five New York–based textile firms on 15 September 1920, which would bring an initial installment of 600,000 yards of woolen cloth to Soviet Russia, was leaked to reporters from the *Manchester Guardian,* the *Daily Herald,* and the *Morning Post:* the deal was worth more than a million pounds sterling in cold, hard cash. "The publication of this deal," Krasin wrote proudly from London to Foreign Minister Chicherin on 18 September 1920, "produced a sensation in the City."[21]

This was no exaggeration. The City of London was full of tsarist Russian bond and property holders who remained adamantly opposed to any settlement with the Bolsheviks and therefore looked warily at any hint of a regularization of trade relations. Among the opponents of Lloyd George's ongoing efforts to legitimize Bolshevik rule were Montagu Norman, chairman of the Bank of England; R. W. Hanna, the national secretary of the British Chambers of Commerce; and the chairmen of eight large insurance companies deeply invested in Russian bonds.[22] The most prominent single creditor was the Russo-Asiatic Consolidated Corporation chaired by John Leslie Urquhart, which before 1917 had owned many of Russia's largest gold and platinum mines. (Despite the similarity in their names, Russo-Asiatic Consolidated was unconnected to the mostly French-owned Banque Russo-Asiatique.) Urquhart had filed a claim against the Soviet government for restitution of stolen property worth no less than 56 million sterling, or $280 million.[23] Krasin wrote to Moscow in October 1920, "The campaign against having any relations with us is being led by the Urquhart group."[24]

To end the gold blockade without having to pay off creditors like Urquhart, Krasin needed to create a countercoalition of businessmen eager for a trade accord that would allow them to negotiate profitable gold-securitized deals with Soviet Russia legally. The bigger the corporate names, the better. In addition to Standard Oil, Krasin negotiated with the London offices of automotive firms like Packard, Rolls-Royce, and Fiat, the last two of which also produced aero-engines for deluxe civilian as well as military aircraft.[25] That many leading aviation firms were English, French, or Italian was an added bonus. The Entente powers were already at odds over everything from the Turkish-Greek war to German reparations, including, not incidentally, the colossal matter of Russian debt. Competition over Bolshevik concessions would not only drive down prices but also lead the firms involved to lobby their governments to be the first to legalize trade with Soviet Russia.[26]

It was not a fair fight. French firms desiring to do business with the Bolsheviks faced enormous political opposition, as literally millions of bondholding "Urquharts" backed the Millerand government's adamant refusal to sign an accord with Soviet Russia. In England, tsarist Russian creditors in the City of London, however influential, had to contend with an ever-expanding cohort eager to do business with Bolshevism, from coal miners and textile factory workers (and the Labour Party politicians who spoke for them) to companies like Rolls-Royce. Krasin won over nearly the entire city of Newcastle when he dangled an offer before Armstrong, Whitworth and Company even bigger than the Nydquist and Holm deal, for the renovation of 1,500 Russian locomotives over a period of five years, along with an exclusive concession for the reconstruction of the port of Petrograd. The Armstrong deal alone would be worth 100 million pounds sterling, or $500 million—the rough equivalent of $20 billion in today's terms. Such an enormous contract would have to await the conclusion of a formal trade accord, of course, but merely by placing it on the table Krasin created a powerful lobby to push for ratification. In effect, the Armstrong group now had a financial stake even larger than the Urquhart group in the Anglo-Soviet trade negotiations, and from the opposite side.[27]

Momentum toward a rapprochement between Soviet Russia and Western business was building in fall 1920, and not only in London and Stockholm. The Nydquist and Holm rail deal itself took on greater force in October, as German firms including Krupp, Borsig,

Henschel and Son, and the German-Russian Transport Company (which would handle the shipping on the Hamburg-Amerika line) began signing on. Lomonosov and Krasin, it will be recalled, had first promoted the German-Swedish-Soviet railway blockbuster in summer 1919, but the German firms had hesitated for fear Entente creditors would seize any Bolshevik gold transferred to German banks. Lomonosov returned to Berlin in August 1920 to put final touches on the deal, accompanied by a multilingual Bulgarian trade negotiator named Boris Stomoniakov. Max Laserson carefully drafted a contract designed to insulate all parties from possible legal complications involving the unofficial gold blockade. By November, despite the Quai d'Orsay having denounced the Krupp deal with the Bolsheviks as a "new treason" committed by Germany in violation of the Versailles Treaty, the German side was ready. Laserson's contract, even the French admitted, was ironclad.[28] In addition to the initial 1,000 rail engines Krasin had ordered in Stockholm, German factories would produce another 700 locomotives and 5 million poods (about 90,000 tons) worth of rolling stock, at a cost of 3 billion marks, or roughly $100 million.[29]

There was money to be made in Soviet Russia, and word was getting around fast. Across Europe in autumn 1920, Soviet trade officials reported a surge in interest about opening trade with Moscow, from industrialists and union representatives in Scandinavia, Germany, Austria and Italy. By December, even the French were beginning to consider authorizing trade deals with Moscow, for fear France would miss out on the Bolshevik gold boom entirely. In practice, a Quai d'Orsay policy memorandum noted with regret, France's principled stand "had simply excluded the French from purchases of [Russian] gold which France needs more than the other Allied countries."[30]

All eyes, however, remained focused on London, where the crucial Anglo-Soviet negotiations would decide the legal status of looted Russian gold in Western capital markets. A Danish delegation even opened official trade talks with the Soviet government—at Krasin's Tsentrosoiuz headquarters in London. Krasin, though frustrated that Lloyd George had not yet lifted the gold blockade, knew his hand was strong. If he was forced to leave London without signing an accord, Krasin wrote in a 16 October 1920 telegram to Moscow,

"We will liquidate our mission here, hoping to continue trade negotiations while focusing on Scandinavia, Germany and Italy."[31]

Krasin's implied threat to leave London for good was not idle. It is likely he even intended this telegram to be read by the British secret services, who had decoded the Soviet ciphers. Krasin, along with Lev Kamenev (seconded to the Tsentrosoiuz mission in July), had attended a tense meeting on Downing Street in September, at which "Lloyd George had virtually told Kamenev that the British government was reading the mission's telegraphic traffic."[32] Krasin's threat to leave was a clever way to put pressure on the British prime minister, who had invested huge political capital in the trade negotiations and did not want his most trusted negotiating partner to abandon him.

With typical stubbornness, Lloyd George continued ignoring evidence of Krasin's duplicity. Just as Lloyd George had promoted Krasin as the palatable Soviet alternative to Litvinov at the inter-Allied conference at San Remo in April, so he weathered a burgeoning controversy inside his cabinet over Bolshevik subversion in England by differentiating between Kamenev and Krasin. The telegrams deciphered by British intelligence revealed not only how cynically the Bolsheviks viewed the debt repayment issue, but also that Kamenev and Krasin had sold on the London market that summer more than 40,000 sterling worth of diamonds and turned over the proceeds to the British Communist Party. Another 35,000 pounds was turned over to the Communist newspaper, the *Daily Herald*. Throughout August and September, as the Polish-Soviet war reached its climax, the telegraphic communication from Moscow revealed a deliberate, well-funded plot to manipulate public opinion in Britain against Poland. While both Curzon and Churchill thought such evidence of Bolshevik interference in British politics warranted the immediate expulsion of all Soviet personnel, Lloyd George insisted on sparing Krasin, who was only a "trade" negotiator and not a "political" representative like Kamenev. To put the issue to rest, Lloyd George leaned on Kamenev to leave London, and the latter obliged on 11 September. Krasin was allowed to stay.[33]

Lloyd George's claim that Krasin was innocent of meddling in British politics was just as false as his earlier protestations that Tsentrosoiuz was independent of the Soviet government: the Politburo files show clearly that Krasin was in constant communication with the Kremlin on political matters all through 1920 and 1921.[34] It was also naïve. Krasin himself deliberately promoted the idea that his own "policy of moderation" was viewed suspiciously in the Kremlin. In a November 1920 meeting with E. F. Wise of the British Ministry of Food, Krasin cleverly hinted that the Moscow hardliners would triumph if he did not get his way. Wise dutifully forwarded Krasin's warning on to the cabinet as evidence that the Soviet Politburo was split between "two tendencies, the one towards trade and economic development and the other towards [revolutionary] propaganda in the East"—that is, against the British Empire.[35] Wise's blinkered assessment of Bolshevism was remarkably insular in its assumptions: the idea that Politburo debates turned on the issue of whether to trade with, or to overthrow, the British Empire is one which can only have occurred to a British trade official. Still more astonishing was that Lloyd George, a man with considerably more political experience than Wise, subscribed to the same benign view of Krasin.

Not everyone at Whitehall was so sanguine. Predictably, it was the Tories in Lloyd George's coalition cabinet who led the opposition. Curzon, the conservative foreign minister, refused to correspond personally with Krasin, let alone meet with him, after his unpleasant encounter in May. For this reason, the British Foreign Office played almost no role in drafting the proposed Anglo-Soviet trade accord. In November, as negotiations grew more serious, the war minister, Winston Churchill, threatened to resign if Lloyd George signed any sort of accord with Krasin. "One might as well legalize sodomy," Churchill objected, "as recognize the Bolsheviks."[†] Lloyd George was, Churchill fumed, "on the high road to embrace Bolshevism."[36]

The objections of Curzon and Churchill notwithstanding, by mid-November Lloyd George had won over the most important Tory cabinet member, Andrew Bonar Law, Lord Privy Seal and leader of the House of Commons. Stunningly, Bonar Law now dismissed the crucial debt problem out of hand, demanding of critics like Curzon and Churchill: "What is the use of our saying that we won't do trade

---

[†]As Daniel Johnson recently noted, Churchill's objections showed how out of touch he was with the postwar sensibilities of the West: both sodomy and Bolshevism were well on their way to widespread social acceptance.

because we cannot get the old debts paid? We have been shilly-shal-lying for two years." Echoing the E. F. Wise–Lloyd George belief that trade would moderate Bolshevism, Bonar Law promised his Tory colleagues that "we shall have far more chance of exercising pressure on Russia after an agreement." Reluctantly, the cabinet as-sented, agreeing to submit a draft trade accord to Krasin on 29 No-vember 1920, which was somewhat stiffened over earlier drafts in its prohibitions against Soviet propaganda on British imperial territory and also in stipulating that each side could terminate the agreement with only three months' notice if evidence emerged that it was being violated.[37] To reassure the Quai d'Orsay (which had submitted a formal request to Lloyd George on 25 November), the final British draft proposal explicitly demanded Soviet acknowledgment, in prin-ciple, of "all its foreign obligations."[38] Churchill, although aban-doning his threat to resign if an accord was offered to Soviet Russia, insisted that cabinet members recognize that "signing this agreement in no way alters the general position we have taken up as to the Bol-sheviks, namely, that Ministers shall be free to point out the odious character of the regime."[39] But in the end even Churchill went along.

As Churchill's dissent suggested, merely the submission of a draft Anglo-Soviet trade accord by Whitehall represented the crossing of a moral Rubicon, an abandonment of the anti-Bolshevik crusade. However strong the provisions condemning Soviet-sponsored sub-version of foreign countries, there was not even a pro forma condem-nation of Bolshevik behavior *inside* Soviet Russia. The more British negotiators foregrounded concerns about Soviet manipulation in "Asia Minor, Persia, Afghanistan and India," the further the essential moral and political problems posed by Bolshevism receded into the background. Even on the issue of revolutionary propaganda against the British Empire, Lloyd George displayed a characteristic uncon-cern over matters that greatly exercised his own ministers. Against Curzon's protestations that Moscow must promise unambiguously to cease anti-British agitation, for example, Lloyd George countered, "Even with the best will in the world with Bolshevik outbreaks you will not be able to restrain [Soviet propaganda]."[40] This was cer-tainly true, but it does raise the interesting question of why Lloyd George felt the need to sign an accord with the Bolsheviks at all.[41]

So far as the mindset of the British prime minister can be ascertained during the historic final negotiations over the Anglo-Soviet trade accord, Lloyd George thought he was in a race against time to bail Britain out of recession by opening up the Russian market to British exports. In his defense, the economic indicators in the winter of 1920–21 were indeed distressing, with Britain sinking into recession and unemployment reaching into the millions, including in the textile-related industries, which stood to benefit most from the opening of the Russian market. Not for nothing was Krasin placing conspicuous orders for British wool all winter. In addition to the high-profile purchases discussed above, by March 1921 Krasin had ordered another 1.7 million pounds sterling (or $8.5 million) worth of English woolen cloth for Red Army greatcoats, full-dress uniforms, and shirts, to be shipped via Reval.[42] This was only the beginning of a major textile boom that would occur, men like Bonar Law, Wise, and Lloyd George hoped with some justification, after the legalization of trade with Soviet Russia.

Krasin was drawing Lloyd George in, hook, line, and sinker. As his telegraphic correspondence with Litvinov and Chicherin makes clear, his goal in London was never to seek full diplomatic recognition or a final peace treaty. Flare-ups over such seemingly contentious matters as "propaganda" were useful distractions from the Bolsheviks' real aim, which was to get the gold blockade lifted without having to recognize any of Russia's debt obligations. As Krasin wrote Chicherin in late December 1920, "We must first draw England and other countries into commercial and business intercourse with us; it is necessary that new commercial concessional interests should become so firm, that our refusal at the peace conference to pay old debts shall not result in a new blockade or intervention."[43]

The Bolsheviks' goal was, quite simply, to gain something for nothing. Britain would lift the gold blockade and allow its wool, boot, and coal producers to supply Soviet Russia, which is to say, the Red Army and Cheka, legally. In exchange, the Bolsheviks would give promises of better behavior in the future. Even the relatively innocuous provisions in the November draft regarding the suppression of Soviet propaganda in regions bordering the British Empire were watered down all winter to appease Krasin, with specific mention of Persia and Kemalist Turkey stricken from the final treaty.[44]

The final draft of the Anglo-Soviet trade accord, ratified on 16

March 1921, was nearly as favorable to Bolshevik interests as the Tartu Treaty with Estonia drafted the previous year. This is rather astonishing when we consider that Estonia was a tiny country with an even tinier army, whose newly won independence rested at the mercy of the Soviet Russian giant enveloping its territory, whereas Great Britain was still the preeminent global power, with miles of blue water and the world's largest navy to protect it from Bolshevik subversion. The issue of propaganda, which so obsessed many British negotiators, was reduced to a few innocuous phrases in the final preamble, which made the agreement conditional on promises "that each party refrains from hostile action or undertakings against the other," along with "any official propaganda direct or indirect against the institutions of the British Empire or the Russian Soviet Republic." As for the crucial matter of debt, Krasin did agree to a declaration that the Soviet government "recognizes in principle that it is liable to pay compensation to private persons who have supplied goods or services to Russia for which they have not been paid." Significantly, however, this "liability" was referred to a "general Peace Treaty" to be negotiated later.[45]

In exchange for these toothless promises to refrain from inflammatory propaganda (so long as the British would too) and to consider, just possibly, compensating the millions of individuals they had expropriated (after some general peace conference, to be held sometime in the future), the Bolsheviks immediately received everything Krasin had asked for. Article 1 formally lifted the British blockade of Soviet goods and guaranteed that London would no longer "place any impediments in the way of banking, credit and financial operations for the purpose of such trade." Article 2 granted merchant ships full docking and coaling privileges in all British ports. In Article 3, the British navy was enjoined to complete "the clearance of the seas adjacent to their own coasts and also certain parts of the Baltic," to facilitate trade with Russia. Article 5 granted Soviet trade officials in England unmolested use of post, telegraph, "wireless telegraphy in cipher," and the ability "to receive and dispatch couriers with sealed bags subject to a limitation of 3 kilograms per week which shall be exempt from examination." Article 8 guaranteed the recognition of "passports, documents of identity, Powers of Attorney and similar documents by the competent authorities in either country for the purpose of enabling trade." Most important of all was Article 9, in which the British government declared "that it will not initiate any steps with a view to attach or to take possession of any gold, funds, securities or commodities not being articles identifiable as the property of the British Government which may be exported from Russia in payment for imports or as securities for such payment, or of any movable or immovable property which may be acquired by the Russian Soviet Government within the United Kingdom." Further, Britain formally assured the Bolsheviks that it "will not take steps to obtain any special legislation not applicable to other countries against the importation into the United Kingdom of precious metals from Russia whether specie (other than British or Allied) or bullion or manufactures or the storing, analyzing, refining, melting, mortgaging or disposing thereof in the United Kingdom, and will not requisition such metals."[46]

By agreeing to Krasin's conditions regarding the gold blockade, Lloyd George had forfeited any leverage the Entente powers still had over the Soviet government. Once the Bolsheviks could sell gold in England, they could effectively sell it anywhere, as London set the standard for the world's financial markets. By giving up the right to seize "gold, funds, securities or commodities" coming from Soviet Russia, the British government undercut its own case that the Bolsheviks were "liable to pay compensation to private persons" they had expropriated, by recognizing the loot thereby obtained as legal Soviet property. The Quai d'Orsay had recognized the full legal implications of Lloyd George's appeasement policy as early as June 1920, while realizing also that there was nothing France could do to force him to change course.[47] Amazingly, Soviet gold imported into Britain was given better terms for reexport than gold coming from South Africa—a member of the British Commonwealth!—the former was granted an export license good for six months after arrival, against forty-two days for the latter.[48] Krasin could not have asked for a more ironclad guarantee of the legal status of Bolshevik gold.

Just as he had earlier differentiated between Krasin and other Bolsheviks, so Lloyd George insisted in the House of Commons that the Anglo-Soviet accord did not confer diplomatic recognition on Moscow but was "purely a trading agreement." This was rank sophistry. The legal guarantees accorded Soviet and British trade representatives were equivalent to those given embassy and consular personnel, from the use of ciphers and sealed diplomatic bags to the recognition of valid passports. At Lloyd George's own urging, the British Court of Appeals overturned, in May 1921, an earlier High Court decision which had allowed the sequestration of Bolshevik assets by creditors of tsarist Russia. The High Court itself ruled in July that Soviet gold imported into the United Kingdom was legally inviolable. Both rulings referenced the 16 March trade accord, noting that the de facto recognition granted Soviet Russia meant that no British court could "pretend to express an opinion upon the legality or otherwise of its acts."[49]

With the British courts now guaranteeing the legal status of Bolshevik gold and other looted properties, there was no longer any reason for other countries to pay lip service to the concerns of dispossessed Russian creditors like the French. By the end of 1921, Soviet Russia had signed trade agreements with Sweden, Norway, Finland, Estonia, Latvia, Lithuania, Poland, Germany, Czechoslovakia, Austria, and Italy and had sent trade missions to Turkey, Persia, and China. The only holdouts of note were France, Japan, and the United States, all interventionist powers whose leaders refused to give in as the British had.[50] Not surprisingly, the volume of imported wares reaching Soviet Russia increased geometrically after the signing of the trade accord, from a mere 736,713 poods (about 13,000 tons) in the month of January 1921 to 5.4 million poods, or some 100,000 tons, in July. In all, Soviet imports for 1921 totaled 86 million poods (1.6 million tons), an increase by a factor of sixteen over the 5.2 million poods imported in 1920 (just under 100,000 tons) and 160 times greater than the 520,000 poods (about 10,000 tons) imported in 1919, while the British blockade was active.

This is not to say the trade accord turned Bolshevik Russia into an ordinary trading nation. Soviet imports still totaled a mere fraction of their prewar volume, and exports remained negligible—an anemic 160,000 tons of gold, flax, hemp, and a few oil products in 1921, or about 6 percent of the volume of imports—because the Soviet economy was still producing almost nothing worthy of export.[51] Those trading with Soviet Russia could reliably receive only one commodity in return, as Lloyd George's conservative critics and French officials had tried to warn him: gold.

Krasin had pulled off a stupendous feat of diplomatic negotiation. Without giving any ground on such issues as Soviet debt repayment or even the red herring of "propaganda," he had put an end to the gold blockade that had been hindering Soviet imports of war matériel ever since the October Revolution. Not only did this allow European manufacturers to sell supplies to the Red Army without fear of legal hassles, it also dramatically lowered the risk premium paid for such deals as Soviet gold no longer needed to be melted down in Stockholm. No longer could Litvinov complain about the expense necessitated by Krasin's complex contracts. Commissions that had reached as high as 25 percent in 1920 now dwindled to 10, 5, and as little as 1–2 percent.[52]

Krasin's coup in London came just in time for Bolshevism, surpassing even the Tartu Treaty and the Nydquist and Holm deal in Stockholm in its long-term impact on the strategic position of Soviet Russia. The timing was uncanny. The Anglo-Soviet accord was signed on the morning of 16 March, just hours before Trotsky ordered the final assault on Kronstadt. Kerzhentsev's ultimatum to the Swedish Foreign Office, in which he threatened to cut off lucrative Swedish contracts with Moscow unless Stockholm prevented supplies from reaching the Kronstadt rebels, was delivered the same day. Also, on the seventeeth the recently enlarged German Communist Party (VKPD), urged on by the Bolshevik emissary Bela Kun, launched a violent Soviet-style insurrection in Germany.[53] When Germany's laborers refused to heed Moscow's call for a general strike, bloody clashes ensued as VKPD activists attacked workers trying to reach their factories and were beaten in turn. Hundreds of Communist activists died, and thousands more were arrested. The VKPD itself was decimated, as nearly 170,000 party members quit in disgust.[54] There was a gruesome irony to all this, as if the governments of Sweden and Great Britain had decided to beatify Bolshevism at the moment it most blatantly revealed its various hypocrisies, crushing a rebellion led by workers' and soldiers' soviets in Russia while waging war on workers in Germany. The French, by contrast, though offered a similar Soviet trade deal later in March, refused to open talks.[55]

With characteristically inappropriate timing, Lloyd George addressed the Commons on 22 March 1921—shortly after the last

Kronstadt rebels had been rounded up, the "March Action" had cut its destructive swathe through Germany, and just before Tukhachevsky's army of class enforcers descended on Tambov province to murder and deport its rebellious peasants en masse—to announce that a new era of Communist moderation was at hand. "There is a great change in Russia itself," Lloyd George declaimed, "there is a change from the wild extravagant Communism of a year or two ago, or even a few months ago . . . a complete change in the attitude of the Bolshevik Government to what is called capitalism, towards private enterprise, towards communal effort, towards nationalization."[56]

This was wishful thinking of the most naïve kind. Lloyd George had fallen, yet again, for the Bolshevik bait, interpreting the onset of the so-called New Economic Policy Lenin announced in March 1921 exactly as Lenin wanted him to: as a harbinger of genuine reform that would ultimately restore some form of capitalism in Russia.[57] Far from moderating Soviet Russia through trade, as Lloyd George promised it would, the Anglo-Soviet accord sealed the transformation of the Bolshevik regime from a beleaguered conspiracy of political activists into a wealthy criminal oligarchy, which could draw on Western capital markets to fund its war with its own people. That millions of these people were on the brink of starvation in spring 1921 as famine rapidly spread through south Russia would hardly make the Bolsheviks blink as they dumped gold abroad on high-end military purchases. Krasin himself, in his first major public address in Moscow following his triumph at Whitehall, took on a much different tone than he had in London when he boasted openly that the Anglo-Soviet trade accord "authorized the import of War Equipment and aeroplanes."[58]

Just as the Tartu Treaty had allowed Moscow to realize a historic gold-for-locomotives deal over a year in the making, the Anglo-Soviet trade accord allowed the Bolsheviks to clear military aircraft orders they had been working on for months. In October 1920, Frederick Ström, the Swedish front man for the Soviet Trade Mission, had held confidential meetings in Stockholm with Swedish and German aircraft engineers.[59] In November, the Bolsheviks sent their leading aviation expert, G. K. Linno, to Reval, where he met with fifteen separate firms. Linno was partial to planes mounting German aero-engines, both for quality and reliability and because the rapidly weakening German mark meant they would be a bargain. Before the Anglo-Soviet accord, though, there was still the worry that payment would be seized by Entente creditors, and so Linno ordered only 80 German planes that winter and 50 extra Mercedes engines (260 horsepower), the former via a Danish front company, the latter in Stockholm.[60]

Still more sensitive was the deal negotiated with the Belgian firm Breget in February 1921, which would have been inconceivable were not the Anglo-Soviet accord on the horizon. Breget was offering 500 planes, three hundred mounting 120-horsepower Renault engines, and two hundred with 300 HP Fiat motors, along with spare parts. Best of all for the Bolsheviks, Breguet would mount a machine-gun chassis on each plane, with 100,000 rounds for each gun, including flares and incendiaries (zazhigatel'nykh). This single deal alone would cost nearly 14 million gold rubles ($7 million). It would, of course, take several years to fulfill, but Breget was insisting on advance payment.[61]

Bolshevik gold went much further in Germany, as Linno had advised. A complex deal, negotiated in January–February 1921, saw the Bolsheviks order one hundred German-made military aircraft, twenty-five spare motors (Mercedes-Benz, BMW, and Maibach), along with enough spare parts; lubricants; and electrical, radio, and telegraphic fixtures for the entire Soviet air force. In all, nearly a half dozen German firms would be involved, in Berlin, Bavaria, and Stuttgart. Of course, such a massive order would take several years to fulfill, but unlike the Breget deal, it would require the Bolsheviks to make only a relatively reasonable deposit of 20 million German marks (under $1 million, so far had the mark tumbled since the end of the war).[62]

So many arms deals were being struck in Germany that Bolshevik purchasing agents began talking them up as a prelude to a strategic partnership against the Entente.[63] Lenin himself was keenly interested in the prospect: in mid-March 1921 he issued a formal request that German military advisers "help reorganize the Red Army."[64] The Germans, too, were interested, and this included both elusive army General Hans von Seeckt (who deployed his own emissaries) and the Foreign Office, which had sent Moritz Schlesinger to Moscow in January 1921. A provisional Soviet-German trade accord, with secret military provisions, was duly dispatched to Berlin in February. Had revolutionary politics not intervened, in the form of Bela Kun's ill-fated March Action, which so disturbed Berlin that German Foreign Minister Walter Simons refused to discuss the draft, the notorious Rapallo agreement between the two anti-Allied pariah states might well have come in April 1921 instead of April 1922.[65] The disastrous March Action also damaged Bolshevik business interests, as German aviation firms began hesitating about supplying Moscow just when the Anglo-Soviet accord should have cleared away the last legal hurdles. By 1922, only 18 of the German warplanes ordered in winter 1920–21 had been manufactured, and most of these were still lying in warehouses in Stockholm.[66] Rapallo would have to wait.

The (temporarily) negative impact of the German March Action on Soviet import prospects was more than offset, however, by the possibilities opened up in 1921 by the Anglo-Soviet trade accord with other European suppliers. Dutch aviation firms, for example, had hesitated to deal with Soviet procurement agents before March 1921 for the same reasons German ones had, fearing sequestration of payment by Entente creditors. Although there were still no diplomatic relations between Amsterdam and Moscow—not even a Soviet trade mission—Dutch companies enjoyed a low enough profile that they could work through middlemen without exciting too much scrutiny. Both Fokker of Amsterdam and Aero-Industrie of Rotterdam had sales offices in Berlin, where they could negotiate with the Soviet Trade Mission without being hassled by the Dutch government. Payment in Dutch guilders was required by both, although this was easy to arrange now that Bolshevik gold could be legally sold in the City of London. In late October and early November 1921, two installments of 6 million gold rubles each were transferred to Krasin in London from a special "12 million fund" for arms purchases, of which about 1 million was used to buy 500,000 Dutch guilders.[67] These were used to make deposits on several large aviation orders placed in Berlin with Fokker and Aero-Industrie. The Aero-Industrie contract, for fifteen L.V.9. C VI military planes with spare parts and double machine-gun batteries on each, was most urgent and thus a bulk payment of 70,000 Dutch guilders was made in advance: the first ten were delivered by January 1922. The Fokker orders, totaling over a million Dutch guilders, of which only a fraction was deposited in 1921, were longer-term and included luxury civilian passenger aircraft; about thirty of the eighty ordered had reached Petrograd by March 1922.[68]

Another promising aviation market opened up by the Anglo-Soviet accord was, of course, the one in Britain itself. English orders emphasized luxury over volume, targeting not the Soviet air force but the commuting needs of top Soviet officials. Competing bids were taken on all through 1921, from specialty firms like Blackburn Aeroplane and Motor Company of Leeds, which had been contracted during the war to produce a twin-engined "General Purpose Seaplane . . . suitable for use either on night bombing raids or (and more especially) on anti-submarine patrol duties." The resulting product, the "Kangeroo Bombing Aeroplane," had now been modified for civilian use, seating seven or eight in "enclosed cabins," with two Rolls-Royce 275-horsepower engines.[69]

More powerful still was the deluxe 0/400 airplane manufactured by the Handley Page Company, a converted bomber now used for passenger traffic between London and Paris. The 0/400, which could seat as many as nine, with "considerable cargo space," mounted twin Rolls-Royce Eagle VIII 350-horsepower engines capable of powering the 630-kilometer trip from Moscow to St. Petersburg in just five and a half hours. Handley-Page also offered a lighter three-seater, the D.H.9 Machine, which had set a world speed record on a nonstop flight from Strasbourg to London, averaging 110 miles per hour. But it was the 0/400 that interested the Bolsheviks, so long as it could be specially mounted with "combined aircraft transmitter and receiver suitable for transmission and reception of wireless telephony or telegraphy, complete with remote control, wind driven generator with propellor and boss, aerial winch, wire and weight, etc., together with complete high frequency selective receiver." The initial order for one 0/400 would cost Moscow 7,245 pounds sterling, or $36,000, not including customs and shipping after "delivery will be made f.o.b. London docks."[70]

It was the English A. V. Roe and Company, however, that finally won the competition to supply the Bolsheviks with a machine meeting all of their peculiar requirements. The deluxe airplane was made to order for the Politburo. "As requested," an A.V. and Roe salesman wrote to the Soviet Trade Delegation in London, "we now have pleasure in quoting you for a machine fitted with a Rolls Royce Condor Engine 750 H.P. complete with all instruments, gun racks, one Vickers and one Lewis gun, parachutes, wireless and photographic apparatus, packed C.I.F. Reval, for the sum of £16,000 (sixteen thousand pounds)."[71] Whether used by the Bolsheviks for surveillance, targeting, aerial assault, or simply for commuting in style between Moscow and Petrograd, this machine was hard to beat.

In addition to supplying engines for deluxe armored Bolshevik airplanes, Rolls-Royce also provided spare parts for Lenin's famous motorcar. Driving a Rolls-Royce had been something of a symbol of sovereignty for Kerensky too: he had requisitioned one back in July 1917.[72] Lenin's 1915 model Rolls-Royce had belonged to Mikhail Romanov, younger brother of the murdered tsar (it can be viewed today at the Gorki Leninskie museum, south of Moscow). Despite its august provenance, Lenin's Rolls-Royce required maintenance like all other cars, and spare parts for his luxury model were particularly hard to come by. Not the least of the benefits accruing to Moscow from the Anglo-Soviet trade accord was that these could now be imported from England without hassles, along with newer models like the "Silver Ghost" ordered in 1921. Because of the politically sensitive nature of the transactions, Krasin himself took charge of all negotiations with Rolls-Royce, paying in cash so as to minimize public exposure.[73]

Still, these luxury aircraft and automobile orders, however indicative of the regal attitude prevailing in the Politburo, did not eat up more than a fraction of the Bolsheviks' import budget. The bulk of the special "12 million fund" sent to London, for example, went to Red Army uniforms (4.7 million), spare parts for military vehicles (2 million) and airplanes (3 million), and supplies for the Red Army artillery command (1.72 million)—this last for movable gun mounts, gunsights, 200,000 steel balls (stal'nye shariki), and binoculars.[74] Similarly huge amounts were spent on practical German products, like Bosch spark plugs, boots, binoculars, field telephones, paper, and pencils.[75]

As these orders suggest, the Bolsheviks' military import priorities had shifted somewhat now that the peasant wars were winding down, away from small arms and ammunition and toward better-targeted heavy artillery, automobiles, and aircraft. The constants were wool and boots, for which the Red Army had a seemingly insatiable appetite. In the first half of 1921, SPOTEKZAK ordered 3,296,875 pairs of deluxe foreign-made military boots, which at 10 rubles a pair came to 32 million gold rubles ($16 million).[76] English textile orders in 1921 totaled 2.2 million sterling, or $11 million, more than ARCOS spent on any other item, even on coal.[77]

Lloyd George could certainly point to this as an achievement of sorts, as Soviet import orders did stimulate England's politically sensitive coal and textile industries. Because these orders were paid in gold and cash, however, they were renewable only so long as the Bolsheviks remained liquid. And as Krasin himself warned in an interview with the Berlin-based newspaper *Novy Mir,* Soviet gold bars being sold off to pay for imports priced in "pounds and dollars" would eventually run out. "Europe and America will need to realize," Krasin hinted, "that the recovery of the entire world economy depends on the recovery of Russian industry," which itself would require "that they open credit for Russia." Without new loans, Russia's credit for foreign purchases remained nothing more than its (ever-dwindling) precious metals reserves.[78]

It was an extraordinary situation. The Russian economy was in ruins, with the prime "black earth" lands of the fertile Volga basin, which before 1914 had produced the world's largest grain surpluses and the vast bulk of Russia's exports, a barren wasteland. Although the Bolsheviks tried to suppress news of the Volga famine, by summer 1921 it was so enormous—threatening to kill 25 million people, as *Pravda* conceded on 26 June—that Lenin hired Herbert Hoover's American Relief Administration (ARA) to feed Russia's peasants and provide seed for the next year's harvest, though not without infiltrating the ARA with Cheka agents and launching an international smear campaign against Hoover's relief workers.[79] Russia's one remaining aviation factory burned to the ground in July. Consumer goods were a bitter memory. The Russian oil industry was virtually dead, despite the reconquest of Baku, with Caspian wells yielding only 2.5 million tons of crude in the first half of 1921, compared to 10 million in 1915.[80] The last Siberian gold and platinum mines still functioning ground to a halt in October 1921, as starving miners began roaming the countryside looking for food.[81]

And yet all through summer and fall 1921, as their people began starving in droves, the Bolsheviks continued importing airplanes, automobiles, arms, and artillery, along with boots and uniforms for the Red Army. They even imported food—not primarily grain or seed for the famine regions (Hoover's ARA and other Western "capitalist" charities were taking care of that, the ARA alone spending $60 million, the bulk contributed by U.S. taxpayers), but luxury items for themselves, like the 30 million tsarist rubles worth of chocolate ordered in London, the 63 million rubles worth of fruit, tobacco, and opium from Persia, along with seaborne perishables like Swedish herring (40,000 tons), Finnish salted fish (250 tons), German bacon (7,000 tons), and French pig fat.[82] As Georgi Solomon later recalled, the Soviet elites were consuming delicacies like "truffles, pineapples, mandarin oranges, bananas, dried fruits, sardines and lord knows what else" while everywhere else in Russia "the people were dying of hunger."[83]

As expensive imports of all kinds poured into Russia from European countries no longer fearing sequestration of Bolshevik payment for them, Soviet gold predictably poured out even faster than before. In the first four months after the ratification of the Anglo-Soviet trade accord on 16 March 1921, 75 million gold rubles ($37.5 million) worth of looted Russian imperial ingots were invoiced departing from the Reval Customs House, nearly half aboard Olof Aschberg's favorite steamer, the *Kalewipoeg*.[84] Aschberg's ship was even busier in August, as the *Kalewipoeg* and another Swedish vessel, the *Egil*, together carried $40 million worth of gold to Stockholm.[85] Another $6 million in gold was shipped in September, before the outflow tapered off, with no gold shipments being registered in the Reval Customs House in the first half of October.[86] A "special fund" of 12 million gold rubles was sent to Krasin in London later in October, but this was in coin, not ingots, intended to be converted into hard currency (dollars, Dutch guilders, pounds sterling, German marks, Swedish crowns).[87]

If Lloyd George's intention in guaranteeing the legal status of Bolshevik gold was to cause that gold to disappear more quickly as Moscow gorged itself on Western imports, then we must rate the Anglo-Soviet trade accord a success, with $100 million worth dispatched abroad just in the first six months, or nearly 150 metric tons. Was the gold reserve running out? Entente intelligence officers were beginning to think so. It seemed significant that many shipments of Soviet gold, beginning in summer 1921, were in coin instead of ingots.[88] In part this was because the French government, while still forbidding the import of gold bars with a tsarist stamp (these still needed to be melted down in Stockholm), legalized the import of Russian gold coin on 11 August 1921. This set off a frenzy on the gold market in Paris, as Charles Westcott noted with alarm in a special report to Washington.[89] Westcott's well-circulated April 1921 report on the "Origin and Disposition of the Former Russian Imperial Gold Reserve" called the "constantly accelerated exports of Soviet gold . . . one of the most portentous developments of [his] investigation." A Russian informant just in from Moscow offered an intriguing theory to explain the phenomenon. As Westcott reported the Russian's remarks, "Lenin and Trotsky are now preparing for precipitate flight, by a premonitory looting of the Russian Imperial Gold Reserve, because in imminent peril of destruction by the Bolshevik Frankenstein which they themselves have created. . . . There is such a thing as hell becoming too hot for the Devil himself."[90] Backing up this theory, another Bolshevik defector told the U.S. commissioner in Riga that "the gold fund of the Bolsheviks on July 15, 1921, amounted to thirty-seven millions in coin," along with 250 poods (about 5 tons) of platinum: "all other resources were exhausted."[91] At about the same time, Irving Linnell, U.S. consul in London, reported that it was a "well-known circumstance that Mr. Krassin in London, as well as Kopp in Berlin, have both been lately stinted of funds for commercial transactions."[92]

Even Swedish officials, despite their generally favorable disposition toward the Bolsheviks, were becoming concerned that the great Russian gold rush was coming to an end. Sweden's own informants from the Soviet Finance Commissariat estimated, in November 1921, that Bolshevik reserves were down to some "25–27 million gold rubles." But this was buttressed by a foreign currency fund at the State Bank, which "consists of approximately 180 boxes each weight 18 lbs and containing English, Scandinavian, Italian etc. paper and gold currency." Then there was the separate "precious stone fund and other valuables"—i.e., the Gokhran—the value of which was "very difficult to define as Government members themselves do not know." Interestingly, the Swedish agent's informant believed the Gokhran vaults to contain treasures "equal to 800–900 million gold roubles."[93] Another informant, though, thought that Gokhran holdings would barely "suffice for 6 month's expenditure."[94] The first informant's higher estimate of Gokhran resources was probably closer to the truth, if we are to credit Olof Aschberg's estimate that he alone processed 200 million Swedish crowns (nearly $50 million) worth of "platinum, gold, precious stones, diamonds, and pearls" from the Gokhran between 1921 and 1924.[95]

Bolshevik reserves were thus more resilient than Westcott and his informants suspected, but they were not wrong to point to a sense of financial panic engulfing Moscow. The Gokhran treasures, immensely valuable in theory, remained difficult to sell abroad, due in part to the De Beers monopoly discussed above (see chapter 3). Georgi Solomon, the Bolsheviks' most experienced contraband smuggler, complained that he had been forced to "haggle as if in a street bazaar" to sell off a Gokhran jewelry collection Krasin had entrusted to him in 1921. The Gokhran had had the jewels appraised at 1 million pounds sterling ($5 million); Solomon's final sale offer, rejected by his buyer, was for £675,000. Maxim Litvinov, taking over after Solomon had given up in frustration, finally sold the looted jewel collection for 365,000 pounds.[96] Litvinov did have more luck later that year, selling jewels worth 20 million gold rubles ($10 million) to an English buyer in August and reporting (optimistically) that the same buyer was prepared to purchase $100 million worth of Gokhran treasures.[97] In general, however, such lucrative sales were the exception, not the rule. "The sale of valuables," Litvinov wrote Lenin somewhat apologetically in June 1921, "has run into immense difficulties. The capacity of the market, given the current economic crisis, is extremely limited. Only an insignificant portion of the [Gokhran] valuables . . . has been sold. This commodity must be removed from the calculations of our hard-currency plans." Revenues from platinum sales, meanwhile, were plunging. After fetching 42 pounds sterling an ounce in Copenhagen in 1920, it now sold for barely 15. Litvinov claimed in his letter to Lenin, rather curiously, "With the disappearance of [platinum] from the world market, the demand has also disappeared." More likely he and Krasin had depressed the price by flooding the market. Despite holding significant

platinum reserves and untold quantities of looted jewelry and diamonds, Litvinov lamented, the Bolsheviks could still reliably finance
imports only with gold. "Everything else," he concluded sadly, "does
not amount to anything."[98]

The gold reserves, alas, would not last forever. An ominous por-
tent came in July, when the Politburo resolved to begin covering major expenses, such as food purchases in Persia and Red Army officer
salaries, with silver.[99] (Interestingly, however, Soviet Russian border
guards would still be paid in gold coin, for as long as it lasted.)[100] Silver rubles would now be cast for the Bolsheviks (where else?) in Sweden, where the Helsingfors Mint took on an (optimistic) contract to
coin over 500 million of them.[101] Some of this silver would come
from the Bokharan loot stored in Tashkent, which the Politburo ordered to be transferred to Moscow beginning in October 1921.[102]

Meanwhile, the Politburo began a seriocomic tradition of setting
up one emergency commission on top of another to account for the
disappearing gold reserves. The first was established under A. O.
Al'skii on 14 September 1921; two days later D. I. Kurskii replaced
Al'skii.[103] V. I. Novitsky, the former Allied gold informant hired by
the Politburo in November 1921, made no more headway than the
others. At the same meeting at which Novitsky was hired, a second
gold commission was created under Krestinsky to limit gold expenses, with a subbranch, under Trotsky, devoted to maximizing
hard currency revenues from foreign sales of Gokhran metals other
than gold (this was the commission which would handle the church
confiscations in 1922).[104]

The Gokhran was indeed flush with silver, platinum, diamonds,
and other metals, but these, as Litvinov had discovered, were not as
easy to convert into cash as gold bars. Luckily, the Bolsheviks still
had some gold. After the lull in October 1921, the Politburo commissions seem to have restored liquidity. Between 26 October 1921
and 6 February 1922, $56 million worth of Soviet gold, altogether
some 80 metric tons, was registered leaving Reval. Yet after the last
major shipment, of 40 metric tons aboard the Estonian steamer
Gladiator on 6 February, exports of Russian gold tapered off for
good, no longer registering on the radar of Entente intelligence.[105]
Krasin himself, the principal architect of the entire gold-financed Soviet import boom, received an urgent telegram on 8 February 1922,

which informed him that his credit line was being revoked in one week. Krasin had been rebuked for excessive spending before, but this was different. Credit for import orders was being withdrawn for *all* Soviet purchasing agents abroad on Trotsky's orders.[106] The Russian imperial gold reserves, once Europe's largest, had run out.

It had been an extraordinary run. In less than two years, since the Stockholm gold-laundering boom began in May 1920, the Bolsheviks had exported over 500 metric tons of gold—raising $353 million in foreign exchange, or more than $35 billion in today's terms.[107] For this they had received hundreds (soon to be thousands) of locomotive engines and rolling stock; tens of millions of boots, greatcoats, and woolen uniforms for the Red Army; rifles, artillery, shell, and hundreds of millions of machine-gun rounds; ferrous metals and ball bearings to reinvigorate Russia's own ailing arms factories; spark plugs and spare parts for military vehicles and for the luxury cars driven by high party officials like Lenin; an entire fleet of armored airplanes; Scandinavian fish, European delicacies, Persian fruit, tobacco, and opium, to satisfy the tastes of Bolshevik elites; and not least, enormous volumes of paper, chemicals to treat it, along with the ink and film stock needed to maintain the drumbeat of Communist propaganda. It was not enough to make Russia prosperous again, but it was plenty enough to keep the Bolsheviks in power through four long years of civil war, in which the vast majority of their people were—unlike regime supporters in the Red Army and Cheka, now well fed, well clothed, mobile, and well armed—reduced to bitter poverty.

Were the Bolsheviks broke? The signs were ominous. With gold all but gone, it was not surprising that the paper ruble plunged to the lowest depths yet reached. Although the Russian inflation of 1917–22 is less generally well known to economic historians than the concurrent Germany hyperinflation, it was no less dramatic. In September 1921, at the same time the Politburo convened its first gold commissions, monthly currency emissions passed the trillion barrier for the first time; nearly 2 trillion rubles were printed in October, and 3.35 trillion in November. In December, emissions doubled again, to over 7 trillion.[108] The reason was obvious: little gold coin remained to pay even high-priority government officials like Red Army officers, Cheka enforcers, and border guards, and—ambitious Swedish minting contract notwithstanding—there was nowhere near enough silver to make up the gap. Tax collection remained anemic. According to Grigory Sokol'nikov, by early 1922, no less than 97 percent of the domestic operating expenses of the Soviet government (then running at 13.5 trillion paper rubles per month) were being met with the printing press.[109]

With neither gold nor taxes to pay for the ordinary operations of government, the Bolsheviks had come full circle, to where they had been between the October Revolution and the breaking of the bank strike in March 1918. True, the Soviet regime was far more firmly entrenched in power in 1922 than in 1917–18, but this was because of the creation of massive, revenue-hungry armies of class enforcers: in this sense the regime was more financially desperate than ever. The whiff of déja vu was hard to miss, not least in the replay of the loot-the-looters campaign of 1918. The most audacious new expropriation of 1922, which saw Catherine the Great's necklace removed from her tomb in Petrograd, even registered on Allied intelligence. Another sign of Soviet financial desperation was the frantic search for the Romanov crown jewels, finally discovered hidden away in the Kremlin Armory in March 1922, in the hope of dumping them abroad to the highest bidder. The Bolsheviks' efforts to launder tsarist plunder that spring and summer were so widely publicized that a Russian passenger ship arriving in New York, the *White Star,* was searched by U.S. Treasury agents who had been (falsely) tipped off that the crown jewels were on board.[110]

Despite its macabre appeal to the Bolshevik mentality, the seizure of tsarist booty from the grave was not likely to yield ready cash anytime soon. Glittering though it was, the Romanov treasure Sokol'nikov was waving before prospective buyers presented the seller with an insuperable dilemma. The whole point of assembling all these otherwise disparate earrings, emblems, diadems, necklaces, brooches, rings, stones, and official regalia together as "the Romanov treasure" was to inflate their value because of their famous provenance. This worked well enough in theory. Sokol'nikov received a promising appraisal (which he unsurprisingly forwarded to Trotsky and the Politburo) of some 900 million gold rubles, or $450 million, for the collection sold as a whole. And yet who on earth would front this kind of money for the world's most famous stolen treasure, on which innumerable Romanov relatives were already staking legal claims? If, in contrast, the buyer wished only to enjoy owning the treasures anonymously, in secret, having no intention of reselling it at a profit (which would require public disclosure of the august provenance of the illegally looted jewelry), then why pay that much, or anywhere close? Finding a purchaser of the entire collection *as the Romanov treasure* was a quixotic fantasy, which Sokol'nikov himself likely suspected was unrealistic.[111]

More financially promising in the short term was the renewed assault on church property ordered by the Politburo in early January 1922. This campaign has been analyzed by a number of scholars, although until now it has not been appreciated just how closely tied it was to Moscow's impending bankruptcy. Jonathan Daly, echoing Richard Pipes, emphasizes the opportunistic timing of the campaign, during the Volga famine.[112] This was certainly the political rationale for the Bolsheviks' church-looting campaign, encompassed in Trotsky's cynical slogan, "Turn Gold into Bread." But at the level of root causation, the renewed church robberies of 1922 were mostly about replenishing Russia's strategic gold reserves, which, as we have seen, ran out in February. It was not to be: Russia's churches and monasteries turned out to be flush with silver (over 500 tons collected by 1923), not gold (less than half a ton, not even $1 million worth). The silver, moreover, was mostly kitchenwares, of little intrinsic value. As there "were practically no demands for Russian silver on the foreign market," Max Laserson later recalled, it could be sold "only at prices slightly above that of the metal when melted down."[113] Russia's church silver, sold by volume, would yield less than $10 million by 1923, barely enough to finance a month's worth of strategic imports.[114] The solution to the Soviet liquidity crisis would have to be sought elsewhere.

Absent a magic financial elixir—say, the discovery of saleable new tsarist-era treasures not already stolen—the Bolsheviks would soon have to swallow Communist pride and borrow money from capitalist banking institutions. But what could they use as collateral? Having sold off the greater portion of Russia's national patrimony and ruined her economy, there was not much left to recommend the Bolsheviks for a loan—not in the Entente countries whose colossal bond holdings they had repudiated, at least. It was therefore logical that the Politburo resolved, in October 1921, to focus a Soviet loan drive primarily on "capitalists from neutral countries."[115] There were two "neutral" countries in particular that interested the Politburo, without whose subtle cooperation the Bolsheviks would never have come to power in 1917: Germany and Sweden. Brought near to financial ruin by the very success of the Anglo-Soviet trade accord, Lenin's beleaguered regime would now pull back closer to its roots.

9   Rapallo

Lenin received [Aschberg] for a long meeting and charged him officially with improving the gold exchange, with organizing the possibility of selling paper rubles abroad, and finally with selling concessions to exploit Russian resources. In Scandinavia and Germany he will have the exclusive right to direct Soviet financial operations.

— LOUIS DELAVAUD, reporting from Stockholm, August 1921

The Bolsheviks must save us from Bolshevism.

— GERMAN FOREIGN OFFICE slogan

AS RUSSIA'S GOLD RESERVES began running down in winter 1921–22, it became increasingly clear to the Bolsheviks that there was no way to rob and loot their way out of their financial crisis. Trotsky's church confiscations initiative could go only so far in restoring temporary liquidity in gold and silver bullion: in the long run the Soviet regime would not survive without being able to import weapons on credit. It was significant that the Politburo established a special foreign bond commission in October 1921, alongside the crisis gold commissions. Its task was not easy: the Bolsheviks, on the verge of bankruptcy and with a credit rating in Western capitals somewhere between negligible and nonexistent, had almost nothing to offer as collateral. Ideally, concessions could be offered to Western companies that would cost the regime nothing, such as the right to search for oil and copper in the Soviet far north, an idea avidly discussed by Lenin, Trotsky, Kalinin, Molotov, and Stalin.[1] But with the regime's notorious record of default on Russia's foreign obligations, who would take the risk?

It is unlikely the Bolsheviks seriously expected Entente statesmen to fall for the bait. Chicherin's draft proposal for what would eventually become the Genoa conference, sent to London and Paris on 28 October 1921, had implied that the Bolsheviks might pay back at least Russia's pre-1914 debts (but not any of the much larger loans contracted during the war). The final preconference conditions set by the Politburo, however, stipulated that any Russian debt repayments would begin only fifteen years later—and would not be made at all unless the Entente powers gave Moscow "an immediate large loan (approximately one billion dollars)."[2] Chicherin himself likely knew that Allied acceptance of such conditions was a fantasy; Krasin had made almost exactly the same offer to the French government in 1920 and been rejected outright.[3]

The diplomatic problem facing Chicherin and Krasin was how to disappoint Entente hopes politely, without giving "a resounding slap in the face to Lloyd George"—whom the Bolsheviks now regarded, with reason, as their greatest partisan in the Entente camp.[4] To cushion the blow for Lloyd George after the inevitable breakdown over the debt issue, Trotsky revealingly suggested to his Politburo colleagues at one point, "We should announce that in the event that the governments of the Entente were to confiscate all the capital of Russian capitalists abroad, we would treat this as an act of international reciprocity and would commit ourselves not to protest."[5] Here was cold comfort for Western bondholders hoping to salvage some scrap of compensation at Genoa: having been robbed blind by the Bolsheviks, they were being invited to rob others in turn. The contempt with which the Soviet government approached the debt negotiations at Genoa was so complete that not even Lloyd George would be able to salvage the conference.

The real target of the Soviet loan drive of 1921–22 was not France and Britain, but Sweden and, if all else failed, Germany. "Neutral" Stockholm had been the Bolsheviks' preferred destination of illicit Romanov ruble sales in 1918 and gold dumping in 1920–21, so it was perhaps inevitable that it would be their first choice for credit now that there was no more cash and gold to launder. The high priority the Politburo placed on exploiting the Stockholm loan market was evident in the personnel chosen for the mission in late October 1921, men who combined high Bolshevik rank with low international profile. Litvinov, who remained persona non grata in Entente countries, would lead the loan mission to Sweden, while Krasin and Foreign Minister Chicherin handled the far more public (and likely insincere) Genoa initiative. Accompanying Litvinov were three men already familiar in the present narrative, although then largely unknown outside Soviet Russia and Sweden: the railway expert Georgi Lomonosov; Platon Kerzhentsev, president of the Soviet Trade Mission in Stockholm; and Aaron Sheinman, the most trusted official in the Finance Commissariat. Their instructions were to "enter negotiations with the Swedish government, Swedish banks, and Swedish commercial and industrial firms about the realization in Sweden of loans of money or goods" (o zakliuchenii v Shvetsii denezhnogo ili tovarnogo zaima).[6]

There was a neat symmetry to the latest Stockholm mission. Swedish bankers had been so successful in helping part the Bolsheviks from their money that it was only fitting that they also pony up the necessary loans when this money ran out. Stepping in yet again to occupy the role of Swedish middleman between the Communist regime and Western capital was Olof Aschberg, a longtime associate of Kerzhentsev, Lomonosov, and Sheinman. Aschberg, because of his contacts and his fluency in Swedish, German, and Russian, was the perfect link between the Stockholm banking community and the Bolshevik regime. He was also ideally placed to negotiate simultaneously with Berlin, in secret. Aschberg's Stockholm-based Svenska Ekonomie Aktiebolaget had set up a branch office in Berlin in 1918, located at 69a Unter den Linden—directly across the street from the Soviet Embassy. His Berlin manager had been head clerk of Deutsche Bank. Another key official of Aschberg's Berlin branch was Isaak "the engineer" Steinberg, the same who was notorious for his alleged role in laundering German Foreign Office funds for the Bolsheviks in 1917.[7] Aschberg's closest friend in Germany was Emil Wittenberg, a longtime Sweden and Russia hand and director of the Nationalbank für Deutschland. Wittenberg's codirectors, Jacob Goldschmidt and Hjalmar Schacht, were also committed to opening up the Russian market, though not for the same reasons. Goldschmidt and Schacht were both anticommunist—Schacht would later become famous as "Hitler's banker"—and were maneuvering for Russian concessions they hoped might turn huge profits once the Bolsheviks were overthrown. Aschberg and Wittenberg, by contrast, sympathized with the Soviet regime, believing that the Entente blockade had destroyed Russia's economy and that the country deserved generous foreign credits. Aschberg was also closely acquainted with Count Ulrich von Brockdorff-Rantzau, the former German ambassador to Denmark who had been instrumental in arranging a liaison with the Bolsheviks in Copenhagen, through Parvus-Helphand, in 1917. Brockdorff-Rantzau was one of the most prominent "easterners" in the Foreign Office and favored dealing with Soviet Russia instead of the Entente powers.[8]

Aschberg's semiofficial coronation as the Bolsheviks' foreign banker came in March 1921, when he was authorized by the Kremlin to negotiate an ambitious Soviet trade treaty with Paris to accompany the Anglo-Soviet accord. Remarkably, the man who had complained for years of unjust persecution by the Entente due to (presumably unfounded) rumors that he had helped the German government finance the Bolsheviks' October Revolution now presented himself openly to the French Embassy in Berlin as their fully accredited representative. Aschberg even boasted that he had no need of French government approval to sell Bolshevik gold, even in France, as "such transactions were quite easy to perform in practice at Reval through agents of Comptoir Lyon-Allemand." Rather, what Aschberg wanted was to be officially removed from the old Entente blacklist dating to 1917, preliminary to a sweeping settlement of Entente claims against Soviet Russia. Aschberg's proposal, which put even Krasin to shame for its audacity, was for the Bolsheviks to recognize a certain figure of total debt owed the French government, which in turn would open for Soviet Russia new credits equaling that amount, to be used by the Bolsheviks to purchase French products. For canceling all of Moscow's colossal obligations—for, in effect, taking them over itself—the French government would receive "a guaranty of substantial concessions [in Soviet Russia], for example in mining and petroleum." To sweeten the offer, Aschberg promised to sell the French government 100 million rubles of Soviet gold, so long as he was allowed to open a branch office of Svenska Ekonomie Aktiebolaget in Paris to handle all transactions relating to the French-Soviet financial settlement.[9]

What is significant about Aschberg's French gambit is not so much that Paris rejected his brazen offer, but that the Soviet government authorized him to make it at all. So secure did the Bolsheviks imagine their position, in legal terms, after the conclusion of the Anglo-Soviet accord, that they were willing to openly expose their most prized, heretofore secret financier as a Bolshevik agent to representatives of the most hostile Entente power, perhaps believing he might have been able to work his wizardry on them. It was not to be. Aschberg returned to Stockholm in April without a deal. In late May 1921, the Swedish financier left for Berlin, accompanied by Nikolai Krestinsky, who was to succeed Victor Kopp as Soviet plenipotentiary in Germany.[10]

Far from being chastened by France's rejection of Aschberg's overtures, the Bolsheviks now entrusted Aschberg with his most lucrative commission yet. In August 1921, Lenin personally gave Aschberg the "exclusive right to direct financial operations for the Soviet government in Scandinavia and Germany," along with titles (written up by Krasin) bearing rights to Russia's raw materials and petroleum reserves to be sold abroad. As indication of the confidence Lenin now invested in the Bolsheviks' favorite banker, Aschberg was given 50 metric tons of gold, 100 million tsarist and Kerensky rubles, plus 25 million Romanian lei. The rubles were to be unloaded in eastern Germany and Poland, the lei to finance imports from Romania. As for the gold—the last major hoard of imperial bullion left in Russia—this was intended as bait for Berlin.[11]

Not surprisingly, in light of their long history together, German officials responded to Aschberg's advances more favorably than the French did. Trade talks between Moscow and Berlin had been suspended temporarily following the disastrous Communist March Action, but commercial relations were never broken off entirely. On 6 May 1921, a tentative trade accord was signed between the two governments. In June and July, as the Soviet money men—Aschberg and Krestinsky—made the rounds in Berlin, the Bolsheviks' leading arms buyer, Victor Kopp, showed a secret team of German arms experts styled "Sondergruppe Russland" around Moscow and Petrograd, where they inspected Russian arms factories (now mostly defunct) that might benefit from German investment or be used by the Germans to produce their own weapons. Long before the notorious Rapallo agreement between the two pariah states was signed in April

1922, the logistical groundwork—concerning the secret manufacture on Russian territory of airplanes, submarines, guns, and shell by such German firms as Albatrosswerke, Blöhm and Voss, Junkers, and Krupp—had been thoroughly prepared.[12] So, too, had the Bolsheviks already placed long-term orders worth hundreds of millions of gold rubles for German military imports in 1920 and 1921. All that remained to be arranged was the financing.

This is where Aschberg came in. The chief worry of Hans von Seeckt and the German generals was that their plans to rearm secretly in Russia would be scotched by the Allied control commission, which scrutinized German government finance in minute detail, looking to pounce on any improprieties. The French, in particular, were on the lookout for any secret slush funds being used to circumvent reparations payments or finance German rearmament. The Bolsheviks, not without reason, were afraid that such Allied scrutiny would make the Germans hesitate before sending weapons exports east to Moscow, as they had already done on several occasions, most recently after the March Action of 1921. Camouflaging the financing of German-Russian arms deals would be no less crucial now than in 1917, when the Foreign Office needed plausible deniability that it was sending funds to Lenin. Then, the transactions had been processed principally through Aschberg's "neutral" Nya Banken. In 1921–22, the secret channel chosen by Berlin would be Aschberg's *Svenska Ekonomie Aktiebolaget,* which name, mercifully, would now be shortened to S.E.A. in diplomatic shorthand.

The S.E.A. financial negotiations began in earnest on 24 August 1921 in the Berlin offices of the German Reichsbank. (Meanwhile, "Sondergruppe Russland," hashing out the future Rapallo arms deals, began holding regular meetings that September in the Berlin apartment of future Reich chancellor Kurt von Schleicher.)[13] Aschberg himself, still en route from Moscow, was not present, but this may have been by design. Taking his place was Boris Stomoniakov, who had been the main Soviet negotiator in Berlin as the Swedish-German rail deal was put together in 1920–21, working together with Aschberg, Laserson, Lomonosov, Kerzhentsev, and of course Krasin. Stomoniakov was less well known to the Allies than either Aschberg or the new Soviet plenipotentiary (and former Gokhran director) Nikolai Krestinsky and for that reason was thought to be better able to fly under Entente radar, although the French were not fooled.[14] The representatives of the Foreign Office insisted that Soviet-German trade be handled "strictly on a private institutional basis" (auf rein privatwirtschaftlichem Boden). Stomoniakov agreed, so long as this would be done through Aschberg's S.E.A.[15] The Reichsbank, when told that Aschberg's bank was willing to sell Soviet gold—38 metric tons worth—for import credits, jumped at the chance to stockpile gold, increasingly scarce in inflation-ridden Germany. The S.E.A. contract, written up in great haste by Reichsbank executives (and cosigned by Heinz Behrendt of the Foreign Office's Eastern Department), specified that the gold be shipped to Germany in two installments, the first on 15 September 1921—virtually three years to the day from the time the Bolsheviks had sent off the first shipment of Brest-Litovsk gold—and the second one month later. The Reichsbank would then extend dollar-denominated import credits against this gold, calculated at the base rate of $664.60 per kilo of fine ingots, to "the S.E.A. or its assignee" (i.e., the Soviet government).[16]

In exchange, the Germans expected Soviet Russia to place new orders with German industry worth at least 2 billion reichsmarks—or about $50 million at the current rate of exchange. Remarkably, however, the Reichsbank was willing to allow the Bolsheviks to use the import credits they obtained from S.E.A. gold to place orders with other countries' firms if prices offered by German companies were "not competitive" (although this was an unlikely scenario, in light of the collapsing value of the mark). The Germans were even offering rent-free facilities in Berlin for the Soviet trade team. The only provision that indicated the slightest skepticism about Bolshevik good faith was a German demand that Moscow would promise not to resell wares imported from Germany to third parties for profit.[17]

It was a golden deal for the Bolsheviks. Boldly, however, they decided to hold out for better terms: Stomoniakov insisted on full political recognition. His diplomatic instincts were sound. Scarcely had the Foreign Office learned that the deal with Aschberg's bank had fallen through before a crisis meeting was arranged to try to save it. As the Bolsheviks knew, the German government was more desperate than they to reach a sweeping settlement. The Wilhelmstrasse had been willing to overlook repeated attempts by the Communists, in 1919 and 1921, to overthrow the German government by putsch, apparently on the paradoxical principle that only cutting a long-term deal with the Bolsheviks could "save Germany from Bolshevism." And so Stomoniakov's refusal to sign the S.E.A. deal prompted from Behrendt not an outburst of anger or frustration, but rather the solemn promise that Berlin would "take pains to fulfill the wishes of the Russian government . . . to the furthest extent possible."[18]

Behrendt's desire to please Soviet representatives was genuine and reflected widespread opinion in both the Reichsbank and the Foreign Office—he was in fact something of a Moscow skeptic among the "easterners," more cognizant of the risks of dealing with the Bolsheviks than most of his colleagues.[19] Whereas Hans von Seeckt and the generals were willing to use the Bolsheviks to help Germany rearm, without trusting them in the least, officials in the Wilhelmstrasse and Reichsbank had never entirely given up a sentimental attachment to the regime they had helped spawn in 1917. Throughout autumn and winter 1921, the S.E.A. deal was reconfigured time and time again, each time in a direction more favorable to the Bolsheviks. At Stomoniakov's insistence, the Foreign Office agreed to exempt Soviet exports and imports to and from Germany from all customs fees, tolls, and taxes. The Germans were even ready to confer full ambassadorial privileges—immunity from prosecution and so forth—on Soviet trade officials, although the Foreign Office insisted this could be approved only by decree of President Friedrich Ebert's cabinet. Since Ebert was known to be hostile to the Bolsheviks, this was an unlikely prospect. But even the suggestion was revealing: the Foreign Office was willing to go the distance to meet Bolshevik conditions, declaring that the "fulfillment" of Moscow's demand for formal diplomatic recognition would be "from now on regarded as . . . completely desirable."[20]

The Bolsheviks were playing a clever game with the Wilhelmstrasse. By stalling trade negotiations on the pretext of holding out for full diplomatic recognition, they further inflamed the desire of many on the German side for a sweeping anti-Allied accord. As Krasin informed Lenin in September 1921, the "easterners" at the Foreign Office on Wilhelmstrasse, dazzled by thoughts of "revenge," would give anything for an anti-Entente deal with Moscow.[21] The

German generals were not quite so naïve, but they were hardly less eager: Hans von Seeckt himself made an appearance at Kurt von Schleicher's apartment on 8 December 1921 to push the Rapallo arms negotiations along, meeting there, for the first time, the new Soviet plenipotentiary—and former Gokhran director—Nikolai Krestinsky.[22] Here was a moment flush with world-historical importance, linking together the eras of Brest-Litovsk, Rapallo, and the Nazi-Soviet Pact. The principal Rapallo conspirators exposed themselves (if only to each other) for the first time, with the chief of the German General Staff shaking hands with the looter-in-chief of Bolshevik Russia, and this in the home of the future chancellor whose machinations would put the Weimar Republic to sleep and usher in Nazi rule.*

It is not by any means clear that the Bolsheviks wanted a public treaty with the German government. The shared enmity of the Entente had brought the two parties together in 1917 and was pushing them strongly in the same direction in 1921–22, but in both cases the Germans were much the more enthusiastic suitors, courting the Bolsheviks in the (largely mistaken) view that they would become loyal dependents of Berlin in an eastern economic empire. All along, Lenin and his key agents had preferred dealing with "neutral" Swedes to Germans, camouflaging their undeniable dependence on German industry and arms through as many inoculating Swedish layers as possible. The Bolsheviks had not needed political recognition to import locomotives, planes, airplanes, lorries, machine guns, and spare parts from German manufacturers in 1920–21, when they were still flush with huge volumes of moveable gold bullion. They did not need diplomatic recognition to facilitate German arms orders now, either. But with Russia's gold reserves running out, they needed new loans to pay for them.

Ideally, as we saw in the dispatch of a Politburo loan mission to Stockholm, the Bolsheviks would have liked to secure these loans in Sweden, not Germany. But Swedish bankers and industrialists had always been shrewder in their dealings with Moscow than their German counterparts, who tended to be blinded by imperial greed whenever they cast their eyes east. During the German and British

---

*On Schleicher's role in Hitler's unlikely appointment as chancellor in January 1933, see Henry Turner, *Hitler's Thirty Days to Power.*

Baltic blockades, Swedish firms were careful never to risk shipping their wares to Russia without obtaining substantial cash deposits first, along with security guarantees. Not for nothing did Stockholm become the capital of the gold-laundering boom of 1920–21: Swedish firms like Nydquist and Holm and Eastern Trading insisted on advance payment in gold. In Germany, by contrast, Viktor Kopp had purchased most of Moscow's military wares on credit, backed by little more than a promise to pay via Reval middlemen. The Swedes drove a harder bargain.

It is not surprising, then, that most of the S.E.A. gold Aschberg had offered to the Germans in August 1921 as a sweetener for a major trade accord ended up being moved in Sweden instead. In a bitter blow to the German Reichsbank, Aschberg sold the last major consignment of imperial Russian gold bullion (about $10 million worth) to the Stockholm branch of a *French* bank, Marret Bonnin Lebel and Guieu.[23] Adding insult to injury, Stomoniakov's deputy at the Soviet Trade Delegation in Berlin informed the German government, on 20 April 1922, that any remaining Soviet gold reserves were earmarked for American buyers and would not be sold to the Reichsbank after all. "No more gold sales," he informed the Germans, "are envisioned in the near future."[24]

Why, then, had the German government signed the Rapallo Treaty on 16 April 1922, just four days before the Soviet delegation in Berlin confessed that Moscow's gold reserves had run out? It is hard to avoid the conclusion that the Bolsheviks played the Germans for fools, exploiting their greed and impatience for an anti-Allied accord just as Krasin had tempted Lloyd George into signing away the store the previous year. The financial carrot was the S.E.A. gold, dangled tantalizingly before hungry Reichsbank executives, only to be snatched away after they had been reeled in at Rapallo. With the German generals, the Bolsheviks employed the stick of blackmail, as when Radek threatened, in January 1922, to cut a deal with France if Berlin did not settle, thus reproducing the two-front hostility that had cost the Germans the war. If the Germans would help Moscow rearm on credit, Radek had implied, the Red Army might help Germany carve up Poland. In both his threats and promises, Radek was lying through his teeth: the Bolsheviks were no more willing to accede to French demands to pay back Russia's colossal sovereign debt than the cash-starved Red Army was prepared for a Polish offensive in spring 1922. But the German generals had taken Radek seriously, even initiating staff discussions that winter with Red Army liaison officers "on the imaginary invasion of Poland." The Foreign Office fell even harder for Radek's lies, offering the Bolsheviks a bribe of 50–60 million gold marks (about $15 million at then-rates; or the equivalent of $1.5 billion today) to prevent them from cutting a deal with Paris. Radek rejected this offer as insultingly inadequate; the Bolsheviks preferring to hold out, as ever, for more.[25] So unequal was the leverage enjoyed by the Bolsheviks at Rapallo in April 1922, so eager the Germans for a deal, that Germany's Foreign Minister Walter Rathenau signed the Soviet draft without even altering it.[26]

It should not surprise us, then, that the terms of the Rapallo Treaty turned out to be far more favorable to Moscow than Berlin. In essence, the deal was similar to the one Krasin (and Aschberg) had offered the French: Berlin wrote off everything it was owed by Russia, from prewar and wartime tsarist bonds to more recent Soviet arms import orders placed via the German government, in exchange for concessions. True, these concessions were strategically significant, none more so than the right to design and test new weapons on Soviet territory: Seeckt and the generals certainly got what they wanted. But in diplomatic-financial terms, Rapallo was absurdly generous to Moscow: not only were all of Russia's substantial debt obligations cancelled, but the Bolsheviks would now have a virtually unlimited credit line for buying new German weapons, without having to turn over any gold at all. In fact, the Germans were themselves pledged to provide the capital needed to get Russia's arms factories working again. The Junkers aircraft factory at Fili in the western Moscow suburbs, for example, required an initial capital outlay of 600 million (paper) marks from the German side: it proved such a money pit that Junkers went bankrupt in 1925.[†27] The commercial

---

†In a curious twist to the Junkers-Fili story, the German arms expert who negotiated the deal, Oskar von Niedermayer, had a secret motive for writing in generous terms for the Bolsheviks: he was trying at the time to recover, via Soviet intermediaries in Afghanistan, twenty-two trunks of personal property he had left behind in Herat while returning from his wartime mission to Kabul in 1916. (Niedermayer had been tasked by Berlin with inciting the Afghan emir to incite a jihad against British India.) Junkers went bust, but Niedermayer did recover his luggage.

provisions in Article 5 of the Rapallo Treaty, in which Berlin promised to "give all possible encouragement" to the fulfillment of Soviet procurement contracts in Germany, gave the game away: the Germans were so desperate for the Bolsheviks' business that they did not even bother to ask how Moscow would pay.[28]

The French reaction to Rapallo, though predictably hostile, was tinged with an intriguing hint of schadenfreude. Quai d'Orsay officials, having read the fine print of Aschberg's extraordinary offer for a debt write-off settlement in 1921, understood perfectly well what the Bolsheviks were really up to at Rapallo. Without new "foreign credits," the French knew, the Bolsheviks "would not be able to finance their propaganda, or to pay for their import orders in Sweden, England, and Germany." Most of all, it meant the Bolsheviks would no longer be able to "equip their army with the materials it needed [to fight]." Had the Germans not been so blinded by anti-Allied rage and imperial greed, they would have realized that the essential question at Genoa had been whether or not the Bolsheviks, whose "last gold reserves were exhausted," would be forced to agree "to pay Russia's debts" in order to obtain new credits (ob Russland seine Schulden bezahlen wird oder nicht).[29] The answer given at nearby Rapallo was emphatic: no, thank you, the Bolsheviks would not be paying back Russia's debts anytime soon.

The Germans had not done their homework. On 18 April 1922, two days *after* Rathenau and Chicherin signed the Rapallo Treaty, the German representative in Moscow informed Berlin that Bolshevik gold exports had been cut off, in part so that the little bullion remaining in the Soviet government's possession could be used to back a new gold-based ruble, the *chervonetz*.[30] On the twentieth, as we have seen, the Soviet delegation in Berlin confessed that the Reichsbank would not be able to purchase Soviet gold as previously promised. In a sudden panic, the German trade team at Genoa sent an urgent telegram to Berlin on 3 May 1922, demanding copies of the various S.E.A. gold contracts and counteroffers.[31] But it was too late: Aschberg had already sold the last S.E.A. gold to the French, as the Germans would learn to their chagrin from the Swedish newspapers later that week.[32] The Reichsbank would get no gold at all out of Rapallo, nor would other German banks—with the partial exception of Emil Wittenberg's Nationalbank für Deutschland, which,

likely due to its director's personal ties to Aschberg, was able to secure a paltry 15 kilograms.[33]

Despite appearances, Aschberg had not entirely sold out the Germans. It was not his fault, for example, that Stomoniakov had
blocked the S.E.A. gold deal with the Reichsbank. Never one to play
favorites based on nationality, Aschberg would have been perfectly
happy to sell the Reichsbank as much gold as the Bolsheviks had allowed him to. After April 1922 there was no more Bolshevik gold on
offer, but Aschberg had other tricks up his sleeve. On his many visits
to Berlin in 1921, Aschberg had been accompanied by Nikolai
Krestinsky, the founder of the Gokhran, who would become, after
Rapallo, Soviet ambassador to Germany. Together, Aschberg and
Krestinsky had quietly prepared the groundwork for the illicit sale of
Gokhran treasures in Germany, proposing to Chancellor Joseph
Wirth that some 300 to 600 million Swedish crowns (about $70 mil-
lion to $140 million) worth of looted Russian art and jewels might
be sold via German auction houses to help lubricate Soviet-German
trade, especially in arms.[‡] The first foreign exhibition of looted Russian arts and antiquities, held in Berlin in October 1922, raised million of marks for this purpose. By 1923, the Bolsheviks had worked
out a standing agreement with Rudolf Lepke's Berlin Kunst-Auction-
Haus on Potsdamer Straße. Lepke's appraisers were given exclusive
access to inspect Gokhran art objects and antiques in Moscow and
Petrograd and were allowed to auction the most promising items in
Berlin to interested bidders from all over the world, at a 7.5 percent
commission. The revenue obtained from these sales would help pay
down debt on yet more German arms exports to Soviet Russia,
bought, as usual, on credit.[34]

The real beneficiary of Aschberg's financial maneuvers, however,
was the Bolshevik regime. In November 1922, Aschberg opened a
bank in Moscow to handle wire transfers with Stockholm and
Berlin. As part of the New Economic Policy (NEP), the Bolsheviks
now allowed private banks to be chartered, though under strict supervision. Aschberg's Russian Bank of Commerce, or *Ruskombank*,
was the flagship, designed to attract both Russian savings deposits

---

[‡]Wirth may have been anxious to recoup his own government's investment of 150 million
marks in "Sondergruppe Russland." See Freund, *Unholy Alliance*, 98.

(relegalized in April 1922) and foreign capital, especially that raised by Aschberg's network of Bolshevik-friendly banks abroad.[35] Chartered with an initial capital of $5 million, Ruskombank was a grand affair, installed just a stone's throw from the Kremlin in "a magnificent building at the corner of Petrovka and Kuznetsky Most." Its director of operations was Max May, who had bought Russian gold from Aschberg for Guaranty Trust of New York. With Aschberg's contacts in Stockholm and Berlin, and May's on Wall Street, Ruskombank brought in "many millions of dollars" in foreign capital. Some capital came into Russia via the sale of bonds in Stockholm and Berlin. Millions more churned through Ruskombank in the form of "an incredible amount of remittances" from Russians abroad, "mostly in 5 and 10 dollars." Then, too, there was the credit the Bolsheviks obtained by depositing in Aschberg's Ruskombank "gold, platinum, precious stones, diamonds and pearls" from the Gokhran, which were then sold to foreign buyers in Moscow or sent on to brokers in Stockholm and Berlin. Lepke's auction house was the principal conduit for foreign sales but by no means the only one. In all, as Aschberg himself later confessed under French police interrogation, he personally sold off $50 million worth of Gokhran treasures between 1921 and 1924, raising the foreign exchange equivalent of some $5 billion today for the Soviet government. Combined together with his leading role in the Stockholm gold-smelting trade in 1920–21 (which netted Moscow $350 million in all, or $35 billion in today's terms, of which trade Aschberg had roughly a third share), Aschberg's Gokhran gold and jewelry sell-off in the early 1920s amounts to a historically unprecedented achievement in money laundering, with the monies he alone raised for Bolshevism— $200 million, or about $20 billion in current value—comparable to the combined output of all the bankers of Switzerland in processing looted Nazi gold during the Second World War.[36]

The ultimate goal of these sales, of course, was to capitalize purchases of German weapons exported to Soviet Russia. In January 1923, the Bolsheviks formally requested some 300 million gold marks (about $75 million) worth of German arms be sent to Moscow on credit, with Gokhran loot as collateral.[37] To facilitate the financing and help throw the Allied Control Commission off the scent, Aschberg now dissolved the Berlin branch of S.E.A. and replaced it with a front bank he had spent years preparing. Not long after the armistice in 1918, Aschberg had quietly purchased "the whole of the stock in an old German provincial bank which had been granted a charter to carry on complete banking business throughout Germany." In November 1922, Aschberg transferred this charter to the new Garantie- und Kreditbank für den Osten, ostensibly independent but actually affiliated with Det Nordiske Kreditselskabet, Aschberg's bank in Copenhagen, S.E.A. in Stockholm, and Ruskombank in Moscow, which was chartered simultaneously. Garantie- und Kreditbank was given favorable treatment by the German government, which used it as the official banking institution of the Soviet government: its seat on the Berlin bourse was specially arranged by the Foreign Office.[38] Aschberg's new bank also spun off an affiliated corporation given a monopoly over processing the sale of Gokhran loot in Germany, the Russische Edelmetallvertriebs-A.G.[39]

With Aschberg's help, Garantie- und Kreditbank raised hundreds of millions of gold marks to pay down debt accrued from Bolshevik arms purchases in Germany, through stock issue on the Berlin bourse, sales of Gokhran treasures, and even by floating special "worker bonds" with German unions.[40] Amazingly, the outflow of gold from Soviet Russia reversed under the Rapallo system, with German gold sent to Russia in 1926, reputedly in exchange for a particularly lucrative sale of some of the Russian crown jewels.[41] That year, the German government had finally agreed to organize the first major Bolshevik bonds, 100 million reichsmarks ($25 million) worth, used to securitize Soviet arms purchases in Germany equal to more than three times that amount.[42] The Bolshevik bonds, floated by a consortium of banks including the Reichsbank, Dresdner Bank, and provincial affiliates, were to be repaid through Aschberg's Garantie- und Kreditbank over five to ten years. Amazingly, the German government allowed the Bolsheviks to place another 420 million reichsmarks in import orders (about $100 million worth, akin to $10 billion in today's terms) by the terms of the Piatakov Agreement in April 1931—just several months before the Soviet government, pleading poverty, defaulted on the earlier loans.[43] Predictably, the German government was saddled with the bill.[44] Before defaulting in 1931, of course, the Bolsheviks had imported enough German Mausers, machine guns, and motor cars to ensure that resistance to

Stalin's collectivization offensive in the Ukraine could be suppressed with ease by army and secret police enforcers.

Rapallo marked the coming of age of the Bolshevik regime. What had begun as an alliance of convenience between the German government and a motley band of revolutionary conspirators had now come full circle, with the Bolsheviks formally recognized as sovereign equals—and curiously treated with great deference, as if they were superiors—by their onetime benefactors in Berlin. Both partners, to be sure, remained pariahs in the Versailles system created by the victorious Entente powers, but this did not mean either was isolated. Linking together the Rapallo partners was the same intermediary that had midwifed Bolshevism into power: the banking community in Stockholm, embodied in the person of Olof Aschberg.

Without Aschberg's Nya Banken wire transfers of money to Petrograd, the October Revolution may never have happened. Without Aschberg's help in selling off rubles in Sweden to obtain hard currency, the Bolsheviks would have been cut off from the world during the Baltic blockades of 1918–19, with no access to the Scandinavian, German, and Persian imports that preserved Red morale against the White armies. Without Aschberg's assistance in laundering the imperial gold reserves and Gokhran treasures to finance imports of military wares needed to replace those exhausted during the war with the Whites, the Soviet regime would likely have been defeated by the peasant wars of 1920–22. With Aschberg's creation of an international network of Soviet credit institutions to lubricate the Rapallo agreement of 1922, Bolshevism was bailed out of bankruptcy at the very moment the Russian imperial gold reserves ran out.

Germany, it is true, was no longer the world-beating power it had seemed to be during the war, which arguably made Rapallo less impressive a diplomatic triumph than had Moscow been recognized by one of the victorious powers, Britain, France, or the United States. But the Entente itself was a spent force in 1922, split apart at the seams. Had Lloyd George wanted to keep the alliance together, he could have shut off the Germano-Swedish-Bolshevik nexus at any point between the launching of the Stockholm gold boom in May

1920 and the ratification of the Rapallo Treaty two years later simply by reactivating the Baltic blockade. This gesture, more than anything, would have won back the French, themselves powerless to stem the Bolshevik gold outflow from Reval, and produced a united front on such crucial matters as German reparations.

Instead, Lloyd George, by first allowing and then formally sanctioning the Bolsheviks' laundering of the Russian national patrimony they had acquired during the revolution and civil war, effectively sold out the Western alliance in exchange for the temporary stimulation of the English coal and textile industries. By so doing, the British prime minister forfeited any legal or financial leverage that the civilized Western powers had over the Kremlin, ensuring the Bolsheviks would never have to make more than hollow promises to pay back all the people they had robbed since 1917. Rapallo was the inevitable result. No matter how hard Allied officials tried to revive the debt issue at Genoa in April 1922, at The Hague that July, or at any of the dozens of conferences that followed over the succeeding decades, they could make little headway. By guaranteeing the inviolability of Bolshevik loot against lawsuits filed by Russian creditors, Britain's courts had, in effect, legalized the Russian Revolution. There was no going back.

Epilogue
From Stockholm to Sotheby's

TAKEN TOGETHER, the Anglo-Soviet accord of 1921 and the Rapallo Treaty of 1922 washed clean the stolen loot the Bolsheviks had previously had to launder, on the sly, in Estonia and Sweden. Although Krestinsky and Aschberg remained somewhat cautious at first in auctioning off the Gokhran treasures in Germany, the periodic auctions at Rudolf Lepke's on Potsdamer Straße inevitably excited public interest in the phenomenon of Bolshevik art and antique dumping. By 1928, when the first major Soviet sales of paintings by European Old Masters began, Lepke's auction catalogue was selling out in London, Paris, Vienna, and New York, despite a price tag of $25. It is not hard to see why: the first major Old Masters auction at Lepke's included 450 paintings "from Italian, Dutch, and French schools of the fifteenth and eighteenth centuries, among them works by Rembrandt, Rubens, Van Dyck, Jordeans, Greuze, Tintoretto, Bassano and Natoire," along with "some fine examples of French furniture" and "a collection of jeweled snuff boxes" assembled from Romanov palaces.[1] Although the high-profile sales occasioned a lawsuit by Russian émigrés in Berlin, the importance of Lepke's auction house for helping lubricate the Rapallo arms trade ensured the plaintiffs' case would be quickly dismissed by the German courts.[2]

Lepke was not the only lucky dealer of looted Bolshevik treasures in the Rapallo era. Just as Krasin's manipulation of Lloyd George had helped broaden the Soviet gold market and lower premiums, it made sense for the Bolsheviks to expand the Rapallo auction market. And so Lepke's monopoly in Germany was limited to high-end paintings and Romanov antiques, while a Berlin dealer named Stepan Mikhailovich Mussuri, a joint German-Greek citizen, was granted a license in July 1927 to "buy and resell on commission antiquities and luxury articles anywhere on the territory of the Soviet Union, such as: antique furniture, items of daily use, religious artifacts, artifacts made of bronze, porcelain, crystal, silver, brocade, carpets, tapestries, paintings, original manuscripts, Russian precious stones, and craft and artistic items not worthy of museum display." Alongside the Mussuri deal, the Soviet commissar for foreign trade, Anastas Mikoyan, opened up the Vienna auction market, offering small-scale deals to Austrian houses and galleries, including Dorotheum, E. and A. Silbermann, Sanct Lucas, and Pollak and Winternitz. Viennese antique and carpet dealers also did a booming business with the Gokhran, in particular an ambitious buyer named Bernhard Altmann, who used a Moscow knitwear factory (Strickwarenfabrik) as cover for exporting to Vienna rare Caucasian- and Persian-style carpets and tapestries captured by the Red Army: Altmann's firm exported no less than twenty-three trunks full of such antiques in spring 1928 alone. No item of war booty from central Asia's bazaars was too petty for the Bolsheviks to dump abroad: Altmann also moved simple children's wooden toys, small lacquered antiques, and a large stash of headwear and headscarves (Schals und Tücher) captured at Orenburg.[3] Stockholm, like Vienna and Berlin, remained a hot market for Gokhran loot. As ever, the Swedes charged the highest commissions. One antique shop in Stockholm sold "tapestries, rugs, porcelain, and other art objects confiscated from private families" on a 10 percent commission, beating Lepke's 7.5 percent with room to spare.[4]

By the end of the 1920s, the galleries, antique shops and auction houses of Berlin, Vienna, and Stockholm were flush with looted Russian wares, from diamonds and rubies to simple bronze and wooden artifacts, and just about everything in between. Even Jewish relics looted from the Pale of Settlement during the civil war were dumped by Mikoyan's men, mostly in Vienna. Then there were the thousands of Orthodox icons swooped up in Trotsky's church expropriation campaign of 1922—those, at least, that had survived the depredations of Gokhran silver sorters. Paraded before potential buyers in Europe, many of the most sacred icons of the Orthodox faith were now pawned off to nonbelieving collectors. The most imposing hoard of all was Olof Aschberg's 277 icons, which easily comprised the "largest private collection of icons, public or private . . . outside the frontiers of Soviet Russia." Aschberg donated the bulk of his collection to the National Museum in Stockholm in 1933, where they remain on display to this day.[5]

With good money to be made auctioning off such treasures, it was unlikely dealers in Stockholm, Berlin, and Vienna would be able to keep the market to themselves for long, especially considering the prominent position of such London houses as Christie's and Sotheby's in the business. Britain, followed by Italy and France, had formally recognized the Soviet Union in 1924, but as we saw in the court decisions following the trade accord of 1921, diplomatic recognition was really no more than a formality. The courts continued referencing Lloyd George's trade accord while upholding the right of Soviet agents to sell off looted treasures on British territory, as in the denial of the claim of Princess Olga Paley to sequester stolen property sold by Soviet agents in 1928.[6] Christie's did not even need to ask the government's permission before announcing an auction on 16 March 1927 of "an important assemblage of magnificent jewelry mostly dating from the eighteenth century, which formed part of the Russian State Jewels." Among these Romanov crown jewels was the nuptial crown Empress Alexandra had worn at her 1894 wedding, "entirely composed of diamonds, diamond necklaces, tiaras, pendants, bracelets and earrings." It was sold for 6,100 pounds sterling, the equivalent of over $2 million today.[7] Sotheby's director, G. D. Hobson, at least, took the precaution of informing the Foreign Office in December 1928 that Sotheby's had "been approached—very tentatively & circuitously—with regard to a possible sale of Bolshevik treasures," and requesting to be informed "whether the F.O. would be likely to raise any objections." The reply, by Stephen Gaselee of the Foreign Office, spoke volumes about the consequences of Lloyd George's surrender in 1921 and the Rapallo Treaty following hard on its heels:

In reply to your letter of December 10th it would seem probable from the recent decision in the case of Princess Olga Paley . . . that, if you sold property entrusted to you for that purpose by the Soviet Government or their agents, the English law courts would not interfere. . . . I suppose that if you refused to act, the articles would be sold in Germany: and from a Berlin telegram . . . it looks as if the German Court of Appeal took much the same view as our own. We don't much want to help the Bolsheviks to despoil their unfortunate fellow-countrymen: but we should do no good by advising you to refuse and for the articles to be sold in another country, so I really don't see why you should not go ahead. But don't quote the Foreign Office as having expressed approval![8]

With such a laissez-faire attitude toward sales of Bolshevik loot, it is not surprising the British government itself bought the single most famous looted item of all, a fourth-century Codex Bible purchased for the British Museum in 1931 for 100,000 pounds sterling.[9]

Mikoyan had designs on the Parisian auction houses as well, but in keeping with the general discomfiture of the French regarding Bolshevik usurpation of property from its rightful owners, these plans ran badly aground. Germain Seligman, whose father Jacques had been one of France's leading dealers in Russian art before the revolution, was invited to Moscow by Mikoyan in fall 1927 to inspect items the Bolsheviks wished to sell in Paris. Taken on a tour of the Gokhran's jewelry storerooms, Seligman later recalled the impression that he had been ushered into "a great cave of ormolu and gilt bronze, with stalactites and stalagmites of gold and crystal. Hanging from the ceiling . . . was an incredible array of chandeliers and candelabra." Although impressed by the sheer volume of gilt objects on display, Seligman informed Mikoyan that he was an *art* dealer, not a jewelry thief: he refused the commission outright.[10]

The Bolsheviks had much better luck dumping art and jewels in the United States, despite the fact that the Soviet Union was not officially recognized by Washington until 1933. In part, this was for the obvious reason that the richest American collectors simply had more cash to burn than their European counterparts. When Armand Hammer organized his famous department store auctions of "Romanov treasures" in 1930, there was no shortage of wealthy women shoppers. Some of the items Hammer displayed, to be sure, were fakes, but not the dozen-odd Fabergé and imperial Easter eggs purchased by Lillian Thomas Pratt, India Early Marshall, and Mathilda Geddings Gray, most of which are now on display in American museums. Steel magnate Andrew Mellon alone bought $6.6 million worth of paintings by Old Masters from the Hermitage in 1930 and 1931, including a multitude of Rembrandts, Van Dycks, Botticellis, and single works by Rubens, Raphael, and Titian. In a curiously sinister twist, Mellon was Treasury secretary at the time, responsible for enforcing American antidumping laws against the Soviet Union. Far from regretting this stunning display of hypocrisy, Mellon claimed his Soviet art purchases as charitable deductions on his income tax returns for 1931.[11]

In one of the most grotesque ironies of Communism, it was Western fat-cat capitalists like Mellon who inherited the greater part of Russia's patrimony, while the Russian proletariat received only the lash. It is hard to imagine a better program for destroying a country's wealth than by robbing and murdering its most successful wealth-producers and shipping their riches out of the country. In this way the Russian people were robbed not only of their cultural past, but of their economic future as well.

As for the Mellons who acquired pieces of Russia's lost national patrimony at cut-rate prices, one can only marvel at their good fortune and hope, for the sake of their emotional health, that most remained unaware of the ultimate consequences of their actions. Russian ruble and gold buyers cashing in on the great Stockholm booms of 1918 and 1920–22 may have had little idea that the money they fronted was used to finance the Red Terror or the brutal Bolshevik wars against Russia's peasants and parishioners, but it might have behooved them to ask a few questions before signing the contracts. Likewise, the lucky purchasers of previously Russian-owned Rembrandts, antique carpets, jewelry, and Fabergé eggs sold in the late 1920s and early 1930s may not have known that their money was being used to pay for Stalin's campaign to exterminate the Ukrainian peasantry or his brutal force-march to industrialization. And yet there is no longer any doubt that Stalin's sprawlingly murderous collective farms, steel plants, and tank factories were substantially funded by art and antique sales to Western collectors. Mellon's millions, for example, were "transferred to Soviet accounts in Germany" almost immediately after he paid for his paintings in New

York, where they would help finance Bolshevik imports of German weapons and machinery.[12]

The saddest part of the entire sordid story of the looting and laundering of Russia's national patrimony is that so few people know the first thing about it. Thanks to hundreds of novels, plays, and movies, the victims of Nazi slave labor and death camps have entered the world's consciousness, and recently some few survivors have been compensated, however little, however late. Although the victims of Stalin's Gulag camps have received no comparable renown or compensation, the efforts of Alexander Solzhenitsyn and a small but growing group of chroniclers have brought their descendants at least some belated attention and sympathy.

But who will speak for the prerevolutionary Russian aristocracy; the icon-artists and icon-worshippers; the monks and church elders; the proud merchants, bankers, army officers and state servants who lovingly furnished their offices and estates; the hard-working, cash-saving town artisans and peasant kulaks; the central Asian emirs and khans and horse traders, the émigré intelligentsia who lost their homes and their entire beloved civilization? The patrimony of Russia belonged above all to them, these unfashionable bourgeois "class enemies," until it was robbed from them at gunpoint, laundered by cynical middlemen, bought by incurious foreigners, and finally scattered to the far corners of the earth. *Gospodi upokoi ikh dushi.* May their souls rest in peace.

Dramatis Personae

Andersson, Gunnar. Lawyer and principal negotiator for Nydquist and
  Holm, a consortium of Swedish locomotive and railway supply firms.
  Signed historic deal with Soviet Russia in May 1920, which kicked off
  the gold-laundering boom in Stockholm.

Andreeva, Maria Fyedorovna. Actress and common-law wife of Maxim
  Gorky, with whom she helped oversee Bolshevik fund-raising balls and
  charity events in prewar St. Petersburg; charged in fall 1918, along with
  Gorky and Leonid Krasin, with the formation of a "Commission for the
  Storage and Registration of Artistic and Historical Monuments," which
  later evolved into the Gokhran. Reputed to be an obsessive thief.

Aschberg, Olof. Swedish financier, born of Russian Jewish parents. Procured for Russia, through J. P. Morgan's Guaranty Trust Co., its first
  major American loan, in 1916. Instrumental in floating the Liberty Loan
  on the U.S. capital market for the Russian Provisional Government in
  spring 1917. Founder of Stockholm's Nya Banken, or New Bank, a
  socialist lending institution that acquired notoriety for its alleged wire
  transfers to Bolshevik agents in Petrograd, later in 1917 (though Nya
  Banken also lent money to Kerensky); after being put on the Allied
  blacklist, sold his shares in Nya Banken and formed Svenska Ekonomie
  Aktiebolaget (the Swedish Finance Co. Ltd.) out of his own capital to
  trade with Bolshevik Russia. Heavily involved in arranging transit of
  Bolshevik gold for Svenska Ekonomie Aktiebolaget, through Reval and
  Stockholm; sold this gold in turn to Western banks, primarily French

and American. Later chairman of the first Soviet commercial bank in Moscow, Ruskombank, with Max May, formerly of the U.S. Guaranty Trust Co., as chief deputy in charge of foreign transactions. Later founded Soviet banks in Germany helping to lubricate the Rapallo agreement and pay for German military imports. Proud collector of stolen Russian icons, later donated to Swedish museums. Sometimes referred to as "the Bolsheviks' banker."

Berzin, Jan Antonovich. Dispatched as chairman of the Soviet Foreign Mission to Switzerland in May 1918. Holder of a numbered account at Bern's Kantonalbank. Expelled from Switzerland with retinue in November 1918, due in part to Entente pressure, for his role in financing Communist propaganda in Western Europe with monies of suspicious origin.

Borodin, Mikhail, alias "Michel Gruzenberg" or "Michael Berg." Russian-born U.S. citizen and Chicago resident; after 1917 suspected to be Bolshevik agent by numerous intelligence services, operating out of Switzerland, Norway, Sweden; liaison between Lomonosov and a consortium of Wall Street bankers and lawyers regarding a railway contract with Soviet Russia in 1919; deposited 500,000 tsarist rubles in a numbered account in Geneva, then transferred the key to a suspected Bolshevik agent named Julius Fox; later smuggled to United States 1 million rubles worth of diamonds sewed into the lining of two leather suitcases; later still masterminded Comintern operations in China in 1926–27, including the Shanghai uprising.

Branting, Hjalmar. Swedish prime minister from March to October 1920, when the Bolshevik gold-laundering boom kicked off in Stockholm. Responded contemptuously to French complaints, making clear he would do nothing to block Soviet gold sales.

Chicherin, Georgi Vasilevich. Second Soviet foreign minister (after Trotsky); nominal superior to Litvinov and Krasin, although largely deferring to their judgment on commercial matters; Soviet signatory to the Rapallo Treaty of 1922 with Weimar Germany.

Churchill, Winston. British minister of war in Lloyd George's cabinet, 1919–21. Principal advocate of the Allied intervention in Soviet Russia and principal scapegoat for the failure thereof. Passionate critic of Lloyd George's halfway policy.

Delavaud, Louis. French ambassador to Stockholm during the great gold boom of 1920–21. Protested with great vigor and moral passion against the laundering of the looted patrimony of Imperial Russia, to absolutely no effect whatsoever.

Fuchs, Joseph, alias "Joseph Fox." Russian-born American citizen, California resident, journalist, and businessman; surfaced in Geneva with a key given him by "Gruzenberg" to a numbered account containing 500,000 rubles; also turned up in Berlin to help Steinberg negotiate, through Bank of Mendelssohn, a Soviet order for one million scythes.

Fürstenberg, Jakob, alias "Hanecki" (Ganetski), alias "Kuba." Polish socialist, banker, business partner of "Parvus" in Copenhagen from 1915 to 1917; associate of Aschberg at Nya Banken in 1917; a key figure in the German financing allegations plaguing the Bolsheviks in summer 1917. An original member of the "triumvirate" of the Bolshevik Foreign Mission in Stockholm, with Radek and Vorovsky; later appointed director of the Soviet National Bank.

Gorky, Maxim. Celebrated Russian novelist and Bolshevik sympathizer who, with his common-law wife Maria Fedorovna, helped raise money for Lenin's party by arranging charity events in prewar St. Petersburg, and on one literary tour of the United States; after 1917 lent his name and prestige to the Soviet regime, though with certain reservations; his sometime criticism of Bolshevik excesses, especially their persecution of artists and writers, was reluctantly tolerated by Lenin due to his worldwide fame; charged in fall 1918, along with Andreeva and Leonid Krasin, with the formation of the "Commission for the Storage and Registration of Artistic and Historical Monuments," which would later evolve into the Gokhran.

Gukovsky, Isidor Emanuilovich. Treasurer of Bolshevik party, 1917; Soviet commissar of finance, 1918; in such capacity entrusted with 50 million rubles as far as Stockholm. Soviet commercial agent in Reval (Tallinn), Estonia, 1920, in which capacity he was reputed to have enriched himself unduly; subject of scandalous corruption rumors, including one involving the theft of a tsarist diadem and as many as 8 million rubles. Close associate of Aschberg, Krasin, Litvinov, and Lomonosov, and bitter rival of Solomon.

Hellberg, Wilhelm. Swedish lawyer employed by Soviet Foreign Mission in Stockholm; associate of Aschberg, Scheiman, and Vorovsky; signatory to a number of important trade contracts between Swedish firms and the Soviet government. Also deeply involved in the gold-laundering boom of 1920–21; like Aschberg, notorious in Entente capitals, particularly Paris, as an unofficial Bolshevik agent.

Helphand, Alexander Israel, aka "Parvus." Tsarist exile, multilingual Ukrainian Jew, German Social Democrat, estranged revolutionary, arms merchant and war profiteer, the key figure in the allegations surrounding German financing of Lenin levied by the beleaguered Russian Provisional Government in summer 1917.

Joffe, Adolf Abromovich. Appointed first Soviet ambassador to Berlin, May 1918. Expelled, due in part to Entente pressure, in November 1918 for financing Communist propaganda in Western Europe with monies of suspicious origin.

Kerzhentsev, Platon Mikhailovich. Soviet commercial agent, appointed director of the Soviet Trade Mission in Stockholm, 1920–21; heavily involved in the Swedish-German railway negotiations; because of the enormous scale of Bolshevik gold sales and factory orders placed in Sweden, was known on occasion to give orders to Swedish government officials.

Kolchak, Admiral Aleksandr Vasilevich. White general and "supreme dictator" of the independent Russian government of Siberia, 1918–19. Acquired the imperial Russian gold reserve from Kazan, some of which financed White arms purchases in San Francisco, by way of Vladivostok. Later captured by Bolsheviks, expropriated of remaining gold, and executed.

Kopp, Viktor Leontevich. Accredited Soviet representative in Berlin, 1920–21. Specialist in quiet, under-the-radar deals for war matériel, including boots, wool, and greatcoats; Bolshevik liaison with numerous suppliers of surplus German automatic rifles and ammunition; purchased military airplanes with Mercedes engines for the embryonic Soviet air force; also operated, on occasion, under cover of the Russian Red Cross.

Krasin, Leonid Borisovich. Electrical engineer; onetime director of Siemens-Schukert's Petrograd branch office; expert in explosives, the counterfeiting of currencies, smuggling, money laundering. Mastermind of Bolshevik finance from 1904–9 (including the supervision of numerous bank heists and holdups of tsarist cash transports) and again after the Russian Revolution, as chief negotiator of the Soviet Commissariat for Foreign Trade (Narkomvneshtorg), commissar for transportation, and unofficial éminence grise of the Gorky-Andreeva arts and antiques registration commission, which would evolve into the Gokhran. Authorized to sell millions of dollars worth of gold, diamonds, and other precious stones. Used the Central Board of Russian Cooperative Organizations (Tsentrosoiuz) as ostensibly independent-of-Moscow front for trade negotiations with the Allied powers, especially Britain under Lloyd George; in fact worked under close supervision of the Soviet Politburo. Founder (in 1920) of ARCOS, the Bolsheviks' procurement front corporation in London; principal Bolshevik negotiator of the Anglo-Soviet trade accord of March 1921. Bitter rival of Litvinov.

Krestinsky, Nikolai Nikolaevich. Second Soviet minister of finance. Specialized in the appraisal of valuables obtained through the nationalization of bank safe-deposit boxes. Founder and first director of Gokhran, the State Treasury for the Preservation of Valuables. Later Soviet plenipotentiary, then ambassador to Weimar Germany, 1921–30, in which capacity he oversaw the auctioning off of Gokhran treasures to help lubricate the Rapallo agreement. Purged by Stalin in 1938 and executed.

Kühlmann, Richard von. State secretary of the German Foreign Office, 1917–18. Architect of Lenin's famous "sealed train car" voyage from Switzerland to Petrograd's Finland Station, by way of Germany, Denmark, Sweden, and Finland. After the Bolshevik coup, leaned heavily on the neutral governments of Sweden and Switzerland to recognize Lenin's regime.

Laidoner, Johan, General. Hero of Estonia's war of independence against Soviet Russia, 1918–20; after the Tartu peace treaty was signed on 2 February 1920, appointed chairman of Estonia's Harju Bank; in this capacity signed off on a large number of Bolshevik gold sales registered in Reval (Tallinn); close working associate of Aschberg.

Larsons, M. J. (Max Laserson). Lawyer and banker, of Russian Jewish heritage, with an economics degree from the Polytechnical Institute in Riga and a law degree from the Russian Imperial University of Dorpat (Tartu); expert on the Baltic region; fluent in Russian, German, English, and French, with working knowledge of Yiddish, Swedish, and Lettish; commercial director of the Shuvalov Mining Company in Petrograd before serving, on and off, as an adviser to the Bolsheviks on legal and financial matters, 1917–24. Negotiated the conclusion of the nationwide anti-Bolshevik bank strike of winter 1917–18. Deputy chief of Soviet Railway Mission in Stockholm in 1920–21 and principal legal draftsman of the blockbuster German-Swedish-Soviet railway contract of 1920. Later hired, in 1923, as deputy chief of the Currency Administration in Moscow and as chief appraiser at Gokhran, the State Treasury for the Preservation of Valuables. Associate of Aschberg, Scheinman, Krestinsky, Lomonosov, Krasin.

Lenin, Vladimir Ilyich. Bolshevik party leader and, after 1918, dictator; ultimate Bolshevik authority on all matters both political and financial; driving force behind the bank nationalizations, the varied looting campaigns against capitalist "expropriators"; also gave the impetus to the renewed assault on church property in 1922.

Lifschitz, Boris, Dr. Russian-born, naturalized Swiss citizen and Bern lawyer; witnessed selling millions of prerevolutionary Russian rubles to a number of Swiss banks in 1918; owing to Swiss citizenship and law degree was not expelled in November 1918; holder of large account at Kantonalbank Bern; believed to have millions more deposited at banks in Geneva, Lucerne, and Zurich; later chairman, from 1929, of Swiss Communist party.

Litvinov, Maxim Maximovich. First Soviet ambassador to independent Estonia. Also masterminded a number of complex arms deals in Copenhagen and sold off large quantities of looted Russian gold, diamonds, and jewelry, mostly in Reval and Copenhagen. Bitter rival of Krasin. Later a favorite Jewish punching bag of the Nazis (as "Finkelstein").

Lloyd George, David. British prime minister who "won the war," was notably less enthusiastic about enforcing the peace. Pursued the holy grail of an Anglo-Soviet trade accord.

Lomonosov, Georgi, "Professor." Engineer, railway consultant for Kerensky's Provisional Government in 1917; later one of the Bolsheviks' principal commercial agents in Stockholm, 1918–22. Technical specialist in the rail procurement requirements of the Red Army. Working associate of Aschberg, Borodin/Gruzenberg, Laserson, Krasin.

May, Max. As bank vice president and head of the U.S. Guaranty Trust Company's foreign department, Aschberg's principal contact on Wall Street; helped Aschberg arrange credit for the tsarist government in 1916 and for Kerensky in 1917; from 1920 was Aschberg's principal Wall Street buyer of Bolshevik gold after it was melted down in Stockholm; named director, in 1922, of the foreign department of the first Soviet commercial bank, Ruskombank.

Mirbach, Count Wilhelm von. First German ambassador to Soviet Russia; strong advocate of Berlin's support for the continuation of Bolshevik rule; assassinated 6 July 1918.

Moor, Karl. Swiss journalist, friend, and financier of Lenin during his Swiss exile, inheritor of a suspiciously timed fortune in summer 1917, immediately donated to the Central Committee of the Bolshevik Party; liaison between Kurt Riezler and the Bolsheviks in spring 1918; colleague of Berzin's Soviet Mission in 1918; from 1919 a distributor of cash handouts to Communists in Berlin and Bern. Close associate of Berzin, Shklovsky, Radek, Riezler.

Novitsky, W. J. (V. I.). Finance minister for Kolchak's ill-fated Siberian White government; hired in 1920 by the Entente powers as chief informant on Russia's fast-depleting gold reserves; in 1921 defected to the Bolsheviks and advised the Politburo.

Palmstierna, Erik, Baron de. Swedish foreign minister during the great Stockholm gold boom, 1920–21. Justified his policy of noninterference on the grounds that Britain had already de facto legalized Soviet gold traffic by receiving a Soviet trade delegation in London.

Platten, Fritz. Swiss radical labor leader and socialist member of parliament; accompanied Lenin on the famous "sealed train car" from Switzerland in 1917; initiator of the single most audacious attempt at Bolshevik money smuggling, involving 100 million rubles, in cash, carried in his personal luggage, confiscated by the Finnish government. Later entrusted abroad by the Soviet government with 20 million rubles in gold coin and a commercial license signed by Lenin. Associate of Berzin, Lenin, Moor, and Shklovsky.

Putilov, Alexei. Owner and son of the founder of the Putilov locomotive works, the largest factory in Petrograd, later converted to war production, principally for artillery shell but also for naval wares; involved in wartime scandals related to nonfulfillment of large government commissions, especially for artillery shell; famous villain of the revolutions of both 1905 and 1917, owing to his labor layoffs; one of the principal targets of the Bolshevik nationalization/confiscation campaign of winter 1917–18. Also the president of Banque Russo-Asiatique from 1914 and of the exiled Paris rump of same bank after 1918. One of the principal financiers of various White Russian conspirators-in-exile.

Radek, Karl. Polish Jew, tsarist exile, German Social Democrat, journalist, close associate of Lenin, whom he accompanied in the famous sealed train car from Switzerland; member of the original triumvirate, with Fürstenberg and Vorovsky, in the Bolshevik Foreign Mission in Stockholm; editor of *Russische Korrespondenz Prawda;* distributor of diplomatic passports for Bolshevik agents in Germany, Sweden, and Switzerland.

Rauch, Franz. German-speaking tsarist Russian subject from the Volga German communes, arrested by the Czechoslovak legion in summer 1918 near Orenburg. Later dispatched to Berlin as part of Joffe's diplomatic retinue; after Joffe's departure became an unaccredited commercial agent of the Bolsheviks in Germany. Tried, nearly single-handedly, to break the Allied blockade on Soviet Russia in 1919 overland.

Reich, James, alias "Fatty." Philosophy major and college dropout from Galicia; editor of *Russische Nachrichten,* the main propaganda organ of the Bolsheviks in Bern, 1918; expelled with same in November 1918; first director of the Comintern's Western European bureau, based in Berlin; distributed cash to Comintern agents there in 1918 and 1919.

Riezler, Karl. German diplomat, liaison between German Foreign Office and General Staff during World War I; also liaison between both and Russian revolutionaries, through the German Legation in Stockholm, in 1917; in 1918 chief deputy of Count Mirbach, first German ambassador to Soviet Russia; famously wired the Foreign Office, warning his fellow conspirators to contain their "joy" after the Bolsheviks' October Revolution. Associate of Fürstenberg, Mirbach, Moor, "Parvus," Vorovsky.

Schreider, Alexander. Bolshevik courier and money smuggler; claimed on several occasions to hold a numbered account in a Lausanne bank under an assumed name; reputed liar rumored to be fleeing from gambling debts, often using Persian costume for disguise.

Sheinman, Aaron. Bolshevik financial adviser, sales and purchasing agent, expert on the gold and platinum markets; served on various commissions with the Ministry of Finance (Narkomfin) and the Soviet State Bank (Gosbank); entrusted with 17 million tsarist and Kerensky rubles on voyage to Stockholm in 1918; later involved, with Vorovsky and Aschberg, in arranging gold sales in Reval and Stockholm; headed Bolshevik trade missions to Berlin, London, Tbilisi, and Peking; arranged orders with West European aviation firms in Tbilisi; headed a foreign loan mission to Stockholm in 1921; assisted Sokol'nikov in appraisal and attempted sale of Romanov treasure and looted church valuables, 1922. Working associate of Aschberg, Krasin, Sokol'nikov, Vorovsky, Litvinov, Lomonosov.

Shklovsky, Grigory, also "Hirsh" or "Doctor." Treasurer and legal counsel of the Bolshevik Foreign Mission in Bern, 1918; holder of numbered account at Schweizerisches Volksbank. Expelled from Switzerland in November 1918; later appointed Soviet consul in Hamburg. Associate of Berzin, Lifschitz, Moor, Platten, and Radek.

Sokol'nikov, Grigory Yakovlovich. First director of the Russian State Bank after the October Revolution and then "commissar of formerly private banks"; sacrificial lamb chosen to sign humiliating terms of Brest-Litovsk Treaty in March 1918, which led to him losing his ministry. Also headed ad hoc committees to appraise and liquidate the Romanov treasure, in 1922, and to appraise the Gokhran vaults, in 1923.

Solomon, Georgi Aleksandrovich. Associate of Krasin at Siemens-Schukert, where he worked, mostly in the Stockholm office, during the First World War; served under Joffe at the Soviet Mission in Berlin, 1918; later became (from 1920) chairman of the Soviet Trade Delegation in Reval, Estonia, which oversaw the outflow of Soviet gold and also the sale of Gokhran treasures. Associate of Aschberg, Vorovsky, Krasin; bitter rival to Gukovsky.

Steinberg, Joseph, also Isaak, aka "the Engineer" Steinberg. Implicated in the German-financing scandals plaguing the Bolsheviks in summer 1917; Bolshevik commercial agent in Stockholm, April 1918; courier for Berzin and the Soviet Mission in Bern, summer 1918. Later surfaced in Berlin as Bolshevik commercial agent, tasked with the purchase of one million scythes; later still Aschberg's confidence man at the Berlin branch of Svenska Ekonomie Aktiebolaget, who negotiated on Aschberg's behalf with the Reichsbank and the German Foreign Office in the lead-up to Rapallo. Associate of Fürstenberg, "Parvus," and Krasin.

Stomoniakov, Boris Spiridonovich. Bulgarian Bolshevik, also fluent in German. Replaced Kopp as chief Soviet trade negotiator in Berlin from 1920 to 1925. Handled ongoing negotiations with German locomotive firms; took on competing bids for the renovation of the port of Petrograd; was principal liaison between the Reichsbank and Foreign Office, and Aschberg's Svenska Ekonomie Aktiebolaget, in the financial negotiations leading up to Rapallo. Associate of Aschberg, Lomonosov, Krasin; sometime rival to Kopp.

Tikhon, Patriarch (born Vasilii Ivanovich Belavin). Elected Orthodox patriarch by church elders in Moscow shortly after the Bolshevik coup in October 1918, Tikhon would reach an accommodation with the Soviet regime while remaining harshly critical of the violent excesses of the Red Terror. Protested strongly against the renewed Soviet assault on church property, which began in 1922, for which "criminal resistance" he was made the principal scapegoat and forced to stand trial as an "enemy of the people." Imprisoned in the Donskoy Monastery until 1923, Tikhon was forced to sign a declaration of loyalty to the Soviet regime before dying a broken man in 1925. Tikhon was sainted by the Orthodox Church in 1989.

Trotsky, Lev. Onetime Menshevik, later the Bolsheviks' first foreign minister and first commander-in-chief of the Red Army. In the present narrative, the Red Army's foremost railway and arms procurement advocate (in particular, a devotee of American-manufactured Browning and Westinghouse rifles) and the Politburo commissioner for the liquidation of looted church valuables in 1921–22, of which campaign he was the principal architect.

Vorovsky, Vatslav Vatslavovich. Engineer, formerly of the "Lux" company of Stockholm; original member, with Fürstenberg and Radek, of the triumvirate comprising the Bolshevik Foreign Mission in Stockholm, from 1917; negotiated far-reaching trade accords with Sweden in 1918; witnessed buying large quantities of British pounds in Stockholm in 1918–19. Many of his public duties were later assumed by Hellberg, Kerzhentsev, and Ström, largely because he was too well known to Allied consuls in Stockholm. Later assassinated in Lausanne. Close working associate of Aschberg, Krasin, Litvinov, Lomonosov, and Scheinman.

Westcott, Charles. Commercial attaché to the U.S. Embassy in Paris during and after the Allied intervention in Soviet Russia. Prepared, in spring 1921, the most thorough single report on the history of Russian gold reserves and gold movements from 1914 to 1921. Lonely though vigorous advocate for enforcement of the "gold blockade" against Soviet Russia.

Yurovsky, Yakov. Head of the Ekaterinburg Cheka, tasked with overseeing the Romanov murder-robberies in July 1918.

Notes

A Note on the Relative Value of Money Then and Now

1. The price figures for fourth-generation jet fighters are widely available, at sources ranging from *Jane's Defense Weekly* to Wikipedia. For the prices the Bolsheviks paid for imported warplanes, see chapter 8, below.

2. Forty-to-one is the conversion figure used by, for example, Clarke, in *Lost Fortune of the Tsars*. Clarke was comparing the relative historical values of British pounds circa 1917–18 against those of 1994; the pound's value relative to many other currencies has since risen. The dollar, of course, has plunged in value since the 1990s, against the pound and against most other currencies. Such currency fluctuations only underscore the necessity of using purchasing power as the relevant criterion of comparison; what matters is what targeted goods a hoard of gold or cash can buy at a given time, not what its nominal value would be according to a sliding scale of traded currencies.

3. See "Despite Its $168 Billion Budget, the Army Faces a Cash Crunch," *Wall Street Journal,* 11 December 2006; and chapter 7, below.

Prologue: The Patrimony of Imperial Russia

1. Stone, *Europe Transformed,* 143. The Russian obsession of Germany's leaders is one of the major themes of Fritz Fischer's classic study of *Germany's Aims in the First World War,* although Fischer's conclusions remain controversial. For more recent discussions of the subject, see David Fromkin, *Europe's Last Summer: Who Started the Great War in 1914?* and David Stevenson, *Cataclysm: The First World War as Political Tragedy,* chap. 1.

2. Moulton and Pasvolsky, *Russian Debts and Russian Reconstruction,* 27–29.

On the gold figures, see Charles Westcott, "Origin and Disposition of the Former Russian Imperial Gold Reserve," 21 April 1921, in NAA, M 316, roll 120. For a general discussion of the Russian economy on the eve of the war, with emphasis on the military build-up, see Peter Gatrell, *Government, Industry and Rearmament in Russia, 1900–1914.*

3. Miller, *Economic Development of Russia*, 61.

4. Moulton and Pazvolsky, *Russian Debts and Russian Reconstruction*, 17. See also Stone, *Eastern Front*, 18.

5. Cited in Kochan, *Last Days of Imperial Russia*, 186–187.

6. Laserson, *Expert in the Service of the Soviet*, 61–62; Clarke, *Lost Fortune of the Tsars*, 9–10; and "Won't Let Czar Go: Ex-Imperial Family's Wealth Put at $9,000,000,000," *New York Times*, 12 May 1917. For pictures of surviving remnants of the imperial collection, see, e.g., *Sokrovitsa Almaznogo Fonda SSSR/Treasures of the USSR Diamond Fund/Les Joyaux du Fonds Diamantaire de l'URSS.*

7. Kochan, *Last Days of Imperial Russia*, 34–36.

8. Stone, *Eastern Front*, 208.

9. Ibid., esp. chap. 13.

10. Hew Strachan, *Financing the First World War*, 117–118, 133–134; "Russian Debt to France: Investment in Old Empire Put at 22,351,000,000 Francs," *New York Times*, 17 January 1922; Malle, *Economic Organization of War Communism*, 43.

INTRODUCTION TO BOLSHEVIK GOLD: THE NATURE OF A FORGOTTEN PROBLEM

1. Lebor, *Hitler's Secret Bankers*, xvii. See also Bower, *Nazi Gold*. For a sampling of media reactions to the controversy, see "The Greatest Theft in History," BBC online, 1 December 1997; Steve Hurst, "'Harsh Report' Critical of Swiss-Nazi Gold," CNN online, 6 May 1997; David E. Sanger, "Goblins of Zurich," *New York Times Sunday Book Review*, 22 June 1997; "Study: Swiss Bank Stashed Gold Taken from Nazi Camp Victims," CNN online, 25 May 1998.

2. The best overview of Operation Safehaven is contained in the 1997 U.S. government "Report on Looted Gold and German Assets," also known as the "Eizenstat report," which can be viewed online at http://www.usembassy-israel.org.il/publish/report/.

3. Roughly $214 million worth of gold was exported from Soviet Russia via Reval, Estonia, between May 1920 and April 1921, according to Charles Westcott's report submitted from the U.S. consulate in Paris to Washington, 21 April 1921, in NAA, M 316, roll 120. Another $80 million worth of gold was shipped by the Bolsheviks through Reval from May to November 1921, according to the report of Captain Kelley submitted to Washington, 20 March 1922, in NAA, M 316, roll 121. The amount of illegal Bolshevik gold exported via Reval alone in eighteen months, then, surpasses the $289 million in looted Nazi gold processed by Swiss banks during the Second World War. Lebor, *Hitler's Secret Bankers*, 68–69.

4. Lebor never does arrive at an estimate for the amount of Nazi gold sent to Switzerland that had its origins in the tooth fillings and crowns of Holocaust victims, which "dental gold" was processed through the so-called Melmer system. The closest to a concrete estimate of quantity Lebor found was in a postwar U.S. intelli-

gence report describing "4,173 bags said to contain 8,307 gold bars inasmuch as these gold bars may . . . be determined to represent melted down teeth fillings and therefore classifiable as non-monetary gold." Lebor, *Hitler's Secret Bankers,* 63. As such inferior gold was valued much less than fine gold bars (which sold at roughly $700 per kilo), this could not have represented more than a few million dollars (and it had not been sent to Switzerland, anyway).

Irregular Bolshevik looting of aristocrats, kulaks, private bank accounts, abandoned households, and churches between 1917 and 1922 was on a much larger scale. The Gokhran, or State Treasury for the Preservation of Valuables, founded in February 1920 to handle an ever-increasing volume of intake, processed many thousands of tons of loot, including fine gold and high-quality diamonds and other easily saleable jewelry. Just between 6 April and 18 July 1920, for example, the Gokhran received 21,500 carats worth of diamonds, 20,000 carats of pearls, 6,300 carats in gold-plated jewels, plus 20 million tsarist rubles ($10 million) worth of fine gold ingots and coin. See the Gokhran files at RGAE, fond 7632, opis 1, del' 4, list' 8.

5. The best overall survey of Bolshevik looting and laundering of arts and antiquities is *Verkaufte Kultur: Die sowjetischen Kunst- und Antiquitätenexporte, 1919–1938,* ed. Waltraud Bayer, although the coverage of the civil war years is spotty. The most thorough study of the claims by Romanov descendants is William Clarke's *The Lost Fortune of the Tsars.* On artwork specifically, see Robert Williams, *Russian Art and American Money, 1900–1940.* On antiquities, early memoir accounts include Percy Muir, "A Russian Adventure," *The Colophon.* An up-to-date bibliography, including an impressive guide to related materials catalogued in the New York Public Library, is provided by Robert H. Davis et al. in *A Dark Mirror.* For details on which Russian imperial art treasures ended up where in American museums, galleries, and private collections, see, e.g., Anne Odom and Liana Paredes Arend, *A Taste for Splendor.* In recent years, a traveling exhibition of "The Jewels of the Romanovs" made its way through America in 1997, prompting renewed interest in the subject. See Jo Ann Lewis, "Crowning Glories: The Romanov Treasures," *Washington Post,* 31 January 1997.

6. The best overview of all the peasant revolts is Figes, *Peasant Russia, Civil War.* For a more recent overview of the literature, see Osipova, "Peasant Rebellions," 154–176. On the economics of the peasant rebellions, see esp. Alessandro Stanziani, "De la guerre contre les blancs a la guerre contre les paysans (1920–1922)," in *L'Economie en Révolution,* 281–304. For recent accounts of the church campaign, see Georgii Mitrofanov, *Istoriia russkoi pravoslavnoi tserkvi, 1900–1927;* Natalya Alexandrovna Krivova, *Vlast' i Tserkov' v 1922–1925 gg. Politbiuro i GPU v borb'e za tserkovnye tsennosti.* In English, see Jonathan Daly, "'Storming the Last Citadel,'" in *Bolsheviks in Russian Society.*

7. The monthly figure of small arms rounds fired for 1919, Orlando Figes estimates, ranged from 70 and 90 million; only 20 million rounds a month were being turned out at Tula. Figes, *People's Tragedy,* 598. Soviet authors agree that the upper ceiling on production was 30 million rounds/month. See Kovalenko, *Oboronnaia promyshlennost' sovetskoi rossii,* 274–278. From Trotsky's well-publicized complaints about ammunition shortages and eyewitness reports that suggest that maybe

one Red Army soldier in ten carried adequate rounds, it is clear even such an amount was nowhere near enough.

8. The mother-source remains W. J. Novitsky, "Russian Gold Reserve," unpub. MS, NAA, M 316, roll 119. Novitsky's analysis is also available at Columbia University's Rare Book and Manuscript Library; a streamlined version was also published in the 4 July 1920 *New York Times* as "Russian Gold Fund's Adventures and Present Status." An updated, and slightly more accurate, report is the 21 April 1921 report of U.S. commercial attaché Charles Westcott, "Origin and Disposition of the Former Russian Imperial Gold Reserve," also at NAA, M 316, roll 120. Novitsky and Westcott, along with those who relied on their reports, tended to underestimate Bolshevik precious metal reserves, unaware as they were of the enormous scope of confiscations beyond the Bolshevik-captured portions of the imperial gold reserve, such as the gold, platinum, silver, and diamonds hoarded at the Gokhran. In addition to the Gokhran files in RGAE, fond 7632, opis 1, Gokhran-related material, such as the files of the "Safes Commission" (*seifovaia kommissia*), can also be found in RGAE, fond 7733, opis 1.

9. The phrase "financiers of genocide" is Lebor's.

10. The inimitable Olof Aschberg, while being questioned at the Paris Préfecture de Police, see chapters 5, 6, 7, 8, and 9, below.

11. Krasin, *O vneshnei torgovle i otnoshenii k nei russkoi kooperatsii; Voprosy vneshnei torgovli;* and *Dela davno minuvshikh dnei (Vospominaniia).*

12. Interestingly, though, the problem of White gold and silver movements during the civil war has found an able chronicler in Oleg Budnitsky, who wrote a three-part series on the subject for *Diaspora* between 2002 and 2004: "Kolchakovskoe zoloto," *Diaspora* 4 (2002): 457–508; "Natsional'ny fond," *Diaspora* 5 (2003): 283–332; and "Generaly i den'gi, ili 'Vrangelevskoe Serebro," *Diaspora* 6 (2004): 134–173. Although his study sheds little light on Bolshevik gold movements, Budnitsky's series will likely remain the final word on the murky finances of Kolchak and Wrangel.

CHAPTER 1. THE BANKS

Epigraph: Francis O. Lindley dispatch to British Foreign Office from Petrograd, "Report on Recent Events in Russia," 25 November 1917, in PRO, FO 371/3000.

1. Marx, *Manifesto of the Communist Party* (1848), in *The Marx-Engels Reader*, 490.

2. Lenin, "Will the Bolsheviks Retain State Power?" (1917), excerpted in Bunyan and Fisher, *Bolshevik Revolution*, 318–319. Bunyan's translation.

3. Stone, *Eastern Front*, 283.

4. Pipes, *Russian Revolution*, 528.

5. F. O. Lindley, "Report on Recent Events in Russia," 25 November 1917, in PRO, FO 371/3000; and V. Obolensky-Osinsky, "How We Got Control of the State Bank," first published in *Ekonomicheskaia Zhizn* on 6 November 1918, translated and reproduced in Bunyan and Fisher, *Bolshevik Revolution*, 319. Lindley's account is consistent with that of Obolensky-Osinsky, right down to the band accompanying the Bolshevik detachment.

6. Pipes, *Russian Revolution,* 528.

7. V. Obolensky-Osinsky, "How We Got Control of the State Bank," in Bunyan and Fisher, *Bolshevik Revolution,* 321.

8. Ibid., 322.

9. "Seizure and nationalization of the banks," enclosure in Sir George Buchanan's dispatch no. 405 Commercial, 31 December 1917, in PRO, FO 368/1965.

10. Obolensky-Osinsky, "How We Got Control of the State Bank," 322–323.

11. Laserson, *Expert in the Service of the Soviet,* 18–19.

12. Letter from Burmeister, manager of the Russian and English Bank, Petrograd, sent from Petrograd 24 January 1918 to the bank's London office, forwarded to the British Foreign Office, in PRO, FO 371 / 3701; and "The bank position," enclosure in Sir George Buchanan's dispatch no. 6 Commercial, 6 January 1918, in PRO, FO 371/3294.

13. Cited by Werth, "Iron Fist of the Dictatorship of the Proletariat," 103.

14. Sokol'nikov, telegram sent from Petrograd to "Moskva, Ekaterinburg,' Arkhangel'sk, Velikii-Ustiug, Vologda, Vyborg,' Viatka, Novgorod' . . . " (etc.), 8 December 1917 (old calendar) in RGASPI, 670-1-15, 29.

15. "Proekt dekreta o provedenii v zhizn' nationalizatsii bankov i o neobkhodimykh v sviazi s etim' merakh,'" in RGASPI, 670-1-35, 19–21.

16. "Letter from the Director of the Russian and English Bank, Petrograd," 24 January 1918, in PRO, FO 371/3701.

17. "Search of Safe Deposit Boxes: Decree of the Central Executive Committee, December 27, 1917," in Bunyan and Fisher, *Bolshevik Revolution,* 324. Bunyan's translation.

18. Pipes, *Russian Revolution,* 550–552.

19. Aschberg, "A Wandering Jew from Glasbruksgatan" (*Ein vandrande jude fran Glasbruksgatan*) (henceforth *Wandering Jew*), 35–36, 41–42.

20. "The bank position," 6 January 1918, in PRO, FO 371/3294.

21. "Opening of safes at banks," enclosure in Sir G. Buchanan's 5 January 1918 dispatch, in PRO, FO 371/3294.

22. Report from the British consulate general, Moscow, forwarded to London via F. O. Lindley in Petrograd, 28 January 1918, in PRO, FO 368/1965.

23. "The bank position," 6 January 1918, in PRO, FO 371/3294.

24. Laserson, *Im Sowjet-Labyrinth,* 64–65.

25. As reported in the 27 July 1918 *Izvestiia,* in Bunyan and Fisher, *Bolshevik Revolution,* 324.

26. Strachan, *Financing the First World War,* 117.

27. Laserson, *Im Sowjet-Labyrinth,* 16–17. On Krestinsky, see chapter 3, below.

28. Undated Doklad, circa late December 1917, "Upravliaiushchemu Komissariatom byvsh. Chastnykh bankov tov. Sokol'nikovu," in RGASPI, 670-1-35, 54.

29. "Naimenovanie Bankov. Adres.' NoNo Telefonov . . . ," etc., circa late December 1917, in the Sokol'nikov fond at RGASPI, 670-1-35, 5–8 (and verso).

30. Undated Doklad, circa late December 1917, "Upravliaiushchemu Komissariatom byvsh. chastnykh bankov tov. Sokol'nikovu," in RGASPI, 670-1-35, 54.

31. Ibid.

32. "Tablitsa tsennykh bumag' prinadlezhavshikh byvshimi chastnimi Bankami v Moskve na 15/31 dekabria 1917 goda/po nominal'noi stoimosti," in RGASPI, 670-1-35, 35. The sum total of national, municipal, and corporate bonds (along with some equities) arrived at in this inquiry was 188,538,743 rubles.

33. "Spisok neoplachannykh chekov," prepared by the People's Bank (i.e., the State Bank) of Moscow, circa late December 1917, in RGASPI, 670-1-35, 59.

34. "Discontinuance of Interest and Dividend Payments," Decree of the Sovnarkom, 11 January 1918, in Bunyan and Fisher, *Bolshevik Revolution,* 326. Bunyan's translation.

35. Telegram Lindley to London, 8 February 1918, in PRO, FO 371/3294.

36. Laserson, *Expert in the Service of the Soviet,* 16–17.

37. "Confiscation of Works by the Bolshevik Government," translated and reported to London by F. O. Lindley, 31 January 1918, in PRO, FO 368/1965; and follow-up report on the "Confiscation of Companies and Works by the Bolshevik Government," 17 February 1918, in PRO, FO 368/1966.

38. "Decree of High Economic Council Concerning Gold and Platinum," translated and reported to London by F. O. Lindley, 29 January 1918, in PRO, FO 368/1965.

39. Lindley report from Petrograd, 5 February 1918, in PRO, FO 368/1965.

40. Lindley report from Petrograd, 10 February 1918, in PRO, FO 368/1965.

41. Pipes, *Russian Revolution,* 672.

42. Malle, *Economic Organization of War Communism,* 50, 161.

43. See Pipes, *Russian Revolution,* 24–26.

44. "Confiscation of Works by the Bolshevik Government," 31 January 1918.

45. Ibid. On Putilov's shell production contracts during the war and the controversy surrounding the loans he took on to fill them, see Stone, *Eastern Front,* 199–200.

46. "Note sur la Banque Russo-Asiatique," 29 June 1930, AN, BB 18/6727.

47. Gatrell, *Government, Industry and Rearmament in Russia,* 219.

48. "Quelques faits et précisions concernant la banque russo-asiatique. La situation des actionnaires," marked 1929 (circa late June), in AN, BB 18/6727. The date of the final Banque Russo-Asiatique statement was June 1917.

49. Pipes, *Russian Revolution,* 561.

50. "Quelques faits et précisions concernant la banque russo-asiatique. La situation des actionnaires," marked 1929 (circa late June), in AN, BB 18/6727.

51. The inventories of Banque Russo-Asiatique taken by Sokol'nikov at Petrograd headquarters list assets of only 9.826 million rubles (on 15 December 1917) and 8.797 million rubles (on 22 January 1918). "Spravka o sostoianii svobodnogo kredita chastnykh bankov po spets. tek. schetov . . . ," 22 January 1918, in RGASPI, 670-1-15, 72.

52. "Svedeniia o kolichestve osvobozhdennykh, vzlomanykh i podlezhashchikh vzlomu seifov vo vsekh stal'nykh kladovykh byvsh. chastnykh bankov g. Moskvy," in RGAE, 7733-1-248, 6 (and verso), 7.

53. From banks such as Russo-Asiatique, Mezhdunarodny, Uchetny i Ssudnoi, Petrogradsky, Ryssky vnesh. Torg. Bank, the balance of "free credit" available on current account (sostoianii svobodnogo kredita . . . po spets. tek. schetov) was deb-

ited by sums ranging from 500,000 to 2 million rubles between 15 December 1917 and 22 January 1918. "Spravka o sostoianii svobodnogo kredita chastnykh bankov po spets. Tek. Schetov . . . ," 22 January 1918, in RGASPI, 670-1-15, 72. The document does not specify for what purpose these funds were debited, but as the period coincides exactly with the beginning of the Bolsheviks' safe-deposit-box confiscation campaign, it seems likely any bank credit available was transferred to the Soviet authorities. The positive exceptions to the rule of generally meager returns were the Russian and English Bank (with the bemused manager), which seems to have yielded the impressive sum of 5.18 million rubles' credit, of 13 million listed in the current account; and the Azov-Don Bank, where 6 million rubles (of 166 million listed) were debited in December and January.

54. See "Proshenie" filed with the Bolshevik Commissar of Finance by the "Pravleniia Niderlandskago banka dlia russkoi torgovli," RGAE, 7733-1-91, 80 (verso) and the reply by Nikolai Krestinsky, in RGAE, 7733-1-91, 86. The bank's shareholders are listed in an attachment to the Proshenie, RGAE, 7733-1-91, 84 (and verso).

55. Pipes, *Russia under the Bolshevik Regime,* 218.

56. See "Russian Debt to France: Investment in Old Empire Put at 22,351,000,000 Francs," *New York Times,* 17 January 1922.

57. Although, to be sure, many of these bondholders had earned a great deal in interest *before* the war brought the interruption of regular dividend payments, even if they ultimately lost the bond principal. According to Olga Crisp, French bondholders had already earned 6 billion francs on their Russian investments between 1889 and 1914, which represented more than half the amount originally invested. See Crisp, *Studies in the Russian Economy before 1914,* 208. Most of those who had bought Russian war bonds, however, lost nearly everything.

58. "Report of the Commissar of Finance, Gukovsky, to the Central Committee Executive Committee, 15 April 1918," cited by Bunyan and Fisher, *Bolshevik Revolution,* 605–606. Bunyan's translation.

59. Lindley report to Arthur Balfour, sent from Petrograd 8 February 1918, in PRO, FO 371/3294; Pipes, *Russian Revolution,* 234–235, 685. On the Russian inflation during and after the First World War, see Katzenellenbaum, *Russian Currency and Banking.*

60. F. O. Lindley report to Arthur Balfour, sent from Petrograd 8 February 1918, in PRO, FO 371/3294.

61. Cited by Malle, 161. Malle's translation.

62. Both Pipes, in *Russian Revolution* (528–529) and Figes, who follows Pipes in *People's Tragedy* (500–502), suggest that the bank strike was effectively brought under control after the dissolution of the Constituent Assembly in January, when most state employees went back to work. But Laserson, who figured prominently in the negotiations, insists that the strikers relented only "towards the end of March." Laserson, *Expert in the Service of the Soviet,* 19. Laserson's account accords well with the reports of F. O. Lindley in Petrograd, who followed the bank strike closely. See, e.g., Lindley's 2 February 1918 dispatch on "The banking position": "the position at the Petrograd banks remains the same, the strike of the bank employees continuing, the banks, when open at all for an hour or so daily, confining themselves,

with the attendance of a few officials, to issuing cheques on the State Bank for payment of factory wages. For normal or private banking operations the banks remain closed." Lenin's 4 March 1918 complaint about a "money famine" seems to confirm that the strike endured into March. By contrast, Bolshevik policy statements from April 1918 onwards begin blandly emphasizing the need for "accounting and control"—suggesting that the party at last had money to account for.

63. Laserson, *Expert in the Service of the Soviet,* 19.

64. Pipes, *Russian Revolution,* 520.

65. See Isarescu, Paunescu, and Stefan, *Tezaurul Bancii Nationale a Romaniei la Moscova.*

66. I have followed the estimates of Charles Westcott, in "Origin and Disposition of the Former Russian Imperial Gold Reserve," 21 April 1921, in NAA, M 316, roll 120. Westcott, with minor revisions, largely draws on W. J. Novitsky, "Russian Gold Reserve," unpub. MS, in NAA , M 316, roll 119. Westcott's estimates of Russia's remaining gold reserves in 1921, as we shall see below (chaps. 7–8) erred significantly on the low side, but the information up to 1917 is fairly accurate, based on information on the tsarist and Kerensky-era reserves widely available to the Entente powers.

67. Westcott, "Origin and Disposition of the Former Russian Imperial Gold Reserve." Westcott's estimate of $160 million worth of gold shipped to Germany is double the real amount. The likely source of confusion is that half of the $160 million shipped to Germany in September was in the form of tsarist rubles. See chapter 5, below.

CHAPTER 2. THE PEOPLE

Epigraph: V. I. Lenin, *Sochineniia,* 22:231. Originally published in *Pravda* on 24 January/6 February 1918.

1. The requisition order, dated 3 July 1917, is preserved in RGAE, 413-3-2, 3.

2. Marx, *Capital,* vol. 1, in *The Marx Engels Reader,* 438.

3. Lenin, *Sochineniia,* 22:231.

4. Ibid.

5. Cited by Figes, *People's Tragedy,* 526. Figes's translation.

6. Arbenina (Baroness Meyendorff), *Through Terror to Freedom,* 158.

7. Clarke, *Lost Fortune of the Tsars,* 134.

8. Stites, *Revolutionary Dreams,* 129.

9. Figes, *People's Tragedy,* 530.

10. Reiss, *Orientalist,* 43–45.

11. Clarke, *Lost Fortune of the Tsars,* 53–55, 128.

12. Yevgenii Zhirnov, "Kak Zakalialsia Brend. O role 'Rolls-Roisa' v rossisskoi istorii," *Kommersant-Den'gi* 10 (15 March 2004): 98. See also chapter 8, below.

13. The official reason the Provisional Government gave for transferring the crown jewels from Petrograd to Moscow in July 1917 was the German military threat. But the Germans did not take Riga until October. The real pretext, according to German intelligence, was the failed Bolshevik putsch in early July. In summer 1917, Bolshevik influence in Moscow was still quite weak in comparison to Petrograd, which suggests the crown jewels would be safer in the Kremlin. See telegram

to Berlin from Freiherr Lucius von Stoedten, German consul in Stockholm, 20 July 1917, in PAAA, R 10080.

14. Pipes, *Russian Revolution*, 770–772.

15. "Yakov Yurovsky's note on the execution of the imperial family and the concealment of the corpses, 1920," translated by Elizabeth Tucker and reproduced in Khrustalëv and Steinberg, *Fall of the Romanovs*, 353. On the executions, see also Sokolov, *Sokolov Investigation of the Alleged Murder of the Russian Imperial Family*, 112–119; Clarke, *Lost Fortune of the Tsars*, 83–85; and Pipes, *Russian Revolution*, 774–777.

16. "Yakov Yurovsky's note on the execution of the imperial family and the concealment of the corpses, 1920," in Khrustalëv and Steinberg, *Fall of the Romanovs*, 353–354.

17. Pipes, *Russian Revolution*, 779–780.

18. "Yakov Yurovsky's note on the execution of the imperial family and the concealment of the corpses, 1920," in Khrustalëv and Steinberg, *Fall of the Romanovs*, 365.

19. Cited by Radzinsky, *Last Tsar,* 392.

20. Pipes, *Russian Revolution*, 784.

21. Radzinsky, *Nicolas II* (updated French ed.), trans. Anne Coldefy-Faucard, 355–357.

22. Sokolov, *Sokolov Investigation*, 91–107.

23. Clements, *Bolshevik Feminist*, 132.

24. Daly, "'Storming the Last Citadel,'" 237; and Curtiss, *Russian Church*, 66.

25. Curtiss, *Russian Church,* 84; Pipes, *Russia under the Bolshevik Regime*, 340–346.

26. Cited by Edward E. Roslof, in *Red Priests,* 28. Roslof's translation.

27. Curtiss, *Russian Church*, 73.

28. Buchanan letter to Mr. Balfour, 15 December 1917, in PRO, FO 368/1965.

29. Letter from H. H. Charnock to the British consulate in Stockholm, 14 October 1918, in PRO, FO 368/1966.

30. Letter from Foreign Office London to the British consulate in Moscow, 3 January 1918, in PRO, FO 368/1965.

31. Letter of apology from Foreign Secretary Arthur Balfour to Frank Reddaway, 30 March 1918, in PRO, FO 368/1965.

32. Letter to Foreign Office London from Margherita Ashton Johnson, circa early February 1918, in PRO, FO 371/3294.

33. Letter from E. M. Nicolson to Foreign Office London, 27 November 1918, in PRO, FO 371/3294.

34. Letter from Mrs. Tatiana Walton to Foreign Office London, 18 January 1918, in PRO, FO 368/1965.

35. Letter from Frank W. Taylor to the Foreign Office London, circa late January 1918, in PRO, FO 371/3294.

36. "Claims against Russia," British Foreign Office memorandum, circa March 1921, in PRO, FO 371/6933.

37. On these claims, see chapters 8 and 9, below.

38. See report from Leutnant Rey, head of the German military commission in Petrograd, sent to Petrograd on 19 November 1918, in PAAA, R 11207.

39. See Franz Rauch's 12 April 1919 report to the German Foreign Office in Berlin after his return from Moscow, in DBB, R 901/82082, 22–25.

40. "Sokhrannaia rospiska no. 300 Saratovskaia Trudovaia Artel' . . . Priniato ot Annyi Ivanovny Nozhinoi na khranenie I strakh. Raznago roda imushchestvo na usloviiakh, izlozhennykh na oborot,'" in RGAE, 7733-1-195, 77.

41. Letter from Sergei Nozhin and Anna Nozhina "V glavnuiu seifovuiu komissiiu," dated Saratov, 8 February 1921, in RGAE, 7733-1-195, 76 (and verso).

42. Stites, *Revolutionary Dreams*, 128.

43. Pipes, *Russian Revolution*, 684.

44. Figes, *People's Tragedy*, 527.

45. To protect his friend's identity, Laserson renders him only by his initials, N. N. Laserson, *Im Sowjet-Labyrinth*, 57–58. On the sum Gukovsky was entrusted with (50 million, or 30 more than Laserson himself believed), see "Stokgol'msky valiutny rynok v 1918 g.," in RGAE, 413-3-18, 11. According to German intelligence, Gukovsky was also carrying 500 kilograms of platinum. See report from Lucius von Stoedten in Stockholm, 11 October 1918, in PAAA, 11207.

46. Pipes, *Russian Revolution*, 719.

47. "Report of [Finance Commissar] Gukovsky to the Central Committee, April 15, 1918," cited by Bunyan and Fisher, *Bolshevik Revolution*, 605–606. Bunyan's translation.

48. Pipes, *Russian Revolution*, 736–737. Pipes's translation.

49. Citations in Werth, "Red Terror," in *Black Book of Communism*, 72–73. The translations are by Jonathan Murphy and Mark Kramer.

50. Pipes, *Russian Revolution*, 742.

51. Meyendorff, *Through Terror*, 102.

52. "Vremennoe Postanovlenie o naloge na dragotsennosti, nakhodiashchiesia v seifakh, lombardakh, ssudnykh kassakh i t.p. ustanovleniiakh g. Moskvy i Moskovskoi oblasti," 11 May 1918, in RGAE, 7733-1-28, 4.

CHAPTER 3. THE GOKHRAN

Epigraph: Laserson, *Expert in the Service of the Soviet*, 58.

1. See Werth, "Red Terror," in *Black Book of Communism*, 68, 73–80.

2. "Spetsial'nago naloga na dragotsennye izdeliia, khraniashchiesia v seifakh mestnykh bankov,' v pol'zu soveta," 10 November 1918, in RGAE, 7733-1-10, 14.

3. Bayer, "Revolutionäre Beute," in *Verkaufte Kultur*, 23.

4. According to Dr. Sandy Berkovski of Bilkent University, whose great-aunt knew Gorky's wife well in the 1920s, Andreeva was commonly known among her close acquaintances to be a compulsive thief.

5. O'Connor, *Engineer of Revolution*, 8–15.

6. Ibid., 51–52, 75, 80, 85–86. On Krasin's success in charming the elites of Baku, see also Reiss, *Orientalist*, 21, 41.

7. Volkogonov, *Lenin*, 55; and O'Connor, *Engineer of Revolution*, 86–89.

8. Figes, *People's Tragedy*, 606–607; and Pipes, *Russia under the Bolshevik Regime*, 298–299.

9. Bayer, "Revolutionäre Beute," in *Verkaufte Kultur*, 23.

10. On the "maniacal" accounting predilection of tsarist bureaucrats, see Stone, *Eastern Front,* 17.

11. "Akt na osnovanii ordera Komendanta Petrogradskogo Ukreplennogo Raiona . . . ot 5-go Oktiabria 1919 g. proizveden obysk v d. no. 30, kv. 9 po naberezhnoi . . . ulitsa koresa," in RGAE, 7733-1-931, 4.

12. "Akt na osnovanii ordera Komendanta Petrogradskogo Ukreplennogo Raiona . . . ot 14 Oktiabria 1919 g. proizveden obysk v d. no. 30, kv. 9 po ulitse KORESA/b. Frantsuzskaia Naberezhnaia," in RGAE, 7733-1-931, 2.

13. Bayer, "Revolutionäre Beute," in *Verkaufte Kultur,* 26.

14. "Opis' veshei osmotrenny . . . po vskritiiu i osnotru iashikov rasformirovan-nykh voinskikh chastei nakhodiashchikhsia na khranenii v Tambovskom Kaz-nacheistve i podlezhashchikh, soglasno telegrammy za Narkomfina Chutskaeva no. 261 ot 27 ianvaria 1919 g. otpravleniiu f gor. Moskvu," and similar opisi for individual containers sent in, in RGAE, 7632-1-11, 1–8.

15. Krasin telegram to the Petrograd headquarters of the Commissariat of Foreign Trade (NKVT), 16 February 1920, in RGAE, 413-3-242, 46 and verso.

16. Laserson, *Im Sowjet-Labyrinth,* 14.

17. Ibid., 14–15, 22–23.

18. "Postanovlenie soveta narodnykh komissarov ob uchrezhdenii gosudarst-vennogo khranilishcha tsennostei Rossisskoi Sotsialisticheskoi Federativnoi Sovet-skoi Respubliki," 3 February 1920, type-signed by V. Ulyanov (Lenin) for Sovnar-kom, in RGAE, 7632-1-1, 1. On the location of the Gokhran, see Laserson, *Expert in the Service of the Soviet,* 58.

19. Nikolai Krestinsky, "Polozhenie o gosudarstvennom khranilishche Tsennos-tei/Gokhran," 16 March 1920, in RGAE, 7632-1-1, 4.

20. "Instruktsia po operatsiiam, deloproizvodstvu schetovodstvu i otchetnosti gosudarstvennogo khranilischa tsennostei/Gokhran," 16 March 1920, in RGAE, 7632-1-1, 68.

21. Gokhran budget report submitted to Narkomfin, 15 April 1920, in RGAE, 7632-1-1, 5.

22. "Protokol soveshchaniia po vyrabotk' tarifa dlia sotrudnikov Narodnago Banka RFSR," 3 September 1920, in RGAE, 7733-1-931, 49–50 (and verso).

23. "Instruktsia po operatsiiam, deloproizvodstvu schetovodstvu i otchetnosti gosudarstvennogo khranilischa tsennostei/Gokhran," 16 March 1920, in RGAE, 7632-1-1, 68–69.

24. "Kratkii Otchet o rezul'tatakh raboty Gokhrana za vremia s 6-go Aprelia po 18 Iiulia vkliuchitel'no 1920 g.," in RGAE, 7632-1-4, 8.

25. "Spravka o nalichnosti tsennostei v kladovykh Gokhrana na 1-oe Dekabria 1920 g.," in RGAE, 7632-1-6, 17; and spreadsheet labeled "Postupilo s 6-go Apre-lia po 30 Noiabria vkliuchitel'no," in RGAE, 7632-1-6, 12 (verso).

26. "Obshchii Uchet otsortivorannykh brilliantov, zhemchuga, dragotsennikh kamnei i izdelii iz zolota ne podlezhashchikh slomu. Gokhran s 1-go po 15-oe Apre-lia," and similar accounts for January, February, March, and so forth, in RGAE, 7632-1-12, 1–3 (and verso).

27. Swedish agent's report from Reval, 1 December 1921, in RSU, HP 495.

28. "Svedeniia o kolichestve osvobozhdennykh, vzlomanykh i podlezhashchikh

vzlomu seifov vo vsekh stal'nykh kladovykh . . . g. Moskvy," in RGAE, 7733-1-248, 6 (and verso), 7.

29. "Otchet o rabotakh, proizvedennykh Seifovoi Komissii za vremia s 10-go sentiabria 1920 g. po 25-go Maia 1921 g. Seifovaia komissiia obrazovalas' v kontse avgusta mesiatsa 1920g. po soglasheniiu N.K.F. R.K.I. i M. Ch. K. dlia rukovodstva delom vskrytiia seifov, iz'iatiia iz nikh tsennostei v peredachi ikh v Gokhran . . . ," in RGAE, 7733-1-248, 1 (and verso), 2.

30. "Protokol no. 2 Zasedaniia seifovoi Komisii za 13-e sentiabria 1920 goda," in RGAE, 7733-1-377, 4, point no. 6.

31. "Otchet o rabotakh, proizvedennykh Seifovoi Komissii za vremia s 10-go sentiabria 1920 g. po 25-go Maia 1921 g.," in RGAE, 7733-1-248, 2 and verso.

32. "Opis' chasov firmy g. Mozer, iz'iatikh iz seifov b. Chastnogo Kommer-chestkogo Banka, otpravlennykh v Gokhran," dated 9 September 1920, 15 January and 5 March 1921, in RGAE, 7733-1-2109, 309 (and verso), 310, 311, 312.

33. "Kratkii Otchet o rezul'tatakh Raboty Gokhrana za vremia s 16-go po 30 Sentiabria vkliuchit' 1920 g.," in RGAE, 7632-1-4, 4.

34. "Obshchii Uchet otsortivorannykh brilliantov, zhemchuga, dragotsennikh kamnei i izdelii iz zolota ne podlezhashchikh slomu. Gokhran s 1-go po 15-oe Apre-lia," in RGAE, 7632-1-12, 2 (verso).

35. See telegram sent from Frunze, now back in Moscow, to Sokol'nikov in Tashkent, 9 September 1920, in RGASPI, 670-1-57, 15.

36. "Kniga Tsennostei Turkkomissii," 1 September 1920, in RGASPI, 670-1-57, 25 and verso.

37. "Telegramma G.Ia. Sokol'nikova na imia V.V. Kuibushev o vyvoze bu-kharskikh tsennostei v Tashkent dlia khraneniia," 11 October 1920, in RGASPI, 670-1-57, 49.

38. RKI/Fininspektsii letter sent to Sokol'nikov at Narkomfin, 6 May 1922, in RGAE, 7733-1-573, 58.

39. RKI/Fininspektsii report dated 21 December 1921, in RGAE, 7733-1-573, 3.

40. RKI/Fininspektsii report dated 16 March 1922, in RGAE, 7733-1-573, 41.

41. Narkomfin request lodged with the Finansovaia Inspektsiia (Fininspektsiia) of RKI, 9 March 1922, in RGAE, 7733-1-573, 34.

42. RKI/Fininspektsii report dated 25 March 1922, in RGAE, 7733-1-573, 45.

43. RKI/Fininspektsii reports dated 1 and 22 July 1922, in RGAE, 7733-1-573, 92–93.

44. Report from the Irkutsk Gubfinotdel sent into RKI Fininspektsiia, 14 February 1923, in RGAE, 7733-1-814, 10.

45. "Pravila proizvodstva fakticheskoi revizii raboche-Krest'ianskoi Inspektsii bankovskikh vagonov," circa early 1922, in RGAE, 7733–1-573, 68 (and verso).

46. Ibid.

47. Laserson, Expert in the Service of the Soviet, 58.

48. Ibid., 59.

49. Swedish agent's report from Reval, 1 December 1921, in RSU, HP 495.

50. Swedish agent's report from Reval, 12 January 1922, in RSU, HP 495.

51. Solomon, Unter den Roten Machthabern, 219–221. On this deal and foreign sales more generally, see chapters 7–8, below.

52. On the De Beers monopoly and the "diamond invention," see Epstein, "Have You Ever Tried to Sell a Diamond?"

53. See Pipes, *Russia under the Bolshevik Regime*, 353.

54. See Litvinov reply to Lenin's query on the Bolsheviks' financial situation, 29 June 1921, reproduced in Pipes, *Unknown Lenin*, 126–127. All translations from *The Unknown Lenin* below are those of Catherine A. Fitzpatrick. On the gold and platinum markets, and Bolshevik efforts to exploit them, see chapters 7–8, below.

55. See the report of the U.S. consul in Viborg, Finland, based on articles in *Krasnaia Gazeta* dated 3 and 12 November 1921, sent to Washington 30 November 1921, in NAA, M 316, roll 121.

56. See Laserson, *Expert in the Service of the Soviet*, 83–84.

CHAPTER 4. THE CHURCH

Epigraph: RGASPI, 2-1-22947, 2.

1. Roslof, *Red Priests*, 27.

2. Citations in Pipes, *Russia under the Bolshevik Regime*, 343, 345. Pipes's translations.

3. Curtiss, *Russian Church*, 67.

4. Cited in Daly, "'Storming the Last Citadel,'" 235. Daly's translation.

5. On the peasant wars of 1920–21, see chapter 7, below.

6. On the politics of famine relief, see McMeekin, "Selling the Famine," in *Red Millionaire*, 103–122.

7. Trotsky's commission was given a number of different official mandates before finally, after March 1922, being placed in charge of the sale of "church valuables." See Politburo minutes of, e.g., 11 November 1921, in RGASPI, 17-3-229; 8 December 1921, in RGASPI, 17-3-242; 31 December 1921, in RGASPI, 17-3-247; and 20 March 1922, in RGASPI, 17-3-283.

8. Citation in Curtiss, *Russian Church*, 108. Curtiss's translations. On the letter-writing campaign, see esp. Daly, "'Storming the Last Citadel,'" 240–24; and Pipes, *Russia under the Bolshevik Regime*, 347–348.

9. On these luxury food imports, see the statistics provided in "Aussenhandel," in the 19 October 1921 *Revaler Bote;* "Sowjetrusslands Import" and "Der Aussenhandel Sowjetrusslands," 6 and 7 December 1921 *Revaler Bote.* On the import drive for the embryonic Soviet air force, see chapter 8, below.

10. "Spravka o sostoianii kreditov 1921 g. Voennogo Vedomstva. V Spotekzak, Srochno. Sekretno. NKVT Finansovo-Schetnoe Upravleniia" circa December 1921, in RGAE, 413-6-36, 219 and back. On these expenditures, see chapter 8, below.

11. See Russian Trade Delegation in London budget report sent to Moscow 17 January 1922, in RGAE, 413-6-36, 89–90, which specifies that "T. Krasina . . . otpravliautsia avtochasti dlia 'Rol's-Rois," to the tune of 16,400 gold rubles.

12. Politburo minutes, 15 March 1922, in RGASPI, 17-3-283.

13. Citations in Krivova, *Vlast' i Tserkov'*, 31. On the dissolution of the church committee, see British intelligence dispatch from Mr. Hodgson Moscow to the Marquess Curzon, 21 August 1922, in in PRO, FO 371/8212; and Curtiss, *Russian Church*, 107.

14. Citations in Mitrofanov, *Istoriia russkoi pravoslavnoi tserkvi*, 210–213; Daly, "'Storming the Last Citadel,'" 242; and Pipes, *Russia under the Bolshevik Regime*, 349.

15. See Hoover letters to U.S. President Warren Harding, 9 February 1922 (reporting the Soviet request to slow down aid shipments) and 26 July 1922, on the prospects for the harvest, both reproduced in Fisher, in *Famine in Soviet Russia*, 545, 550.

16. See Chicherin telegram to Krasin/Solomon, which passes on Trotsky's order, 7 February 1922, in RGAE, 413-6-36, 96. On the 6 February 1922 gold shipment from Reval, see report of Captain Kelley, assistant military observer at the U.S. Commission in Reval, 20 March 1922, in NAA, M 316, roll 121. For more on these gold shipments, see chapters 7–8, below.

17. On the chain of command in the church operations, see Krivova, *Vlast' i Tserkov'*, 34–36.

18. Citations in ibid., 35–36.

19. Cited by Pipes, in *Russia under the Bolshevik Regime*, 349.

20. Ibid.

21. Politburo minutes for 16 and 20 March 1922, in RGASPI, 17-3-282 (item 12), and 17-3-283 (item 6). See also Daly, "'Storming the Last Citadel,'" 243.

22. The original of this notorious document can be found in RGASPI, 2-1-22947, 1–4. Long excerpts in the original Russian can also be found in Mitrofanov, *Istoriia russkoi pravoslavnoi tserkvi*, 217–218. An English-language translation of the entire document (on which I have largely relied, with subtle changes of emphasis) is in Pipes, *Russia under the Bolshevik Regime*, 350–352. The document is also excerpted in Pipes, *Unknown Lenin*, 152–155, and in Daly "'Storming the Last Citadel,'" 244. On Lenin's whereabouts in March 1922, see Volkogonov, *Lenin*, 377.

23. Cited by Curtiss, *Russian Church*, 115. Curtiss's translation.

24. Pipes, *Russia under the Bolshevik Regime*, 353–355; Volkogonov, *Lenin*, 69; Figes, *People's Tragedy*, 748–749. On the anticlerical show trials, see Daly, "'Storming the Last Citadel,'" 252–253.

25. "Report on the Removal of Valuables by the Soviet Authorities from Petropavlovsk Cathedral," forwarded from British intelligence in Petrograd to the Foreign Office, 9 July 1922. The source of the report is unstated, but it seems to have arisen from widespread gossip about the grave-robbing episode. As the informant writes, "The news that the coffins of the Tsars had been opened quickly spread in Petrograd, evoking great indignation amongst the inhabitants." Of course it may be fictitious; but in the tenor of the times it has a great ring of truth.

26. Volkogonov, *Lenin*, 374.

27. As recited in the diary entry of Frank Golder of 19 March 1922, in Emmons and Patenaude, *War, Revolution, and Peace in Russia*, 148.

28. Krivova, *Vlast' i Tserkov'*, 102, 105–109.

29. Ibid., 109.

30. Still later, the Church of Christ the Savior would be restored, at colossal expense, under the stewardship of Moscow mayor Yuri Luzhkov in the 1990s. For a fine account, from which I have taken many of these details, see Remnick, *Resurrection*, 169–173.

31. Report of the British commercial attaché in Moscow to the Foreign Office, 11 April 1922, in PRO, FO 371/8212; Krivova, *Vlast' i Tserkov'*, 106.

32. The putative ownership of these materials—many of which had belonged to private British subjects, who had deposited them in the church in the hope they would remain safe from Bolshevik depredations—was later transferred from the Commissariat of Finance to the Soviet Foreign Ministry, where they would be held in a kind of diplomatic escrow, used as a bargaining chip in debt negotiations with London. "Opis' imushchestva kladovoi v Anglikanskoi tserkvi," in RGAE, 7632-1-19, 2–4 (and verso).

33. Krivova, *Vlast' i Tserkov'*, 116.

34. Report of the British commercial attaché in Moscow to the Foreign Office, 31 May 1922, in PRO, FO 371/8212. See also Krivova, *Vlast' i Tserkov'*, 117–118.

35. Volkogonov, *Lenin*, 381.

36. Laserson, *Expert in the Service of the Soviet*, 72; Krivova, *Vlast' i Tserkov'*, 118.

37. Aschberg, *Wandering Jew*, 135–138.

38. Laserson, *Expert in the Service of the Soviet*, 68–73.

39. Report of the British commercial attaché in Moscow to the Foreign Office, 26 September 1922, in PRO, FO 371/8212.

40. "Otchet Gokhrana s 1 Ianvaria do 1 oktiabria 1922 g.," in RGAE, 7632-1-16, 2. On revenues from the Church campaign see also Pipes, 356, and Krivova, *Vlast' i Tserkov'*, 118–119. On the sums being spent on Soviet imports in 1921–22, see chapter 8 below.

41. Laserson, *Expert in the Service of the Soviet*, 69.

42. See Sokol'nikov's 27 May 1922 memorandum to M. K. Vladimirov, A. I. Rykov and A. D. Tsiurupy, labeled *o pereotsenke romanovskikh tsennostei*, and the more detailed private letters to M. K. Vladimirov and Trotsky, in RGASPI, 670-1-36, 26–30.

43. The Bolsheviks proposed a collateral value for the crown jewels of 1 billion rubles ($500 million) to James P. Goodrich, the former Republican governor of the state of Indiana posted to Russia as ARA political representative in 1922. British commercial attaché in Moscow to the Foreign Office, 27 June 1922, in PRO, FO 371/8212.

CHAPTER 5. BREST-LITOVSK AND THE DIPLOMATIC BAG

Epigraph: V. A. Nik, "Stokgol'msky valiutny rynok v 1918 g.," in RGAE, 413-3-18, 10.

1. "Condition of the Bolshevik Party" (Sverdlov's report to the Seventh Party Congress, March 6, 1918), cited by Bunyan and Fisher, *Bolshevik Revolution*, 543–544. Bunyan's translation.

2. Pipes, *Russian Revolution*, 520.

3. Lenin's "Theses Presented at the Conference of Bolshevik Leaders, April 4, 1918," cited by Bunyan and Fisher, *Bolshevik Revolution*, 555.

4. On the Latvian Rifles and their crucial role in defending the Bolshevik regime in 1918, see Pipes, *Russian Revolution*, 544–550, 628–644, and 654–661.

5. "Report of the Commissar of Finance, Gukovsky, to the Central Committee Executive Committee, April 15, 1918," cited by Bunyan and Fisher, *Bolshevik Revolution*, 605–606. Bunyan's translation.

6. Kennan, *Soviet-American Relations, 1917–1920*, 2:223.

7. Pipes, *Russian Revolution*, 602.

8. The Brest-Litovsk Treaty, in the original German, is reproduced in full in Hahlweg, ed., *Der Friede von Brest-Litovsk*, 656–659. For an annotated English translation, see Wheeler-Bennett, *Brest-Litovsk*, 269–275. More recent studies include Winfried Baumgart, *Deutsche Ostpolitik, 1918*.

9. Wheeler-Bennett, *Brest-Litovsk*, 84, 348–349; and Solomon, *Unter den Roten Machthabern*, 29–34.

10. Baumgart, *Deutsche Ostpolitik*, 274–275. The Foreign Office memorandum is cited in Pipes, *Russian Revolution*, 633. Pipes's translation.

11. The German estimates of diplomatic couriers who passed through Joffe's embassy in 1918 were generally lower, ranging between 100 and 200. Wheeler-Bennett, *Brest-Litovsk*, 348. French intelligence, perhaps prone to exaggeration, claimed 300: 19 November 1918 report from Bern, in French police générale files, in AN, F7/13506.

12. There is still some dispute about the sums involved, and the precise channels through which German funds were transmitted to the Bolsheviks in Russia. Pipes, in *Russian Revolution* (411), accepts the estimate of Eduard Bernstein, that the German government spent in all "more than 50 million deutsche marks in gold" on the Bolsheviks. Semion Lyandres, in *The Bolshevik's German Gold Revisited*, argues that German Foreign Office files confirm only 40 million gold marks in appropriations for propaganda in Russia, not all of it going to the Bolsheviks. In any case, there is no doubt that the German Foreign Office appropriated monies expressly for the purpose of aiding the Bolsheviks as early as April 1917 and as late as May 1918. For the former, see the citation in Z. A. B. Zeman's editorial note in his *Germany and the Revolution in Russia*, 24; for the latter, see, e.g., Kühlmann telegram to German Ambassador Mirbach in Moscow, 18 May 1918, in which he expressly instructs, "Please use larger sums, as it is greatly in our interests that Bolsheviks should survive. Riezler's funds at your disposal. If further money required, please telegraph how much." Zeman, 128. As late as June 1918, the German treasury secretary placed 40 million marks at Kühlmann's disposal for supporting the Bolsheviks, though only a small consignment of these funds is likely to have been sent, owing to the assassination of Ambassador Mirbach in early July, which cooled relations considerably. Zeman, 137. The most thorough investigation in Russian is Sergei Mel'gunov's *'Zolotoi nemetskii kliuch' k bol'shevitskoi revolutsii*.

13. Kühlmann report dated 3 December 1917, in Zeman, *Germany and the Revolution in Russia*, 94. This document is also excerpted at length in Pipes, *Russian Revolution*, 411.

14. Riezler telegram from Stockholm to Foreign Office headquarters in Berlin, 26 November 1917, in PAAA, R 2000.

15. Telegram from Lersner at Gr. Hauptquartier to the Foreign Office in Berlin, 25 November 1917, in PAAA, R 10085.

16. Quoted by Wheeler-Bennett, *Brest-Litovsk*, 259.

17. Futrell, *Northern Underground*.

18. Decipher of telegram from Sir E. Howard in Stockholm, 22 December 1917, in PRO, FO 371/3000. As Howard complained, the Swedish government's indulgence of the Bolshevik Mission "would seem to be coming very near recognition."

19. ""Schweden und der Separatfrieden," from *Aftonbladet* 4 December 1917, as clipped and translated by the German Legation in Stockholm, along with reproductions in such newspapers as *Stockholms Dagblad* and *Nya Dagligt Allehanda*, in a report headlined "Zeitungsnachricht. *Schwedische Hoffnungen bei einem deutsch-russischen Separatfrieden*," in PAAA, R 11207.

20. Cited in Volkogonov, *Lenin*, 121.

21. Aschberg, *Wandering Jew*, 38.

22. Both *Nya Banken* (until roughly September) and *Svenska Ekonomie Aktiebolaget* knowingly purchased millions of rubles from Bolshevik agents in 1918, mostly in exchange for Swedish crowns. See Nik, "Stokgol'msky valiutny rynok v 1918 g.," in RGAE, 413-3-18, 10.

23. Aschberg, *Wandering Jew*, 31–35.

24. On the gold deposit, see W. J. Novitsky, "Russian Gold Reserve," unpub. MS prepared for the U.S. State Department, August 1920, in NAA, M 316, roll 119, p. 10.

25. See 9 December 1917 Kühlmann telegram to the German Legation in Stockholm, reproduced in Zeman, *Germany and the Revolution in Russia*, 101.

26. Cited in ibid., 109.

27. Telegram from Reichskommissar für Aus- und Einfuhrbewilligung to the German Foreign Office, 2 April 1918, in German Foreign Office files, at DBB, R 901/86984, 12.

28. "Kassaberattelse frau Svenska Handelsdelegationen i Moskva Juni–Oktober 1918," in RSU, vol. 4467.

29. See Mirbach's telegram to the Foreign Office in Berlin, in DBB, R 901/86984, 45.

30. See German intelligence dispatch from Stockholm, 22 May 1918, in DBB, R 901/86984, 47–49.

31. "Kommissionens för varuutbyte mellan Sverige och Ryssland protokoll fran sammanträdet den 29 april 1918," in RSU, vol. 4466. On the general parameters of the trade negotiations for Swedish imports in spring 1918, see R. Karpova, *Sovetskii diplomat*, 48–49.

32. "Stokgol'msky valiutny rynok v 1918 g.," in RGAE, 413-3-18, 10. For the allegations surrounding Steinberg, see Kerensky's own postmortem, *The Russian Provisional Government, 1917*, 3:1374, 1379; and Mel'gunov, '*Zolotoi nemetskii kliuch*,' 101–104.

33. "Otchet torgovogo otdela pri Stokgol'mskoi missii RSFSR o deiatelnosti za 1919 g.," in RGAE, 413-3-267, 7, 12.

34. These deals, dating from April to June 1918, are discussed at length in a lengthy 1919 transcript titled "Otchet torgovogo otdela pri Stokgol'mskoi missii RSFSR o deiatelnosti za 1919 g.," (henceforth "Stokgol'mskoi missii") in RGAE, 413-3-267, 2–12, 25–28, 45–57.

35. Ibid., RGAE, 413-3-267, 70. In Swedish crowns, the order came to 11,150,000.

36. Ibid., RGAE, 413-3-267, 2–3, 15–17, 70. Strictly military orders were placed only in late November 1918, after the German collapse.

37. See dispatches dated 2 and 8 July 1918, with attached Soviet news clippings, from the German consul in Petrograd to the Foreign Office in Berlin, in DBB, R 901/86984, 86–96.

38. "Stokgol'mskoi missii," in RGAE, 413-3-267, 15–18, 71–74, 89–93, 96.

39. The Swiss sting operation to root out subversion carried out by Berzin's "Soviet Mission" produced an enormous trail of papers, in the BB, E 21 "Polizeiwesen 1848–1930" files.

40. Berzin did grant an interview to *Izvestiia* after his expulsion from Switzerland but confined his remarks to the general goal of his mission, which he claimed, rather blandly, was to establish a kind of news service to link the Bolsheviks with their supporters in the West. This was the standard line, also used by Vorovsky in Stockholm: not entirely untrue, it nevertheless left a great deal unsaid, such as why tens of millions of rubles were needed to fund anodyne reprints of Soviet propaganda in cheap newssheets like *Korrespondenz Prawda* and *Russische Nachrichten*. See the interview as reproduced from *Izvestiia* in Swiss public prosecutor's 5 February 1920 report to the Swiss parliament, BB, E 21/10528, pp. 5–6. See also Pipes, *Russian Revolution*, 621.

41. Swiss public prosecutor's 11 March 1919 report to the Swiss government, in BB, E 21/10452, pp. 20–21.

42. Schreider was a known gambler who often boasted that he had large sums of money hidden away in various bank accounts, ostensibly to foster a reputation for liquidity that could secure new lines of credit. That he was entrusted by the Bolsheviks with carrying such a large sum to Switzerland in June 1918 is thus unlikely, although he did have some 50,000 Swiss francs deposited in his own name in a Bern bank, and another account opened on his behalf (in another name) in Lausanne turned out to have nearly 100,000 rubles in it. See Scheider's written confession while in prison in Bern, 9 August 1920, and various Swiss public prosecutor reports from 1919 and 1920 in BB, E 21/9447.

43. On the currency hand-offs, see the 16 February 1919 Swiss intelligence report from Bern, in BB, E 21/10484.

44. Swiss public prosecutor's 11 March 1919 report to the Swiss government, in BB, E 21/10452, pp. 20–21.

45. See W. Tschudy's deposition to the Cantonal magistrate in Bern, 17 March 1919, in BB, E 21/10484.

46. See Adolf Dätwyler's deposition to Dr. Bickel, the Cantonal magistrate in Zurich, 24 March 1919, in BB, E 21/10484.

47. See the enormous 11 January 1919 report on Bolshevik money-laundering activities from the magistrate of Zurich to Bern, in BB, E 21/10527, pp. 64–65.

48. Report from Swiss intelligence at Neuchâtel, 18 January 1919, to the federal judge at Aarau, in BB, E 21/10484.

49. Lifschitz would return later to become, in 1929, chairman of the Swiss Communist Party. The Lifschitz queries yielded a ream of paperwork, including replies from some four banks in which he had held accounts, including the Berner Handelsbank, Volksbank Bern, Spar- und Leihkasse Bern, and the Kantonalbank Bern,

all in BB, E 21/10489. The Kantonalbank was the only one to report a significant re-maining balance, circa 3 January 1919 (date of last transaction), in BB, E 21/10489. On Lifschitz, see also the Swiss intelligence report from Neuchâtel, 7 March 1919, to the federal judge in Bern, in BB, E 21/10484.

50. See the final 27 February 1920 Swiss government report "betr. Die Bol-schewikuntersuchung," in BB, E 21/10528.

51. See 11 January 1919 report from Zurich magistrate to Bern, in BB, E 21/10527, p. 9.

52. Swiss public prosecutor's 11 March 1919 report to the Swiss government, in BB, E 21/10452, p. 36.

53. See final 27 February 1920 Swiss government report "betr. Die Bolsche-wikuntersuchung," in BB, E 21/10528.

54. See 11 January 1919 report on Bolshevik money-laundering activities from the magistrate of Zurich to Bern, BB, E 21/10527, pp. 17–18, and reply of Schweizerische Volksbank Bern to police inquiry, 20 November 1918, in BB, E 21/10383.

55. The files relating to the Borodin(Gruzenberg)-Fox incident are in BB, E 21/10540. This was the same Borodin who would later direct Comintern operations in China.

56. See British consul's report to Balfour from Bern, 15 November 1918, in PRO, FO 371/3317; and similar French reports from Geneva, dated 18 and 19 November, in AN, F7/13506.

57. Citations in Pipes, *Russian Revolution,* 620–621, 666. Pipes's translations. The "Supplementary Treaty to the Treaty of Peace between Russia and the Central Powers," signed at Berlin, 27 August 1918, is reproduced in Wheeler-Bennett, *Brest-Litovsk,* 427–446.

58. Pipes, *Russian Revolution,* 667; and Wheeler-Bennett, *Brest-Litovsk,* 356.

59. See the 7 April 1919 German Foreign Office postmortem on the Brest-Litovsk Supplementary Treaty, titled "Aufzeichnung betreffend unsere handelspoli-tischen Beziehungen zu Russland," in DBB, R 901/81069, 339–345.

60. Baumgart, *Deutsche Ostpolitik,* 298–299.

61. Pipes, *Russian Revolution,* 664.

62. This is one of Wheeler-Bennett's principal arguments in *Brest-Litovsk.*

63. At 200 gold marks per ton. Both sources agree on the amount of coal and coke delivered to Petrograd (the Russian source is more precise, counting 35,423 tons of coal and 3,453 tons of coke to fire it). The Russians claim to have paid in gold, which presumably excused the tardiness in shipping requested raw materials to Germany. Clearly, the Bolsheviks had little to ship but gold.

The German Foreign Office later claimed nothing at all had been delivered. In re-ply, the Bolsheviks claimed to have shipped ferrous metal scrap (zheleznogo loma) and brass shavings (latunoi struzhki) to Germany aboard the steamer *Hugo Stinnes* in September. See table of shipments to and from the port of Petrograd, in RGAE, 413-3-252, 22 and back. For the German side, see "Aufzeichnung betreffend unsere handelspolitischen Beziehungen zu Russland," in DBB, R 901/81069, 339–345. For more on the coal negotiations between Berlin and the Bolsheviks, see Baumgart, *Deutsche Ostpolitik,* 283–284.

64. According to the Germans, some of the gold the Bolsheviks shipped came from the Romanian treasure sent to Moscow for safekeeping back in 1916. See Baumgart, *Deutsche Ostpolitik*, 298–299 n166.

65. Pipes, *Russian Revolution*, 666.

66. Wheeler-Bennett, *Brest-Litovsk*, 358, 360–361.

67. See the files in folder marked "Ablieferung des von der russischen Regierung geliefertes Goldes an die Westmächte Nov.–Dez. 1918," in DBB, R 901/80919.

68. See A. Rosemeyer "Abschrift" sent from Moscow to Berlin, 10 October 1918, in DBB, R 901/86976, 84–87.

69. See report from Leutnant Rey, head of the German military commission in Petrograd, sent to Petrograd on 19 November 1918, in PAAA, R 11207.

70. See Franz Rauch's 12 April 1919 report to the German Foreign Office in Berlin after his return from Moscow, in DBB, R 901/82082, 22–25.

71. Axel Christiernsson, which today deals in lubricating grease and other petroleum products, may have been only the logistical front for these orders, which were likely spread across a range of Swedish firms. The aero-engines, for example, were to be supplied by the "Ensk Tulip" factory. But the 9.466 million Swedish crowns deposited by the Bolsheviks in November 1918 went into the accounts of Axel Christiernsson. "Otchet torgovogo otdela pri Stokgol'mskoi missii RSFSR o deiatel'nosti za 1919 g.," in RGAE, 413-3-267, 58–59.

72. These orders are detailed in "Otchet torgovogo otdela pri Stokgol'mskoi missii RSFSR o deiatel'nosti za 1919 g.," in RGAE, 413-3-267, 65–68.

73. Dogovor dated 9 November 1918, between "Vneshnei Torgovli Narodnogo Komissariata Torgovli i Promyshlennosti" and "Aktsionernoe Obshchestvo 'Separator' v Stokgol'me," in RGAE, 413-4-18, 1–4.

74. "Svenskt motforslag. Avtal," 28 October 1918, with Russian translation, "Dogovor o tovaroobmen' mezhdu Sovetskoi Respublikoi, v lits Narodnogo Komissariata Torgovli i Promyshlennosti, i Shvedskoi Torgovoi Delegatsii v Petrograde," in RSU, box 4456, 153–158. This deal was also noted by German intelligence, while it was being negotiated in Petrograd, in a 25 October 1918 dispatch to Berlin, in DBB, R 901/81080, 236 and verso.

75. This and other addendums to the 28 October 1928 trade agreement, the final version of which was dated 14 November 1918, can be found in RSU, box 4466b.

76. See British Foreign Office dispatches from Stockholm to London dated 12 and 20 November 1918, in PRO, FO 371/3317. The first dispatch was a "paraphrase of a cable from the American Legation," sent to John Maynard Keynes at the Inter-Ally Council of War Purchases and Finance; the second a telegram from Mr. Clive in Stockholm. The report about Vorovsky hoarding British pounds, U.S. dollars, and French francs came from French military intelligence, dispatched from Stockholm to Paris on 28 December 1918, in AN, F7/13506.

77. "Stokgol'msky valiutny rynok v 1918 g.," in RGAE, 413-3-18, 11. On Gukovsky's platinum, see report from Lucius von Stoedten in Stockholm, 11 October 1918, in PAAA, 11207.

78. Swiss assets in Russia were worth some 500 million Swiss francs, which in Swedish crowns would have been over 600 million. "Memorandum on Switzerland as a Bolshevik Centre," 2 November 1918, in PRO, FO 371/3317.

79. A copy of this decree can be found in DBB, R 901/86984, 203–204. It was announced on 31 December 1918, although in practice the ban was only applied on 11 January 1919. See "Stokgol'msky valiutny rynok v 1918 g.," in RGAE, 413-3-18, 13.

80. From the "paraphrase of a cable from the American Legation" in Stockholm, sent to John Maynard Keynes at Whitehall, 12 November 1918, in PRO, FO 371/3317. See also "Stokgol'msky valiutny rynok v 1918 g.," in RGAE, 413-3-18, 9.

81. Berlin Reichsbank report sent to the German Foreign Office, 20 May 1919, in DBB, R 901/82082, 178–180; German Foreign Office memorandum on the consequences of the 27 August Finanzabkommen, in DBB, R 901/86986, 136; and Baumgart, *Deutsche Ostpolitik,* 299n167.

82. See dispatch from the German Legation at Stockholm to Berlin, 8 April 1919, with attachments, in DBB, R 901/86986, 256–264. On the booming business in Russian rubles, see Adolf Dätwyler's deposition in Zurich, 24 March 1919, in BB, E 21/10484: Dätwyler bought rubles because it was so easy to unload them on German and Austrian banks at a quick profit.

83. The German government took the ruble problem quite seriously: see "Massnahmen gegen die 'Währungspolitik der Sowjetregierung,'" 5 March 1919, in DBB, R 901/86986, 218–219.

Chapter 6. Blockade

Epigraph: Letter from French Legation in Stockholm to Swedish Foreign Ministry, 5 April 1919, in RSU, vol. 4477.

1. Cited by Pipes, *Russian Revolution,* 657.

2. The most thorough account of the Allied intervention in Russia is Richard Ullman's three-volume history, *Anglo-Soviet Relations, 1917–1921.* For the American side, the best account remains George Kennan's two-volume account, *Soviet-American Relations, 1917–1920.* For the French perspective, see the memoirs of Joseph Noulens, *Mon ambassade en Russie soviétique, 1917–1919,* 2 vols.

3. Saul, *War and Revolution,* 351. On the Japanese intervention, see Morley, *Japanese Thrust into Siberia.*

4. Quoted by Ullman, vol. 2, *Britain and the Russian Civil War,* 125–126.

5. Citations in Arno Mayer, *Politics and Diplomacy of Peacemaking,* 309, 314.

6. Contracts for these deals, which fell under the category of *snabzheniia krasnoi armii,* can be found at RGAE, in 413-3-245, 19, 28, 56–57.

7. "Spetsifikatsiia predmetov, vkliuchenniykh v plan vvoza iz za granitisy," 24 March 1919, and accompanying contracts, in RGAE, 413-3-245, 23–25, 110, 115 and verso.

8. German secret agent report from Petrograd, 1 January 1919, labeled "Betrifft: Warenaustausch mit Russland," in DBB, R 901/81080, 316–317.

9. RGAE, 413-3-242, 9.

10. See 1 January 1919 report "Betrifft: Warenaustausch mit Russland," in DBB, R 901/81080, 318–319.

11. See 7 February 1919 request from Narkomvneshtorg, "Glavnomu upravleniiu predpriiatiia mekhovoi promyshlennosti 'Glavmekh,'" and accompanying reply, in RGAE, 413-3-245, 23–24.

12. Soviet Trade Commission letter "Schvedskomu Poverennomu Advokatu Khellbergu," 27 May 1919, in RGAE, 413-3-243, 96.

13. See 27 May 1919 *Doverennost'* for Hellberg, signed by Krasin for the People's Commissariat of Trade and Industry (Narkomtorgprom) and Neiman for the Foreign Trade Commissariat (Narkomvneshtorg), in RSU, vol. 4467.

14. Wilhelm Hellberg letter to Kungl, Utrikesdepartement, 27 August 1919, in RSU, vol. 4467. See also the earlier 24 May 1919 letter from Narkomtorgprom to Glavnoe Artilleriiskoe Upravlenie, which promises that Hellberg will attempt to place orders for gun barrels (oruzheinye stvoly) after he returns to Stockholm, in RGAE, 413-3-243, 86.

15. Red Army procurement budget report, in RGAE, 413-3-253, 17 and verso; and dispatches sent to the Soviet Foreign Trade Commission by the captain of the Port of Petrograd, in RGAE, 413-3-252, 19, 33–34.

16. For an account of Estonia's path to independence, see Arthur Ruhl, *New Masters of the Baltic,* 60–122.

17. See Pasvolsky and Moulton, *Russian Debts and Russian Reconstruction,* 28–41.

18. "Der Außenhandel Sowjetrußlands," *Beilage des 'Revaler Boten,'* 7 December 1921. On the dramatic arrival of the Eskilstuna, see Solomon, *Unter den Roten Machthabern,* 131–132.

19. See, e.g., Soviet Foreign Minister Georgi Chicherin's 4 February 1919 telegram to Vorovsky in Stockholm, in RSU, vol. 4477.

20. Copies of the Danish, Norwegian, and Swedish bans on ruble transactions can be found in DBB, R 901/86984.

21. Letter from French Legation in Stockholm to Swedish Foreign Ministry, 5 April 1919, in RSU, vol. 4477.

22. Reynolds, "Ottoman-Russian Struggle for Eastern Anatolia and the Caucasus," 600–601.

23. See funding request for 63,425,000 rubles sent by the directors of Narkomtorgprom and Narkomvneshtorg to the Soviet Commissariat of Finance, 3 July 1919, and accompanying transit requests for the merchants (Ali Aga Darrudi, Mirsa Abbas Ali Agaev, the brothers Abduliga, Iskander and Abbedin Mamedovym, Mamed Mekhdi Kasman, the brothers Ibrahim, Gadzhi Iusuff, David, Rakhim, and Murad Aminovym) who contracted to supply the Bolshevik with Persian goods, in RGAE, 413-3-243, 161–162, 179, 238.

24. RGAE, 413-3-245, 57, 106, 111–114, 116, 126, 135; and RGAE, 413-3-252, 12–18.

25. See the complaint lodged by the Foreign Trade Commission on 19 June 1919 against the Cheka, which had arrested Levshin, in RGAE, 413-3-243, 130 and verso.

26. See, e.g., the list labeled "V Chrezvychainuiu komissiiu po borbe so spekulatsiei. Vedomost' Udostovreniiam,' vydannym otd'lom' vneshnei torgovli komissariata torgovli i promyshlennosti, na vyvoz' tovarov' za granitsu za 30 ianvaria 1918 g.," in RGAE, 413-3-8, 34 and back.

27. Solomon, *Unter den Roten Machthabern,* 112–113.

28. See, e.g., the 30 December 1919 contract given Movshe Izrailevich Kulangiev

for purchasing medicines and medical products across the demarcation lines in White Russia, in RGAE, 413-3-241, 2. Solomon (112) claims to have given his purchasing agents 15 percent, but this is contradicted by the data now available in the Soviet archives. For a typical low priority civilian goods contract, with a 3 percent commission, see the 8 December 1919 contract signed with Solomon Moiseevich Rubinstein, in RGAE, 413-3-240, 7.

29. Authorization form from Narkomvneshtorg to "Agronomu Leontiiu Terent'evich Luk'iankovu," in RGAE, 413-3-243, 65.

30. Letter from Narkomtorgprom to the People's Commissariat of Foreign Affairs, 20 May 1919, in RGAE, 413-3-243, 72.

31. Laserson, *Im Sowjet-Labyrinth,* 126–152. The engineer's initials, Laserson informs us, were R. L., although to protect the identity of this Bolshevik buyer, he does not give the name.

32. Narkomvneshtorg import plan for March 1919, RGAE, 413-3-245, 109.

33. "Svidetel'stvo" signed by director of Narkomtorgproma, 8 June 1919, in RGAE, 413-3-243, 175.

34. Bela Kun did receive a shipment of smuggled gold in Budapest in spring 1919, but it was the relatively insubstantial amount of 8 million Czech crowns, or $6,000 dollars worth, barely enough to register on the radar of Allied inspectors. Confidential 9 March 1921 report of the U.S. consul in Prague, in U.S. State Department Reports on Russia, NAA, M 316, roll 120. For an overview of the amounts of Bolshevik gold movements being detected in different countries in 1919, see the confidential memorandum of Paul Jameson prepared for the U.S. State Department on 31 January 1921, NAA, M 316, roll 119. Almost certainly, Kun, like most Moscow agents in 1919, also carried Russian diamonds or jewelry in his luggage to help finance the Hungarian Communist Party, but it is impossible to estimate how much. Swiss intelligence also picked up a rumor that Kun received tsarist rubles via Fritz Platten, the radical Swiss socialist who had accompanied Lenin on the train ride across Germany in 1917, but aside from getting Platten to admit ties to Kun was unable to confirm the rumor or the amount. See reports dated 20 and 24 March 1919, in BB, E 21/11418.

35. Agnew and McDermott, *Comintern,* 21.

36. Jacobs, *Borodin,* 60–61.

37. On James Reich and the short-lived "Western European Bureau" in distributing Comintern cash, see also Andrew and Gordievsky, *KGB,* 85; Lazitch, "Two Instruments of Control by the Comintern," 45–65. On Karl Moor specifically, see Barthel, *Kein Bedarf an Weltgeschichte.*

38. Letter from Swedish consul general in Moscow, sent to the German Foreign Office on 13 November 1918, in DBB, R 901/81081, 284

39. Rauch's written prospectus, attached to Swedish consul general's letter of 13 November 1918, in DBB, R 901/81081, 286–287.

40. Rauch telegram from Moscow to Berlin describing the route by which he arrived, 5 March 1919, with attachment of itinerary, in DBB, R 90/81081, 199–201.

41. Report dated 5 August 1919 and addressed "Herrn Ministerialdirektor Freiherrn von Stockhammern Wirkl Geheimer Legationsrat, Berlin," in DBB, R 901/81083, 115.

42. The relevant title given Krasin was actually commissar of ways of communication (Narodny kommissar putei soobshcheniia, or NKPS), but the position was generally understood and intended to be something akin to special commissar of the railways, which were, of course, Russia's principal means of communication and transport in 1919. The position retained a similar emphasis in responsibility primarily for the railways well into the Stalinist era. See O'Connor, *Engineer of Revolution*, 159.

43. Rauch report datelined Berlin, 12 April 1919, in DBB, R 901/81082, 22–25.

44. Ibid.

45. German army dispatch from Kovno to Berlin Foreign Office, 27 April 1919, in DBB, R 901/81082, 75–77.

46. German Foreign Office reply to Kovno, 28 April 1919, in DBB, R 901/81082, 78.

47. The final verdict on Rauch's lawsuit is reproduced in DBB, R 901/81083, 276.

48. Baehr letters to German Foreign Office, 21 January and 23 February 1919, in DBB, R 901/81081, 205 and 320.

49. German Foreign Office letter to Baehr, 31 July 1919, in DBB, R 901/81083, 96.

50. German Foreign Office report on Steinberg's scythe negotiations, dated 4 April 1919, in DBB, R 901/81082, 13 and verso, 14 and verso.

51. Niederschrift über die Besprechung im Auswärtigen Amt am 11. April 1919, betreffend private Versuche der Wiederaufnahme unserer Handelsbeziehungen zu Russland," in DBB, R 901/81081, 332 and verso, 333 and verso.

52. This deal is outlined in a letter from the German Foreign Office to Krasin, in R 901/81083, 235.

53. See report of the Staatssekretär des Reichswirtchaftsamts, "Betrifft: Ausfuhr von Arzneimitterln nach Großrußland," 22 October 1918, a reply to a Russian query about the delay in delivery dated 3 September 1918, in DBB, R 901/81080, 62.

54. *Udostoverenie* signed by Krasin for Narkomtorgprom and Neiman for Narkomvneshtorg, 16 May 1919, in RGAE, 413-3-243, 52–53.

55. See the questionnaire Brendel filled out in his application for a visa from the German Foreign Office, DBB, R 901/81083, 88–89.

56. DBB, R 901/81083, 264

57. DBB, R 901/81083, 155, 227.

58. German Foreign Office report, 14 August 1919, in DBB, R 901/81083, 163–164.

59. German intelligence report sent to Foreign Office headquarters in Berlin, 4 June 1919, in DBB, R 901/81082, 251–254.

60. Lomonosov's Wall Street contact was Thomas L. Chadbourne, director of the U.S. Russian Bureau Inc., an offshoot of the War Trade Board. The Chadbourne-Lomonosov correspondence of winter 1919 is discussed at length in Antony C. Sutton, *Wall Street and the Bolshevik Revolution*, chap. 9. In his rather overheated account, Sutton makes a great deal out of a figure of $25,000 deposited in Stockholm in Lomonosov's name but never explains how exactly that implicated anyone on

Wall Street in Lomonosov's deals. In fact Sutton seems unaware that Lomonosov did later arrange an enormous railway deal, not with Wall Street but with Swedish and German firms.

61. German Foreign Office report, 14 August 1919, in DBB, R 901/81083, 164. Twelve telegrams were sent back and forth between Lomonosov and Krasin that summer.

62. Laserson, *Expert in the Service of the Soviet,* 40–41.

63. Although initial rumors varied as to the size of the sum, by summer all Entente sources were agreed that the sum was 100 million rubles, at least according to the Finnish authorities who reported the arrest. See letter from Swiss intelligence to the public prosecutor, 11 April 1919, based on American and British intelligence reports, in BB, E 21/11427. The French reports on Platten's arrest, which occupied a great deal of attention in May and June 1919, are filed in the folder labeled "Introduction en France de billets de banque altérés et d'origine douteuse," in AN, F7/14769.

64. In the 2 May 1919 *Tageszeitung,* reproduced in BB, E 21/11423.

65. See numerous reports on rumors of Bolshevik counterfeiting of British pounds, French francs, and German marks, dating from April to September 1919, in folder labeled "Introduction en France de billets de banque altérés et d'origine douteuse," in AN, F7/14769; list of "suspected German and Bolshevik agents in Stockholm" sent to Paris by French intelligence on 31 July 1919, in AN, F7/13506; and French intelligence reports from Stockholm, 30 July 1919; Copenhagen, 2 August 1919; and Helsingfors, 28 and 30 September 1919, in AN, F7/13507.

66. Swiss intelligence report from Copenhagen, 15 July 1920, in BB, E 21/11429.

67. For rumors regarding Gukovsky and Sheinman (the latter was believed to have "125 million rubles in his apartment"), see French intelligence dispatches from Stockholm, 17 and 18 December 1918, in AN, F7/13506.

68. The telegrams and supporting material relating to the ill-fated Zaudig deal can be found in RGAE, 413-3-268, 1–12. Lukhianov's original commission, dated 20 May 1919, is in RGAE, 413-243, 65.

69. Citations in Ullman, vol. 2, *Britain and the Russian Civil War,* 306–307; and Pipes, *Concise History of the Russian Revolution,* 270. For the course of military events, I have mainly relied on Pipes, *Concise History,* 267–270.

70. Quoted by Saul, *War and Revolution,* 372.

71. On the effect of Lloyd George's announcement on Estonian morale, see Ruhl, *New Masters of the Baltic,* 118–119.

72. Karpova, *Sovetskii diplomat,* 51–53; Ullman, vol. 2, *Britain and the Russian Civil War,* 257–258, 282–287.

73. Solomon, *Unter den Roten Machthabern,* 135–136.

74. O'Connor, *Engineer of Revolution,* 231–232.

75. Quoted by Ullman, vol. 2, *Britain and the Russian Civil War,* 293.

76. See report from Lucius von Stoedten, the German minister in Stockholm, 16 October 1919, in PAAA, R 11207.

77. See above, chapter 3. A copy of the Gokhran's founding document can be found in RGAE, 7632-1-1, 1. On the connection between the Tartu Treaty and the

foundation of the Gokhran, see also Bayer, "Revolutionaere Beute," in *Verkaufte Kultur,* 27–28.

78. Krasin telegram to the Petrograd headquarters of NKVT, 16 February 1920, in RGAE, 413-3-242, 46 and verso.

CHAPTER 7. STOCKHOLM

Epigraph: Aschberg, *Wandering Jew,* 107.

1. Budnitsky, "Kolchakovskoe Zoloto," in *Diaspora* 4 (2002): 458.

2. Pipes, *Concise History,* 265.

3. Colonel Ryan's observations, as reported by Robert E. Olds, American Red Cross commissioner to Europe, in a 15 April 1920 letter to Dr. Livingston Farrand, Red Cross chairman in Washington, in RSU, HP 494, p. 2.

4. Ibid., 4; Figes, *People's Tragedy,* 605.

5. Citation in Pipes, *Russia under the Bolshevik Regime,* 394.

6. Quoted by Lubov Krassin, in *Leonid Krassin,* 105.

7. *Nya Dagligt Allehand,* 8 juin 1920, in the French Foreign Ministry files at the Quai d'Orsay, section URSS (henceforth QOURSS), 481, 68–69.

8. Solomon, *Unter den Roten Machthabern,* 131.

9. This agreement is reproduced in Aschberg, *Wandering Jew,* 46–47.

10. Krasin, *Voprosy vneshnei torgovli,* 245; Karpova, *Sovetskii diplomat,* 57.

11. *Echo de Paris,* 19 June 1920, in QOURSS 481, 121. See also Krasin, *Voprosy vneshnei torgovli,* 245–249; and *O vneshnei torgovle i otnoshenii k nei russkoi kooperatsii,* 20–21. On the Copenhagen negotiations, see O'Connor, *Engineer of Revolution,* 235–336.

12. Quoted by Ullman, in vol. 3, *Anglo-Soviet Accord,* 37.

13. Citations in ibid., 43–44.

14. Citations in ibid., 40–41.

15. On the Nydquist and Holm gold deposit, see letter from Gunnar W. Anderson to "Centrosojus" headquarters in Stockholm, 25 October 1920, in RGAE, 413-3-523, 39–40; and Krasin, *Voprosy vneshnei torgovli,* 246; Karpova, *Sovetskii diplomat,* 57–58. On the arrival of Tsentrosoiuz in London, see Ullman, vol. 3, *Anglo-Soviet Accord,* 91–92.

16. Citations in Ullman, vol. 3, *Anglo-Soviet Accord,* 51, 54.

17. "Note sur l'Or Bolchévique," submitted by M. Delavaud, French ambassador in Stockholm, to the Quai d'Orsay on 2 June 1920, in QOURSS 481, 48–49.

18. Note from Delavaud to Baron de Palmstierna, the Swedish foreign minister, 2 June 1920, in QOURSS 481, 14.

19. *Times of London,* 16 June 1920, clipped and translated into French, in QOURSS 481, 112.

20. French translation of Branting interview with *Svenska Dagbladet,* 2 June 1920, in QUORSS 481, 15.

21. Text of telegram to Krasin, approved in the 11 May 1920 Politburo minutes, in RGASPI, 17-3-77.

22. Text of telegram to Krasin, approved in the 10 June 1920 Politburo minutes, in RGASPI, 17-3-87.

23. Solomon, *Unter den Roten Machthabern,* 18–21, 149–157.

24. See, e.g., Delavaud's dispatches from Stockholm dated 10, 12, and 15 June 1920, QOURSS 481, 71, 103–104 (and verso), 107.

25. Solomon, *Unter den Roten Machthabern,* 151, 158.

26. Aschberg, *Wandering Jew,* 48.

27. "Lokomotiven aus dem Ausland," in the 8 September 1921, *Revaler Bote.*

28. *Rosta-Wien,* édition française, 18 February 1922, clipped in AN, F7/13507.

29. Copy of contract between "Messrs All Russian Co-operative Society" and "Ralph L. Fuller & Co., LTD.," signed in London, 20 July 1920, in RGAE, 413-6-27, 5–6. The first installment was to cost roughly 30,000 British pounds, to be paid in gold.

30. Dispatch from Charles Albrecht, American representative in Reval to the State Department in Washington, 1 February 1921, in NAA, M 316, roll 119. Solomon (163–164) confirms that he dealt directly with G. Scheel and Co.

31. The Roche contracts are in RGAE, 413-6-8, 33–47.

32. Figes, *People's Tragedy,* 729.

33. From the ARCOS contracts with Hjalmar Hartmann and Co. and Theodore Jensen and Co., both of Copenhagen, Denmark, 17 November 1920, 7 December 1920, etc., in RGAE, 413-6-8, 18–32.

34. From the 17 November 1920 ARCOS-Jensen contract, in RGAE, 413-6-8, 30–31.

35. Krasin, *Voprosy vneshnei torgovli,* 248.

36. Ibid.; "Protokol no. 1 Zasedaniia pri Chusosnabarme ot 27-go Oktiabria 1920 g.," in RGAE, 413-6-2, 25; "Svedeniia o vypolnenii plana SPOTEKZAKA po 1 Noiabria 1920 goda," in RGAE, 413-6-3, 1 and verso, 2 and verso; and "Spravka o sostoianii zakazov s 1 po 6 noiabria 1920 goda," in RGAE, 413-6-3, 15 and verso.

37. Dispatch from M. Soussay of the French Embassy in Stockholm, 7 August 1920, in QOURSS 482, 14.

38. H. Kershaw, of the Commercial Secretariat of the British Legation in Stockholm, "Memorandum. British Trading with the Baltic Provinces via Sweden," 2 November 1920, in PRO, FO 371/5421, pp. 6–7. On the Eastern Trading Company, see also "L'armeé rouge approvisionnée par la contrebande," *Echo de Paris,* 20 November 1920.

39. "Svedeniia o vypolnenii plana SPOTEKZAKA po 1 Noiabria 1920 goda," in RGAE, 413-6-3, 1 and verso, 2 and verso, 7 and verso, 8 and verso; and "Protokol no. 1 Zasedaniia pri Chusosnabarme ot 27-go Oktiabria 1920 g.," in RGAE, 413-6-2, 25. On the British Communist Party subsidy, see Agnew and McDermott, *Comintern,* 22.

40. Request form for disbursement, signed by directors of Narkomtorgprom and Narkomvneshtorg, addressed "v Sukharevskoe Otdelenie Narodnogo Banka RSRSR," 5 May 1919, in RGAE, 413-3-243, 64.

41. "Svedeniia o vypolnenii plana SPOTEKZAKA po 1 Noiabria 1920 goda," in RGAE, 413-6-3, 15 and verso, 16 and verso; and O'Connor, *Engineer of Revolution,* 250.

42. The telegrams relating to this German arms offer are in RGAE, 413-6-10, 29–35.

43. Chicherin/Sheinman telegram to Litvinov in Copenhagen, 7 June 1920, in RGAE, 413-6-10, 36.

44. Telegram from Kopp to Lezhav, and Lezhav's reply, 7 and 10 September 1920, in RGAE, 413-6-10, 43–44.

45. Telegram from Kopp to Lezhav, and Lezhav's reply, 30 October and 18 November 1920, in RGAE, 413-3-10, 47, 53. See also "Spravka o sostanii zakazov s 1 po 6 noiabria 1920 goda," in RGAE, 413-6-3, 15 and verso.

46. German Foreign Office "Aufzeichnung" marked urgent, 29 October 1920, in PAAA, R 83649. The report notes, to justify permitting the suspicious wire transfer from Reval, that Kopp then found himself in "embarrassing financial straits" (Herr Kopp sich in großer Geldverlegenheit befindet).

47. Telegram from Minsk, forwarded by Trotsky to Lenin, Krestinsky, Lezhav et al., 18 August 1920, with Trotsky recommending approval, in RGAE, 413-3-10, 40–41.

48. Krasin telegram to Chicherin, 17 November 1920, forwarded to Lenin and Trotsky, and their replies, in RGAE, 413-3-10, 52–53, 57–59.

49. On the Treaty of Riga, see Ullman, vol. 3, *Anglo-Soviet Accord*, 310–311.

50. "Svodnaia Vedomost' raskhoda artilleriiskago imushchestva na grazhdanskuiu voinu/s 1/II–18–IV 20 g.," in RGAE, 413-6-5, 82; and "Vedomost' Predmetam Artilleriiskogo Imushchestva Podlezhaschikh Zakazu," 7 October 1920, in RGAE, 413-6-10, 155 and verso, 156 and verso.

51. "Izvlechenie iz Obshei Svodnoi Vedomosti otdela Metalla V.S.N.Kh. Predmety vypisyvaemye dlia voennoi nadobnosti," 2 June 1920, in RGAE, 413-6-2, 27; "Svedeniia o vypolnenii plana SPOTEKZAKA po 1 Noiabria 1920 goda," in RGAE, 413-6-3, 3 and verso; and "Vedemost' gruzov, pribyvshikh iz zagranitsei," 12 January 1921, in RGAE, 413-6-3, 28. There is no mention in either of the two later inventories of the wolfram having arrived in Soviet Russia, as of November 1920 or January 1921.

52. "Report of Commander, U.S. Naval Forces Operating in European Waters, Passage Reval to Danzig, 29 August, 1920," in NAA, M 316, roll 120.

53. "L'armeé rouge approvisionnée par la contrebande," in *Echo de Paris,* 20 November 1920.

54. "Vedemost' gruzov, pribyvshikh iz zagranitsei," 12 January 1921, in RGAE, 413-6-3, 28. For the orders, see "Spravka o sostanii zakazov s 1 po 6 noiabria 1920 goda," in RGAE, 413-6-3, 15 and verso; and "Svedeniia o vypolnenii plana SPOTEKZAKA po 1 Noiabria 1920 goda," in RGAE, 413-6-3, 1 and verso, 2 and verso.

A large rubber tire deal, printed on the letterhead of Goodrich's Stockholm office, is in RGAE, 413-6-6, 9–11. Documents relating to the Michelin deal, worked out in Christiania, Norway, are in RGAE, 413-6-7. An 11 December 1920 Dunlop deal is in RGAE, 413-6-11, 30. Fiat spare parts were ordered by Krasin himself in London in November 1920: "Spravka no. 3 o sostaianii zakazov s 9 po 20 Noiabria 1920 goda," in RGAE, 413-6-3, 16 and verso.

55. "Svedeniia o vypolnenii plana SPOTEKZAKA po 1 Noiabria 1920 goda," RGAE, 413-6-3, 2 (verso), 3; 8 and verso, 9 and verso. On these orders, more below.

56. Contract dated Tiflis 3 November 1920, between Siono, Gella and Co., and

Sheinman, in RGAE, 413-6-14, 16; and "Spravka no. 3 o sostaianii zakazov s 9 po 20 Noiabria 1920 goda," in RGAE, 413-6-3, 16 (verso). That Sheinman was "officially loaded" with Kremlin funds is confirmed by Frank Golder, who met with him in Tiflis in 1921 to discuss the possibility of financing imports from the United States. See Golder's diary entry for 1 April 1922 in Emmons and Patenaude, *Frank Golder*, 153.

57. "Vedomost' gruzov, pribyvshikh iz zagranitsy," 12 January 1921, in RGAE, 413-6-3, 28.

58. "Export of Russian Gold (Bullion & Coin) through the Reval Customs House for the period from Nov. 1, 1920 to March 26, 1921," in NAA, M 316, roll 120.

59. By October, Red Army foreign arms purchases in 1920 amounted to 286 million gold rubles, or $143 million, according to the "Vedemost' predmetam artilleriiskogo imushchestva podlezhashchikh zakazu zagranitsei," 7 October 1920, in RGAE, 413-6-10, 158. See also "Note. Releve Recapitulatif des Exportations d'or russe," 31 decembre 1920, in QOURSS 482, 139–140.

60. Delavaud dispatch from Stockholm, 14 October 1920, QOURSS 482, 63.

61. "L'armeé rouge approvisionnée par la contrebande," *Echo de Paris,* 20 November 1920.

62. Werth, "Dirty War," in *Black Book of Communism,* 106.

63. Ullman, vol. 3, *Anglo-Soviet Accord,* 310–313.

64. The most thorough study of these conflicts in English is Figes, *Peasant Russia, Civil War.* For a more recent study, see Stanziani, "De la guerre contre les blancs a la guerre contre les paysans, 1920–1922," in *L'Economie en Révolution,* 281–304.

65. Werth, "Dirty War," in *Black Book of Communism,* 90–97, 102.

66. Pipes, *Concise History,* 344.

67. Citations in Werth, "Dirty War," in *Black Book of Communism,* 101; and Figes, in *Peasant Russia, Civil War,* 321. The casualty figures are in Pipes, *Russia under the Bolshevik Regime,* 373.

68. Quotes and citations in Figes, *Peasant Russia, Civil War,* 260–262; and *People's Tragedy,* 727, 752, 754.

69. This contract is preserved in RGAE, 413-6-10, 63.

70. "Vedomost' no. 1 gruzov pribyvshikh iz zagranitsy na 7 fevralia 1921 g.," in RGAE, 413-6-3, 29; and "Vedemost' no. 4 gruzov, idushchikh iz zagranitsy v Revel' na 7-e Fevralia 1921 g.," in RGAE, 413-6-3, 33.

71. "Protokol no. 1. Soveshchaniia pri Spotekzake po voprosu o sokrashchenii ekstrennoi ocheredi Plana Zagranichnogo Snabzheniia GAU na 25 percent," 27 January 1921, in RGAE, 413-6-2, 106.

72. "Vedomost' no. 5 gruzov pribyvshikh iz zagranitsy na 7 fevralia 1921 g.," in RGAE, 413-6-3, 34.

73. See letter from Chr. Henriksen, sent via Kobenhavns Handelsbank to the Soviet Trade Delegation in Stockholm, 25 June 1921, in RGAE, 413-6-10, 206–207.

74. Ferguson, *Cash Nexus.*

75. Swedish intelligence agent's report from Reval, "Strängt förtrolig," 10 May 1921, in RSU, HP 495.

76. Minutes of 14 February 1921 Politburo meeting, item 20, "predlozhenie tov.

Krasina o sposobe realizatsii brilliantov," in RGASPI, 17-3-132; and 16 February 1921, item 5, "o prodazhe tsennostei zagranitsii," RGASPI, 17-3-133.

77. Kershaw's "Memorandum. British Trading with the Baltic Provinces via Sweden," 2 November 1920, in PRO, FO/371, box 5421, p. 5.

78. Karpova, *Sovetskii diplomat*, 62. Nydquist and Holm, however, did value Krasin's gold deposit at 3,000 crowns per kilo.

79. Kershaw "Memorandum. British Trading with the Baltic Provinces via Sweden," 2 November 1920, in PRO, FO/371, box 5421, pp. 2–4.

80. On the half-hearted U.S. military intervention in Russia, see Saul, *War and Revolution*, 366–375.

81. "Certificate of Ownership" form, circa November 1920, in NAA, M 316, roll 119.

82. Treasury superintendant to Mr. James Heckscher, vice president, Irving National Bank of NY, 17 November 1920, in NAA, M 316, roll 119.

83. S. P. Gilbert, assistant secretary of the treasury, to the director of the Mint, Washington, DC, 26 November 1920, in NAA, M 316, roll 119.

84. Compare, e.g., the "Export of Russian Gold (Bullion & Coin) through the Reval Customs House for the period from Nov. 1, 1920 to March 26, 1921," in NAA, M 316, roll 120, with the "Schedule of Gold Invoices Shipped to the U.S." between April 1920 and April 1921, submitted from the U.S. consulate in Paris to Washington on 21 April 1921, in NAA, M 316, roll 120. The former has dates of debarkation, names of ships, destinations, and volumes of gold aboard, but not the names of the gold shippers and consignees. The latter has names of both shippers and consignees, and dates of arrival, but no information on the gold's origin. There is undoubtedly a huge overlap between the gold shipments out of Reval and into New York, but the connection between the two ends has been lost, almost certainly in Stockholm.

85. Westcott, "Origin and Disposition of the Former Russian Imperial Gold Reserve," in NAA, M 316, roll 120, p. 30.

86. See, e.g., French intelligence reports on sales of "precious stones," "pearls, diamonds etc." in Stockholm, 14 and 16 November 1920, QOURSS 482, 110, 115 (and verso).

87. Newsclipping from the 23 April 1921 *Dagens Nyheter,* labeled "GOLD FOR 100 MILLION ROUBLES HAS BEEN MELTED THE SWEDISH ROYAL MINT STATES THAT THE REMELTING OF RUSSIAN GOLD IS NOTHING NEW," and attached to Consul Charles Albricht's dispatch to Washington from Reval, and in NAA, M 316, roll 120.

88. Kerzhentsev letter to His Excellency, Count Herman Wrangel, Minister for Foreign Affairs, Stockholm, 16 March 1921, in RSU, HP 495; and Wrangel letter to "P. M. Kergentzeff," 31 March 1921, which references his earlier letter of 17 March 1921, in RSU, HP 495. (The 17 March letter, apparently handed over personally by Wrangel, was not copied for the Swedish Foreign Office.) The 31 March 1921 letter was dispatched after Wrangel received a telegram from Soviet Foreign Minister Chicherin complaining that no public denial had yet been offered by the Swedish government. Kerzhentsev had been appointed by the Politburo on 11 October 1920. RGASPI, 17-3-114.

89. Werth, "From Tambov to the Great Famine," in *Black Book of Communism,* 113–114; Pipes, *Russia under the Bolshevik Regime,* 382–386.

90. Figes, *People's Tragedy,* 768; Werth, "Tambov to the Great Famine," in *Black Book of Communism,* 116–117; Pipes, *Russia under the Bolshevik Regime,* 388.

91. Report of Captain Kelley, assistant military observer at the U.S. Commission in Reval, 20 March 1922, in NAA, M 316, roll 121.

92. Politburo minutes of 11 November 1921, in RGASPI, 17-3-229, item 3-z.

93. Westcott, "Origin and Disposition of the Former Russian Imperial Gold Reserve," 21 April 1921, in NAA, M 316, roll 120, p. 30.

94. On the personal rivalry between Krasin and Litvinov, see Liberman, *Building Lenin's Russia,* 110–112.

95. "Doklad Maxim Litvinov o proizvedenniykh im za granitsei torgovykh operatsiakh," 30 October 1920, in RGAE, 413-6-15, 6–8.

96. Aschberg's idea was to ship a small amount of gold bullion ($250,000, or about 400 kg) straight to Washington, DC, as a test. See "Doklad Maxim Litvinov o proizvedenniykh im za granitsei torgovykh operatsiakh," 30 October 1920, RGAE, 413-6-15, 9–10. On Aschberg's willingness to charge lower premiums, see transcript of the Aschberg interrogation at the Préfecture de Police, p. 4. Solomon (193–194) confirms that Aschberg bought gold at near parity with world market prices.

97. Solomon, *Unter den Roten Machthabern,* 169–170, 177–179, 186. It was likely for complaining about such corruption that Solomon was later denounced by Gukovsky as a "counterrevolutionary."

98. Krasin interview with *Krasnaia Gazeta,* as reproduced in "Krassin über die 'Goldblokade' und die bevorstehende Anleihe in Frankreich," 21 September 1921, *Revaler Bote.* See also Karpova, *Sovetskii diplomat,* 246.

99. Quoted by O'Connor from a 22 July 1920 letter from Krasin to Narkomvneshtorg, *Engineer of Revolution,* 251. O'Connor's translation.

Chapter 8. London

Epigraph: Quoted by Ullman, vol. 3, *Anglo-Soviet Accord,* 97.

1. Ibid., 9, 99. See also O'Connor, *Engineer of Revolution,* 230.

2. This is Ullman's phrase, in vol. 3, *Anglo-Soviet Accord,* 96.

3. Williams, *Other Bolsheviks,* 113; Volkogonov, *Lenin,* 55.

4. See dispatches from the French ambassadors to Tokyo and Washington, on 3 and 26 June 1920, respectively, in QOURSS 20, 155.

5. Undated "Note," circa December 1929, in folder labeled "Banque russo-asiatique Notes et rapports 1928–1932," in AN, BB 18/6727, 5–6.

6. Ullman, vol. 3, *Anglo-Soviet Accord,* 113.

7. Ibid., 112.

8. Quai d'Orsay "Note," 16 June 1920, sent to (among others) the French Embassy in Stockholm, in QOURSS 481, 107.

9. Ullman, vol. 3, *Anglo-Soviet Accord,* 106–107.

10. Litvinov's 26 June telegram to Krasin, intercepted by British intelligence, cited in Ullman, vol. 3, *Anglo-Soviet Accord,* 123. Ullman's translation; emphasis added.

11. Krasin's June 1920 memorandum is cited in O'Connor, *Engineer of Revolution*, 248–249 (O'Connor's translation), and in Karpova, *Sovetskii diplomat*, 81.

12. Quoted by Karpova, *Sovetskii diplomat*, 69. On the Standard Oil negotiations, see also telegram from Krasin to Lenin, Rykov, Litvinov et al., 29 May 1920, in RGAE, 413-6-17, 24.

13. O'Connor, *Engineer of Revolution*, 248–249; see also Karpova, *Sovetskii diplomat*, 81.

14. See Krasin's letter to Monsieur le Vicomte du Halgouet from London, in QOURSS 421, 81–84 (French translation of the original English, 85–90).

15. Ullman, vol. 3, *Anglo-Soviet Accord*, 109–110.

16. On the formation of ARCOS, see O'Connor, *Engineer of Revolution*, 245, and Karpova, *Sovetskii diplomat*, 82–87.

17. Contract between ARCOS and Siemens Brothers and Company, Limited, 18 August 1920, in RGAE, 413-6-27, 8–9.

18. ARCOS contract with L. B. Ericsson and Co. of Stockholm, 24 September 1920, in RGAE, 413-6-27, 15–16.

19. Contract with Aronstein and Co., Ltd., 6 October 1920, in RGAE, 413-6-27, 22.

20. See ARCOS contracts dated 20 July, 16 and 20 September 1920, in RGAE, 413-6-27, 5–7, 11–13.

21. Cited by Karpova, *Sovetskii diplomat*, 99.

22. Ullman, vol. 3, *Anglo-Soviet Accord*, 414.

23. O'Connor, *Engineer of Revolution*, 266.

24. Cited by Karpova, *Sovetskii diplomat*, 96–97.

25. "Protokol no. 7. Zacedaniia Podkomissii pri SPOTEKZAKE po sokrashcheniiu ekstrennoi ocheredi Importnogo plana TsAS'a na 50 percent sostoiavchegosia 1-go fevralia 1921 g.," afternoon session, in RGAE, 413-6-2, 118 (verso).

26. Such was the strategy laid out in Tsentrosoiuz's 21 January 1921 report to the Soviet Foreign Trade Commissariat and SPOTEKZAK on the "possibility of exploiting the French and English markets for supplying the air force with airplanes and aero-engines." In RGAE, 413-6-14, 26.

27. On the Armstrong negotiations over the locomotive engine repair in Newcastle, see Karpova, *Sovetskii diplomat*, 99–100; O'Connor, *Engineer of Revolution*, 254. On the sums involved, and the deal to reconstruct the port of Petrograd, see "Die Frage der Garantien in der Hungerhilfe für Russland," 31 August 1921, *Revaler Bote*.

28. Quai d'Orsay circular dated 23 October 1920, in QOURSS 482, 87.

29. See "Lokomotiven aus dem Ausland," 8 September 1921, *Revaler Bote*; Laserson, *Expert in the Service of the Soviet*, 40–47; and Krasin, *Voprosy vneshnei torgovli*, 249. See also Stomoniakov interview in *Ekonomicheskaia Zhizn,'* 21 August 1921, and Laserson, *Expert in the Service of the Soviet*, 40–41.

30. Quai d'Orsay memorandum, 14 December 1920, in QOURSS 482, 133–134.

31. Cited by Karpova, *Sovetskii diplomat*, 103.

32. Ullman, vol. 3, *Anglo-Soviet Accord*, 308.

33. Ibid., 272–273, 398; and O'Connor, *Engineer of Revolution*, 253.

34. For examples of the instructions and directives given Krasin, see Politburo discussions dated 11, 15, 19 and 25 May, 10, 15, 29, and 30 June and 7 July (at which Krasin himself was present), 1 September, 21 October, 5 November, and 4 December 1920, 14 and 16 February 1921 RGASPI, 17-3, del' numbers 77, 78, 80, 82, 87, 88, 92, 93, 94, 106, 116, 120, 126, 132, 134.

35. Cited by Ullman, vol. 3, *Anglo-Soviet Accord*, 441–442.

36. Ibid., 411–412, 420; and O'Connor, *Engineer of Revolution*, 253–255. The Daniel Johnson comment is in "Contra Iran," *New Criterion*, May 2007, p. 14.

37. O'Connor, *Engineer of Revolution*, 255.

38. This agreement is referenced, for example, in a Quai d'Orsay memorandum dated 18 March 1921, in QOURSS 423, 15 (back). See also "Dette extérieure russe," 14 December 1920, in QOURSS 421, 165.

39. Ullman, vol. 3, *Anglo-Soviet Accord*, 418–420.

40. Ibid, 418.

41. It is possible, of course, that Lloyd George and Bonar Law, cleverly manipulated by Krasin and his Politburo colleagues, really had been convinced the Bolsheviks would make efforts to tone down anti-British propaganda. According to Edward Jay Epstein, in order to make the Bolsheviks' theoretical climbdown in 1921 on revolutionary propaganda "more credible to British intelligence, orders were subsequently sent to Soviet embassies calling off subversive activities, in diplomatic codes which Soviet intelligence knew the British were intercepting and reading." See Epstein, "Petropower and Soviet Expansion," in the July 1986 issue of *Commentary*.

42. Red Army procurement report labeled "Glavkhozupr," circa mid-March 1921, filed in folder titled "Svodka o khode vypolneniia importnogo plana s 15 sentiabria 1920 g. do 15 mart 1921 goda," in RGAE, 413-6-4, 15 and verso, 16 and verso.

43. Krasin telegram to Chicherin, 24 December 1920, cited in Ullman, vol. 3, *Anglo-Soviet Accord*, 426. Ullman's translation.

44. O'Connor, *Engineer of Revolution*, 258–259.

45. The final Anglo-Soviet accord, signed by R. S. Horne for His Britannic Majesty's Government and Krasin for the Russian Socialist Federated Soviet Republic, is reproduced in Ullman, vol. 3, *Anglo-Soviet Accord*, 474–478.

46. Ibid.

47. See Quai d'Orsay "Note," 16 June 1920, in QOURSS 481, 107.

48. Liubov, *Krassin*, 132.

49. Ullman, vol. 3, *Anglo-Soviet Accord*, 452–453.

50. Krasin, *Voprosy vneshnei torgovli*, 249; Karpova, *Sovetskii diplomat*, 115. For a French critique of the Anglo-Soviet trade accord, see the "Memoire sur l'accord commercial anglo-bolcheviste conclu a Londres le 16 mars 1921" prepared on behalf of the Quai d'Orsay, in AN, F7/13490.

51. For trade figures, see special *Beilage des 'Revaler Boten,'* 14 September 1921; and "Der Außenhandel Sowjetrußlands," *Beilage des 'Revaler Boten,'* 7 December 1921.

52. "Krassin über die 'Goldblokade' und die bevorstehende Anleihe in Frankreich," 21 September 1921, *Revaler Bote*.

53. After the Halle Congress of December 1920, the KPD had absorbed 300,000 new members in a merger with the Independent German Social Democratic Party.

54. See Angress, *Stillborn Revolution*, 105–219.

55. See "Note Séjour à Paris du Financier Suèdois Aschberg" prepared by the Quai d'Orsay's "Service Financier," 22 March 1921, in QOURSS 482, 230. On Aschberg's debt settlement offer to the French, more below.

56. Cited in Ullman, vol. 3, *Anglo-Soviet Accord*, 397.

57. On the cynical use of NEP propaganda to lure Western capital to Russia, see Epstein, "Petropower and Soviet Expansion." For another illuminating recent interpretation of NEP, see Stanziani, *L'Economie en Révolution*, 307–416.

58. Swedish agent's report from Reval, 31 May 1921, in RSU, HP 495, p. 1.

59. Letter from Russian Trade Delegation in Stockholm addressed "An Hauptkommando des Rotes Luftflotte der Russische [*sic*] Republik. Die Wissenschaftliche-Teknische Kommitté," 12 October 1920, in RGAE, 413-4-12, 48–50.

60. "Doklad Konsultanta po voprosam Vozdushnogo Flota pri Torgovom Agente NKVT v Revele–Krasvoendeta I Vozdukhoplavatelia G.K. Linno," stamped received by SPOTEKZAK 10 March 1921, in RGAE, 413-6-12, 33–40.

61. "Khodataistvo ob utverzhdenii zaiavki Vozdush. Flota na pokupku vo Frantsii 500 sht. Samoletov BREGE i 500 sht. Motorov," 26 February 1921, RGAE, 413-6-14, 6 and verso, 7.

62. "Doklad tovarishchu Koppu," dated Berlin, 17 January 1921, with attachment, in RGAE, 413-4-12, 148–152; "Doklad tov. Lezhave," from "Gvait" (i.e., White) in Berlin, 5 February 1921, in RGAE, 413-4-12, 145–147; and letter from Linno, in Reval, to Narkomvneshtorg, 21 April 1921, in RAGE, 413-4-12, 21 and verso, 22.

63. See, e.g., the letter from Gvait (White) in Berlin to Narkomvneshtorg, 17 January 1921, in RGAE, 413-4-12, 153–155.

64. Cited by Pipes, in *Russia under the Bolshevik Regime*, 425.

65. Freund, *Unholy Alliance*, 84–85.

66. "Zakazy na samolety, vydannye Berlinskiim Torgpredom za vremia s 1-go sentiabria 21 po 31-oe marta 22," in RGAE, 413-3-36, 327.

67. "Spravka o sostoianii kreditov 1921 g. Voennogo Vedomstva. V Spotekzak, Srochno. Sekretno. NKVT Financovo-Schetnoe Upravleniia" circa December 1921, in RGAE, 413-6-36, 219 and verso; and telegram from the Soviet Trade Mission in Berlin to Narkomvneshtorg, Moscow, 25 December 1921, in RGAE, 413-6-36, 51.

68. "Zakazy na samolety, vydannye Berlinskiim Torgpredom za vremia s 1-go sentiabria 21 po 31-oe marta 22," in RGAE, 413-3-36, 327.

69. Prospectus labeled "Blackburn 'Kangaroo,'" sent to the Russian Trade Delegation in Stockholm, 25 September 1921, in RGAE, 413-6-13, 15–16, 35–38.

70. "Quotation no. 848 for machines for use on the proposed Petrograd-Moscow Line," 27 July 1921, in RGAE, 413-6-13, 17-20.

71. Prospectus from A. V. Roe and Company sent to the Russian Trade Delegation in London, 17 May 1922, in RGAE, 413-6-91, 263.

72. The requisition order, dated 3 July 1917, is preserved in RGAE, 413-3-2, 3.

73. See, e.g., Russian Trade Delegation in London budget report sent to Moscow 17 January 1922, in RGAE, 413-6-36, 89–90, which specifies that "T. Krasina . . .

otpravliautsia avtochasti dlia 'Rol's-Rois." The cost was 16,400 gold rubles, or $8,200. By 18 March 1922, nine containers containing Rolls-Royce spare parts had left London destined for Reval. RGAE, 413-6-36, 143. Another order for Rolls-Royce spare parts, in December 1922, is in RGAE, 413-6-36, 406–407 and backs.

74. "Spravka o realizatsii dvenatsati millionogo fonda," 21 December 1921, in RGAE, 413-6-36, 52–53.

75. "Summy, izraskhodovannye po nariadam SCH.," circa December 1921, in RGAE, 413-6-36, 118.

76. "Spravka na 13-oe Iunia 1921 g.," in RGAE, 413-6-17, 21.

77. *Beilage des 'Revaler Boten,'* 28 December 1921.

78. "Sowjetwirtschaft und Sowjethandel," including excerpts from the Krasin interview with *Novy Mir,* in the 2 June 1921 *Revaler Bote.*

79. On Bolshevik famine propaganda operations, see McMeekin, "Selling the Famine," in *Red Millionaire,* 103–122.

80. Swedish agent's reports from Reval, 4 July and 27 October 1921, in RSU, HP 495.

81. See report of the U.S. consul in Viborg, Finland, based on articles in the *Krasnaia Gazeta,* sent to Washington 30 November 1921, in NAA, M 316, roll 121.

82. See "Aussenhandel," 19 October 1921, *Revaler Bote;* "Sowjetrusslands Import" and "Der Aussenhandel Sowjetrusslands," 6 and 7 December 1921, *Revaler Bote.*

83. Solomon, *Unter den Roten Machthabern,* 198.

84. "Gold Shipments from Soviet Russia from March 26, 1921 to May 25, 1921," and same from May 26, 1921 to July 22, 1921, U.S. intelligence reports from Reval, 14 July and 9 August 1921, in NAA, M 316, roll 120.

85. "Gold Shipments from Soviet Russia from July 23 to September 14, 1921," U.S. intelligence report from Reval, 15 September 1921, in NAA, M 316, roll 120.

86. "Gold Shipments from Soviet Russia from September 14 to October 14, 1921," U.S. intelligence report from Reval, 21 October 1921, in NAA, M 316, roll 120.

87. "Spravka o sostoianii kreditov 1921 g. Voennogo Vedomstva. V Spotekzak, Srochno. Sekretno. NKVT Finansovo-Schetnoe Upravleniia" circa December 1921, in RGAE, 413-6-36, 219 and back.

88. U.S. commissioner's report from Riga, 25 July 1921, in NAA, M 316, roll 120.

89. Westcott, "Gold and Platinum Invoiced through the Paris Consulate General September 29 to October 27, 1921," 15 November 1921, in NAA, M 316, roll 121.

90. Westcott, "Origin and Disposition of the Former Russian Imperial Gold Reserve," 21 April 1921, in NAA, M 316, roll 120, pp. 26–28.

91. U.S. commissioner's report from Riga, 5 August 1921, in NAA, M 316, roll 120.

92. Report of U.S. Consul Irving Linnell, 12 July 1921, in NAA, M 316, roll 120.

93. Swedish agent's dispatch from Reval, 1 December 1921, containing reports dated 1 and 23 November 1921, in RSU, HP 495.

94. Swedish agent's report from Reval, 12 January 1922, in RSU, HP 495.

95. Transcript of Aschberg interrogation at the Paris Préfecture de Police, p. 2.

96. Solomon, *Unter den Roten Machthabern*, 219–221.

97. Pipes, *Russia under the Bolshevik Regime*, 418.

98. Litvinov reply to Lenin's query on the Bolsheviks' financial situation, 29 June 1921, reproduced in Pipes, *Unknown Lenin*, 126–127.

99. Politburo minutes of 7 July 1921 meeting, item 32, authorizing 4 million silver rubles of bread purchases in Persia, in RGASPI, 17-3-184; and 9 July 1921 meeting, item 1, authorizing 500,000 silver rubles to pay salaries in the Fifth Army, RGASPI, 17-3-185.

100. Politburo minutes of 21 September 1921, item 12, RGASPI, 17-3-206.

101. As reported in the 30 August 1921 *Izvestiia*.

102. Politburo minutes of 20 October 1921, item 9, RGASPI, 17-3-219.

103. Minutes of 14 September 1921 Politburo meeting, item 6, RGASPI, 17-3-202; and 16 September 1921, item 3, RGASPI, 17-3-203.

104. Politburo minutes of 11 November 1921, items 3z and 4, RGASPI, 17-3-229. See also Bayer, "Revolutionaere Beute," in *Verkaufte Kultur,* 36–37; and Pipes, *Russian under the Bolshevik Regime,* 353.

105. Report of Captain Kelley, assistant military observer, U.S. Commission in Reval, 20 March 1922, in NAA, M 316, roll 121. See also Delavaud reports from Stockholm, 10 and 13 February 1922, in QOURSS 483, 10 and 12.

106. Chicherin telegram to Krasin/Solomon, 7 Feb. 1922, RGAE, 413-6-36, 96.

107. According to the Estonian minister of finance, $353,134,709.27 in gold was transmitted through the Reval Customs House between May 1920 and December 1922 (the amount transmitted between February and December 1922 was negligible, less than $1 million worth). "Russian gold in transit through Estonia," dispatch of E. L. Packer, U.S. vice consul in Reval, 9 December 1922, in NAA, M 316, roll 121.

108. Sokol'nikov report to Politburo, 9 February 1922, RGASPI, 670-1-25, 11–13.

109. See Sokol'nikov's 1 February 1923 report, "Frantsusky assignat i sovetsky rubl,'" in RGASPI, 670-1-36, 72–99.

110. Clarke, *Lost Fortune of the Tsars,* 218.

111. The best analysis of the legal problems opened up by the looting of the Romanov treasures is Clarke, *Lost Fortune of the Tsars.* For Sokol'nikov's own thinking about these matters, see his 27 May 1922 memo to M. K. Vladimirov, A. I. Rykov, and A. D. Tsiurupy, labeled *o perotsenke romanovskikh tsennostei,* and the more detailed private letters to M. K. Vladimirov and Trotsky, in RGASPI, 670-1-36, 26–30.

112. See Daly, "'Storming the Last Citadel,'" esp. 244.

113. Laserson, *Expert in the Service of the Soviet,* 75.

114. Daly, "'Storming the Last Citadel,'" 258.

115. Politburo minutes, 17 October 1921, RGASPI, 17-3-217, item 6.

CHAPTER 9. RAPALLO

Epigraph 1: Delavaud report to the Quai d'Orsay from Stockholm, 2 September 1921, in QOURSS 482, 258 (and verso).

Epigraph 2: Widely attributed, e.g., in Wipert von Blücher, *Deutschlands Weg nach Rapallo,* 151; Freund, *Unholy Alliance,* 90; and Pipes, *Russia under the Bolshevik Regime,* 231.

1. Transcript of Politburo telephone conversations, 11 October 1921, RGASPI, 17-3-214, item 2.

2. Telegram from the Politburo to Chicherin, 17 April 1922, reproduced in Pipes, *Unknown Lenin,* 159.

3. Krasin letter to Halgouet sent from London, in QOURSS 421, 81–84.

4. "Ultrasecret" message from Chicherin to Lenin, 30 January 1922, reproduced in Pipes, *Unknown Lenin,* 184–185.

5. "Extremely Urgent Top Secret" letter from Trotsky to the Politburo, 28 April 1922, reproduced in Pipes, *Unknown Lenin,* 162–163.

6. Politburo minutes, 28 October 1921, RGASPI, 17-3-224, item 3.

7. See the draft of a gold contract prepared by I. V. Steinberg of the Svenska Ekonomie Aktiebolaget for the German Economics Ministry (Reichswirtschaftsministerium), forwarded on to the Reichsbank and Foreign Office, 5 December 1921, in R 31956.

8. Aschberg, *Wandering Jew,* 50–53, 56–57.

9. Report of a conversation with Aschberg by Saint-Quentin, chargé d'affaires of the French Embassy in Berlin, submitted to the Quai d'Orsay on 19 March 1921, in QOURSS 482, 227 (and verso), 228; and "Note Séjour à Paris du Financier Suèdois Aschberg" prepared by the Quai d'Orsay's "Service Financier," 22 March 1921, in QOURSS 482, 230.

10. Report from Saint-Quentin, chargé d'affaires of the French Embassy in Berlin, submitted to the Quai d'Orsay on 24 March 1921, in QOURSS 482, 244.

11. See Quai d'Orsay report labeled "Exportation des fonds d'Etat russes [*sic*]," 25 August 1921, in QOURSS 482, 252–253; and Delavaud report to the Quai d'Orsay from Stockholm, 2 September 1921, in QOURSS 482, 258 (and verso).

12. See Hans-Ulrich Seidt, *Berlin, Kabul, Moskau,* 145–151; Freund, *Unholy Alliance,* 84–99; Pipes, *Russia under the Bolshevik Regime,* 425–427.

13. Seidt, *Berlin, Kabul, Moskau,* 149–150; Freund, *Unholy Alliance,* 96.

14. See Delavaud report to the Quai d'Orsay from Stockholm, 2 September 1921, in QOURSS 482, 258 (and verso), which mentions a certain "STOMANIOKOF?" as a probable Soviet agent.

15. See "Vertraulich" report from the Reichswirtschaftsminister to the Reichsbankdirektorium, 29 August 1921, in PAAA, R 31956.

16. "Entwurf eines Vertrages zwischen der Reichsbank und der Svenska Ekonomie Aktibolaget Stockholm," attachment to protocol of the meeting held in the Reichsbank on 24 August 1921, "betreffend Goldankauf von der Svenska Ekonomie Aktiebolaget Stockholm durch die Reichsbank und Abshluss eines deutsch-russischen Wirtschaftsabkommens," in PAAA, R 31956.

17. Ibid., attachment labeled "Entwurf des Herrn Stomoniakow."

18. From the minutes of a meeting at the German Foreign Office, 6 September 1921, with Behrendt and a number of Reichsbank officials present, in PAAA, R 31956.

19. At the 24 August 1921 meeting at the Reichsbank, for example, Behrendt was cautious about the S.E.A. deal, thinking it might have been better to camouflage

payments further by shipping the gold through "neutral" countries (i.e., Sweden) in case the Allies might sequester it in Berlin. See protocol of Reichsbank meeting held on 24 August 1921, in PAAA, R 31956.

20. German Foreign Office "Aufzeichnung," re. "Entwurf eines Vertrages zwischen der Reichsbank und der Svenska Ekonomie Aktiebolaget Stockholm," 10 December 1921, in PAAA, R 31956.

21. Cited by Pipes, in *Russia under the Bolshevik Regime*, 426.

22. Seidt, *Berlin, Kabul, Moskau*, 150.

23. See the clipping from the *Svenska Dagbladet*, 5 May 1922, sent in to the German Foreign Office the next day, in PAAA, R 31956.

24. Letter from gez. Pieper of the Soviet Trade Delegation in Berlin to the Ministry of Economics (Reichswirtschaftsministerium), 20 April 1922, in PAAA, R 31956.

25. See Pipes, *Russia under the Bolshevik Regime*, 427.

26. The original draft from 1921 had been somewhat revised over the winter with the help of a few German experts in Moscow, but Rathenau himself does not seem to have read it very closely, or to have insisted on any changes. In one of the cruelest ironies of Weimar history, Rathenau had been the greatest skeptic in the Foreign Office about dealing with the Bolsheviks, yet because his signature was affixed to Rapallo he would take the lion's share of the blame among those who disapproved of the deal. Two months after signing the treaty, Rathenau was murdered by *völkisch* nationalists for being, it seems, a pro-Communist Jew.

27. Freund, *Unholy Alliance*, 96; and Seidt, *Berlin, Kabul, Moskau*, 150–153.

28. For a Russian-language version of the Rapallo Treaty, see *Sovetsko-Germanskie Otnosheniia ot peregovorov v Brest-Litovske do Podpisaniia Rapall'skogo Dogovora*, 479–481.

29. French intelligence reports, as intercepted by German intelligence and translated on 20 and 24 May 1922, in DBB, R 43/I/132, 525, 533.

30. Report from the German minister in Moscow sent to Foreign Office Berlin, 18 April 1922, in PAAA, R 31956.

31. Telegram from gez. Reuter, in Genoa, to the Foreign Office in Berlin. 3 May 1922, "Durch Eilboten abtragen!": "sendet unsere letzte Fassung des Schwedenbankvertrages mit Gegenentwurf." In PAAA, R 31956. That Reuter is referring to the S.E.A. deal is confirmed in his reference to "Steinberg": this was Isaak "the engineer" Steinberg, Aschberg's confidence man at S.E.A. Berlin headquarters.

32. See the clipping from the *Svenska Dagbladet*, 5 May 1922, sent in to the German Foreign Office the next day, in PAAA, R 31956.

33. Letter from Emil Wittenberg to Herrn Ministerialdirektor Freiherrn Maltzan of the Foreign Office, 4 April 1922, in PAAA, R 31956.

34. Waltraud Bayer, "Erste Verkaufsoffensive: Exporte nach Deutschland und Österreich," in *Verkaufte Kultur*, 102; Nesbit, "Some Facts on the Organizational History of the Van Diemen Exhibition," in *First Russian Show*, 67–72; and Williams, *Russia Imagined*, 243. On the Aschberg-Krestinsky-Wirth negotiations, see also French intelligence report from Berlin, 24 May 1921, in QOURSS 482, 244. On Bolshevik sales of jewels to finance German arms purchases, see also Rolf Dieter-Müller, *Das Tor zur Weltmacht*, 123.

35. On the chartering of Ruskombank, and its connection to the financing of German-Soviet trade, see Brockdorff-Rantzau's telegram from Moscow to the Foreign Office, 17 November 1922, in PAAA, R 94575.

36. Of course Aschberg does not use the word "launder" to describe his sales of Bolshevik gold and other Gokhran loot: in his mind he was simply helping the Soviet government recover from its isolation and begin trading again. Aschberg does not estimate how much gold he helped launder in Stockholm during the gold boom of 1920–21, but judging from the volumes registered leaving Reval on his preferred vessel, the *Kalewipoeg*, it was likely to have been somewhere in the vicinity of 150 million dollars worth, or the equivalent of $15 billion today. In his memoirs, Aschberg sticks to vague generalizations, but at one point he casually boasts, in describing a "typical voyage" of the *Kalewipoeg*, that it was carrying "a consignment of gold representing many millions of kroner." Aschberg, *Wandering Jew*, 48. If we add this gold-laundering sum to the amount of jewels and diamonds Aschberg himself confessed to laundering between 1921 and 1924 (200 million crowns, or $50 million), we reach an estimate of Aschberg's money laundering "yield" for the Bolsheviks of $200 million, the equivalent of $20 billion today in international arms purchasing power. However we look at it, it is an impressive achievement. See transcript of the Aschberg interrogation at the Paris Préfecture de Police, p. 2; and Aschberg, *Wandering Jew*, 56–63.

37. Müller, *Das Tor zur Weltmacht*, 106.

38. German Foreign Office Memorandum "An die Bevollmächtigte Vertretung (Botschaft) der Russischen Sozialistischen Föderativen Sowjet-Republik in Deutschland," 12 June 1923, in PAAA, R 94575.

39. See the complaint lodged with the Foreign Office about Aschberg's monopoly by the Handelskammer of Pforzheim, 13 March 1926, in PAAA, R 94426.

40. On the "worker bonds," see Aschberg, *Wandering Jew*, 62–63.

41. See French intelligence report sent from Kovno to Paris, 20 April 1926, in QOURSS 483, 31.

42. Müller, *Das Tor zur Weltmacht*, 163. See also article on the "sogenannte 300 = Millionen = Kredit," in *Deutsche Allgemeine Zeitung*, 11 September 1926, as clipped in PAAA, R 94575.

43. Letter from Kastl, "Geschäftsführende Präsidialmitglied für den Russland-Ausschuss der deutschen Wirtschaft Reichsverband," to Reichsbank President Luther, 15 August 1931, in PAAA, R 94575: "Seit Abschluss des Abkommens . . . vom 14. April ds.Js. (Pjatakoff-Abkommen) sind russische Lieferungsaufträge im Gesamtbetrage von rund 420 Millionenen Reichsmark an deutsche Firmen vergeben werden."

44. See the memorandum prepared by Heintze of the Reichswirtschaftsministerium for the German Foreign Office, 4 August 1931, "Betrifft: Finanzierung der Russengeschäfte; Protesterhebung bei Prolongationswechseln," in PAAA, R 94575.

EPILOGUE: FROM STOCKHOLM TO SOTHEBY'S

1. "Royal Russian Art for Sale in Berlin: Soviet Asserts Auction of Treasures Is to Dispose of Oversupply," *New York Times*, 1 October 1928.

2. "Germany Will Permit Sale of Russian Art: Berlin Courts Refuse Injunction Asked for by Exiles Who Claim Property," *New York Times,* 2 November 1928.

3. Citations in Bayer, "Erste Verkaufsoffensive," in *Verkaufte Kultur,* 102–106.

4. Williams, *Russian Art and American Money,* 213. On the organization of Soviet art "exhibitions" generally, see the VOKS files in the Government Archive of the Russian Federation (GARF), Fond 5283, opis 11, del. 42.

5. *Icones Russes. Collection Olof Aschberg Donation faite au Musée National,* 1. On sales of Russian icons in the late 1920s and 1930s generally, see Bayer, "Erste Verkaufsoffensive," in *Verkaufte Kultur,* 117–123.

6. See, e.g., "Russian Laws of Confiscation. Sale by Soviet. Princess's Claim for Valuables," *Daily Telegraph,* 1 December 1982.

7. Christie's Auction Notice, *New York Times,* 6 March 1927, p. X13. See also Anne Odom, "The Selling of Russian Art and the Origins of the Hillwood Collection," in Arend and Odom, *Taste for Splendor,* 45.

8. Letter from G. D. Hobson to Stephen Gaselee of the Foreign Office, 10 December 1928, and 15 December reply by Stephen Gaselee, in PRO, FO 371/13324.

9. Davis et al., in *Dark Mirror,* 12–14.

10. Odom, "Selling of Russian Art," in Arend and Odom, *Taste for Splendor,* 46.

11. Williams, *Russian Art and American Money,* 7, 173; Odom, "Selling of Russian Art," in Arend and Odom, *Taste for Splendor,* 46. On Armand Hammer's role in laundering Soviet assets, see Epstein, *Dossier.*

12. Williams, *Russian Art and American Money,* 175.

Selected Bibliography

The subject of Bolshevik precious metals exports and their role in funding strategic imports has been largely ignored in the historical literature on the Russian Revolution. This is a bit surprising when we consider the number of works devoted to German financial support for Lenin in 1917 and to the Rapallo Treaty signed five years later. It is as if the civil war and Allied blockade opened up a critical caesura in the subject between 1917 and 1922, with most historians simply assuming that Russian imports of war matériel—and the Stockholm banking connection used to finance them, what I call the Germano-Swedish-Bolshevik nexus—must have been bottled up entirely.

The bulk of the sources used in writing this book were thus of a primary nature. The most important material on foreign trade and military procurement in the first years of the Soviet regime is found in fond 413 of the Russian Government Archive of Economics (RGAE) in Moscow. Most of these materials are in Russian, but there are also a number of German-, Swedish-, and English-language contracts. The Gokhran files (exclusively in Russian) are in fond 7632. The Finance Commissariat and "Safes Commission" files are in fond 7733. A good deal of material relating to art and antique dumping later in the 1920s, handled through the Society for Foreign Cultural Relations (VOKS), can be found at GARF (in the same building as RGAE).

At the Russian Government Archive for Social-Political History (RGASPI), near the Kremlin in Moscow, the Politburo files give a fine overview of Soviet financial policymaking and strategizing at the highest level. I have also found a great deal of helpful information on currency policy, Red Army looting in Central Asia, and the appraisal of the Romanov treasure ordered in 1922 in the Grigory Sokol'nikov papers.

Because of the transnational nature of the subject, I have also relied on non-Russian archival material to a particularly large extent, seeking to corroborate evidence of Bolshevik money laundering with as many sources as possible. The nature of the files available differs greatly from country to country. The Swiss Bundesarchiv in Bern is particularly good on international Bolshevism in 1918, because of a nation-wide sting operation carried out that year by the Swiss police. The paperwork from the investigation of Bolshevik money laundering and propaganda operations inside Switzerland can be found in the E 21, "Polizeiwesen" files.

The British Foreign Office files, located at the Public Record Office (now known as the National Archives of the United Kingdom) in Kew Gardens, London, are the richest overall in terms of diplomatic correspondence. Consular and intelligence dispatches from Petrograd, Stockholm, Christiania (Oslo), Copenhagen, and Reval (Tallinn) for the years 1917–22 are abundant if not always entirely reliable: the British have a rich appetite for amusing anecdotes and rumor of all kinds. The file-ordering system is a bit perplexing. I have referenced most of the Foreign Office files in the footnotes as FO/371 for consular reports or FO/368 for commercial correspondence, and then given simply the document date and the box number in which the document is located, while ignoring the mostly five- and six-digit "file numbers," which seem to follow consecutively both inside boxes and from one box to another, except for when they don't.

The files relating to Soviet gold movements at the National Archives in Washington, by contrast, are much less voluminous than those in London, but more concentrated. They are largely confined, in fact, to three compact microfilms housed at the National Archives Annex in College Park, Maryland. In general, U.S. intelligence was very good on gold movements because the American delegation at Reval was the best at cataloguing the port statistics provided by the Estonian government. Charles Westcott's consular reports from Paris on Bolshevik gold outflow across the Baltic were well researched and colorfully written, especially his April 1921 report "Origin and Disposition of the Former Russian Imperial Gold Reserve."

The French files are also extremely informative, though in a manner informed by the extreme anti-Bolshevik bias of the government, the police, and the Foreign Ministry (Quai d'Orsay). At the Archives Nationales, the files relating to Bolshevism and Bolshevik gold movements are abundant though a bit lacking in focus. French consuls and spies liberally passed on rumors and reports from everywhere in Europe without pausing to sift between the more and less informative. The *police générale* section (the "F7s") has some good surveillance on Bolshevik cash and gold movements. Materials relating to French creditors and bondholders whose property was confiscated by the Bolsheviks can be found in the "BB 18" files, although most of these are available only through a special "dérogation" from the French Interior Ministry. Of these, I have found BB 18/6727, on the Banque Russo-Asiatique, particularly useful.

The Swedish Foreign Ministry files in Stockholm, by contrast, provide the opposite side to the story, which is to say the commercial *opportunities* opened by the advent of a rogue anticapitalist regime in Moscow. In general, Swedish government officials were reticent about their friendly relations with the Bolsheviks. But a number of the most sensitive trade contracts and correspondence from 1917 to 1922 are still preserved in the Riksarkivet Stockholm Utrikesdepartement, most in both Swedish and Russian duplicates (they can thus be cross-checked against commercial contracts filed at RGAE in Moscow). Swedish Foreign Office employees also clipped hundreds of relevant articles from the German-language Estonian newspaper *Revaler Bote,* which is by far the most informative source on the Baltic trade during and after Soviet blockade years.

Of special interest in Stockholm are the Olof Aschberg Papers, stored at the Swedish Labour Movement Archive (Arbettörelsens Arkiv och Bibliothek). These include the notes and supporting materials for Aschberg's memoirs and also an unpublished English typescript translation by Alan Blair, in box 4, along with an assortment of translations in other languages, including German. Aschberg is not shy in his memoirs about detailing his role in laundering Bolshevik gold, money, and other confiscated treasures (although he does not use the word "launder"). Still, perhaps sensing that not everything he accomplished was worthy of the public's interest, Aschberg does not go into as much detail in his published memoirs about the colossal cash sums involved in his Bolshevik precious metals laundering as he did while under hostile interrogation in Paris.

Finally, there is the Politisches Archiv des Auswärtigen Amtes in Berlin at Werderscher Markt, containing the files of the German Foreign Office where, we might say, Bolshevism was born. These include the notorious documents relating to German financing of Lenin in 1917, Parvus-Helphand, and so on. As far as Bolshevik finances and illicit trade after the October Revolution, the suspicious German consular reports from Stockholm ("Beziehungen Schweden zu Rußland") housed at Werderscher Markt are extremely informative. There is also rich material on Bolshevik gold movements, and on pre- and post-1922 German-Soviet trade, in particular the murky financial arrangements of Rapallo, in the section labeled "Russland Akten betreffend finanzielle Beziehungen Russland zu Deutschland."

Despite a heavy reliance on primary archival material, I could not have written this book without the efforts of those trailblazers who first explored the secrets of Soviet Russian history. The problems of the late tsarist economy are ably discussed in Margaret Miller, *The Economic Development of Russia, 1905–1914,* and Olga Crisp, *Studies in the Russian Economy before 1914.* Robert C. Allen's recent *Farm to Factory: A Reinterpretation of the Soviet Industrial Revolution* takes a more skeptical line on the potential of the tsarist economy. Peter Gatrell gives a good introduction to Russian war industry in *Government, Industry and Rearmament in Russia, 1900–1914.* The story is carried through the war years, with particular emphasis on the paper inflation and its relation to the collapse of the tsarist government, in Norman Stone, *The Eastern Front, 1914–1917.* Up-to-date statistics on war finance, covering not only Russia but all the belligerent powers, can be found in Hew Strachan, *Financing the First World War.*

To explore the Lenin-and-the-Germans controversy, the place to begin is still with the primary documents first published in Hahlweg, *Lenins Rückkehr nach Russland, 1917: Die deutschen Akten,* and in English translation in Zeman's *Germany and the Russian Revolution.* On the Parvus connection, the biography by Zeman and Scharlau, *The Merchant of Revolution,* remains the most informative. On the Stockholm connection used by Russian revolutionaries going back to the nineteenth century, and the wartime smuggling trade at Haparanda on the Swedish-Finnish border, Michael Futrell's *Northern Underground* is illuminating although frustrating: Futrell cuts off his story in October 1917, just when things were becoming interesting.

On the question of how (and how much) German money made it to Lenin in 1917 and 1918, there is no one definitive source but a number of competing accounts. In Russian, the best studies are Sergei Mel'gunov's *'Zolotoi nemetskii kliuch'*, and more recently Dmitri Volkogonov's biography *Lenin*. Richard Pipes, in *The Russian Revolution*, covers the topic quite thoroughly, although his conclusions about the sums spent by the German government on the Bolsheviks are disputed by Semion Lyandres in *The Bolshevik's German Gold Revisited*.

On nearly all factual questions relating to the Russian Revolution and civil war, the two-volume history by Richard Pipes—*The Russian Revolution* and *Russia under the Bolshevik Regime*—remains indispensable. Orlando Figes's *Peasant Russia, Civil War* and his *A People's Tragedy* together help fill in the blanks relating to the civil war, especially the peasant wars behind the front lines. So, too, does Nicolas Werth's long essay on Soviet Russia in *The Black Book of Communism*, especially on the Cheka and the Red Terror. Many of the most important primary documents on the revolution are available in English translation, such as in James Bunyan, *Intervention, Civil War, and Communism in Russia*, and Bunyan and H. H. Fisher, eds., *The Bolshevik Revolution, 1917–1918: Documents and Materials*. Jane Degras's *Soviet Documents on Foreign Policy* is still a handy reference. The collected works of Lenin, widely available both in the original Russian and in English translation, are essential for studies of the revolution.

On the Brest-Litovsk era, the most thorough investigations are in German. On the hidden financial maneuverings and German plans for the Russian economy, the best study is Winfried Baumgart, *Deutsche Ostpolitik, 1918*. The best introduction in English remains that of John Wheeler-Bennett in *Brest-Litovsk: The Forgotten Peace*.

On Bolshevik finances and the domestic policies of War Communism, there are a number of helpful works, although most were written before the Soviet archives were opened in 1991. Of these, Sylvana Malle's *The Economic Organization of War Communism* remains the best. S. S. Katzenellenbaum, *Russian Currency and Banking, 1914–1924* is also useful. For official Soviet estimates of armaments production during the civil war, see especially D. A. Kovalenko, *Oboronnaia promyishlennost' sovetskoi rossii v 1918–1920 gg*. Alessandro Stanziani's more recent *L'Economie en Révolution* does not treat the revolution exclusively, but it is very good on the Russian economy, especially the agricultural sector during the peasant wars.

On the Allied intervention in Soviet Russia, particularly matters relating to the Baltic blockade, by far the most informative resource is Richard Ullman's masterful three-volume *Anglo-Soviet Relations, 1917–1921*. Arno Mayer's *Politics and Diplomacy of Peacemaking* is also informative on the Entente perspective. George Kennan covers the American angle well in *Soviet-American Relations, 1917–1920*. Kennan's story is updated in Norman Saul, *War and Revolution*.

The Bolshevik assault on the Church in 1922 has recently inspired a healthy output of critical study, most of it by Russians. Georgii Mitrofanov's *Istoriia russkoi pravoslavnoi tserkvi, 1900–1927* is superb. The material "output" of the campaign has been most thoroughly examined by Natalya Krivova in *Vlast' i Tserkov' v 1922–1925 gg: Politbiuro i GPU v borb'e za tserkovnyie tsennosti.* In English, the best short introduction is in Jonathan Daly's article "The Bolshevik Assault on the Church."

On the Rapallo Treaty, the best books are in German, beginning with Wipert von Blücher, *Deutschlands Weg nach Rapallo,* published in 1951. The most informative on financial matters is Rolf-Dieter Müller, *Das Tor zur Weltmacht.* On the arms negotiations, there is a good deal of new information in Hans-Ulrich Seidt, *Berlin, Kabul, Moskau.* In English, the most thorough study is Gerald Freund, *Unholy Alliance.*

On Bolshevik art and antique dumping in the Rapallo era and beyond, the essential resource is the volume edited by Waltraud Bayer, *Verkaufte Kultur,* especially Bayer's own articles, "Revolutionäre Beute" and "Erste Verkaufsoffensive: Exporte nach Deutschland und Österreich." Robert Williams's *Russian Art and American Money* remains informative on Soviet sales of paintings by Old Masters to American collectors in particular. On looted Russian antiquities, especially antique books, the place to begin is Robert H. Davis et al., *A Dark Mirror.* On the claims of Romanov descendants to pieces of crown assets confiscated by the Bolsheviks after the revolution, the most thorough study is William Clarke's *The Lost Fortune of the Tsars.* Max Laserson's memoirs, both *Expert in the Service of the Soviet* and *Im Sowjet-Labyrinth* (available only in German) are also extremely informative, especially on the platinum market and the Gokhran. The Laserson papers, including some correspondence relating to the Swedish-German-Soviet locomotive deal and some extraordinary pictures of the Gokhran, can be found in the Hoover Institution Archives in Stanford, California.

On most of the principal actors in the historical narrative—aside from Lenin, Trotsky, and Stalin—the secondary literature is lacking. Olof Aschberg remains almost unknown outside Sweden, although he remains a social democratic icon there. Michael Futrell is the only non-Swedish historian who seems to have looked into the Stockholm milieu of international Bolshevism, in *Northern Underground.* Aschberg's own memoirs are quite useful but as yet have not been published outside Sweden, although German- and English-language translations are available, as noted, in Stockholm.

On Krasin, there is a bit more information available in print. Timothy Edward O'Connor's *The Engineer of Revolution* is quite useful, although a bit thin on the crucial period directly following the revolution. Rosa Karpova, in *L. B. Krasin, sovetskii diplomat,* made little effort to go beyond hagiography, but at times (as with her informative coverage of the Nydquist and Holm deal of 1920 and Krasin's cynical remarks about his English interlocutors) she gives the game away.

As for the central theme of this book—the Stockholm currency and precious metals laundering market and its role in helping the Bolsheviks break the Allied blockade and import the weapons that allowed them to triumph over the Whites, Poles, and peasant armies—until now it has remained almost completely virgin territory for historians. If there are any previous works on the subject, I have not found them.

LIST OF ARCHIVES AND PRINCIPAL COLLECTIONS USED

Arbetarrölsens Arkiv och Bibliotek (AAB), Stockholm
Olof Aschbergs Arkiv. 12 boxes.

Archives Nationales (AN), Paris
BB 18/6727. Banque Russo-Asiatique.
F 7. Police générale.

Bundesarchiv Bern (BB), Bern
E 21. "Polizeiwesen 1848–1930" files.

Deutsches Bundesarchiv Berlin (DBB), Lichterfelde, Berlin
R 901. Auswärtiges Amt.
R 1501. Reichsministerium des Innern.
R 2. Reichsfinanzministerium.
R 3101. Reichswirtschaftsministerium.

Godudarstvenny Arkhiv Rossiiskoi Federatsii (GARF), Moscow
Fond 5283, opis 11. VOKS (Society for Foreign Cultural Relations).

Hoover Institution Archives, Stanford University, Stanford, CA
Collection: M. J. Larsons (Max Laserson). 2 boxes.

National Archives Annex (NAA), Washington, DC
State Department Reports on Russia, M 316, rolls 119–121.

Politisches Archiv des Auswärtigen Amtes (PAAA), Berlin
Abteilung IV: Rußland.
Geheime Akten: Rußland 61.
Geheime Akten: Deutschland 131.
Geheime Akten: Weltkrieg no. 2

Préfecture de Police, Paris
Dossier "Aschberg, Olof."

Quai d'Orsay Archives (QO), Paris, France.
Angleterre, "Grande-Bretagne-Russie. Janv. 1921–Mai 1922" (folder 61).
URSS: debt (folder 421).
URSS: gold (folders 481–483).

Riksarkivet Stockholm Utrikesdepartement (RSU), Stockholm
Rysslands handel med Sverige 1900–1918 and continuation
(Handel med Sverige 1918 dec.–1919 sept., etc.,–1922),
boxes 4456, 4466, 4466b, 4467, 4477, and HP 495.

Russian Government Archive of Economics (RGAE), Moscow
Fond 413. Ministerstvo vneshnei torgovli SSSR (Minvneshtorg SSSR).
Opis 3. Foreign Trade, 1917–20, especially with Scandinavia.

Opis 4. Founding documents of Narkomvneshtorg (NKVT), etc.
Opis 6. Red Army Procurement, 1917–22 and beyond.
Fond 7733. Ministerstvo Finansov SSSR (Minfin SSSR). 1917–91.
Opis 1. Narkomfin RSFSR, 1917–23, especially the "Seifovaia komissiia" files.
Fond 7632. Gosudarstvennoe khranilishche tsennostei (Gokhran) Narkomfina.
SSSR. 1920–22 (2 opisi).

Russian Government Archive of Social-Political History (RGASPI), Moscow
Fond 17. Politbiuro TsK RKP (b)—VKP (b).
Opis 3. Povestki dnia zasedanii. (Politburo minutes, 1919–23).
Fond 670, opis 1. Grigory Sokol'nikov (lichnoe delo).

PRINTED AND ONLINE WORKS CITED, INCLUDING MEMOIRS

Agnew, Jeremy, and Kevin McDermott. *The Comintern: A History of International Communism from Lenin to Stalin.* London: Macmillan, 1996.
Allen, Robert C. *Farm to Factory: A Reinterpretation of the Soviet Industrial Revolution.* Princeton: Princeton University Press, 2003.
Andrew, Christopher, and Oleg Gordievsky. *KGB: The Inside Story of Its Foreign Operations from Lenin to Gorbachev.* London: Sceptre, 1991.
Angress, Werner T. *Stillborn Revolution: The Communist Bid for Power in Germany, 1921–1923.* Princeton: Princeton University Press, 1963.
Arbenina, Stella (Baroness Meyendorff). *Through Terror to Freedom.* London: Hutchinson, 1929.
Arend, Liana Paredes, and Anne Odom. *A Taste for Splendor: Russian Imperial and European Treasures from the Hillwood Museum.* Alexandria, VA: Art Services International, 1998.
Aschberg, Olof. "A Wandering Jew from Glasbruksgatan" (*Ein vandrande jude fran Glasbruksgatan*). Unpublished English-language typescript translation by Alan Blair, located in Olof Aschbergs Arkiv at the Arbetarrölsens Arkiv och Bibliotek, Stockholm.
———. *Gryningen till en ny tid: Ur Mina Memoarer.* Stockholm: Tidens bokkklubb, 1961.
Barthel, Max. *Kein Bedarf an Weltgeschichte.* Wiesbaden: Limes, 1950.
Baumgart, Winfried. *Deutsche Ostpolitik 1918: Von Brest-Litowsk bis zum Ende des Ersten Weltkrieges.* Vienna/Munich: Oldenbourg, 1966.
Bayer, Waltraud, ed. *Verkaufte Kultur: Die sowjetischen Kunst- und Antiquitätenexporte, 1919–1938.* Frankfurt-am-Main: Peter Lang, 2001.
Blücher, Wipert von. *Deutschlands Weg nach Rapallo.* Wiesbaden: Limes, 1951.

Bower, Tom. *Nazi Gold: The Full Story of the Fifty-Year Swiss-Nazi Conspiracy to Steal Billions from Europe's Jews and Holocaust Survivors.* New York: Harper Collins, 1997.

Budnitsky, Oleg. "Generaly i den'gi, ili 'Vrangelevskoe Serebro." *Diaspora* 6 (2004): 134–173.

———. "Kolchakovskoe zoloto." *Diaspora* 4 (2002): 457–508.

Bunyan, James, and Harold H. Fisher, eds., *The Bolshevik Revolution, 1917–1918:. Documents and Materials.* Stanford: Stanford University Press, 1934.

Clarke, William. *The Lost Fortune of the Tsars: The Search for the Fabulous Legacy of the Romanoffs.* London: Orion, 1996.

Clements, Barbara Evans. *Bolshevik Feminist: The Life of Alexandra Kollontai.* Bloomington: Indiana University Press, 1979.

Crisp, Olga. *Studies in the Russian Economy before 1914.* London: Macmillan, 1976.

Curtiss, John Shelton. *The Russian Church and the Soviet State, 1917–1950.* Boston: Little, Brown, 1953.

Daly, Jonathan. "'Storming the Last Citadel': The Bolshevik Assault on the Church, 1922." In *The Bolsheviks in Russian Society: The Revolution and Civil War,* ed. Vladimir N. Brovkin. New Haven: Yale University Press, 1997.

Davis, Robert H., et al. *A Dark Mirror: Romanov and Imperial Palace Library Materials in the New York Public Library: A Checklist and Agenda for Research.* New York: Norman Ross, 2000.

Dieter-Müller, Rolf. *Das Tor Zur Weltmacht.* Boppard am Rhein: Harald Boldt, 1984.

Emmons, Terence, and Bertrand M. Patenaude. *War, Revolution, and Peace in Russia: The Passages of Frank Golder.* Stanford: Hoover Institution Press, 1992.

Epstein, Edward Jay. *Dossier: The Secret History of Armand Hammer.* New York: Carroll and Graf, 1999.

———. "Have You Ever Tried to Sell a Diamond?" *Atlantic Monthly,* February 1982. Available online at: http://www.theatlantic.com/doc/198202/diamond.

———. "Petropower and Soviet Expansion." *Commentary,* July 1986. Available online at: http://www.edwardjayepstein.com/oilpower.htm.

Eizenstat, Stuart. "Report on Looted Gold and German Assets." Available online at http://www.usembassy-israel.org.il/publish/report/.

Ferguson, Niall. *The Cash Nexus: Money and Power in the Modern World, 1700–2000.* London: Basic Books, 2001.

Figes, Orlando. *Peasant Russia, Civil War: The Volga Countryside in Revolution, 1917–1921.* New York: Oxford University Press, 1989.

————. *A People's Tragedy: The Russian Revolution, 1891–1924*. New York: Penguin, 1998.

Fischer, Fritz. *Germany's Aims in the First World War*. New York: Norton, 1968.

Fisher, Harold H. *The Famine in Soviet Russia, 1919–1923: The Operations of the American Relief Administration*. New York: Macmillan, 1927.

Freund, Gerald. *Unholy Alliance: Russian-German Relations from the Treaty of Brest-Litovsk to the Treaty of Berlin*. London: Chatto and Windus, 1957.

Fromkin, David. *Europe's Last Summer: Who Started the Great War in 1914?* New York: Vintage, 2004.

Futrell, Michael. *Northern Underground: Episodes of Russian Revolutionary Transport and Communications through Scandinavia and Finland, 1863–1917*. London: Faber and Faber, 1963.

Gatrell, Peter. *Government, Industry and Rearmament in Russia, 1900–1914*. Cambridge: Cambridge University Press, 1994.

Gerschenkron, Alexander. "Russia: Patterns and Problems of Economic Development, 1861–1958." In *Economic Backwardness in Historical Perspective: A Book of Essays*. Cambridge: Belknap Press of Harvard University, 1962.

Hahlweg, Werner, ed. *Der Friede von Brest-Litovsk*. Düsseldorf: Droste, 1971.

————. *Lenins Rückkehr nach Russland, 1917: Die deutschen Akten*. Leiden: E. J. Brill, 1957.

Hurst, Steve. "'Harsh Report' Critical of Swiss-Nazi Gold." CNN online, 6 May 1997. Available online at: http://edition.cnn.com/US/9705/06/nazi.gold/.

Isarescu, Mugur, Cristian Paunescu, and Marian Stefan. *Tezaurul Bancii Nationale a Romaniei la Moscova—Documente*. Bucharest: Fundatiei Culturale Magazin Istoric, 1999.

Jacobs, Dan N. *Borodin: Stalin's Man in China*. Cambridge: Harvard University Press, 1981.

Johnson, Daniel. "Contra Iran." *New Criterion*, May 2007.

Karpova, Rosa Federovna. *L. B. Krasin, sovetskii diplomat*. Moscow: Izd. Sotsialno-ekonom. Lit., 1962.

Katzenellenbaum, S. S. *Russian Currency and Banking, 1914–1924*. London: P. S. King and Son, 1925.

Kennan, George. *Soviet-American Relations, 1917–1920*. 2 vols. London: Faber and Faber, 1956 and 1958.

Kerensky, Alexander F., and Robert Paul Browder, eds. *The Russian Provisional Government 1917*. 3 vols. Stanford: Stanford University Press, 1961.

Khrustalëv, Vladimir M., and Mark D. Steinberg. *The Fall of the Romanovs: Political Dreams and Personal Struggles in a Time of Revolution.* New Haven: Yale University Press, 1995.

Kjellin, Helge, ed. *Icones Russes. Collection Olof Aschberg: Donation faite au Musée National.* Stockholm: Kungl. Boktryckeriet. P. A. Norstedt and Söner, 1933.

Kochan, Miriam. *The Last Days of Imperial Russia.* London: Weidenfeld and Nicolson, 1976.

Kovalenko, D. A. *Oboronnaia promyishlennost' sovetskoi rossii v 1918–1920 gg.* Moscow: Nauka, 1970.

Krasin, Leonid Borisovich. *Dela davno minuvshikh dnei (Vospominaniia).* Moscow: Molodaia gvardiia, 1931.

———. *O vneshnei torgovle i otnoshenii k nei russkoi kooperatsii.* Novgorod: Tipografiia Gubsoiuza, 1921.

———. *Voprosy vneshnei torgovli.* Moscow: Gosudarstvennoe izdatel'stvo, 1928.

Krassin, Lubov. *Leonid Krassin: His Life and Work.* London: Skeffington and Son, 1929.

Krivova, Natalya Alexandrovna. *Vlast' i Tserkov' v 1922–1925 gg: Politbiuro i GPU v borb'e za tserkovnyie tsennosti I politicheskoe podchinenie dukhovenstva.* Moscow: Airo-XX, 1997.

Laserson, Max (M. J. Larsons). *An Expert in the Service of the Soviet,* trans. Dr. Angelo S. Rappoport. London: Ernst Benn, 1929.

———. *Im Sowjet-Labyrinth: Episoden und Silhouetten.* Berlin: Transmare, 1931.

Lazitch, Branko. "Two Instruments of Control by the Comintern: The Emissaries of the ECCI and the Party Representatives in Moscow." In *The Comintern: Historical Highlights,* ed. Milorad M. Drachkovitch and Branko Lazitch. Stanford: Hoover Institution Press, 1966.

Lebor, Adam. *Hitler's Secret Bankers: How Switzerland Profited from Nazi Genocide.* London: Simon and Schuster, 1999.

Lenin, V. I. *Sochineniia,* ed. N. I. Bukharin et al. Leningrad: Gosudarstevennoe Sotsial'no Ekonomicheskoe Izdatel'stvo, 1931.

Lewis, Jo Ann. "Crowning Glories: The Romanov Treasures." In *Washington Post,* 31 January 1997. Available online at: http://www.washington post.com/wp-srv/inatl/exussr/feb/19/romanov.htm.

Lyandres, Semion. *The Bolshevik's German Gold Revisited: An Inquiry into the 1917 Accusations.* Pittsburgh: Carl Beck Series, University of Pittsburgh, 1995.

Marx, Karl. *Capital,* vol. 1, and *Manifesto of the Communist Party.* In *The Marx-Engels Reader,* ed. Robert C. Tucker. New York: Norton, 1972.

Mayer, Arno. *Politics and Diplomacy of Peacemaking: Containment and*

Counterrevolution at Versailles, 1918–1919. New York: Alfred A. Knopf, 1967.

Mel'gunov, Sergei. *'Zolotoi nemetskii kliuch' k bol'shevitskoi revolutsii.* Paris: Maison du livre étranger, 1940.

Miller, Margaret. *The Economic Development of Russia, 1905–1914.* London: Frank Cass, 1967. Originally published 1926.

Mitrofanov, Georgii. *Istoriia russkoi pravoslavnoi tserkvi, 1900–1927.* St. Petersburg: Satis, 2002.

Morley, James William. *The Japanese Thrust into Siberia, 1918.* New York: Columbia University Press, 1957.

Moulton, Harold G., and Leo Pasvolsky. *Russian Debts and Russian Reconstruction: A Study of the Relation of Russia's Foreign Debts to Her Economic Recovery.* New York: McGraw-Hill, 1924.

Muir, Percy. "A Russian Adventure." In *The Colophon.* New York: 1932.

Müller, Rolf-Dieter. *Das Tor zur Weltmacht.* Boppard am Rhein: Harald Boldt Verlag, 1984.

Nesbit, Peter. "Some Facts on the Organizational History of the Van Diemen Exhibition." In *The First Russian Show: A Commemoration of the Van Diemen Exhibition, Berlin 1922.* London: Annely Juda Fine Art, 1983.

O'Connor, Timothy Edward. *The Engineer of Revolution: L. B. Krasin and the Bolsheviks, 1870–1926.* Boulder, CO: Westview, 1992.

Osipova, Taisia. "Peasant Rebellions: Origin, Scope, Dynamics, and Consequences." In *The Bolsheviks in Russian Society: The Revolution and Civil War,* ed. Vladimir N. Brovkin. New Haven: Yale University Press, 1997.

Pipes, Richard. *A Concise History of the Russian Revolution.* New York: Random House/Vintage, 1996.

———. *The Russian Revolution.* New York: Random House/Vintage, 1990.

———. *Russia under the Bolshevik Regime.* New York: Vintage, 1994.

———. *The Unknown Lenin: From the Secret Archive.* Trans. Catharine Fitzpatrick. New Haven: Yale University Press, 1999.

Radzinsky, Edvard. *The Last Tsar: The Life and Death of Nicholas II.* Trans. Marian Schwartz. New York: Doubleday, 1992.

———. *Nicolas II, le Dernier Tsar.* Trans. Anne Coldefy-Faucard. Paris: Cherche midi, 2002.

Reiss, Tom. *The Orientalist: In Search of a Man Caught between East and West.* London : Vintage/Random House, 2005.

Remnick, David. *Resurrection: The Struggle for a New Russia.* New York : Random House/Vintage, 1998; orig. pub. 1997.

Reynolds, Michael A. "The Ottoman-Russian Struggle for Eastern Anatolia and the Caucasus, 1908–1918." Ph.D. diss., Princeton University, 2003.

Roslof, Edward E. *Red Priests: Renovationism, Russian Orthodoxy, and Revolution, 1905–1946*. Bloomington: Indiana University Press, 2002.

Ruhl, Arthur. *New Masters of the Baltic*. New York: E. P. Dutton, 1921.

Sanger, David E. "Goblins of Zurich." *New York Times Sunday Book Review*, 22 June 1997. Available online at: http://query.nytimes.com/gst/fullpage.html? res=9B01E0D8143FF931A15755C0A961958260.

Saul, Norman E. *War and Revolution: The United States and Russia, 1914–1921*. Lawrence: University Press of Kansas, 2001.

Scharlau, W. B., and Z. A. B. Zeman. *The Merchant of Revolution: The Life of Alexander Israel Helphand (Parvus), 1867–1924*. Oxford: Oxford University Press, 1965.

Seidt, Hans-Ulrich. *Berlin, Kabul, Moskau: Oskar Ritter von Niedermayer und Deutschlands Ostpolitik*. Munich: Universitas, 2002.

Sokolov, Nicholas A. *The Sokolov Investigation of the Alleged Murder of the Russian Imperial Family*. Trans. John F. O'Connor. New York: Robert Speller and Sons, 1971.

Sokrovitsa Almaznogo Fonda SSSR/Treasures of the USSR Diamond Fund/ Les Joyaux du Fonds Diamantaire de l'URSS. Moscow: Sovetskii Khudozhnik, 1967.

Solomon, Georg. *Unter den Roten Machthabern: Was ich im Dienste der Sowjets persönlich sah und erlebte*. Berlin: Verlag für Kulturpolitik, 1930.

Sovetsko-Germanskie Otnosheniia ot peregovorov v Brest-Litovske do Podpisaniia Rapall'skogo Dogovora. Moscow: Izdatel'stvo Politicheskoi Literatury, 1971.

Stanziani, Alessandro. *L'Economie en Révolution: Le cas russe, 1870–1930*. Paris: Albin Michel, 1998.

Stevenson, David. *Cataclysm: The First World War as Political Tragedy*. New York: Basic Books, 2004.

Stites, Richard. *Revolutionary Dreams: Utopian Vision and Experimental Life in the Russian Revolution*. New York: Oxford University Press, 1989.

Stone, Norman. *The Eastern Front, 1914–1917*. New York: Charles Scribner's Sons, 1975.

———. *Europe Transformed, 1878–1919*. Oxford: Blackwell, 1999.

Strachan, Hew. *Financing the First World War*. Oxford: Oxford University Press, 2004.

Sutton, Antony C. *Wall Street and the Bolshevik Revolution: How Western Capitalists Funded Lenin, the Bolsheviks, and the Soviet Union*. Cutchogue, NY: Buccaneer Books, 1999.

Turner, Henry. *Hitler's Thirty Days to Power: January 1933*. New York: Basic Books, 1997.

Ullman, Richard. *Anglo-Soviet Relations, 1917–1921*. 3 vols. Princeton: Princeton University Press, 1961, 1968, and 1972.

Volkogonov, Dmitri. *Lenin: A New Biography*. Trans. Harold Shukman. New York: Free Press, 1994.

Werth, Nicolas. "The Iron Fist of the Dictatorship of the Proletariat," "The Red Terror," and "The Dirty War." In *The Black Book of Communism: Crimes, Terror, Repression*. Trans. Jonathan Murphy and Mark Kramer. Cambridge: Harvard University Press, 1999.

Wheeler-Bennett, John W. *Brest-Litovsk: The Forgotten Peace, March 1918*. New York: St. Martin's, 1956.

Williams, Robert C. *The Other Bolsheviks: Lenin and His Critics*. Bloomington: Indiana University Press, 1986.

———. *Russian Art and American Money, 1900–1940*. Cambridge: Harvard University Press, 1980.

———. *Russia Imagined: Art, Culture, and National Identity, 1840–1995*. New York: Peter Lang, 1997.

Zeman, Z. A. B. *Germany and the Revolution in Russia, 1915–1918: Documents from the German Foreign Ministry*. London: Oxford University Press, 1958.

Zhirnov, Yevgenii. "Kak Zakalialsia Brend. O role 'Rolls-Roisa' v rossisskoi istorii." *Kommersant-Den'gi*, 15 March 2004.

Acknowledgments

This project could not have been undertaken without financial support from a wide range of sources. Some of my initial scouting in the Moscow archives was helped along by a Foreign Language Area Studies grant for advanced Russian language training from the U.S. Department of Education in summer 2001. A short-term travel grant from the International Research and Exchanges Board the following summer helped kick-start my research at RGAE. Finally, Bilkent University, through its faculty development office, has generously supported trips during the four years I have been privileged to teach in its International Relations Department. In particular, fruitful archival visits to Berlin, Bern, London, Moscow, and Stockholm were funded by Bilkent. For this support I am deeply indebted to Professors Ali Doğramaci, Abdullah Atalar, and Ali Karaosmanoğlu, along with Muge Keller and the friendly staff of the finance office.

In Moscow, thanks go first and foremost to Aleksey Yurasovsky for his hospitality and many long conversations in the kitchen of his comfortable flat overlooking the Church of Christ the Savior. Daniel Repko has also been indispensable in clearing away various logistical hurdles and forwarding my mail. Director Sergei Mironenko helped open several doors at GARF, including those leading to the special collections of RGAE. Alexandr Nazarov, the photocopy workhorse of GARF and RGAE, has put up with many outlandish Xerox requests on short notice and come through with flying colors. I imagine he has never quite figured out why I needed all those spreadsheets of Gokhran loot intake and Red Army expenditures, as asking intrusive questions is not his way. Perhaps this book will go some way toward satisfying his possibly latent curiosity.

At RGASPI, I must single out for special praise the notorious Misha, whose lurching mood swings have scared away many a researcher. Still, despite a short temper, Misha really knows his business. It was Misha who turned me on to the Sokol'nikov papers in 2002, for which I am grateful, not least because they are apparently no longer being given out. I do hope they get the dumbwaiter fixed, if only so poor Vera Stepanova no longer has to explain to exasperated researchers why their materials cannot be retrieved. It is certainly not her fault that the Russian government does not adequately fund its own archives. I am grateful to Vera Stepanova, too, for her assistance, especially for letting me into the reading room after closing time on one special occasion in summer 2005. Director Kirill Anderson was also helpful in arranging access to documents.

At the Bundesarchiv in Berlin-Lichterfelde, I would have been lost without help. I still do not understand why the filing system changes every time I visit the place: I suppose it gives cataloguers something to do. Certainly I would have found little worthwhile material if not for the expertise of Herrs Klein and Göttlicher. At the Foreign Office archives on Werderscher Markt, Dr. Peter Grupp helped smooth away all obstacles, such that I was able to begin my work as soon as I walked in the door.

In Paris, Segolène Barbiche was extremely obliging with my urgent request for a dérogation for the Interior Ministry file on the Banque Russo-Asiatique. The staff of the Préfecture de Police was friendly and helpful as always. To Francine-Dominique Liechtenhan of the Sorbonne, I am grateful for many superb tips and for somehow arranging access to the Quai d'Orsay archives in just one day, whereas everyone else told me it would take a week at least. A minor miracle, that: and without it I would have had to push my timetable back many months.

If there is no one in particular to thank at the national archives in Stockholm, London, and Washington, DC, it is because these are so easy to use that little assistance is required. So, too, the New York and Boston public libraries, the Bibliothèque Nationale in Paris, the Staatsbibliothek in Berlin, Widener Library at Harvard, the Lenin Library in Moscow, and my own Bilkent library.

Visits to more specialized collections, however, can be much more rewarding if inside advice is on offer. Tanya Chebotarev of the Bakhmeteff Archive of Columbia University passed on a fine tip about the Budnitsky articles on White gold movements. Timothy Colton of Harvard's Davis Center for Russian and Eurasian Studies made me feel right at home. Bertil Haggman helped prepare me thoroughly for my visit to the Swedish Labour Archive. Edward Kasinec at the New York Public Library shared his encyclopedic knowledge of Soviet antiquities dumping. Carol Leadenham, Linda Bernard, and Elena Danielson of the Hoover Archives at Stanford have always gone the extra mile for me.

In Bucharest, I was fortunate to meet Mr. Costin Ionescu, director of the Romanian Diplomatic Archives, who regaled me for hours with stories about the national treasure stolen by the Bolsheviks. Costin Fenesan, of the Romanian National Archives, is one of the world's leading experts on the Lenin-and-the-Germans saga, even if his new annotated volume of documents on the subject has not yet been published outside Romania. I learned a great deal from Fenesan, both from his conversation and from his groundbreaking research, although in the end I was not quite certain enough about the authenticity of the new documents he discovered to use them in this project. This is no reflection on Fenesan, whose work deserves much wider attention than it has received.

In the many cities I have visited in the course of researching this book, I have benefited from the hospitality of friends and colleagues. In Washington, DC, Brian Bogart was gracious to host me, even if the price was visiting his favorite watering hole, the Karl Marx Café. Ethan Rundell put me up in his Paris flat, where we had many stimulating conversations on World War I. Ethan also forwarded a crucial Xerox request from the Quai d'Orsay. Andrew MacDowell in New York and Joel Stanforth in Boston have both endured much longer visits than they had reason to expect. My London stay was made infinitely more pleasant (and affordable) by the hospitality of Lord Robert Skidelsky, who also generously shared an unpublished memoir on his own family history, touching on the history of the Banque Russo-Asiatique. Julie Elkner tracked down the latest dirt on Lenin's Rolls-Royce. In Istanbul, Ian Sherwood, vicar of the Crimean Memorial Church, indulged me for a charity lecture on the Bolshevik church robberies, which served as a useful sounding board for my ideas. Ian's breadth of learning is extraordinary, his conversation always a pleasure.

In Berkeley, where my introduction to the Russian language and Soviet history began, Yuri Slezkine, Gerry Feldman, and Peggy Anderson have continued to support my endeavors, though now from afar. Peggy is always a keen critical reader of my work. Yuri Slezkine has set the bar high for Soviet studies with *The Jewish Century:* I was happy to see someone else take some heat for a change. I was pleased to have the chance to try my ideas off Professor Slezkine recently in Moscow, although of course he cannot be held accountable for the final result.

Bilkent University has been my happy home for nearly the entire period I have been at work on this project. I am grateful to Norman Stone, first of all, for helping me get the job there. Norman's company is always entertaining, his conversation sparkling, his advice pointed, his criticism—usually—warranted. In my own small way I have tried to live up to his imposing standards as a historian. Norman also created Bilkent's Russian Studies Centre, where I have been blessed with colleagues such as the one-of-a-kind central Asian scholar Hasan Ali Karasar, the deeply learned Tatar historian Hakan Kirimli, and Sergei Podbolotov, whose Russian patriotism was a healthy tonic helping to put despair at bay as I worked on this often depressing topic. Sandy Berkovski helped generously with many of the trickier renderings from the Russian. Needless to say, Sandy bears no responsibility for any errors of translation or transliteration that remain.

In New Haven, Jonathan Brent has been consistently supportive of my endeavors since shepherding my first book, *The Red Millionaire,* through to publication by Yale University Press. I have always looked forward to my visits to New Haven and to our long conversations on Temple Street. I could not ask for a better editor or advocate. I thank you again, Jonathan, for your time and support.

Finally, there is Nesrin Ersoy, my one true joy in this life, my love.

She has been a rock by my side through the long days and nights, offering a critical ear when needed, at other times just a shoulder to lean on. She, too, grew up under a Communist system, in 1980s Bulgaria, and I have learned a great deal from her family's stories, especially from her parents Yüksel and Süheyla. Although I wouldn't dream of associating Nesrin with such a dark subject as Communist looting, money laundering, and arms smuggling, what little good may come out of this book is due in no small part to her inspiration, her integrity, and her strong moral sense. Thank you, Nesrin, for everything.

Index

Aschberg, Olof, 140, 223, 225, 277; and Bolshevik diamond, platinum, and jewelry
laundering, 193, 212, 214, 218, 223,
271n36, 275; and Bolshevik gold laundering, 137, 144–46, 166–67, 191, 193, 202,
205, 208, 211–12, 223, 275; and Bolshevik loan drive of 1921, 22, 201–05, 208–
09, 211, 214, 223; and financing of Lenin's
return to Russia in 1917, 101–02, 103fn,
202, 214, 223; and Russian bank strike of
1917–18, 18–19. *See also* Bolsheviks; Germany, and financial support for Lenin and
Bolsheviks
Atalar, Abdullah, 286
Austria, 176, 183; art galleries and auction
houses of, 217
A. V. & Roe Company, xiii, 188–89
Axel Christiernsson, 112–13, 119, 252n71.
See also Sweden, Russian business interests
and concessions of; Vorovsky, Vatslav
Azeri Turks, 123
Azov-Don Bank, 14, 22, 28, 47, 48, 239n53

Baehr, Ludwig, 128
Baku's oil wealth, 38, 49, 123, 171, 190
Balfour, Arthur, 46, 119
Baltic Sea ports and shipments, 61, 63, 98,
103, 112, 120–22, 135–36, 137, 142–43,
145
Baltik Company, 104, 120
Banque de l'Union Parisienne, 26
Banque du Nord de la Chine, 26
Banque Russo-Asiatique, 26; assets and safe
deposit boxes of, 26–28, 68, 169, 174,
238n51
Baumgart, Winfried, 276
Bayer, Waltraud, 277
BBC (British Broadcasting Corporation), 1
Behrendt, Heinz, 205–06. *See also* Germany,
Foreign Office of
Benckendorffs, xix
Berkovski, Sandy, 224n4, 289
Bernard, Linda, 288
Berzin, Jan, 105–09, 115, 126, 224, 250n40
Bethmann-Hollweg, Theobald, Chancellor of
Germany, xvi
Bevin, Ernest, 142
Blackburn Aeroplane and Motor Company,
188
Black Sea ports and shipments, 63, 98, 123
Blair, Alan, 275

Blöhm & Voss, 204
Blücher, Wipert von, 277
BMW (Bayerische Motoren Werke AG),
186
Bogosloff Mining Works, 24
Bokhara, sack of, 67
Bolsheviks, xii–xv, xvii, xix, xx, xxii, 2, 3, 4,
and *passim;* abolition of private banks by,
16–17, 18, 21–24, 26–29, 31–33, 39, 91,
96; and assaults on and looting of the Russian Church by, 63, 73–75, 80–91, 194;
Berlin Mission of, 98–99, 109–11; Bern
Mission of, 105–06, 108–09, 224; clothing, boots, and wool imports of, 148–49,
153–54; concentration camps of, 134;
confiscations by, 6, 16–22, 24, 28, 32, 36–
39, 41–49, 54–56, 64–70, 83–90, 95–96,
130, 172, 194, 200, 235n4, 238–39n53;
Economics Commissariat of, 139; finances
and Finance Commissariat of, xii–xiv, 2, 3,
12, 13, 16, 30–31, 50, 51, 53, 56, 62, 63,
65, 70, 72, 96–97, 100, 114–16, 151,
192, 195–96, 240n62, 273; "food armies"
of, 137, 157–58; foreign concessions
stratagem of, 97–98, 104; and foreign
trade, nationalization of, 97; German financing of, 99–100; gold laundering by,
2–5, 7, 136, 143–46, 147, 153–60, 161–
62, 165, 183, 192–95; grain requisitions
by, 51–53, 137, 157–58; and "loot the
looters" drive in 1918, 35–38, 48, 51–52,
60, 95, 112; luxury imports of, 77, 80,
173, 177–78, 189, 191, 198, 266–67n73;
money laundering by, 105–09, 113–15,
131–32; Party bosses of, 88; Politburo of,
73, 75–77, 80–81, 144, 159, 188, 195–
96, 199, 228; procurement agents of, 52,
148–54, 187; propaganda of, 4, 18, 25,
77, 80–83, 101, 109, 117, 149, 162, 179–
80, 184, 195, 266n57; property nationalizations of, 24–29; Red Guards of, 12, 17,
30, 46, 54; and reparations payments to
Imperial Germany, 109–11; and repudiation of Brest-Litovsk Treaty, 112, 123;
Reval Mission of, 144, 147; safe-cracking
efforts of, 50, 65–67; and split with Mensheviks, 58; Stockholm Mission of, 100–
104, 112–14, 119, 126, 148–49, 163,
172; strategic imports of, xiii–xv, 2, 4, 7,
59, 77–78, 80, 185–86
Bonar Law, Andrew, 142, 178–79, 265n41